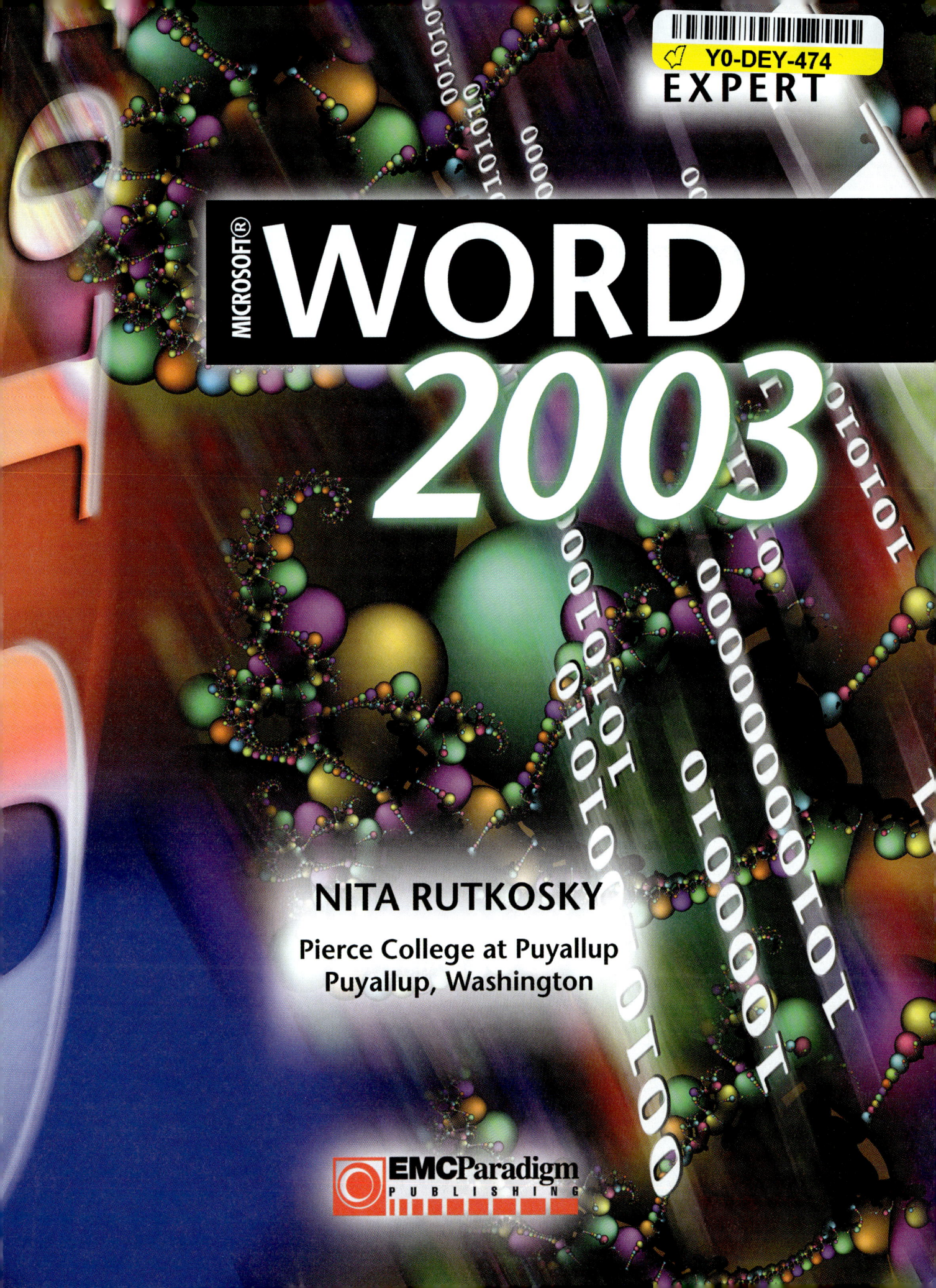

Project Editor	Sonja Brown
Developmental Editor	James Patterson
Senior Designer	Leslie Anderson
Technical Reviewer	Desiree Faulkner
Cover Designer	Jennifer Wreisner
Copyeditor	Susan Capecchi
Desktop Production Specialists	Erica Tava, Lisa Beller
Proofreader	Joy McComb
Indexer	Nancy Fulton
Photo Researcher	Paul Spencer

Publishing Team—George Provol, Publisher; Janice Johnson, Director of Product Development and Instructional Design; Tony Galvin, Acquisitions Editor; Lori Landwer, Marketing Manager; Shelley Clubb, Electronic Design and Production Manager

Acknowledgments—The author and editors wish to thank the following instructors for their technical and academic contributions:

- Nancy Graviett, St. Charles Co. Community College, St. Peters, MO, for preparing the IG materials
- Kay M. Newton, Commonwealth Business College, Michigan City, IN, for testing the exercises and assessing instruction
- Ann Lewis, Ivy Tech State College, Evansville, IN, for creating the Chapter Challenge case studies
- Daphne Press, Ozarks Technical Community College, Springfield, MO, for preparing the Internet Projects and Job Study scenarios
- Rob Krumm, Diablo Valley College, Pleasant Hill, CA, for preparing material on XML
- Denise Seguin, Fanshawe College, London, Ontario, Canada, for writing the introductions to Word 2003, Excel 2003, Access 2003, and PowerPoint 2003

Photo Credit: E3, Images.com/CORBIS

Library of Congress Cataloging-in-Publication Data

Rutkosky, Nita Hewitt.
    Microsoft Word 2003 expert certification / Nita Rutkosky.
      p. cm. — (Benchmark series)
    Includes index.
    ISBN 0-7638-2068-7
 1.Microsoft Word. 2. Word processing. 3. Microsoft Word—Examinations—Study
guides. 4. Word processing—Examinations—Study guides. I. Title. II. Benchmark series
(Saint Paul, Minn.)

Z52.5.M52R9454 2004
005.52--dc22

2003049471

Care has been taken to verify the accuracy of information presented in this book. However, the author, editors, and publisher cannot accept any responsibility for Web, e-mail, newsgroup, or chat room subject matter or content, or for consequences from application of the information in this book, and make no warranty, expressed or implied, with respect to its content.

Trademarks: Some of the product names and company names included in this book have been used for identification purposes only and may be trademarks or registered trademarks of their respective manufacturers and sellers. The author, editors, and publisher disclaim any affiliation, association, or connection with, or sponsorship or endorsement by, such owners.

Microsoft and the Microsoft Office Logo are trademarks or registered trademarks of Microsoft Corporation in the United States and/or other countries, and the Microsoft Office Specialist Logo is used under license from owner.

EMC/Paradigm Publishing is independent from Microsoft Corporation, and not affiliated with Microsoft in any manner. This publication may be used in assisting students to prepare for a Microsoft Office Specialist Exam. Neither Microsoft, its designated program administrator or courseware reviewer, nor EMC/Paradigm Publishing warrants that use of this publication will ensure passing the relevant exam.

Text: ISBN 0-7638-2068-7
Product Number 05626

© 2004 by Paradigm Publishing, Inc.
    Published by **EMC**Paradigm
    875 Montreal Way
    St. Paul, MN 55102

    (800) 535-6865
    E-mail: educate@emcp.com
    Web site: www.emcp.com

All rights reserved. No part of this book may be reproduced, stored in a retrieval system, or transmitted, in any form or by any means, electronic, mechanical photocopying, recording, or otherwise, without prior written permission of Paradigm Publishing, Inc.

Printed in the United States of America
10 9 8 7 6 5 4

CONTENTS

Microsoft Word 2003 Expert — E1

Expert Unit 1 Managing Data and Documents — E5

Unit 1 Microsoft Office Specialist Skills Table — E6

Chapter 1 Merging Documents and Sorting and Selecting Data — E7
Completing a Merge with the Mail Merge Wizard — E7
Preparing Envelopes Using the Mail Merge Wizard — E13
Preparing Labels Using the Mail Merge Wizard — E15
Preparing a Directory Using the Mail Merge Wizard — E17
Completing a Merge Using Outlook Information as the Data Source — E19
Editing Merge Documents — E20
Editing Merge Documents Using the Mail Merge Wizard — E20
Editing Merge Documents Using the Mail Merge Toolbar — E21
Inputting Text during a Merge — E23
Sorting Text — E26
Sorting Text in Paragraphs — E27
Changing Sort Options — E28
Sorting Text in Columns — E30
Sorting on More than One Field — E31
Specifying a Header Row — E33
Sorting Text in Tables — E33
Sorting Records in a Data Source — E35
Selecting Records — E38
Chapter Summary — *E41*
Features Summary — *E43*
Concepts Check — *E43*
Skills Check — *E44*
Chapter Challenge — *E47*

Chapter 2 Formatting with Special Features — E49
Inserting a Nonbreaking Space — E49
Finding and Replacing Special Characters — E51
Inserting a Manual Line Break — E52
Controlling Pagination — E53
Turning On/Off Widow/Orphan Control — E54
Keeping a Paragraph or Paragraphs Together — E54
Creating Footnotes and Endnotes — E55
Printing Footnotes and Endnotes — E58
Viewing and Editing Footnotes and Endnotes — E59
Moving, Copying, or Deleting Footnotes or Endnotes — E60
Automatically Summarizing a Document — E61
Analyzing a Document with Readability Statistics — E63
Performing Calculations on Data in a Table — E64
Modifying Table Formats and Properties — E66
Changing Data Direction in Cell — E67
Recalculating a Formula — E69
Inserting and Modifying Fields — E69
Customizing Toolbars — E72
Customizing Menus — E74
Chapter Summary — *E77*
Features Summary — *E78*
Concepts Check — *E78*
Skills Check — *E79*
Chapter Challenge — *E82*

Chapter 3 Adding Visual Elements — E83
Inserting Page Borders — E83
Inserting Horizontal Lines — E85
Inserting and Customizing Images — E87
Formatting an Image with Buttons on the Picture Toolbar — E87
Sizing and Moving an Image — E88
Formatting an Image at the Format Picture Dialog Box — E90
Displaying Images in an Editable Format — E94
Inserting and Aligning Objects — E95
Flipping and Rotating an Object — E98
Creating a Watermark — E100
Using WordArt — E102
Sizing and Moving WordArt — E104
Customizing WordArt — E105
Customizing WordArt with Buttons on the Drawing Toolbar — E107
Creating and Formatting Web Pages — E109
Applying a Theme — E110
Formatting with Buttons on the Web Tools Toolbar — E110
Applying a Background to a Document — E112
Inserting Frames in a Document — E113
Downloading and Saving Web Pages and Images — E116
Opening and Editing a Saved Web Page — E117
Inserting a Saved Image — E118
Chapter Summary — *E119*
Features Summary — *E120*
Concepts Check — *E121*
Skills Check — *E121*
Chapter Challenge — *E126*

Chapter 4 Formatting with Macros and Styles — E127
Creating Macros — E127
Recording a Macro — E128
Running a Macro — E130
Pausing and Then Resuming a Macro — E131
Deleting a Macro — E131

Assigning a Macro a Keyboard Command	E131
Assigning a Macro to the Toolbar	E133
Recording a Macro with Fill-In Fields	E136
Editing a Macro	E138
Formatting Text with Styles	E140
Formatting with AutoFormat	E141
Creating Styles	E142
Creating a Style by Example	E142
Creating a Style Using the New Style Dialog Box	E143
Applying a Style	E145
Assigning a Shortcut Key Combination to a Style	E146
Modifying a Style	E148
Creating a Style by Modifying an Existing Style	E149
Creating and Modifying a List Style	E151
Removing a Style from Text	E153
Renaming a Style	E153
Deleting a Style	E153
Copying a Style to a Template	E154
Deleting a Style from a Template	E155
Navigating in a Document	E156
Navigating Using the Thumbnails Pane	E156
Navigating Using the Document Map Pane	E157
Using Bookmarks	E158
Creating a Cross-Reference	E160
Chapter Summary	*E161*
Features Summary	*E162*
Concepts Check	*E163*
Skills Check	*E163*
Chapter Challenge	*E167*

Expert Unit 1 Performance Assessment — E169

Assessing Proficiencies	E169
Writing Activity	E176
Internet Project	E177
Job Study	E178

Expert Unit 2 Sharing and Publishing Information — E179

Unit 2 Microsoft Office Specialist Skills Table — E180

Chapter 5 Working with Shared Documents — E181

Tracking Changes to a Document	E181
Controlling the Display of Editing Markings	E182
Customizing Track Changes Options	E183
Creating Multiple Versions of a Document	E186
Saving a Version of a Document	E186
Opening an Earlier Version	E188
Saving a Version as a Separate Document	E188
Deleting a Version	E188
Protecting Documents	E189
Restricting Formatting	E190
Restricting Editing	E191
Allowing Exceptions	E192
Enforcing Restrictions	E192
Protecting a Document with a Password	E197
Identifying a Document as Read-Only	E197
Creating and Applying a Digital Signature	E198
Customizing Document Properties	E200
Changing the Default Font	E202
Searching for Specific Documents	E203
Completing Advanced Searches	E205
Creating a Custom Dictionary	E208
Changing the Default Dictionary	E209
Removing a Dictionary	E209
Creating a Template	E210
Changing the Default File Location for Workgroup Templates	E210
Chapter Summary	*E213*
Features Summary	*E214*
Concepts Check	*E215*
Skills Check	*E215*
Chapter Challenge	*E219*

Chapter 6 Sharing Data — E221

Importing Data	E222
Importing Data into a Chart	E222
Importing a Worksheet into a Table	E224
Copying an Object	E230
Creating a Form	E231
Creating the Form Template	E232
Changing File Locations	E232
Filling in a Form Document	E235
Printing a Form	E236
Editing a Form Template	E237
Opening a Template Document	E238
Customizing Form Field Options	E239
Creating Form Fields with Drop-Down Lists	E239
Changing Text Form Field Options	E240
Changing Check Box Form Field Options	E241
Creating Tables in a Form Template	E245
Creating a Master Document and Subdocuments	E247
Creating a Master Document	E248
Opening and Closing a Master Document and Subdocument	E248
Expanding/Collapsing Subdocuments	E249
Locking/Unlocking a Subdocument	E249
Rearranging Subdocuments	E251
Removing a Subdocument	E252
Splitting/Combining Subdocuments	E252
Renaming a Subdocument	E252

Chapter Summary	*E254*
Features Summary	*E255*
Concepts Check	*E256*
Skills Check	*E256*
Chapter Challenge	*E261*

Chapter 7 Creating Specialized Tables and Indexes — E263

Creating a Table of Contents	E263
Marking Table of Contents Entries as Styles	E264
Compiling a Table of Contents	E264
Assigning Levels to Table of Contents Entries	E267
Marking Table of Contents Entries as Fields	E269
Updating a Table of Contents	E271
Deleting a Table of Contents	E272
Creating an Index	E272
Marking Text for an Index	E273
Compiling an Index	E276
Creating a Concordance File	E277
Updating or Deleting an Index	E280
Creating a Table of Figures	E281
Creating Captions	E281
Compiling a Table of Figures	E282
Updating or Deleting a Table of Figures	E284
Creating a Table of Authorities	E284
Compiling a Table of Authorities	E285
Updating or Deleting a Table of Authorities	E288
Chapter Summary	*E289*
Features Summary	*E290*
Concepts Check	*E290*
Skills Check	*E291*
Chapter Challenge	*E293*

Chapter 8 Using XML in Word 2003 — E295

Introducing XML	E295
Providing Structure with XML Schemas	E296
Working with XML Schemas in Word 2003	E296
Attaching an XML Schema	E298
Extracting Data as XML	E301
Using the XML Data in a Different Application	E305
Using Schemas as Templates	E307
Validating a Schema	E307
Enhancing the Schema	E314
Using XML to Create Fill-In Documents	E316
Generating XML Data with a Form	E317
Transforming XML with Style Sheets	E319
Transforming XML	E320
Streamlining XML in Word	E322
Deleting Schemas and Solutions	E324
Chapter Summary	*E325*
Features Summary	*E326*
Concepts Check	*E326*
Skills Check	*E327*
Chapter Challenge	*E330*

Unit 2 Performance Assessment — E331

Assessing Proficiencies	E331
Writing Activities	E337
Internet Project	E338
Job Study	E339

Index — E341

WELCOME

You are about to begin working with a textbook that is part of the Benchmark Office 2003 Series. The word *Benchmark* in the title holds a special significance in terms of *what* you will learn and *how* you will learn. *Benchmark*, according to *Webster's Dictionary*, means "something that serves as a standard by which others may be measured or judged." In this text, you will learn the Microsoft Office Specialist skills required for certification on the Specialist and/or Expert level of one or more major applications within the Office 2003 suite. These skills are benchmarks by which you will be evaluated, should you choose to take one or more certification exams.

The design and teaching approach of this textbook also serve as a benchmark for instructional materials on software programs. Features and commands are presented in a clear, straightforward way, and each short section of instruction is followed by an exercise that lets you practice using the new feature. Gradually, as you move through each chapter, you will build your skills to the point of mastery. At the end of a chapter, you are offered the opportunity to demonstrate your newly acquired competencies—to prove you have met the benchmarks for using the Office suite or an individual program. At the completion of the text, you are well on your way to becoming a successful computer user.

EMC/Paradigm's Office 2003 Benchmark Series includes textbooks on Office 2003, Word 2003, Excel 2003, Access 2003 and PowerPoint 2003. Each book includes a Student CD, which contains documents and files required for completing the exercises. A CD icon and folder name displayed on the opening page of each chapter indicates that you need to copy a folder of files from the CD before beginning the chapter exercises. *(See the inside back cover for instructions on copying a folder.)*

Introducing Microsoft Office 2003

Microsoft Office 2003 is a suite of programs designed to improve productivity and efficiency in workplace, school, and home settings. A suite is a group of programs that are sold as a package and are designed to be used together, making it possible to exchange files among the programs. The major applications included in Office are Word, a word processing program; Excel, a spreadsheet program; Access, a database management program; and PowerPoint, a slide presentation program.

Using the Office suite offers significant advantages over working with individual programs developed by different software vendors. The programs in the Office suite use similar toolbars, buttons, icons, and menus, which means that once you learn the basic features of one program, you can use those same features in the other programs. This easy transfer of knowledge decreases the learning time and allows you to concentrate on the unique commands and options within each program. The compatibility of the programs creates seamless integration of data within and between programs and lets the operator use the program most appropriate for the required tasks.

New Features in Office 2003

Users of previous editions of Office will find that the essential features that have made Office popular still form the heart of the suite. New enhancements include improved templates for both business and personal use. The Smart Tags introduced in Office XP also have been enhanced in Office 2003 with special customization options. One of the most far-reaching changes is the introduction of XML (eXtensible Markup Language) capabilities. Some elements of this technology were essentially hidden behind the scenes in Office XP. Now XML has been brought to the forefront. XML enables data to be used more flexibly and stored regardless of the computer platform. It can be used between different languages, countries, and across the Internet. XML heralds a revolution in data exchange. At the same time, it makes efficient and effective use of internal data within a business.

Structure of the Benchmark Textbooks

Users of the Specialist Certification texts and the complete application textbooks may begin their course with an overview of computer hardware and software, offered in the *Getting Started* section at the beginning of the book. Your instructor may also ask you to complete the *Windows XP* and the *Internet Explorer* sections so you become familiar with the computer's operating system and the essential tools for using the Internet.

Instruction on the major programs within the Office suite is presented in units of four chapters each. Both the Specialist and Expert levels contain two units, which culminate with performance assessments to check your knowledge and skills. Each chapter contains the following sections:

- performance objectives that identify specifically what you are expected to learn
- instructional text that introduces and explains new concepts and features
- step-by-step, hands-on exercises following each section of instruction
- a chapter summary
- a knowledge self-check called Concepts Check
- skill assessment exercises called Skills Check
- a case study exercise called Chapter Challenge

Exercises offered at the end of units provide writing and research opportunities that will strengthen your performance in other college courses as well as on the job. The final activities simulate interesting projects you could encounter in the workplace.

Benchmark Series Ancillaries

The Benchmark Series includes some important resources that will help you succeed in your computer applications courses:

Snap Training and Assessment

A Web-based program designed to optimize skill-based learning for all of the programs of Microsoft Office 2003, Snap is comprised of:

- a learning management system that creates a virtual classroom on the Web, allowing the instructor to schedule tutorials and tests and to employ an electronic gradebook;
- over 200 interactive, multimedia tutorials, aligned to textbook chapters, that can be used for direct instruction or remediation;
- a test bank of over 1,800 performance skill items that simulate the operation of Microsoft Office and allow the instructor to assign pretests, to administer chapter posttests, and to create practice tests to help students prepare for Microsoft Office Specialist certification exams; and
- over 6,000 concept items that can be used in combined concepts/application courses to monitor student understanding of technical and computer literacy knowledge.

Online Resource Center

Internet Resource Centers hosted by EMC/Paradigm provide additional material for students and instructors using the Benchmark books. Online you will find Web links, updates to textbooks, study tips, quizzes and assignments, and supplementary projects.

Class Connection

Available for both WebCT and Blackboard, EMC/Paradigm's Class Connection is a course management tool for traditional and distance learning.

What does this logo mean?

It means this courseware has been approved by the Microsoft® Office Specialist program to be among the finest available for learning Microsoft Word 2003. It also means that upon completion of this courseware, you may be prepared to take an exam for Microsoft Office Specialist qualification.

What is a Microsoft Office Specialist?

A Microsoft Office Specialist is an individual who has passed exams for certifying his or her skills in one or more of the Microsoft Office desktop applications such as Microsoft Word, Microsoft Excel, Microsoft PowerPoint, Microsoft Outlook, Microsoft Access, or Microsoft Project. The Microsoft Office Specialist Program typically offers certification exams at the Specialist and Expert skill levels. The Microsoft Office Specialist Program is the only program in the world approved by Microsoft for testing proficiency in Microsoft Office desktop applications and Microsoft Project. This testing program can be a valuable asset in any job search or career advancement.

More Information

- To learn more about becoming a Microsoft Office Specialist, visit www.microsoft.com/officespecialist
- To learn about other Microsoft Office Specialist approved courseware from EMC/Paradigm Publishing, visit www.emcp.com

---

The availability of Microsoft Office Specialist certification exams varies by application, application version, and language. Visit www.microsoft.com/officespecialist for information on exam availability.

Microsoft, the Microsoft Office Logo, PowerPoint, and Outlook are trademarks or registered trademarks of Microsoft Corporation in the United States and/or other countries, and the Microsoft Office Specialist Logo is used under license from owner.

EXPERT
MICROSOFT® WORD

A multitude of advanced features in Microsoft Word 2003 allow individuals and companies to efficiently organize, analyze, and present more complex tasks to meet the information needs of the new century. Learning these skills to become an Expert Word professional will help you gain a competitive edge in the workplace.

Organizing Information

Connecting the pages in a long document such as a report, proposal, or essay provides a frame of reference for the reader and visually unifies the pages. Accomplish this effect by incorporating headers and footers that include text and page numbering that print at the top or bottom of each page. Readers will appreciate the continuity.

Need to credit a source or include reference information? Open the Footnote or Endnote pane depending on whether you want the source at the bottom (footnote) or end of the document (endnote) and then type the reference information. Let Word do the job of automatically keeping track of the reference numbers so you can add, modify, or delete references as necessary without the worry of renumbering existing references. In addition to footnotes and endnotes, Word can automatically number captions and cross references.

EXPERT

Making WORD Work for YOU!

Including a table of contents and/or an index at the beginning or end of a long report, proposal, or research paper is easy with Microsoft Word 2003. Mark entries within the document that need to be included in the table or index and then let Word generate the page numbers and text entries for you. Changes made to the document? New entries marked? No problem—just tell Word to update the table and index and watch the screen regenerate the lists. A table of figures and table of authorities can also be generated from the Index and Tables dialog box.

Need to send a standard letter to a list of clients? It's as easy as 1, 2, 3! Creating customized form letters and generating mailing labels or envelopes generally involves two documents that are merged into one. Use Word's Mail Merge Wizard—a series of six task panes—to step you through the process of: (1) creating the data to be included in the mailing list; (2) preparing the standard letter with the codes that tell Word where to insert customized information; and (3) merging the documents.

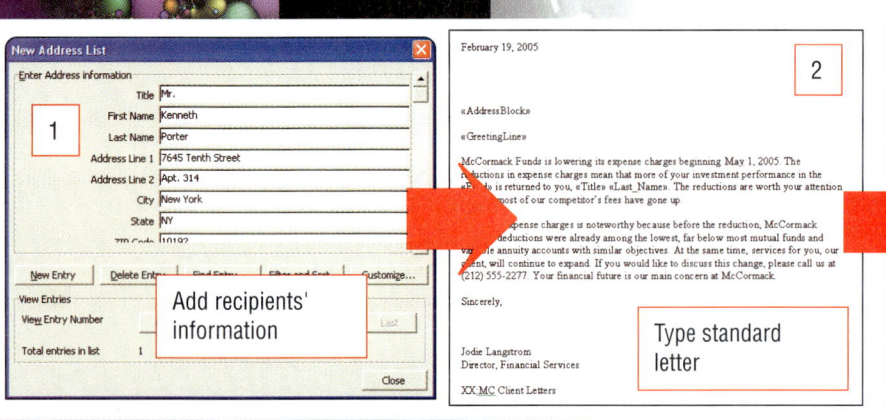

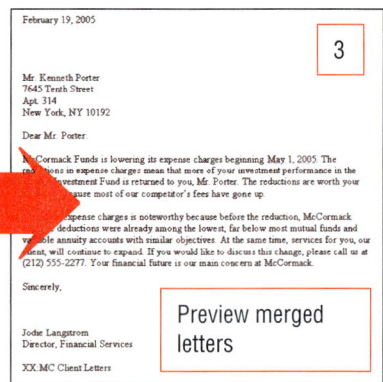

Analyzing Information

XML (Extensible Markup Language) is leading business to a new level of document standardization that will become more commonplace within the next few years. XML standards, developed by various XML Working Groups of the World Wide Web Consortium (W3C), offer flexibility and adaptability to businesses by specifying a file format for the storage and transmission of text and data—both on and off the Web. XML tags in a document are designed to describe the data—what it is as opposed to how the Web browser should display it. Businesses will be eager to produce XML-documents since these files will have the ability to be understood by many different types of applications (word processor, spreadsheet, or database) internal and external to the organization. Stakeholders will be able to share and exchange information without the worry of whether their business partners have compatible systems. Microsoft Word 2003 is XML-ready. Create a document as you normally would and then with an XML schema selected, change the file type to XML document.

When you find yourself repeating the same sequence of steps over and over again for a specific task or document, it's time to think "macro." Use macros to automate repetitive tasks. Assign the macro to a keyboard shortcut and the next time you do the activity all you need to do is press the shortcut keys. Maximize your time with a minimum of effort!

Use the Forms toolbar to create an application or registration document that includes items such as text fields and check boxes. The next time you are planning a conference, seminar, or sales leader follow-up form, use the Forms tools to create a customized form that looks professionally prepared.

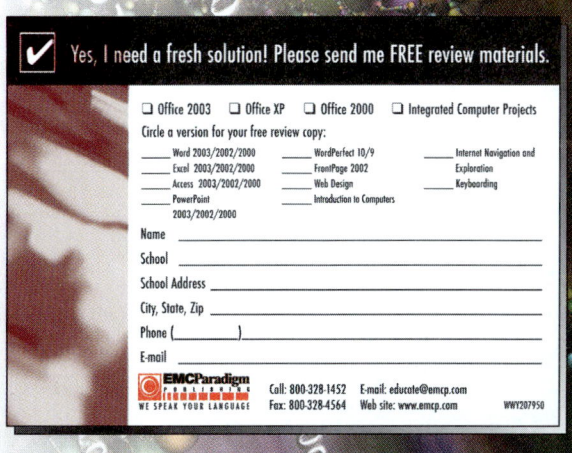

Use the Formula box to perform calculations on columns in tables — similar to a speadsheet

Presenting Information

Create exciting invitations, announcements, signs, fundraising letters, and more using clip art, WordArt, and by drawing graphics using tools on the Drawing toolbar. The Clip Art task pane provides the ability to search for media such as Clip Art, Photographs, Movies, and Sound by descriptive keywords. With an Internet connection, you have access to the Web collection found at Microsoft Office Online where you can search for that perfect clip in over 40 categories of frequently-updated media.

Adding visual appeal to documents by inserting and modifying pictures, drawing lines and shapes, adding watermarks, and creating WordArt will have your business associates, friends, family, and neighbors eagerly anticipating your next event!

Tables are one of the most versatile features in Word. Information presented in a table format is easy to read and comprehend. Readers can quickly grasp the significance of numbers presented in a table rather than poring over long explanatory paragraphs of text. Once the table is created, apply advanced formatting options, sort data in columns within a table, and do simple calculations by adding formulas. A variety of table autoformats are included for you to browse when deciding on a table's appearance.

For any employee who uses Microsoft Word, the more advanced features will help use the program to its fullest capabilities. Learn valuable time-saving tips, how to add visual eye-catching graphics, and master how to manage long documents. It's easier than you think to acquire the skills to become a Word Expert.

EXPERT

MICROSOFT® WORD

Unit 1: Managing Data and Documents

- Merging Documents and Sorting and Selecting Data
- Formatting with Special Features
- Adding Visual Elements
- Formatting with Macros and Styles

BENCHMARK MICROSOFT® WORD 2003

MICROSOFT OFFICE SPECIALIST EXPERT SKILLS—UNIT 1

Reference No.	Skill	Pages
WW03E-1	**Formatting Content**	
WW03E-1-1	Create custom styles for text, tables and lists	
	Format text with styles	E140-E142
	Create styles	E142-E144
	Apply styles	E145-E148
	Modify styles	E148-E156
WW03E-1-2	Control pagination	
	Turn widow/orphan control on/off	E53-E55
	Insert manual line break	E52-E53
WW03E-1-3	Format, position and resize graphics using advanced layout features	
	Insert page borders	E83-E86
	Create, format and customize objects	E87-E95
	Insert and align graphic elements	E95-E99
	Flip, rotate and crop objects	E98-E99
	Apply advanced layout and text wrapping options	E90-E94
	Control image brightness and contrast	E88-E89
	Size and position an object	E88-E94
WW03E-1-4	Insert and modify objects	
	Insert and modify objects	E87-E100
	Insert and modify WordArt	E102-E109
WW03E-2	**Organizing Content**	
WW03E-2-1	Sort content in lists and table	
	Sort text	E26-E30
	Sort text in columns	E30-E33
	Sort text in tables	E33-E35
	Sort records in a data source	E35-E37
WW03E-2-2	Perform calculations in tables	E64-E66
WW03E-2-3	Modify table formats	
	Modify table formats and properties	E66-E69
	Insert and modify fields	E69-E72
WW03E-2-4	Summarize document content using automated tools	
	Automatically summarize document	E61-E63
	Analyze document with readability statistics	E63-E64
WW03E-2-5	Use automated tools for document navigation	
	Navigate using thumbnails	E156-E158
	Navigate using Document Map	E157-E158
	Insert bookmarks	E158-E159
WW03E-2-6	Merge letters with other data sources	E7-E26
WW03E-2-7	Merge labels with other data sources	E15-E17
WW03E-3	**Formatting Documents**	
WW03E-3-2	Create and modify document background	
	Create a watermark	E100-E102
	Apply and modify a theme	E110-E112
	Apply a background color and fill effect	E112-E116
WW03E-3-4	Insert and modify endnotes, footnotes, captions, and cross-references	
	Create and modify footnotes and endnotes	E55-E61
	Insert a cross-reference	E160-E161
WW03E-4	**Collaborating**	
WW03E-4-2	Publish and edit Web documents in Word	
	Create and format Web pages	E109-E116
	Download and save Web pages and images	E116-E118
	Insert and modify frames	E113-E116
WW03E-5	**Customizing Word**	
WW03E-5-1	Create, edit, and run macros	
	Record and run macros	E127-E140
	Assign a macro a keyboard command	E131-E133
	Assign a macro to a toolbar	E133-E135
	Record a macro with a fill-in field	E136-E138
	Edit a macro using the Visual Basic Editor	E138-E140
WW03E-5-2	Customize menus and toolbars	
	Customize toolbars	E72-E74
	Customize menus	E74-E76

CHAPTER 1

MERGING DOCUMENTS AND SORTING AND SELECTING DATA

PERFORMANCE OBJECTIVES

Upon successful completion of Chapter 1, you will be able to:
- Use the Mail Merge Wizard to create letters, envelopes, labels, and a directory
- Create custom fields for a merge
- Edit main documents and data source files
- Input text during a merge
- Sort text in paragraphs, columns, and tables
- Sort records in a data source file
- Sort on more than one field
- Select specific records in a data source file for merging

Word includes a Mail Merge Wizard you can use to create customized letters, envelopes, labels, directories, e-mail messages, and faxes. The Mail Merge Wizard guides you through six steps to create customized documents including steps from selecting a document type to executing the final merge. The Mail Merge Wizard presents a Mail Merge task pane for each step. This allows you to work in your document without having to close the wizard.

Word includes some basic database functions you can use to alphabetize information, arrange numbers numerically, and select specific records from a document. In addition, you can sort text in paragraphs, columns, tables, and data sources and select specific records from a document.

Completing a Merge with the Mail Merge Wizard

A merge generally takes two files—the ***data source*** file and the ***main document***. The data source file contains the variable information that will be inserted in the main document. Before creating a data source file, determine what type of correspondence you will be creating and the type of information you will need to insert in the correspondence. Word provides predetermined field names that can be used when creating the data source file. Use these field names if they represent the data you are creating. Variable information in a data source file is saved as a

Begin Mail Merge Wizard
1. Click Tools.
2. Point to Letters and Mailings.
3. Click Mail Merge.

Merging Documents and Sorting and Selecting Data

record. A record contains all of the information for one unit (for example, a person, family, customer, client, or business). A series of fields makes one record, and a series of records makes a data source file. The main document contains standard text along with fields identifying where variable information is inserted during the merge process.

The Mail Merge Wizard guides you through the merge process and presents six task panes. Begin the Wizard by clicking Tools, pointing to Letters and Mailings, and then clicking Mail Merge. The options in each task pane may vary depending on the type of merge you are performing. Generally, you complete the following steps at each of the six task panes:

> **HINT**
> If you want merged data formatted, you must format the merge fields at the main document.

Step 1: Identify the type of document you are creating (letter, e-mail message, envelope, label, or directory).
Step 2: Specify whether you want to use the current document window to create the document, start from a template, or start from an existing document.
Step 3: Specify whether you are using an existing list (for the variable information), selecting from an Outlook contacts list, or typing a new list. Depending on the choice you make, you may need to select a specific data source file or create a new data source file.
Step 4: Use the items in this task pane to help you prepare the main document. For example, if you are creating a letter, click the Address block hyperlink and the wizard inserts the required codes in the main document for merging names and addresses. Click the Greeting hyperlink and the wizard inserts codes for a greeting.
Step 5: Preview the merged documents.
Step 6: Complete the merge. At this step, you can send the merged document to the printer and/or edit the merged document.

> **HINT**
> View the merged document before printing to ensure that the merged data is correct.

If you choose to type a new list at Step 3, the Mail Merge Wizard saves the completed list in the My Data Sources folder as an Access database file. Microsoft Word looks for data source files in this folder. In a multi-user environment, such as a school, you may want to specify a different location for your list. The Mail Merge Wizard provides a variety of predesigned fields. If these fields do not provide all variable information in a main document, you can create your own custom field. For Exercise 1, you will prepare a data source file using predesigned fields as well as a custom field. You will also prepare a main document and then merge the documents to create form letters. In Exercises 2, 3, and 4, you will use the data source file created in Exercise 1 to prepare envelopes, labels, and a directory.

(Before completing computer exercises, copy to your disk the WordChapter01E subfolder from the Word2003Expert folder on the CD that accompanies this textbook. Steps on how to copy a folder are presented on the inside of the back cover of this textbook. Do this every time you start a chapter's exercises.)

exercise 1

PREPARING FORM LETTERS USING THE MAIL MERGE WIZARD

1. At a clear document screen, click Tools, point to Letters and Mailings, and then click Mail Merge.
2. At the first wizard step at the Mail Merge task pane, make sure the *Letters* option is selected in the *Select document type* section of the task pane, and then click the Next: Starting document hyperlink located toward the bottom of the task pane.

3. At the second wizard step, make sure the *Use the current document* option is selected in the *Select starting document* section of the task pane, and then click the Next: Select recipients hyperlink located toward the bottom of the task pane.
4. At the third wizard step, click *Type a new list* in the *Select recipients* section of the task pane.
5. Click the Create hyperlink that displays in the *Type a new list* section of the task pane.
6. At the New Address List dialog box, the Mail Merge Wizard provides you with a number of predesigned fields. Delete the fields you do not need by completing the following steps:
   a. Click the Customize button.
   b. At the Customize Address List dialog box, click *Company Name* to select it, and then click the Delete button.
   c. At the message asking if you are sure you want to delete the field, click the Yes button.
   d. Complete steps similar to those in Steps 6b and 6c to delete the following fields:
      Country
      Home Phone
      Work Phone
      E-mail Address
   e. Insert a custom field by completing the following steps:
      1) At the Customize Address List box, click the Add button.
      2) At the Add Field dialog box, type **Fund** and then click OK.
   f. Click the OK button to close the Customize Address List dialog box.
7. At the New Address List dialog box, type the information for the first client as shown in Figure 1.1 by completing the following steps:

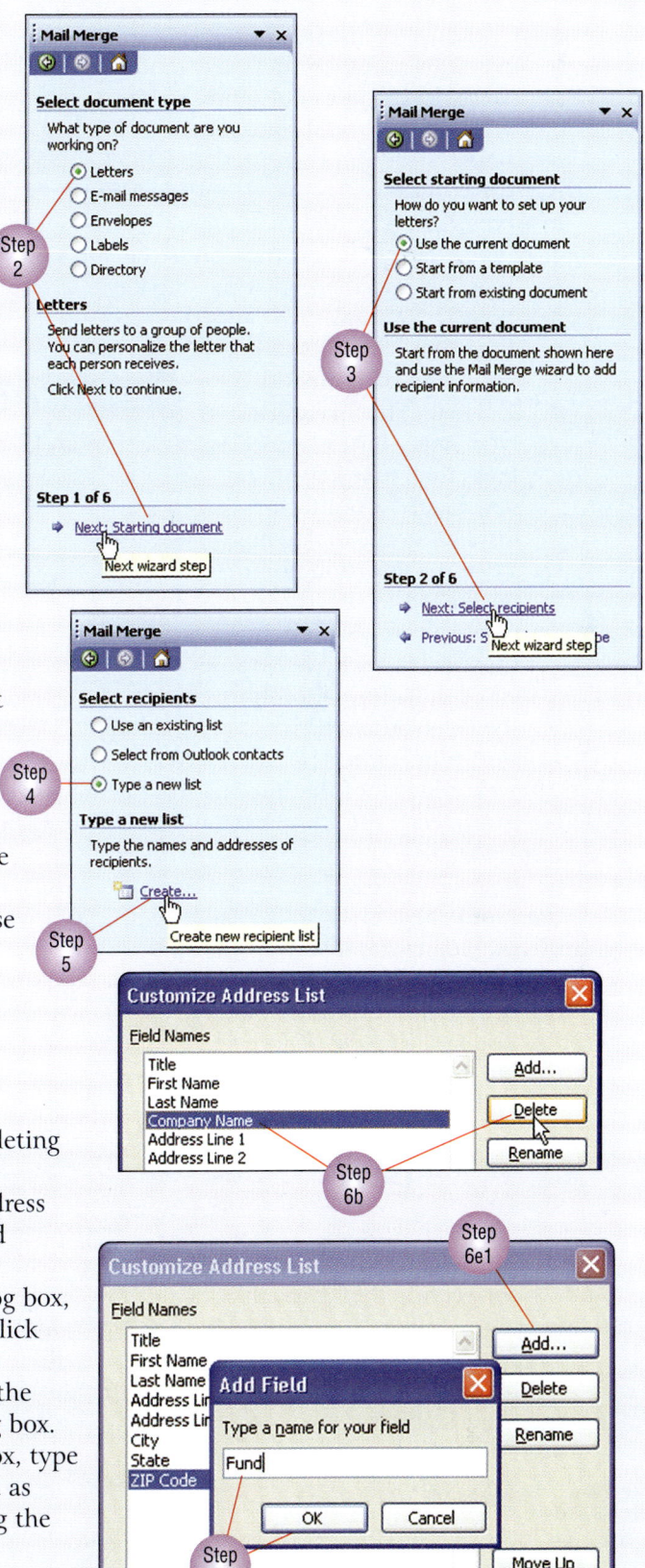

a. Click in the *Title* text box.
b. Type **Mr.** and then press the Tab key. (This moves the insertion point to the *First Name* field. You can also press Shift + Tab to move to the previous field.)
c. Type **Kenneth** and then press the Tab key.
d. Type **Porter** and then press the Tab key.
e. Type **7645 Tenth Street** and then press the Tab key.
f. Type **Apt. 314** and then press the Tab key.
g. Type **New York** and then press the Tab key.
h. Type **NY** and then press the Tab key.
i. Type **10192** and then press the Tab key.
j. Type **Mutual Investment Fund** and then press the Tab key. (This makes the New Entry button active.)
k. Press the Enter key and a new blank record form displays in the dialog box.
l. With the insertion point positioned in the *Title* field, complete steps similar to those in 7b through 7j to enter the information for the three other clients shown in Figure 1.1.

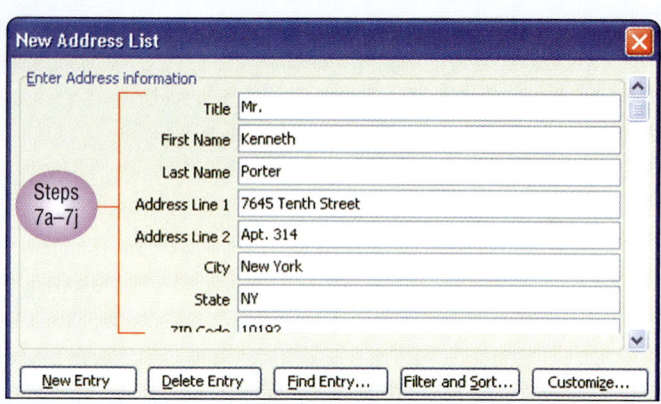

Steps 7a–7j

8. After entering all of the information for the last client in Figure 1.1 (Mrs. Wanda Houston), click the Close button located in the bottom right corner of the New Address List dialog box.
9. At the Save Address List dialog box, specify that you want the data source file saved in the WordChapter01E folder on your disk in drive A and then name the data source file by completing the following steps:
    a. Click the down-pointing arrow at the right of the *Save in* option box.
    b. At the drop-down list that displays, click *3½ Floppy (A:)*.
    c. Double-click the *WordChapter01E* folder.
    d. Click in the *File name* text box and then type **MCClientList**.
    e. Press Enter or click the Save button.
    f. At the Mail Merge Recipients dialog box, check to make sure all four entries are correct and then click the OK button.

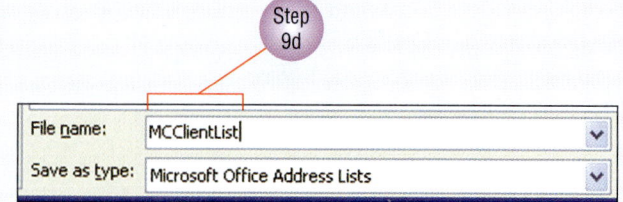

Step 9d

10. Move to the next step by clicking the <u>Next: Write your letter</u> hyperlink that displays toward the bottom of the task pane.
11. At the fourth wizard step, create the letter shown in Figure 1.2 by completing the following steps:
    a. Press the Enter key six times, type **February 21, 2005**, and then press the Enter key five times.

b. Insert the address fields by clicking the Address block hyperlink located in the *Write your letter* section of the task pane.
c. At the Insert Address Block dialog box, click the OK button.
d. Press the Enter key twice and then click the Greeting line hyperlink located in the *Write your letter* section of the task pane.
e. At the Greeting Line dialog box, click the down-pointing arrow at the right of the option box containing the comma (the box to the right of the box containing *Mr. Randall*).
f. At the drop-down list that displays, click the colon.
g. Click OK to close the Greeting Line dialog box.
h. Press the Enter key twice.
i. Type the letter to the point where «Fund» displays and then insert the «Fund» field by completing the following steps:
   1) Click the More items hyperlink in the *Write your letter* section of the task pane.
   2) At the Insert Merge Field dialog box, click *Fund* in the *Fields* list box.
   3) Click the Insert button and then click the Close button.
j. Type the letter to the point where the «Title» field displays and then insert the «Title» field by completing steps similar to those in Step 11i. Press the spacebar and then insert the «Last_Name» field by completing steps similar to those in Step 11i.
k. Type the remainder of the letter shown in Figure 1.2. (Insert your initials instead of the *XX* at the end of the letter.)

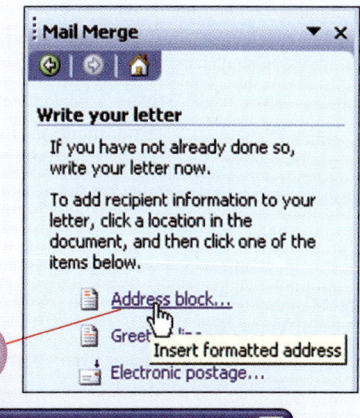
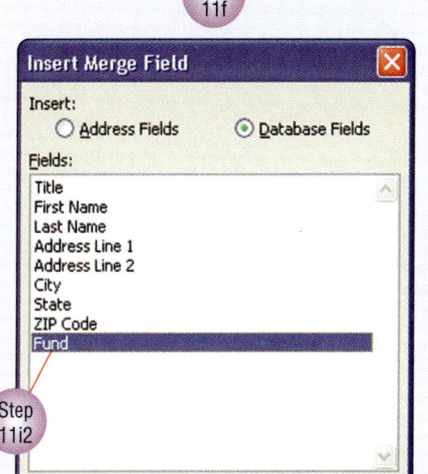

12. When you are finished typing the letter, click the Next: Preview your letters hyperlink located toward the bottom of the task pane.
13. At the fifth wizard step, look over the letter that displays in the document window and make sure the information was merged properly. If you want to see the letters for the other recipients, click the button in the Mail Merge task pane containing the two right-pointing arrows.
14. Click the Next: Complete the merge hyperlink that displays toward the bottom of the task pane.
15. At the sixth wizard step, click the Edit individual letters hyperlink that displays in the *Merge* section of the task pane.

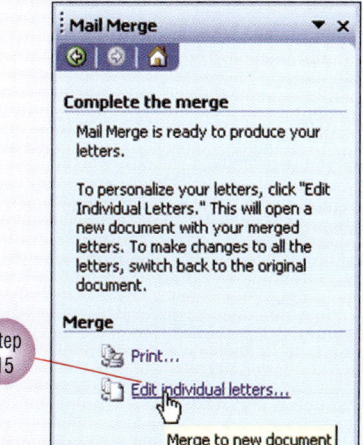

16. At the Merge to New Document dialog box, make sure *All* is selected, and then click the OK button.
17. Save the merged letters in the normal manner in the WordChapter01E folder on your disk in drive A and name the document **MCClientLetters**.
18. Print **MCClientLetters**. (This document will print four letters.)
19. Close **MCClientLetters**.
20. At the sixth wizard step, save the main document in the normal manner in the WordChapter01E folder on your disk in drive A and name it **MCMainDoc**.
21. Close **MCMainDoc** and then close the task pane.

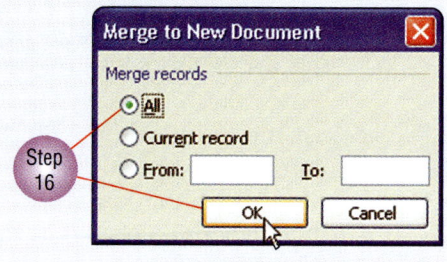

Step 16

FIGURE 1.1 Information for Data Source Fields

Title	=	Mr.	Title	=	Ms.
First Name	=	Kenneth	First Name	=	Carolyn
Last Name	=	Porter	Last Name	=	Renquist
Address Line 1	=	7645 Tenth Street	Address Line 1	=	13255 Meridian Street
Address Line 2	=	Apt. 314	Address Line 2	=	(leave this blank)
City	=	New York	City	=	New York
State	=	NY	State	=	NY
ZIP Code	=	10192	ZIP Code	=	10435
Fund	=	Mutual Investment Fund	Fund	=	Quality Care Fund
Title	=	Dr.	Title	=	Mrs.
First Name	=	Amil	First Name	=	Wanda
Last Name	=	Ranna	Last Name	=	Houston
Address Line 1	=	433 South 17th	Address Line 1	=	566 North 22nd Avenue
Address Line 2	=	Apt. 17-D	Address Line 2	=	(leave this blank)
City	=	New York	City	=	New York
State	=	NY	State	=	NY
ZIP Code	=	10322	ZIP Code	=	10634
Fund	=	Priority One Fund	Fund	=	Quality Care Fund

FIGURE 1.2 Main Document

February 21, 2005

«AddressBlock»

«GreetingLine»

McCormack Funds is lowering its expense charges beginning May 1, 2005. The reductions in expense charges mean that more of your account investment performance in the «Fund» is returned to you, «Title» «Last_Name». The reductions are worth your attention because most of our competitors' fees have gone up.

Lowering expense charges is noteworthy because before the reduction, McCormack expense deductions were already among the lowest, far below most mutual funds and variable annuity accounts with similar objectives. At the same time, services for you, our client, will continue to expand. If you would like to discuss this change, please call us at (212) 555-2277. Your financial future is our main concern at McCormack.

Sincerely,

Jodie Langstrom
Director, Financial Services

XX:MCClientLetters

Preparing Envelopes Using the Mail Merge Wizard

If you create a letter as a main document and then merge it with a data source file, more than likely you will need envelopes properly addressed in which to send the letters. The Mail Merge Wizard guides you through the steps for creating and printing envelopes. For Exercise 2, you will create and print envelopes for the letters you created and printed in Exercise 1.

exercise 2

PREPARING ENVELOPES USING THE MAIL MERGE WIZARD

1. At a clear document screen, click Tools, point to Letters and Mailings, and then click Mail Merge.
2. At the first wizard step at the Mail Merge task pane, click *Envelopes* in the *Select document type* section.
3. Click the Next: Starting document hyperlink.
4. At the second wizard step, make sure the *Change document layout* option is selected in the *Select starting document* section, and then click the Next: Select recipients hyperlink located toward the bottom of the task pane.
5. At the Envelope Options dialog box, make sure the envelope size is 10, and then click OK.
6. At the third wizard step, make sure the *Use an existing list* option is selected in the *Select recipients* section.
7. Click the Browse hyperlink located in the *Use an existing list* section.
8. At the Select Data Source dialog box, complete the following steps:
   a. Change the *Look in* option to *3½ Floppy (A:)*.
   b. Double-click the *WordChapter01E* folder.
   c. Double-click **MCClientList** in the Select Data Source list box. (Notice that **MCClientList** is an Access database file and an Access icon displays before the file name.)
   d. At the Mail Merge Recipients dialog box, click OK.
9. Click the Next: Arrange your envelope hyperlink located toward the bottom of the Mail Merge task pane.
10. At the fourth wizard step, complete the following steps:
    a. Click in the approximate location in the envelope in the document window where the recipient's address will appear. (This causes a box with a dashed gray border to display. If you do not see this box, try clicking in a different location on the envelope.)
    b. Click the Address block hyperlink located in the *Arrange your envelope* section of the task pane.

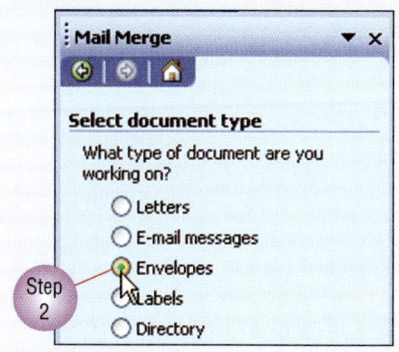
Step 2

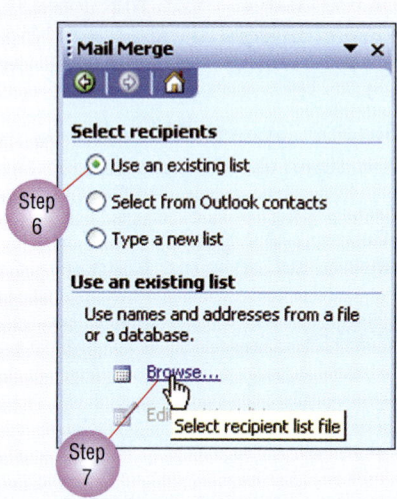
Step 6
Step 7

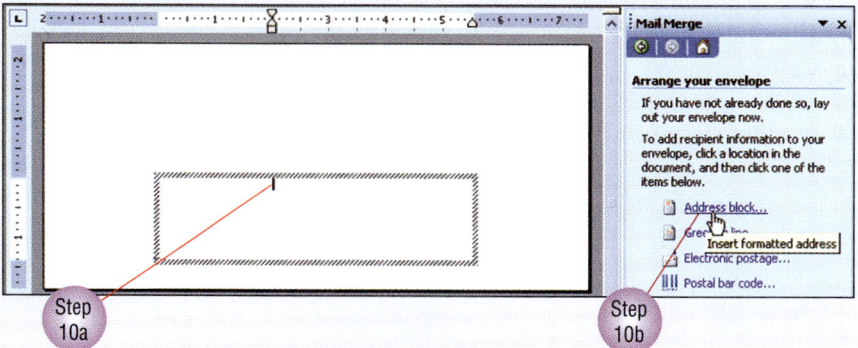
Step 10a
Step 10b

E14 Chapter One

c. At the Insert Address Block dialog box, click OK. (This inserts the field «AddressBlock» inside the box on the envelope.)
11. Click the Next: Preview your envelopes hyperlink located toward the bottom of the Mail Merge task pane.
12. At the fifth wizard step, view the first merged envelope. (To view the other envelopes, click the button located toward the top of the task pane containing the two right-pointing arrows.)
13. Click the Next: Complete the merge hyperlink located toward the bottom of the task pane.
14. At the sixth wizard step, click the Edit individual envelopes hyperlink that displays in the *Merge* section of the task pane.
15. At the Merge to New Document dialog box, make sure *All* is selected, and then click the OK button.
16. Save the merged envelopes in the normal manner in the WordChapter01E folder on your disk in drive A and name the document **MCClientEnvs**.
17. Print **MCClientEnvs**. (This document will print four envelopes. Check with your instructor about specific steps for printing envelopes. You may need to hand-feed envelopes in your printer.)
18. Close **MCClientEnvs**.
19. At the sixth wizard step, save the envelope main document in the normal manner in the WordChapter01E folder on your disk in drive A and name it **MCEnvMainDoc**.
20. Close **MCEnvMainDoc**.

Preparing Labels Using the Mail Merge Wizard

Create mailing labels for records in a data source file in much the same way that you create envelopes. Use the Mail Merge Wizard to guide you through the steps for preparing mailing labels.

exercise 3

PREPARING LABELS USING THE MAIL MERGE WIZARD

1. At a clear document screen, click Tools, point to Letters and Mailings, and then click Mail Merge.
2. At the first wizard step at the Mail Merge task pane, click the *Labels* option in the *Select document type* section.
3. Click the Next: Starting document hyperlink.
4. At the second wizard step, make sure the *Change document layout* option is selected in the *Select starting document* section.
5. Click the Label options hyperlink in the *Change document layout* section of the task pane.
6. At the Label Options dialog box, complete the following steps:
    a. Make sure *Avery standard* displays in the *Label products* option box.

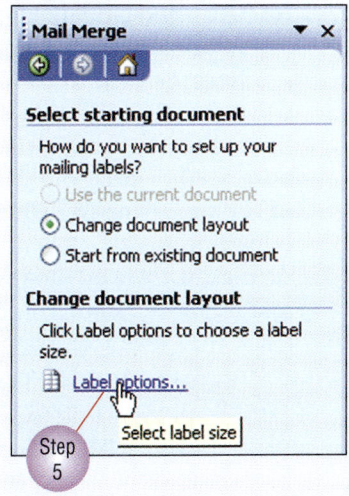
Step 5

b. Scroll down the *Product number* list box until *5260 - Address* is visible, and then click it.
c. Click OK to close the dialog box.
7. Click the Next: Select recipients hyperlink located toward the bottom of the task pane.
8. At the third wizard step, make sure the *Use an existing list* option is selected in the *Select recipients* section.
9. Click the Browse hyperlink located in the *Use an existing list* section.
10. At the Select Data Source dialog box, complete the following steps:
    a. Change the *Look in* option to *3½ Floppy (A:)*.
    b. Double-click the *WordChapter01E* folder.
    c. Double-click **MCClientList** in the *Select Data Source* list box.
    d. At the Mail Merge Recipients dialog box, click OK.
11. Click the Next: Arrange your labels hyperlink located toward the bottom of the Mail Merge task pane.
12. At the fourth wizard step, complete the following steps:
    a. Click the Address block hyperlink located in the *Arrange your labels* section of the task pane.

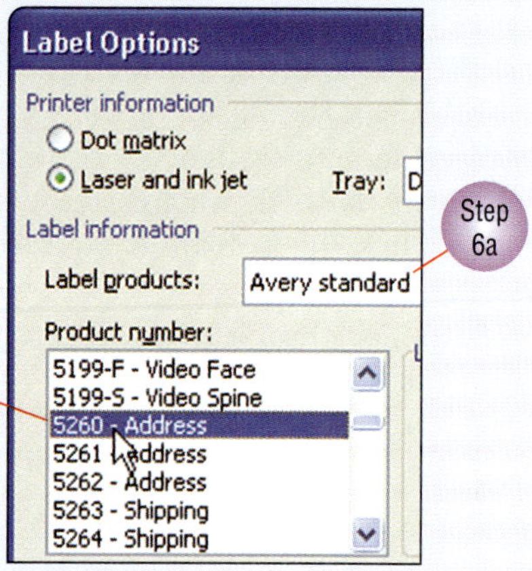

  b. At the Insert Address Block dialog box, click OK. (This inserts «AddressBlock» in the first label. The other labels contain the «Next Record» field.)
  c. Click the Update all labels button in the task pane. (This adds the «AddressBlock» field after each «Next Record» field in the second and subsequent labels.) 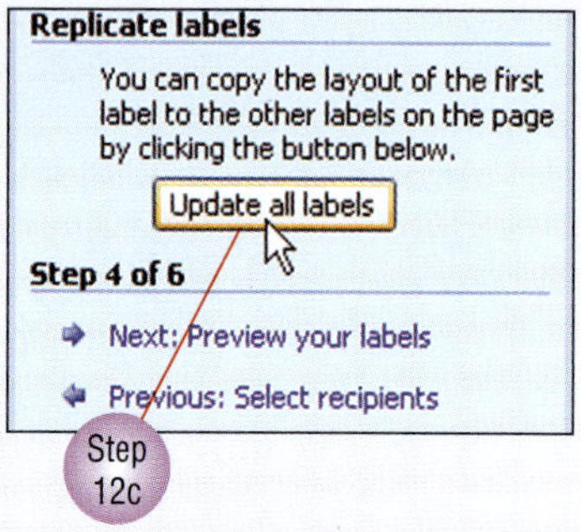
13. Click the Next: Preview your labels hyperlink located toward the bottom of the Mail Merge task pane. (You may need to click the down-pointing arrow at the bottom of the task pane to display the Next: Preview your labels hyperlink.)
14. At the fifth wizard step, view the first merged labels. (Only four labels will contain names and addresses since you only have four records in the **MCClientList** data source file.)
15. Click the Next: Complete the merge hyperlink located toward the bottom of the task pane.
16. At the sixth wizard step, save the merged labels document in the normal manner in the WordChapter01E folder on your disk in drive A and name the document **MCClientLabels**.

17. Print **MCClientLabels**. (Check with your instructor about specific steps for printing labels. You may need to hand-feed paper into the printer.)
18. Close **MCClientLabels**.

Preparing a Directory Using the Mail Merge Wizard

When merging letters, envelopes, or mailing labels, a new form is created for each record. For example, if the data source file merged with the letter contains eight records, eight letters are created. If the data source file merged with a mailing label contains twenty records, twenty labels are created. In some situations, you may want merged information to remain on the same page. This is useful, for example, when creating a list such as a directory or address list. Use the Mail Merge Wizard to create a merged directory. In Exercise 4, you will create a directory that displays the last name, first name, and ZIP Code for the four records in the MCClientList.

PREPARING A DIRECTORY LIST USING THE MAIL MERGE WIZARD

1. At a clear document screen, set left tabs at the 1-inch mark, the 2.5-inch mark, and the 4-inch mark on the Ruler, and then press the Tab key. (This moves the insertion point to the tab set at the 1-inch mark.)
2. Click Tools, point to Letters and Mailings, and then click Mail Merge.
3. At the first wizard step at the Mail Merge task pane, click the *Directory* option in the *Select document type* section.
4. Click the Next: Starting document hyperlink.
5. At the second wizard step, make sure the *Use the current document* option is selected in the *Select starting document* section.
6. Click the Next: Select recipients hyperlink located toward the bottom of the task pane.
7. At the third wizard step, make sure the *Use an existing list* option is selected in the *Select recipients* section.
8. Click the Browse hyperlink located in the *Use an existing list* section.
9. At the Select Data Source dialog box, complete the following steps:
    a. Change the *Look in* option to *3½ Floppy (A:)*.
    b. Double-click the *WordChapter01E* folder.
    c. Double-click **MCClientList** in the *Select Data Source* list box.
    d. At the *Mail Merge Recipients* list box, click OK.
10. Click the Next: Arrange your directory hyperlink located toward the bottom of the Mail Merge task pane.
11. At the fourth wizard step, complete the following steps:

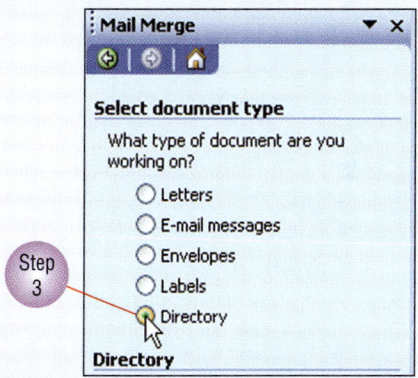

Step 3

a. Click the More items hyperlink located in the *Arrange your directory* section of the task pane.
b. At the Insert Merge Field dialog box, click *Last Name* in the list box, and then click the Insert button. (This inserts the «Last_Name» field in the document.)
c. Click the Close button to close the Insert Merge Field dialog box.
d. Press the Tab key to move the insertion point to the tab set at the 2.5-inch mark.
e. Click the More items hyperlink.

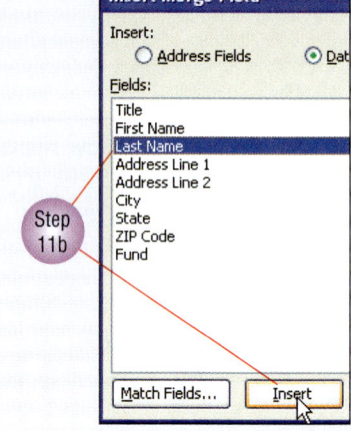
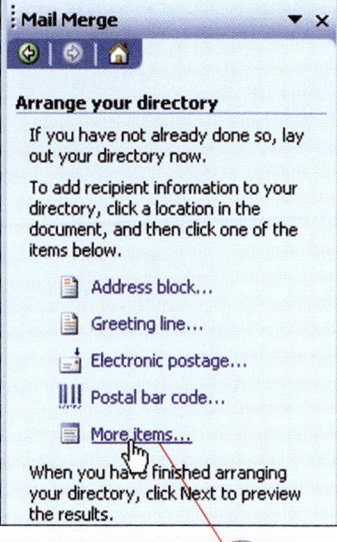

f. At the Insert Merge Field dialog box, click *First Name* in the list box, and then click the Insert button. (This inserts the «First_Name» field in the document.)
g. Click the Close button to close the Insert Merge Field dialog box.
h. Press the Tab key to move the insertion point to the tab set at the 4-inch mark.
i. Click the More items hyperlink.
j. At the Insert Merge Field dialog box, click *ZIP Code* in the list box, and then click the Insert button. (This inserts the «ZIP_Code» field in the document.)
k. Click the Close button to close the Insert Merge Field dialog box.
l. Press the Enter key once.

12. Click the Next: Preview your directory hyperlink located toward the bottom of the Mail Merge task pane.
13. At the fifth wizard step, view the first merged record. (Only the first record displays at this step.)
14. Click the Next: Complete the merge hyperlink located toward the bottom of the task pane.
15. At the sixth wizard step, click the To New Document hyperlink located in the *Merge* section of the task pane.
16. At the Merge to New Document dialog box, make sure *All* is selected, and then click OK.
17. At the document (with the four records displayed), make the following changes:

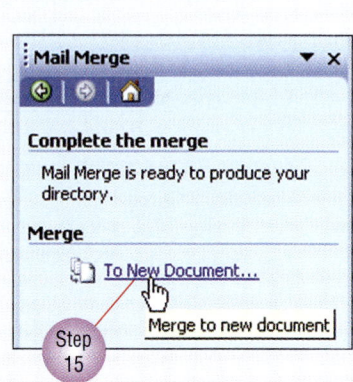

   a. Press the Enter key twice.
   b. Press Ctrl + Home to move the insertion point back to the beginning of the document.
   c. Turn on bold.
   d. Press the Tab key and then type **Last Name**.
   e. Press the Tab key and then type **First Name**.
   f. Press the Tab key and then type **ZIP Code**.
18. Save the directory list document in the normal manner in the WordChapter01E folder on your disk in drive A and name the document **MCDirectory**.
19. Print **MCDirectory**.

20. Close **MCDirectory**.
21. At the sixth wizard step, save the directory list main document in the normal manner in the WordChapter01E folder on your disk in drive A and name it **MCListMainDoc**.
22. Close **MCListMainDoc**.

Completing a Merge Using Outlook Information as the Data Source

If you maintain a contacts list in Microsoft Outlook, you can use the list as the data source to merge with a main document to create form letters, envelopes, labels, directories, and/or e-mail messages. The specific steps for preparing a merge using Outlook information vary depending on your system configuration and contacts data in Outlook. To create and distribute an e-mail message using an Outlook contacts list, you would complete the following basic steps. *(Note: Check with your instructor to determine if you have access to Outlook and an Outlook contacts list and to obtain specific information on completing the steps.)*

exercise
(OPTIONAL EXERCISE) STEPS TO CREATE AN E-MAIL MESSAGE MERGED WITH AN OUTLOOK CONTACT LIST

1. At a clear document screen click Tools, point to Letters and Mailings, and then click Mail Merge.
2. At the first wizard step at the Mail Merge task pane, click *E-mail messages* in the *Select document type* section, and then click the Next: Starting document hyperlink.
3. At the second wizard step, make sure the *Use the current document* option is selected in the *Select starting document* section of the task pane, and then click the Next: Select recipients hyperlink.
4. At the third wizard step, click *Select from Outlook contacts* in the *Select recipients* section of the task pane.
5. Click the Choose Contacts Folder hyperlink.
6. At the Select Contact List folder dialog box, click the desired contact list, and then click OK.
7. At the Mail Merge Recipients dialog box, click OK. (If you do not want all individuals in the Mail Merge Recipients dialog box to receive the e-mail, remove the check mark preceding the name.)
8. Move to the next step by clicking the Next: Write your e-mail message hyperlink.
9. At the fourth wizard step, create the e-mail message in the document screen.
10. When the e-mail message is complete, click the Next: Preview your e-mail message hyperlink.
11. At the fifth wizard step, make sure the information is merged properly, and then click the Next: Complete the merge hyperlink.
12. At the sixth wizard step, click the Electronic Mail hyperlink.
13. At the Merge to E-mail dialog box, specify the distribution settings and then click OK.

Editing Merge Documents

Edit a main document in the normal manner. Open the document, make the required changes, and then save the document. Since a data source is actually an Access database file, you cannot open it in the normal manner. Edit a data source file using the Mail Merge Wizard or with buttons on the Mail Merge toolbar.

Editing Merge Documents Using the Mail Merge Wizard

When you complete the six wizard steps, you create a data source file and a main document. The data source file is associated with the main document. If you need to edit the main document, open it in the normal manner, make the required changes, and then start the Mail Merge Wizard. With a main document open, the Mail Merge Wizard begins with the third step. At this step, click the Edit recipient list hyperlink. At the Mail Merge Recipients dialog box, click the Edit button and then make the necessary edits to the fields in the records. Changes you make to the data source file are automatically saved. If you want to save edits made to a main document, you must save the changes.

exercise 5

EDITING THE MAIN DOCUMENT AND DATA SOURCE

1. Open **MCMainDoc**.
2. Make the following changes to the document:
   a. Change the date *February 21, 2005* to *February 28, 2005*.
   b. Select and then delete the last sentence in the second paragraph of text in the body of the letter. (This is the sentence that begins *Your financial future is our....*)
3. Start the Mail Merge Wizard by clicking Tools, pointing to Letters and Mailings, and then clicking Mail Merge. (Since a main document is open, the Mail Merge Wizard begins with Step 3 instead of Step 1.)
4. Edit the data source file by completing the following steps:
   a. Click the Edit recipient list hyperlink that displays in the *Use an existing list* section of the Mail Merge task pane.
   b. At the Mail Merge Recipients dialog box, click the Edit button. (This displays the fields for the record for Kenneth Porter.)
   c. Click the Next button. (This displays the record for Carolyn Renquist.)
   d. Select the current address in the *Address Line 1* field and then type **7561 South 22nd**.
   e. Click the New Entry button.

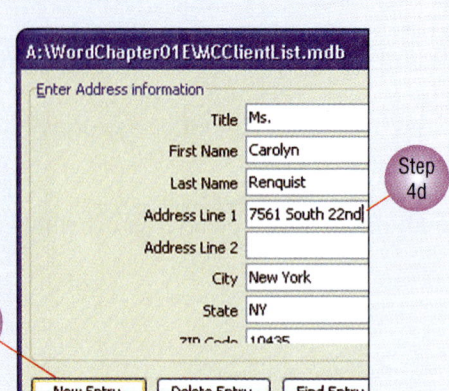
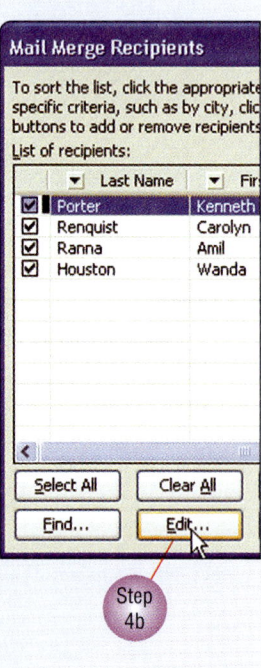

f. Type the following in the specified fields:
Title	=	**Mr.**
First Name	=	**David**
Last Name	=	**Reece**
Address Line 1	=	**1500 East 77th**
Address Line 2	=	**Apt. 2-C**
City	=	**New York**
State	=	**NY**
ZIP Code	=	**14223**
Fund	=	**Mutual Investment Fund**

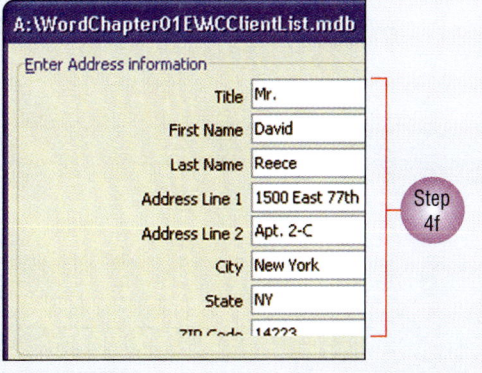

Step 4f

g. Delete the record for Wanda Houston by completing the following steps:
   1) Click the Previous button until the record for Wanda Houston displays.
   2) Click the Delete Entry button.
   3) At the message asking if you want to delete the entry, click the Yes button.
h. Click the Close button.
i. At the Mail Merge Recipients dialog box, click OK.

5. Click the Next: Write your letter hyperlink located toward the bottom of the Mail Merge task pane.
6. At the fourth wizard step, click the Next: Preview your letters hyperlink located toward the bottom of the task pane.
7. At the fifth wizard step, click the Next: Complete the merge hyperlink located toward the bottom of the task pane.
8. At the sixth wizard step, click the Edit individual letters hyperlink located in the *Merge* section of the task pane.
9. At the Merge to New Document dialog box, make sure *All* is selected, and then click OK.
10. Save the merged letters in the normal manner in the WordChapter01E folder on your disk in drive A and name the document **MCClientEditedLtrs01**.
11. Print **MCClientEditedLtrs01**. (This document will print four letters.)
12. Close **MCClientEditedLtrs01**.
13. At the sixth wizard step, save the edited main document with the same name (**MCMainDoc**).
14. Close **MCMainDoc**.

Editing Merge Documents Using the Mail Merge Toolbar

The Mail Merge toolbar shown in Figure 1.3 provides buttons you can use to edit a main document and/or a data source file. Display this toolbar by clicking View, pointing to Toolbars, and then clicking Mail Merge. The Mail Merge toolbar generally displays below the Formatting toolbar (this location may vary).

HINT With buttons on the Mail Merge toolbar, you can prepare merged documents without using the Mail Merge Wizard.

FIGURE 1.3 Mail Merge Toolbar Buttons

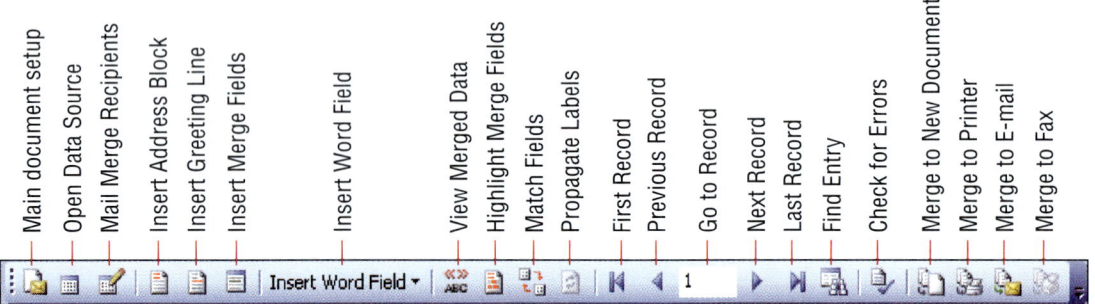

Insert Merge Fields

Merge to New Document

Merge to Printer

Mail Merge Recipients

To edit a main document, open the document in the normal manner. You can insert additional fields in a main document by clicking the Insert Merge Fields button on the Mail Merge toolbar. At the Insert Merge Field dialog box, click the desired field, click the Insert button, and then click the Close button.

After editing the main document, you can merge it with the associated data source file. Click the Merge to New Document button on the Mail Merge toolbar and the main document is merged with the data source file to a new document. You can also merge the main document with the data source file directly to the printer by clicking the Merge to Printer button on the Mail Merge toolbar.

Edit a data source file by clicking the Mail Merge Recipients button on the Mail Merge toolbar. At the Mail Merge Recipients dialog box, click the Edit button, and then make the desired edits to the data source records.

exercise 6

EDITING MERGE DOCUMENTS USING BUTTONS ON THE MAIL MERGE TOOLBAR

1. Open the **MCMainDoc** document in the normal manner. (This was the main document you created in Exercise 1 and edited in Exercise 5.)
2. Display the Mail Merge toolbar by clicking View, pointing to Toolbars, and then clicking Mail Merge.
3. Change the date in the letter from *February 28, 2005* to *March 7, 2005*.
4. Edit the **MCClientList** data source by completing the following steps:
   a. Click the Mail Merge Recipients button on the Mail Merge toolbar.
   b. At the Mail Merge Recipients dialog box, click the Edit button. (This displays the fields for the record for Kenneth Porter.)
   c. Click the Next button. (This displays the record for Carolyn Renquist.)

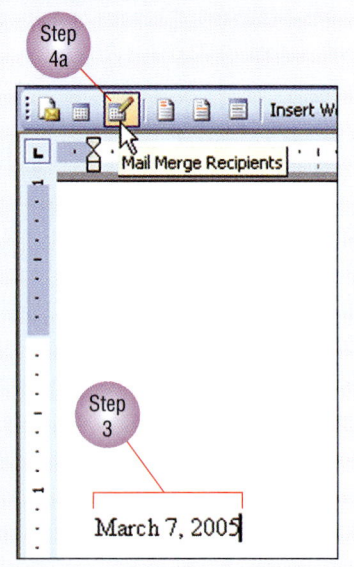

d. Change the last name from *Renquist* to *Fanshaw*.
   e. Display the record for Dr. Amil Ranna and then delete the record.
   f. Click the Close button.
   g. At the Mail Merge Recipients dialog box, click OK.
5. Merge the edited data source file with **MCMainDoc** by completing the following steps:
   a. Click the Merge to New Document button on the Mail Merge toolbar.
   b. At the Merge to New Document dialog box, make sure *All* is selected, and then click OK.
6. Save the merged document in the WordChapter01E folder on your disk in drive A and name it **MCClientEditedLtrs02**.
7. Print and then close **MCClientEditedLtrs02**. (Three letters will print.)
8. Save and then close **MCMainDoc**.

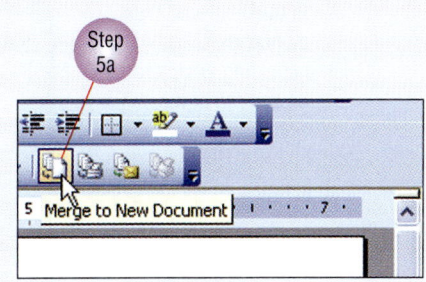

Inputting Text during a Merge

Word's Merge feature contains a large number of Word fields that can be inserted in a main document. In this chapter, you will learn about the ***Fill-in*** field that is used for information input at the keyboard during a merge. For more information on the other Word fields, please refer to the on-screen help.

Situations may arise in which you do not need to keep all variable information in a data source file. For example, variable information that changes on a regular basis might include a customer's monthly balance, a product price, and so on. Word lets you input variable information into a document during the merge using the keyboard. A Fill-in field is inserted in a main document by clicking the Insert Word Field button on the Mail Merge toolbar and then clicking Fill-in at the drop-down menu. A document can contain any number of Fill-in fields.

To insert a Fill-in field, open a main document, and position the insertion point at the location in the document where you want the field to display. Click the Insert Word Field button on the Mail Merge toolbar and then click Fill-in at the drop-down menu that displays. At the Insert Word Field: Fill-in dialog box shown in Figure 1.4, type a short message indicating what should be entered at the keyboard, and then click OK. At the Microsoft Word dialog box with the message you entered displayed in the upper left corner, type text you want to display in the document, and then click OK. When the Fill-in field or fields are added, save the main document in the normal manner.

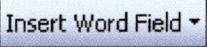

Insert Word Field

Insert Fill-in Field in Main Document
1. Click Insert Word Field button on Mail Merge toolbar.
2. Click Fill-in.
3. Type prompt text.
4. Click OK.
5. Type text to be inserted in document.
6. Click OK.

FIGURE 1.4 Insert Word Field: Fill-in Dialog Box

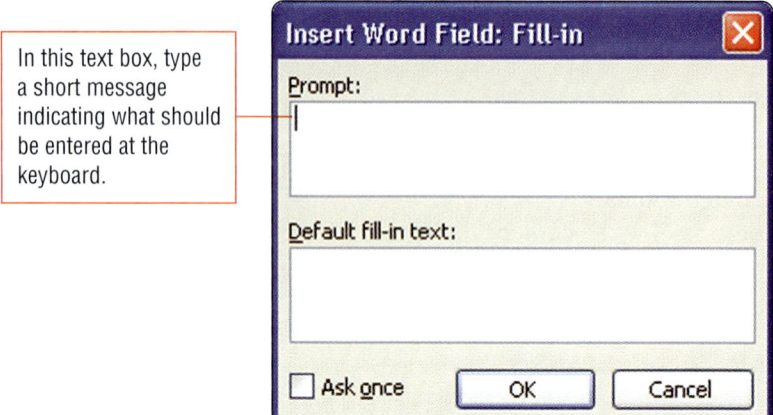

In this text box, type a short message indicating what should be entered at the keyboard.

HINT

Press Alt + Shift + N to display the Merge to New Document dialog box and press Alt + Shift + M to display the Merge to Printer dialog box.

To merge the main document with the data source file, click the Merge to New Document button on the Mail Merge toolbar or the Merge to Printer button. When Word merges the main document with the first record in the data source file, the Microsoft Word dialog box displays with the message you entered displayed in the upper left corner. Type the required information for the first record in the data source file and then click the OK button. If you are using the keyboard, type the required information, press the Tab key to make the OK button active, and then press Enter.

Word displays the dialog box again. Type the required information for the second record in the data source file and then click OK. Continue in this manner until the required information has been entered for each record in the data source file. Word then completes the merge.

exercise 7

ADDING FILL-IN FIELDS TO A DOCUMENT

1. Edit the **MCMainDoc** main document so it includes Fill-in fields by completing the following steps:
    a. Open **MCMainDoc**.
    b. Turn on the display of the Mail Merge toolbar.
    c. Change the second paragraph in the body of the letter to the paragraph shown in Figure 1.5. Insert the first Fill-in field (representative's name) by completing the following steps:
    1) Click the Insert Word Field button on the Mail Merge toolbar. (If this button is not visible, click the Toolbar Options buttons at the right side of the Mail Merge toolbar, point to Add or Remove Buttons, point to Mail Merge, and then click Insert Word Field.)
    2) At the drop-down menu that displays, click Fill-in.

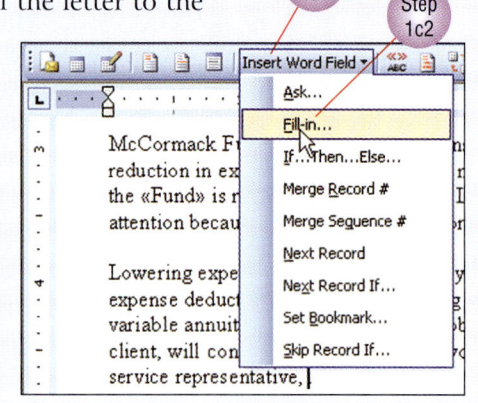

Step 1c1
Step 1c2

3) At the Insert Word Field: Fill-in dialog box, type **Insert rep name** in the *Prompt* text box.
4) Click OK.
5) At the Microsoft Word dialog box with *Insert rep name* displayed in the upper left corner, type **(representative's name)**, and then click OK.

d. Complete steps similar to those in Step 1c to insert the second Fill-in field (phone number), except type **Insert phone number** in the *Prompt* text box at the Insert Word Field: Fill-in dialog box and type **(phone number)** at the Microsoft Word dialog box.

2. When the paragraph is completed, save the document with Save As and name it **MCMainDocLtr2**.
3. Merge the main document with the data source file by completing the following steps:
    a. Click the Merge to New Document button on the Mail Merge toolbar.
    b. At the Merge to New Document dialog box, make sure *All* is selected, and then click OK.
    c. When Word merges the main document with the first record, a dialog box displays with the message *Insert rep name* and the text *(representative's name)* selected. At this dialog box, type **Marilyn Smythe**, and then click OK.
    d. At the dialog box with the message *Insert phone number* and *(phone number)* selected, type **(646) 555-8944**, and then click OK.
    e. At the dialog box with the message *Insert rep name*, type **Anthony Mason** (over *Marilyn Smythe*), and then click OK.
    f. At the dialog box with the message *Insert phone number*, type **(646) 555-8901** (over the previous number), and then click OK.
    g. At the dialog box with the message *Insert rep name*, type **Faith Ostrom** (over *Anthony Mason*), and then click OK.
    h. At the dialog box with the message *Insert phone number*, type **(646) 555-8967** (over the previous number), and then click OK.
4. Save the merged document and name it **ewc1x07**.
5. Print and then close **ewc1x07**.
6. Save and then close **MCMainDocLtr02**.

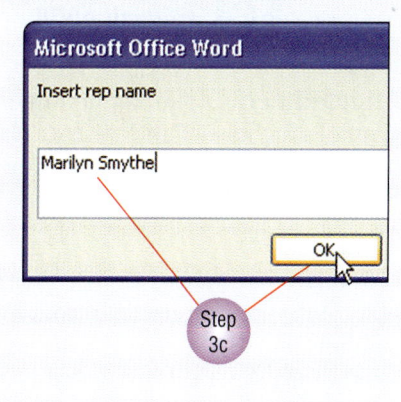

FIGURE 1.5 Exercise 7

Lowering expense charges is noteworthy because before the reduction, McCormack expense deductions were already among the lowest, far below most mutual funds and variable annuity accounts with similar objectives. At the same time, services for you, our client, will continue to expand. If you would like to discuss this change, please call our service representative, **(representative's name)**, at **(phone number)**.

Sorting Text

In Word, you can sort text in paragraphs, text in columns in tables, or records in a data source. Sorting can be done alphabetically, numerically, or by date. You can also select specific records from a data source to be merged with a main document. Word can perform the three types of sorts shown in Table 1.1.

TABLE 1.1 Types of Sorts

Alphanumeric: In an alphanumeric sort, Word arranges the text in the following order: special symbols such as @ and # first, numbers second, and letters third. You can tell Word to sort text in all uppercase letters first, followed by words beginning with uppercase letters, and then words beginning with lowercase letters.

Numeric: In a numeric sort, Word arranges the text in numeric order and ignores any alphabetic text. Only the numbers 0 through 9 and symbols pertaining to numbers are recognized. These symbols include $, %, ( ), a decimal point, a comma, and the symbols for the four basic operations: + (addition), - (subtraction), * (multiplication), and / (division).

Date: In a date sort, Word sorts dates that are expressed in common date format, such as 05-15-05; 05/15/05; May 15, 2005; or 15 May 2005. Word does not sort dates that include abbreviated month names without periods. Dates expressed as months, days, or years by themselves are also not sorted.

Sorting Text in Paragraphs

Text arranged in paragraphs can be sorted by the first character of the paragraph. This character can be a number, a symbol (such as $ or #), or a letter. The paragraphs to be sorted can be typed at the left margin or indented with the Tab key. Unless you select paragraphs to be sorted, Word sorts the entire document.

Paragraphs can be sorted alphanumerically, numerically, or by date. In an alphanumeric sort, punctuation marks or special symbols are sorted first, followed by numbers, and then text. If you sort paragraphs either alphanumerically or numerically, dates are treated as regular numbers.

To sort text in paragraphs, open the document containing the paragraphs to be sorted. (If the document contains text you do not want sorted with the paragraphs, select the paragraphs.) Click Table and then Sort and the Sort Text dialog box displays as shown in Figure 1.6. At this dialog box, make sure *Paragraphs* displays in the *Sort by* option and the *Ascending* option is selected, and then click OK or press Enter.

HINT
Sorting potentially can make substantial changes to a document, so save the document before sorting.

HINT
If you are sorting an extremely important document, practice sorting on a copy of the document first.

FIGURE 1.6 Sort Text Dialog Box

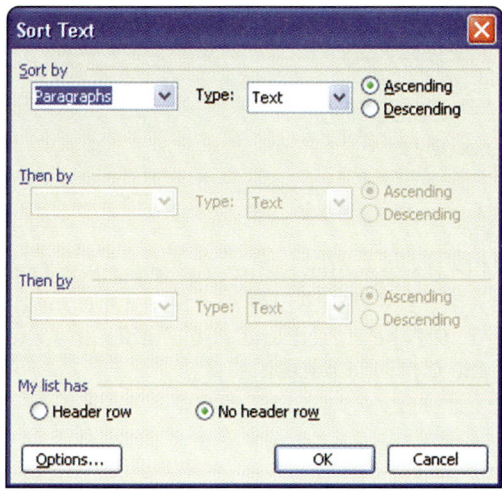

QUICK STEPS

Sort Paragraphs of Text
1. Click Table, Sort.
2. Make any needed changes at Sort Text dialog box.
3. Click OK.

The *Sort by* option at the Sort Text dialog box has a default setting of *Paragraphs*. This default setting changes depending on the text in the document. For example, if you are sorting a table, the *Sort by* option has a default setting of *Column 1*. If you are sorting only the first word of each paragraph in the document, leave the *Sort by* option at the default of *Paragraphs*.

The *Type* option at the Sort Text dialog box has a default setting of *Text*. This can be changed to *Number* or *Date*. Table 1.1 specifies how Word will sort numbers and dates.

When Word sorts paragraphs that are separated by two hard returns (two strokes of the Enter key), the hard returns are removed and inserted at the beginning of the document. If you want the sorted text separated by hard returns, you will need to insert the hard returns by positioning the insertion point where you want the hard return and then pressing the Enter key.

HINT
When sorting paragraphs, any blank lines in a document are moved to the beginning of the document.

SORTING PARAGRAPHS ALPHABETICALLY

1. Open **WordReferences**.
2. Save the document with Save As and name it **ewc1x08**.
3. Sort the paragraphs alphabetically by the last name by completing the following steps:
    a. Click Table and then Sort.
    b. At the Sort Text dialog box, make sure *Paragraphs* displays in the *Sort by* option box and the *Ascending* option is selected.
    c. Click OK.
    d. Deselect the text.
4. Delete the hard returns at the beginning of the document.
5. Add space below each paragraph by completing the following steps:
    a. Press Ctrl + A to select the entire document.
    b. Click Format and then Paragraph.
    c. At the Paragraph dialog box with the Indents and Spacing tab selected, click the up-pointing arrow at the right side of the *After* text box (in the *Spacing* section) until *12 pt* displays in the text box.
    d. Click OK to close the dialog box.
    e. Deselect the text.
6. Save, print, and then close **ewc1x08**.

Display Sort Options Dialog Box
1. Click Table, Sort.
2. Click Options button.

Changing Sort Options

The *Sort by* options will also vary depending on selections at the Sort Options dialog box shown in Figure 1.7. To display the Sort Options dialog box, open a document containing text to be sorted and click Table and then Sort. At the Sort Text dialog box, click the Options button.

FIGURE 1.7 Sort Options Dialog Box

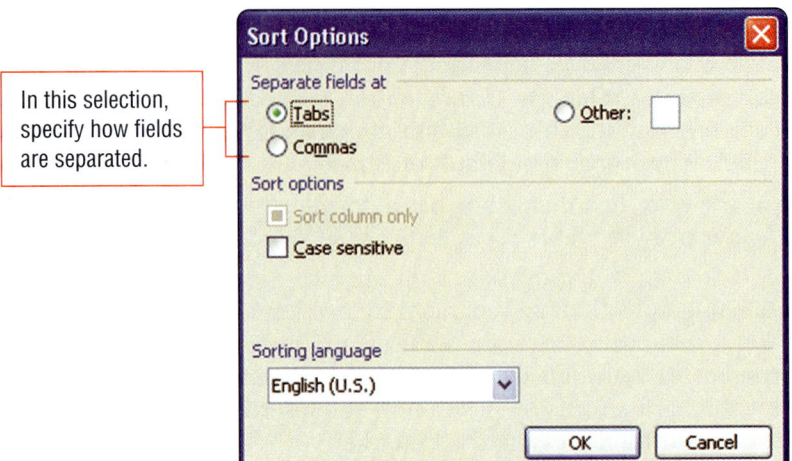

In this selection, specify how fields are separated.

The *Separate fields at* section of the dialog box contains three options. The first option, *Tabs*, is selected by default. At this setting, Word assumes that text to be sorted is divided by tabs. This can be changed to *Commas* or *Other*. With the *Other* setting, you can specify the character that divides text to be sorted. For example, suppose a document contains first and last names in paragraphs separated by a space and you want to sort by the last name. To do this, you would click *Other* at the Sort Options dialog box, and then press the spacebar. (This inserts a space, which is not visible, in the *Other* text box.) If names are separated by a comma, click *Commas* as the separator.

The Sort Options dialog box contains two choices in the *Sort options* section. The first choice, *Sort column only*, sorts only the selected column. This choice is dimmed unless a column of text is selected. If a check mark appears in the *Case sensitive* check box, Word will sort text so that a word whose first letter is a capital letter is sorted before any word with the same first letter in lowercase. This option is available only if *Text* is selected in the *Type* option box at the Sort Text dialog box.

When you make changes at the Sort Options dialog box, the choices available with the *Sort by* option at the Sort Text dialog box will vary. For example, if you click *Other* at the Sort Options dialog box, and then press the spacebar, the choices for the *Sort by* option at the Sort Text dialog box will include *Word 1*, *Word 2*, *Word 3*, and so forth.

exercise 9

SORTING TEXT ALPHABETICALLY BY FIRST AND LAST NAME

1. Open **WordSort01**.
2. Save the document with Save As and name it **ewc1x09**.
3. Sort the text alphabetically by first name by completing the following steps:
    a. Click Table and then Sort.
    b. At the Sort Text dialog box, make sure *Paragraphs* displays in the *Sort by* option box and the *Ascending* option is selected.
    c. Click OK or press Enter.
    d. Deselect the text.
4. Save and then print **ewc1x09**.
5. With **ewc1x09** still displayed, sort the text by the last name (second word) by completing the following steps:
    a. Click Table and then Sort.
    b. At the Sort Text dialog box, click the Options button.
    c. At the Sort Options dialog box, click *Other*, and then press the spacebar.

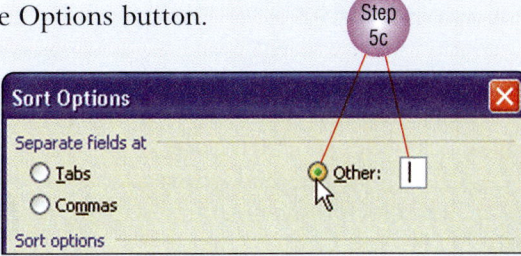

Step 5c

WORD
Merging Documents and Sorting and Selecting Data   E29

d. Click OK or press Enter.
   e. At the Sort Text dialog box, click the down-pointing arrow at the right side of the *Sort by* option box (contains the word *Paragraphs*), and then click *Word 2* at the drop-down list.
   f. Make sure the *Ascending* option is selected.
   g. Click OK or press Enter.
   h. Deselect the text.
6. Save, print, and then close **ewc1x09**.

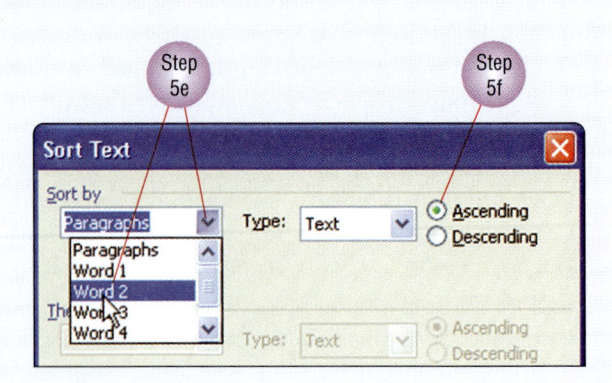

Sorting Text in Columns

HINT Columns of text to be sorted must be separated by tabs.

Text arranged in columns with tabs between the columns can be sorted alphabetically or numerically. Text in columns must be separated with tabs. When sorting text in columns, Word sorts by fields. Text typed at the left margin is considered *Field 1*, text typed at the first tab stop is considered *Field 2*, and so on. To sort text arranged in columns, display the Sort Text dialog box, and then click the Options button. At the Sort Options dialog box, make sure *Tabs* is selected in the *Separate fields at* section of the dialog box, and then click OK or press Enter. At the Sort Text dialog box, display the appropriate field number in the *Sort by* option box, and then click OK or press Enter.

When sorting text in columns, only one tab can be inserted between columns when typing the text. If you press the Tab key more than once between columns, Word recognizes each tab as a separate column. In this case, the field number you specify may correspond to an empty column rather than the desired column.

QUICK STEPS

Sort Text in Columns
1. Select specific text.
2. Click Table, Sort.
3. Click Options button.
4. Specify *Tabs* as separator.
5. Click OK.
6. Make any needed changes at Sort Text dialog box.
7. Click OK.

exercise 10 — SORTING TEXT IN COLUMNS

1. Open **WordSort02**.
2. Save the document with Save As and name it **ewc1x10**.
3. Sort the first column alphabetically by last name by completing the following steps:
   a. Select the text in all three columns except the headings.
   b. Click Table and then Sort.
   c. At the Sort Text dialog box, click the Options button.
   d. At the Sort Options dialog box, click the *Tabs* option in the *Separate fields at* section.
   e. Click OK to close the Sort Options dialog box.

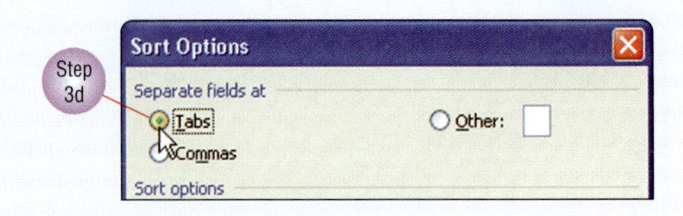

E30 Chapter One

f. At the Sort Text dialog box, make sure *Field 2* displays in the *Sort by* option and that *Ascending* is selected.
   g. Click OK or press Enter.
   h. Deselect the text.
4. Save and then print **ewc1x10**.
5. With **ewc1x10** still open, sort the third column of text numerically by completing the following steps:
   a. Select the text in all three columns except the headings.
   b. Click Table and then Sort.
   c. At the Sort Text dialog box, click the Options button.
   d. At the Sort Options dialog box, click the *Tabs* option in the *Separate fields at* section.
   e. Click OK to close the Sort Options dialog box.
   f. At the Sort Text dialog box, click the down-pointing arrow at the right side of the *Sort by* option box, and then click *Field 4* at the drop-down list. (Field 4 is the third tab stop.)
   g. Make sure *Ascending* is selected and *Numbering* displays in the *Type* text box.
   h. Click OK or press Enter.
   i. Deselect the text.
6. Save, print, and then close **ewc1x10**.

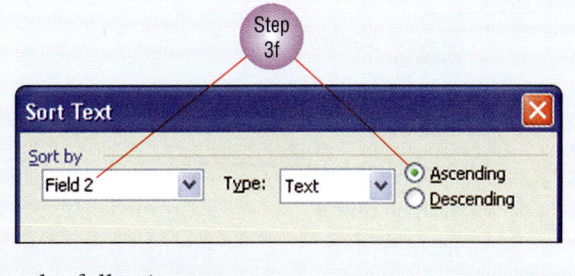

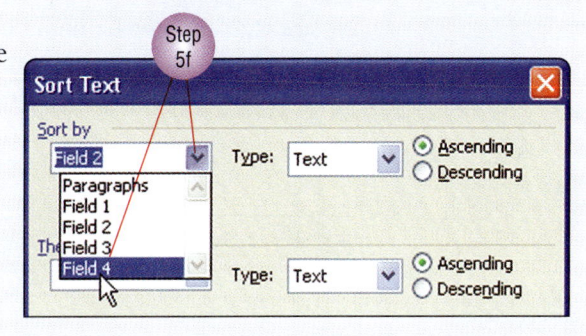

Sorting on More than One Field

When sorting text, you can sort on more than one field. For example, in the text shown in the columns in Figure 1.8, you can sort the text alphabetically by department and then tell Word to sort the last names alphabetically within the departments. To do this, you would tell Word to sort on Field 3 (the second tab stop) and then sort on Field 2 (the first tab stop). Word sorts the second column of text (Field 3) alphabetically by department, and then sorts the names in the first column of text (Field 2) by last name. This results in the columns displaying as shown in Figure 1.9.

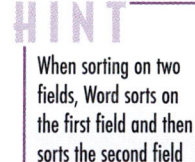

HINT When sorting on two fields, Word sorts on the first field and then sorts the second field within the first.

FIGURE 1.8 Columns

Employee	Department	Ext.
Thomas, Megan	Financial Services	474
Dey, Richard	Administrative Services	122
Lattin, Kim	Financial Services	430
Ebsen, William	Administrative Services	153
Blanchett, Jan	Financial Services	436

FIGURE 1.9 Sorted Columns

Employee	Department	Ext.
Dey, Richard	Administrative Services	122
Ebsen, William	Administrative Services	153
Blanchett, Jan	Financial Services	436
Lattin, Kim	Financial Services	430
Thomas, Megan	Financial Services	474

Notice that the departments in the second column in Figure 1.9 are alphabetized and that the last names *within* the departments are alphabetized. For example, *Dey* is sorted before *Ebsen* within *Administrative Services*.

exercise 11 — SORTING ON TWO FIELDS

1. Open **WordSort02**.
2. Save the document with Save As and name it **ewc1x11**.
3. Sort the text in columns alphabetically by department and then alphabetically by last name by completing the following steps:
   a. Select the text in all three columns except the headings.
   b. Click Table and then Sort.
   c. At the Sort Text dialog box, click the Options button.
   d. At the Sort Options dialog box, click the *Tabs* option in the *Separate fields at* section.
   e. Click OK or press Enter to close the Sort Options dialog box.
   f. At the Sort Text dialog box, click the down-pointing arrow at the right side of the *Sort by* option box, and then click *Field 3* at the drop-down list. (Field 3 is the second tab stop.)
   g. Click the down-pointing arrow at the right side of the *Then by* option box and then click *Field 2* from the drop-down list.
   h. Make sure *Ascending* is selected on both fields.
   i. Click OK or press Enter.
   j. Deselect the text.
4. Save, print, and then close **ewc1x11**.

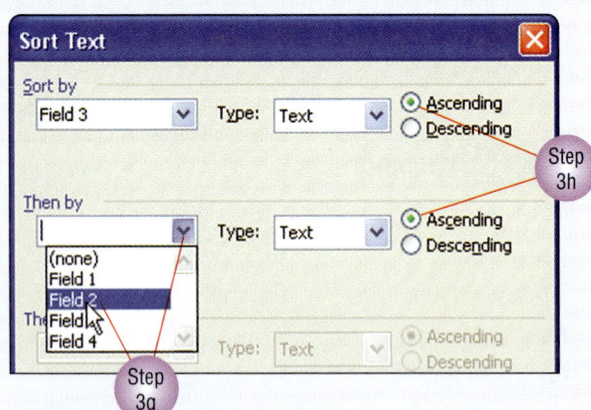

Specifying a Header Row

The Sort Text dialog box contains the option *Header row* in the *My list has* section. If a document contains only columns of text with headings, you can use this option to tell Word to sort all text except for the headings of the columns.

exercise 12 — SORTING TEXT WITH A HEADER ROW

1. Open **WordSort02**.
2. Save the document with Save As and name it **ewc1x12**.
3. Sort the third column of text numerically by the extension number by completing the following steps:
   a. Click Table and then Sort.
   b. At the Sort Text dialog box, click the *Header row* option in the *My list has* section of the dialog box.
   c. Click the Options button.
   d. At the Sort Options dialog box, make sure the *Tabs* option in the *Separate fields at* section.
   e. Click OK to close the Sort Options dialog box.
   f. At the Sort Text dialog box, click the down-pointing arrow at the right side of the *Sort by* option box, and then click *Ext.* at the drop-down list.
   g. Make sure *Ascending* is selected.
   h. If any text displays in the *Then by* option box, click the down-pointing arrow to the right of the box, and then click *(none)* at the drop-down list.
   i. Click OK or press Enter.
   j. Deselect the text.
4. Save, print, and then close **ewc1x12**.

Step 3f

Sorting Text in Tables

Sorting text in columns within tables is very similar to sorting columns of text separated by tabs. The same principles that apply to sorting columns of text also apply to sorting text within table columns. If a table contains a header row, you can tell Word not to include the header row when sorting by clicking *Header row* at the Sort dialog box. (The Sort Text dialog box becomes the Sort dialog box when sorting a table.) You can also select the cells in the table except the header row and then complete the sort.

If *Header row* is selected at the Sort dialog box, the information in the header row becomes the *Sort by* options. For example, in the table shown in Figure 1.10, if *Header row* is selected, the *Sort by* options are *Salesperson, January Sales,* and *February Sales*.

QUICK STEPS

Sort Text in a Table
1. Position insertion point in table.
2. Click Table, Sort.
3. Make any needed change at Sort dialog box.
4. Click OK.

FIGURE 1.10 Table

Salesperson	January Sales	February Sales
Underwood, Gary	214,368.10	208,438.50
Russell, Felicia	243,655.00	230,541.65
Meyers, Alan	198,560.15	187,240.75
Epstein, Byron	215,466.35	204,233.45

exercise 13 — SORTING TEXT ALPHABETICALLY IN A TABLE

1. Open **WordSort03**.
2. Save the document with Save As and name it **ewc1x13**.
3. Sort the text alphabetically in the first column by completing the following steps:
    a. Position the insertion point anywhere within the table.
    b. Click Table and then Sort.
    c. At the Sort dialog box, make sure *Header row* in the *My list has* section of the dialog box is selected.
    d. Make sure *Salesperson* displays in the *Sort by* option box.
    e. Make sure *Ascending* is selected.
    f. Click OK or press Enter.
4. Save, print, and then close **ewc1x13**.

In Exercise 13, the *Header row* option at the Sort dialog box was selected. You can also sort text in a table by first selecting the cells you want sorted and then displaying the Sort dialog box.

exercise 14 — SORTING NUMBERS IN A TABLE IN DESCENDING ORDER

1. Open **WordSort03**.
2. Save the document with Save As and name it **ewc1x14**.
3. Sort the numbers in the second column in descending order by completing the following steps:
    a. Select all of the cells in the table except the cells in the first row.
    b. Click Table and then Sort.
    c. At the Sort dialog box, click the down-pointing arrow at the right side of the *Sort by* option, and then click *Column 2* at the drop-down list.
    d. Click *Descending*.
    e. Click OK or press Enter.

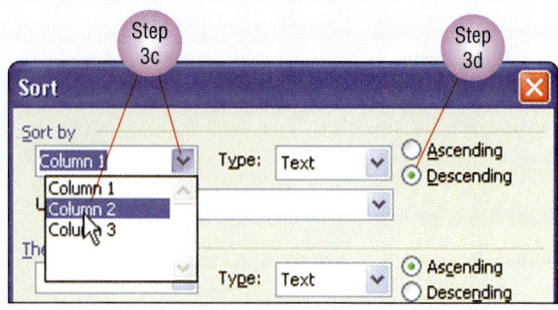

4. With the insertion point positioned anywhere in the table, display the Table AutoFormat dialog box, and then apply the *Table 3D effects 3* table style.
5. Save, print, and then close **ewc1x14**.

Sorting Records in a Data Source

To sort records in a data source, open the main document, display the Mail Merge toolbar, and then click the Mail Merge Recipients button. This displays the Mail Merge Recipients dialog box shown in Figure 1.11 where you can sort the various fields in the data source and/or perform advanced sorts.

QUICK STEPS

Sort Records in Data Source
1. Open main document.
2. Click Mail Merge Recipients button on Mail Merge toolbar.
3. At Mail Merge Recipients dialog box, sort on specific field by clicking field column heading.
4. Click OK.

FIGURE 1.11 *Mail Merge Recipients Dialog Box*

To sort on a specific field, click on the column heading.

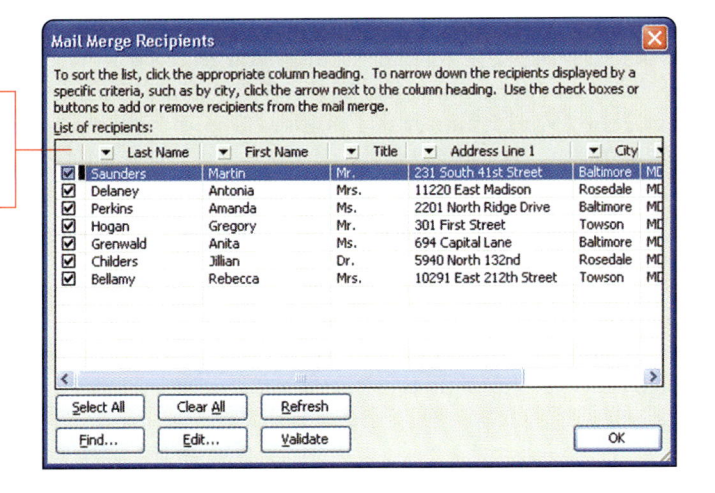

Click the column heading to sort data in a specific column in ascending order. To perform additional types of sorts, click the down-pointing arrow at the left of the column heading, and then click *(Advanced...)* at the drop-down list. This displays the Filter and Sort dialog box. At this dialog box, click the Sort Records tab and the dialog box displays as shown in Figure 1.12. The options at the Filter and Sort dialog box with the Sort Records tab selected are similar to the options available at the Sort Text (and Sort) dialog box.

HINT Decide the order in which you want your merged documents printed and then sort the data before merging.

WORD Merging Documents and Sorting and Selecting Data E35

FIGURE 1.12 Filter and Sort Dialog Box with Sort Records Tab Selected

Use options at this dialog box to specify sort options.

exercise 15 — SORTING DATA IN A DATA SOURCE

1. Open **LFSMainDoc**. (If a message displays telling you that Word cannot find the data source, click the Find Data Source button. At the Select Data Source dialog box, change the *Look in* option to the Word Chapter 01E folder on your disk and then double-click **LFSClients** in the list box.)
2. Save the document with Save As and name it **ewc1LFSMainDoc**.
3. Sort records in the data source attached to this main document alphabetically. To begin, display the Mail Merge toolbar by right-clicking any visible toolbar and then clicking Mail Merge at the pop-up list. (Skip this step if the Mail Merge toolbar is displayed.)
4. Click the Mail Merge Recipients button on the Mail Merge toolbar.
5. At the Mail Merge Recipients dialog box, click the *Last Name* column heading. (This sorts the last names in ascending alphabetical order.)

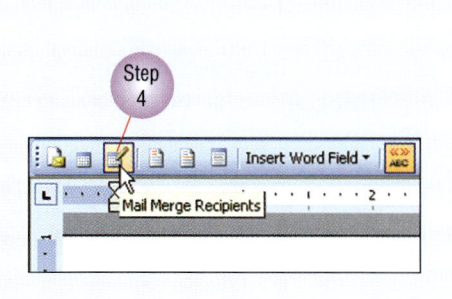

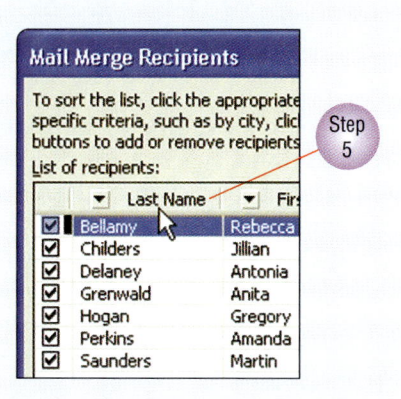

6. Scroll to the right to display the *ZIP Code* field and then click the *ZIP Code* column heading. (This sorts the ZIP Codes in order from lowest to highest.)

7. Sort by ZIP Codes in descending order by completing the following steps:
   a. Click the down-pointing arrow at the left side of the *ZIP Code* column heading.
   b. Click *(Advanced…)* at the drop-down list.
   c. At the Filter and Sort dialog box, click the Sort Records tab.
   d. Make sure *ZIP Code* displays in the *Sort by* option box and that *Descending* is selected.
   e. Click the down-pointing arrow at the right of the *Then by* option and then click *(none)*. 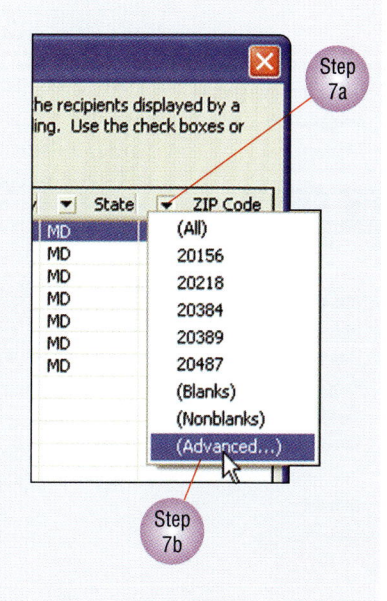 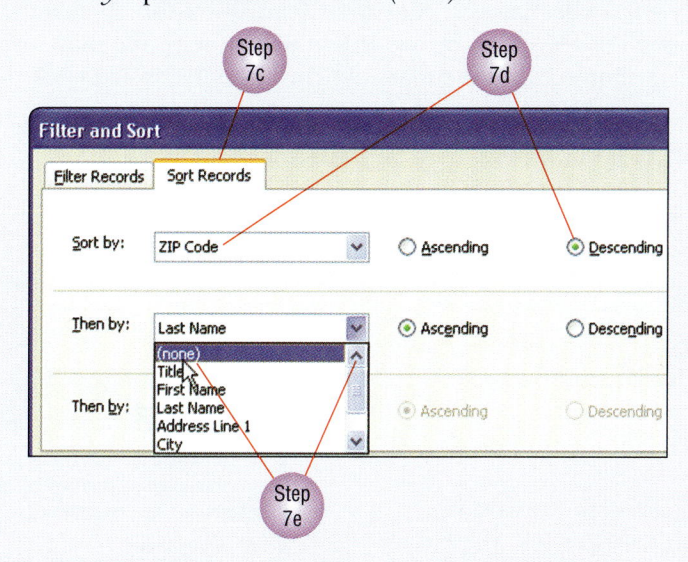
   f. Click OK to close the Filter and Sort dialog box.
   g. Click OK to close the Mail Merge Recipients dialog box.
8. View the first merged letter (for Ms. Amanda Perkins) and then click the Next Record button on the Mail Merge toolbar. 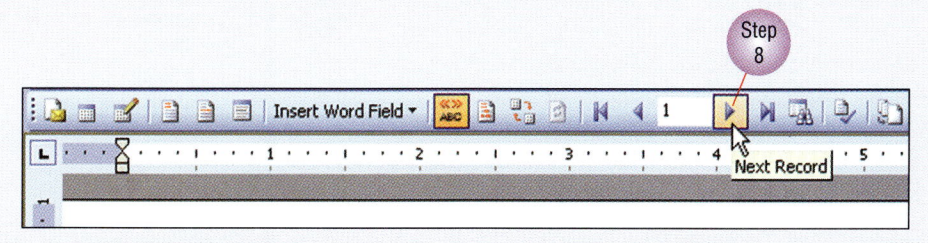
9. Continue clicking the Next Record button to view the sorted letters. (The order of the letters should be—*Perkins, Childers, Delaney, Grenwald, Bellamy, Hogan,* and *Saunders.*)
   (Optional: If you want to print the merged document, click the Merge to Printer button on the Mail Merge toolbar and then click OK at the Merge to Printer dialog box.)
10. Save the document with Save As and name it **ewc1x15**.
11. Close **ewc1x15**.

HINT
Including or excluding certain records from the merge is referred to as *filtering*.

QUICK STEPS

Select Records
1. Open main document.
2. Click Mail Merge Recipients button on Mail Merge toolbar.
3. Remove check marks from records to be excluded.
4. Click OK.

Selecting Records

If you have created a main document and a data source file to create personalized form letters, situations may arise where you want to merge the main document with specific records in the data source. For example, you may want to send a letter to customers with a specific ZIP Code or who live in a certain city.

One method for selecting specific records is to display the Mail Merge Recipients dialog box and then insert or remove check marks from specific records. For example, to select records for a specific city, remove check marks from any record that does not contain the desired city. To remove or insert a check mark, click the check box that displays at the beginning of the record. If you will be selecting only a few check boxes, click the Clear All button. This removes the check marks from all of the check boxes. If you will be selecting most of the records in the data source, leave the marks in the check boxes (or click the Select All button to insert check marks in all check boxes).

exercise 16

SELECTING RECORDS FOR A SPECIFIC CITY

1. Open **ewc1LFSMainDoc**.
2. Save the document with Save As and name it **ewc1x16**.
3. Click the Mail Merge Recipients button on the Mail Merge toolbar.
4. At the Mail Merge Recipients dialog box, select the records of those individuals living in the city of Rosedale by completing the following steps:
   a. Click the check box preceding the last name *Saunders*. (This removes the check mark from the check box.)
   b. Click the check box before the following last names: *Perkins*, *Hogan*, *Grenwald*, and *Bellamy*. (The only records that should be checked are those for *Delaney* and *Childers*. These individuals live in the city of Rosedale.)
   c. Click OK to close the Mail Merge Recipients dialog box.
   d. View the first merged letter and then click the Next Record to view the next letter. Click the Next Record and/or Previous Record button to view the two merged letters.
   (Optional: If you want to print the merged document, click the Merge to Printer button on the Mail Merge toolbar and then click OK at the Merge to Printer dialog box.)
5. Save and then close **ewc1x16**.

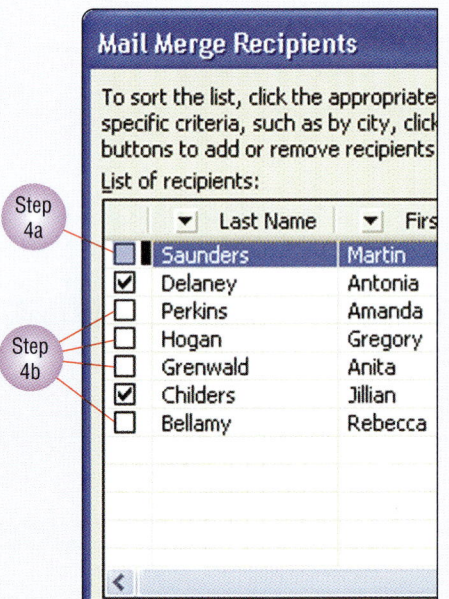

Using check boxes to select specific records is useful in a data source containing a limited number of records, but may not be practical in a data source containing many records. In a large data source, use options from the Filter and Sort dialog box with the Filter Records tab selected, shown in Figure 1.13, to select specific records for merging with the main document that meet certain criteria. For example, in Exercise 17, you will select records of clients with a ZIP Code higher than 20300.

FIGURE 1.13 Filter and Sort Dialog Box with Filter Records Tab Selected

Use the *Field* option to specify on which field you want to select and then use the *Comparison* and *Compare to* options to specify records matching certain criteria.

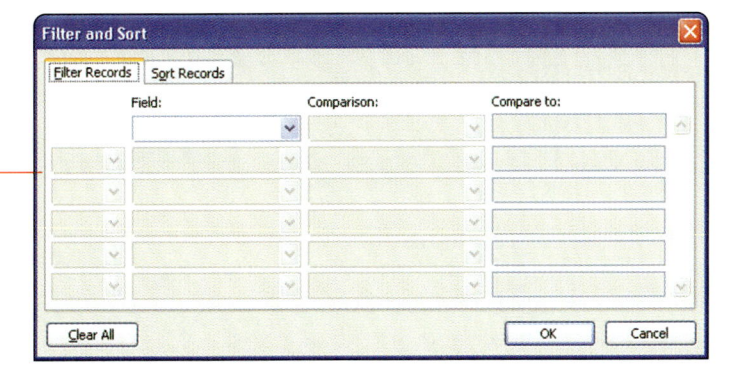

When you select a field from the *Field* drop-down list, Word automatically inserts *Equal to* in the *Comparison* option box. You can make other comparisons. Clicking the down-pointing arrow to the right of the *Comparison* option box causes a drop-down list to display with these additional options: *Not equal to, Less than, Greater than, Less than or equal, Greater than or equal, is blank*, and *is not blank*. Use one of these options to create a select equation. For example, select all customers with a ZIP Code higher than 90543 by clicking *ZIP Code* at the *Field* drop-down list. Click the down-pointing arrow at the right of the *Comparison* option box, click *Greater than*, and then type **90543** in the *Compare to* text box.

exercise 17 — SELECTING RECORDS WITH SPECIFIC ZIP CODES

1. Open **ewc1LFSMainDoc**.
2. Save the document with Save As and name it **ewc1x17**.
3. Select the records with a ZIP Code higher than 20300 by completing the following steps:
   a. Click the Mail Merge Recipients button on the Mail Merge toolbar.
   b. Scroll to the right until the *ZIP Code* field is visible, click the down-pointing arrow at the left of the ZIP Code column heading, and then click *(Advanced...)* at the drop-down list.

Merging Documents and Sorting and Selecting Data

c. At the Filter and Sort dialog box with the Filter Records tab selected, click the down-pointing arrow at the right side of the *Field* option box, and then click *ZIP Code* at the drop-down list. (You will need to scroll down the list to display *ZIP Code*. When *ZIP Code* is inserted in the *Field* option box, *Equal to* is inserted in the *Comparison* option box and the insertion point is positioned in the *Compare to* text box.)
d. Type **20300** in the *Compare to* text box.
e. Click the down-pointing arrow at the right of the *Comparison* option box and then click *Greater than* at the drop-down list.
f. Click OK to close the Filter and Sort dialog box.
g. Click OK to close the Mail Merge Recipients dialog box.
h. View the letters merged with the selected records.
   (Optional: If you want to print the merged document, click the Merge to Printer button on the Mail Merge toolbar and then click OK at the Merge to Printer dialog box.)
4. Save and then close **ewc1x17**.

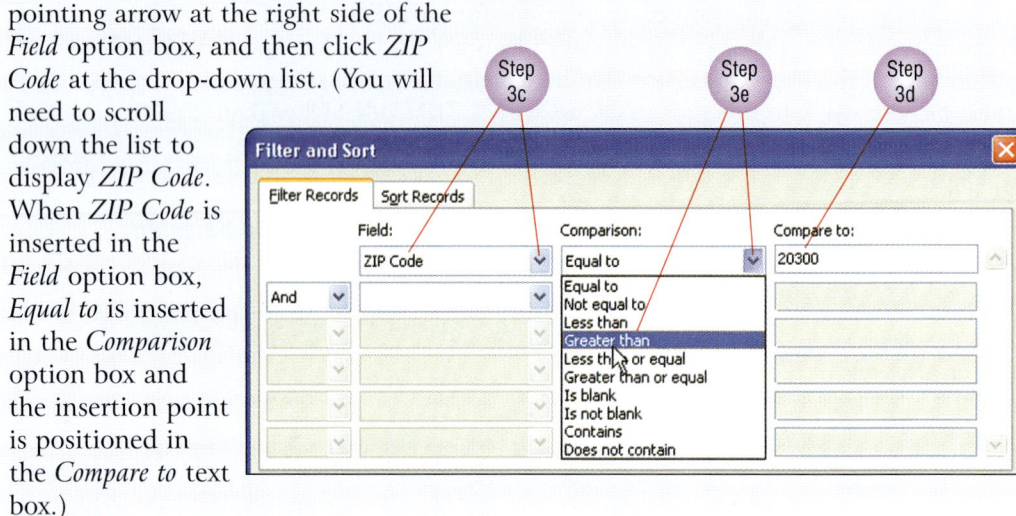

When a field is selected from the *Field* option box, Word automatically inserts *And* in the first box at the left side of the dialog box. This can be changed, if needed, to *Or*. With the *And* and *Or* options, you can specify more than one condition for selecting records. For example, in Exercise 18, you will select all records of clients living in the cities of Rosedale or Towson. If the data source file contained another field such as a specific financial plan for each customer, you could select all customers in a specific city that subscribe to a specific financial plan. For this situation, you would use the *And* option.

If you want to clear the current options at the Filter and Sort dialog box with the Filter Records tab selected, click the Clear All button. This clears any text from text boxes and leaves the dialog box on the screen. Click Cancel if you want to close the Filter and Sort dialog box without specifying any records.

exercise 18 — SELECTING RECORDS CONTAINING SPECIFIC CITIES

1. Open **ewc1LFSMainDoc**.
2. Save the document with Save As and name it **ewc1x18**.
3. Select the records that contain *Rosedale* or *Towson* by completing the following steps:
   a. Click the Mail Merge Recipients button on the Mail Merge toolbar.
   b. Click the down-pointing arrow at the left of the *Last Name* column heading and then click *(Advanced…)* at the drop-down list.

c. At the Filter and Sort dialog box with the Filter Records tab selected, click the down-pointing arrow to the right of the *Field* option box, and then click *City* at the drop-down list. (You will need to scroll down the list to display this field.)
d. With the insertion point positioned in the *Compare to* text box, type **Rosedale**.
e. Click the down-pointing arrow to the right of the option box containing the word *And* (at the left side of the dialog box), and then click *Or* at the drop-down list.
f. Click the down-pointing arrow to the right of the second *Field* option box, and then click *City* at the drop-down list. (You will need to scroll down the list to display this field.)
g. With the insertion point positioned in the second *Compare to* text box (the one below the box containing *Rosedale*), type **Towson**.

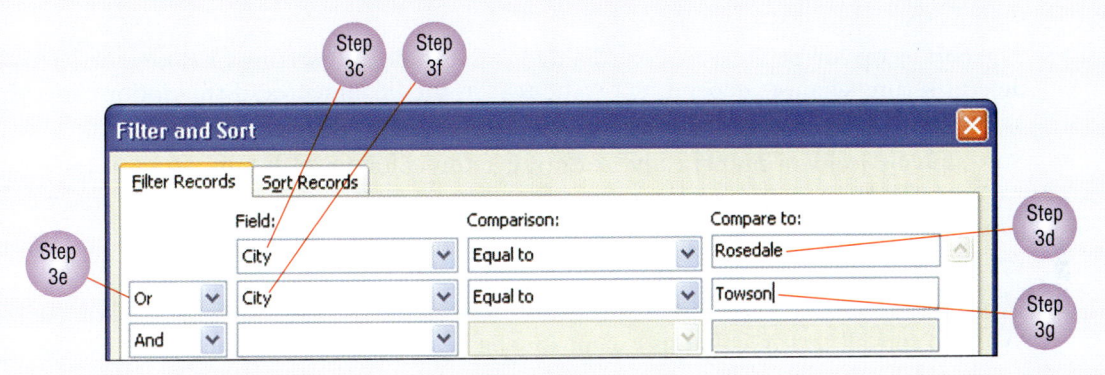

h. Click OK to close the Filter and Sort dialog box.
i. Click OK to close the Mail Merge Recipients dialog box.
j. View the letters merged with the selected records.
  (Optional: If you want to print the merged document, click the Merge to Printer button on the Mail Merge toolbar and then click OK at the Merge to Printer dialog box.)
4. Save and then close **ewc1x18**.

CHAPTER summary

- Word includes a Mail Merge Wizard you can use to create letters, envelopes, labels, directories, e-mail messages, and faxes, all with personalized information.

- Generally, a merge takes two documents—the data source file containing the variable information and the main document containing standard text along with fields identifying where variable information is inserted during the merge process.

- Variable information in a data source file is saved as a record. A record contains all of the information for one unit. A series of fields makes one record, and a series of records makes a data source file.

- The Mail Merge Wizard guides you through six steps for merging documents and presents a Mail Merge task pane for each step.

- You can create your own custom field at the Customize Address List dialog box.

- Edit a main document in the normal manner. Edit a data source file using the Mail Merge Wizard or with buttons on the Mail Merge toolbar.
- The Mail Merge toolbar contains buttons you can use to edit a main document and/or a data source file.
- Word lets you input variable information with the keyboard into a document during the merge. This Fill-in field is inserted in a main document by clicking the Insert Word Field button on the Mail Merge toolbar, and then clicking Fill-in at the drop-down menu.
- You can sort text in paragraphs, text in table columns, or records in a data source. You can also select specific records from a data source to be merged with a main document.
- Word can perform these three types of sorts: alphanumeric, numeric, and date.
- Sort text arranged in paragraphs by the first character of the paragraph at the Sort Text dialog box.
- The *Sort by* option at the Sort Text dialog box has a default setting of *Paragraphs*. This default setting changes depending on the text in the document and the options specified at the Sort Options dialog box.
- Sort alphabetically or numerically text arranged in columns with tabs between the columns. Text typed at the left margin is considered *Field 1*, text typed at the first tab is considered *Field 2*, and so on.
- When sorting text, you can sort on more than one field.
- Use the option *Header row* in the *My list has* section of the Sort Text dialog box to tell Word to sort all text in columns except for the headings of the columns.
- Sorting text in columns within tables is very similar to sorting columns of text separated by tabs.
- Sort records in a data source at the Mail Merge Recipients dialog box. To display this dialog box, open the main document, display the Mail Merge toolbar, and then click the Mail Merge Recipients button on the Mail Merge toolbar.
- At the Mail Merge Recipients dialog box, click the column heading to sort the data in a specific field in ascending order.
- Sort records at the Filter and Sort dialog box with the Sort Records tab selected.
- Select specific records for merging with the main document with options at the Mail Merge Recipients dialog box or with options at the Filter and Sort dialog box with the Filter Records tab selected.

FEATURES summary

FEATURE	BUTTON	MENU	KEYBOARD
Mail Merge Wizard		Tools, Letters and Mailings, Mail Merge	
Mail Merge toolbar		View, Toolbars, Mail Merge	
Merge to New Document dialog box	📋		Alt + Shift + N
Merge to Printer dialog box	🖨		Alt + Shift + M
Mail Merge Recipients dialog box	📝		
Sort Text dialog box		Table, Sort	

CONCEPTS check

Completion: On a blank sheet of paper, indicate the correct term, command, or number for each description.

1. The Mail Merge Wizard guides you through this number of steps to prepare merge documents.
2. Generally, a merge takes two documents: the data source file and this document.
3. Variable information in a data source file is saved as this, which contains all of the information for one unit.
4. A data source file created using the Mail Merge Wizard is created and saved as this type of database file.
5. This inserts records on the same page, rather than creating a new form for each record.
6. Open a main document, start the Mail Merge Wizard, and the Wizard begins with this step number.
7. Click this button on the Mail Merge toolbar and the main document is merged with the data source file to a new document.
8. Edit a data source by clicking this button on the Mail Merge toolbar.
9. This field is used for information input at the keyboard during a merge.
10. With the sorting feature, you can sort text in paragraphs, text in columns in tables, or records in this type of file.
11. These three types of sorts can be performed by Word's sort feature: alphanumeric, numeric, and this.
12. At this dialog box, you can sort text in paragraphs.
13. When sorting columns, text typed at the first tab is considered to be this field number.
14. Click this option at the Sort Text dialog box to tell Word not to include the column headings in the sort.
15. At the Mail Merge Recipients dialog box, click this option to sort data in a specific column in ascending order.
16. Use options from this dialog box with the Filter Records tab selected to select specific records for merging with the main document.

WORD Merging Documents and Sorting and Selecting Data E43

SKILLS check

Assessment 1

1. Look at the information shown in Figure 1.14 and Figure 1.15.
2. Use the Mail Merge Wizard to prepare six letters using the information shown in Figure 1.14 and Figure 1.15. When completing the steps, consider the following:
   a. At Step 3, create a data source file using the information shown in Figure 1.14. Save the data source file in the WordChapter01E folder on your disk and name it **SFClientList**.
   b. At Step 6, complete the following steps:
      1) Click the *Edit individual letters* hyperlink in the task pane.
      2) At the Merge to New Document dialog box, make sure *All* is selected, and then click the OK button.
      3) Save the merged letters in the normal manner in the WordChapter01E folder on your disk and name the document **SFClientLetters**.
      4) Print **SFClientLetters**. (This document will print four letters.)
      5) Close **SFClientLetters**.
      6) Save the main document in the normal manner in the WordChapter01E folder on your disk and name it **SFMainDoc**.

FIGURE 1.14 Assessment 1

Mr. and Mrs. Tony Benedetti
13114 East 203rd Street
Apt. 402
New Rochelle, NY 10342
Supplemental Retirement Plan

Mrs. Mary Arguello
2554 Country Drive
Suite 105
Mount Vernon, NY 10539
Personal Pension Plan

Ms. Theresa Dusek
12044 Ridgway Drive
(leave this blank)
New York, NY 10233
Firstline Retirement Plan

Mr. Preston Miller
120 South Broadway
(leave this blank)
New York, NY 10123
Supplemental Retirement Plan

FIGURE 1.15 Assessment 1

(current date)

«AddressBlock»

«GreetingLine»

Last year, «Title» «Last_Name», a law went into effect that changes the maximum amounts that may be contributed to defined contribution pension and tax-deferred annuity plans, such as those using Stradford Funds annuities. Generally, the changes slow down the rate at which the maximums will increase in the future. A likely result is that more people will reach the maximum and, if they wish to save more for their retirement, they will have to use after-tax savings instruments.

The amount of money you can voluntarily contribute to your «Plan» was expected to rise above the current maximum. The amendments will delay any cost-of-living adjustments, and the limit will probably not go up for several years. The changes in the law will have an effect on your next annuity statement. If you want to increase or decrease the amount you contribute to your «Plan», please let us know.

Sincerely,

Chris Warren
Director of Financial Services

XX:SFClientLetters

Assessment 2

1. Use the Mail Merge Wizard to prepare envelopes for the letters created in Assessment 1.
2. Specify **SFClientList** as the data source file.
3. Save the merged envelope document in the WordChapter01E folder on your disk and name the document **SFClientEnvs**.
4. Print the **SFClientEnvs** document.
5. Do not save the envelope main document.

Assessment 3

1. Use the Mail Merge Wizard to prepare mailing labels for the names and addresses in the **SFClientList**.
2. Save the label document in the WordChapter01E folder on your disk and name the document **SFClientLabels**.
3. Print the **SFClientLabels** document.
4. Do not save the labels main document.

Assessment 4

1. Open the **SFMainDoc** document.
2. Start the Mail Merge Wizard.
3. At the third wizard step, click the *Edit recipient list* hyperlink and then click the Edit button at the Mail Merge Recipients dialog box. Make the following changes to the records:
   a. Display the record for Ms. Theresa Dusek and then change the address from *12044 Ridgway Drive* to *1390 Fourth Avenue*.
   b. Display the record for Mr. Preston Miller and add *and Mrs.* in the title (so the title field displays as *Mr. and Mrs.*).
   c. Display and then delete the record for Mrs. Mary Arguello.
4. At the sixth wizard step, click the *Edit individual letters* hyperlink. At the Merge to New Document dialog box, click OK.
5. Save the merged letters with the name **SFEditedLetters**.
6. Print and then close **SFEditedLetters**.
7. Save and then close **SFMainDoc**.

Assessment 5

1. Open **WordSort04**.
2. Save the document with Save As and name it **ewc1sc05**.
3. Sort the names alphabetically by last name.
4. Save, print, and then close **ewc1sc05**.

Assessment 6

1. Open **WordSort05**.
2. Save the document with Save As and name it **ewc1sc06**.
3. Sort the columns of text alphabetically by last name in the first column. (Display the Sort Options dialog box and make sure *Tabs* is selected in the *Separate fields at* section.) ***(Hint: Select the columns of text but not the title, subtitle, and headings.)***
4. Print **ewc1sc06**.
5. Sort the columns of text by the date of hire in the third column.
6. Print **ewc1sc06**.
7. Sort the columns of text alphabetically by the department name and then alphabetically by last name.
8. Save, print, and then close **ewc1sc06**.

Assessment 7

1. Open **WordSort06**.
2. Save the document with Save As and name it **ewc1sc07**.
3. Sort the text alphabetically by State in the first column of the table. (Make sure no text displays in the *Then by* option box.)
4. Save and then print **ewc1sc07**.
5. Sort the text numerically by First Quarter in ascending order in the second column of the table.
6. Display the Table AutoFormat dialog box and apply a table style of your choosing to the table.
7. Save, print, and then close **ewc1sc07**.

Assessment 8

1. Open **ewc1LFSMainDoc**.
2. Save the document with Save As and name it **ewc1sc08**.
3. Display the Mail Merge Recipients dialog box and then select those clients living in the city of Baltimore.
4. Merge the selected records to the printer.
5. Save and then close **ewc1sc08**.

CHAPTER challenge

You work in the billing department at Shiny and Bright Dental Clinic. Each month you send out a letter to patients providing them with information concerning their last appointment and the fees that were rendered. This letter will be used as a main document to be merged with the patient data source. The data source will include patient information in the form of the following fields: first name, last name, address, city, state, zip code, insured (yes/no), balance due (amount), and any other fields you feel appropriate. Add at least five patients to your data source. The letter should contain at least two paragraphs. Save the letter before merging. Merge (to a new document) the letter with the data source. Print one of the merged letters.

While some patients are covered by insurance, others are not. Those that are covered by insurance will have their bill sent directly to their insurance provider for payment; however, those not covered by insurance will be asked to pay their fees by the end of the month. Use the Help feature to learn about the If...Then...Else... merge field. Using the letter created in the first part of the Chapter Challenge, incorporate the If...Then...Else... merge field. If the patient is insured, insert a statement indicating that the insurance provider will be billed; if the patient is not insured, insert a statement indicating that the balance is due at the end of the month. Save and merge the letter. Print one of the merged letters.

INTEGRATED

Instead of maintaining patients in a data source in Word, you have stored the information in a table called **Patients** in an Access database called **Shiny and Bright**. Merge the letter created in the first part of the Chapter Challenge with the table called **Patients** located in the Access database called **Shiny and Bright**. Print one of the merged letters.

CHAPTER 2

FORMATTING WITH SPECIAL FEATURES

PERFORMANCE OBJECTIVES

Upon successful completion of Chapter 2, you will be able to:
- **Insert a nonbreaking space between words in a document**
- **Find and replace special characters**
- **Insert a manual line break**
- **Control pagination with widow/orphan control and by keeping a paragraph or paragraphs of text together**
- **Create, view, edit, modify, move, copy, and delete footnotes and endnotes**
- **Automatically summarize a document**
- **Analyze content readability**
- **Modify table format, position, direction, and properties and insert and modify fields**
- **Add buttons to and remove buttons from a toolbar**
- **Create custom menus**

In this chapter, you will learn to use a variety of Word features that can control pagination in a document, insert footnotes and endnotes, summarize document content, analyze document readability, and format tables. Control the location of page breaks by inserting a manual line break, using the widow/orphan control feature, and specifying text that is to be kept together on a page. Calculate data in cells in a table with options at the Formula dialog box, modify table formats with options at the Table Properties dialog box, and insert and modify fields with options at the Field dialog box. In this chapter, you will also learn how to customize toolbars and create custom menus.

Inserting a Nonbreaking Space

As you type text in a document, Word makes line-end decisions and automatically wraps text to the next line. In some situations, word wrap may break up words or phrases on separate lines that should remain together. For example, a name such as *Daniel C. Lagasa* can be broken after, but should not be broken before, the initial *C*. The phrase *World War II* can be broken between *World* and *War*, but should not be broken between *War* and *II*.

HINT
A nonbreaking space can be inserted at the Symbol dialog box with the (normal text) font selected.

To control what text is wrapped to the next line, insert a nonbreaking space between words. When a nonbreaking space is inserted, Word considers the words as one unit and will not divide them. To insert a nonbreaking space between words, type the first word, press Ctrl + Shift + spacebar, and then type the second word.

If nonprinting characters are displayed, a normal space displays as a dot and a nonbreaking space displays as a degree symbol. To turn on the display of nonprinting characters, click the Show/Hide ¶ button on the Standard toolbar.

exercise 1

INSERTING NONBREAKING SPACES

1. At a clear document screen, turn on the display of nonprinting characters (click Show/Hide ¶ button on the Standard toolbar), and then type the memo shown in Figure 2.1. Insert nonbreaking spaces within the commands in the memo (for example, within *Ctrl + B* and *Ctrl + I*). Insert a nonbreaking space by pressing Ctrl + Shift + spacebar before and after the plus symbol in all of the shortcut commands.
2. Save the document and name it **ewc2x01**.
3. Turn off the display of nonprinting characters.
4. Print and then close **ewc2x01**.

FIGURE 2.1 *Exercise 1*

DATE: January 12, 2005

TO: All Employees

FROM: Jolene Risse

SUBJECT: SHORTCUT COMMANDS

The transition to Office 2003 is almost complete. During the transition, I will continue to offer helpful hints to all employees. Word offers a variety of shortcut commands to quickly access features. For example, press Ctrl + B to bold selected text and press Ctrl + U to underline text. Italicize selected text with Ctrl + I.

In addition to the shortcut commands for applying character formatting, you can use shortcut commands to display certain dialog boxes. For example, use the command Ctrl + F to display the Find and Replace dialog box with the Find tab selected. Press Ctrl + O to display the Open dialog box.

XX:ewc2x01

Finding and Replacing Special Characters

You can use the find and replace feature to find special text and replace with other text. You can also use this feature to find special formatting, characters, or nonprinting elements in a document. Special formatting, characters, or nonprinting elements can then be removed from the document or replaced with other formatting or characters.

In addition to finding and replacing text and formatting, you can use the find and replace feature to search for special characters such as an en dash or an em dash and search for nonprinting elements such as a paragraph mark, tab character, or nonbreaking space. To display a list of special characters and nonprinting elements, display the Find and Replace dialog box with the Replace tab selected, expand the dialog box, and then click the Special button. This displays a drop-down menu as shown in Figure 2.2.

QUICK STEPS

Find and Replace Special Character
1. Click Edit, Replace.
2. Click More button.
3. Click Special button.
4. Click desired character.
5. Click Replace All.

HINT
Press Ctrl + H to display the Find and Replace dialog box.

FIGURE 2.2 Special Button Drop-Down Menu

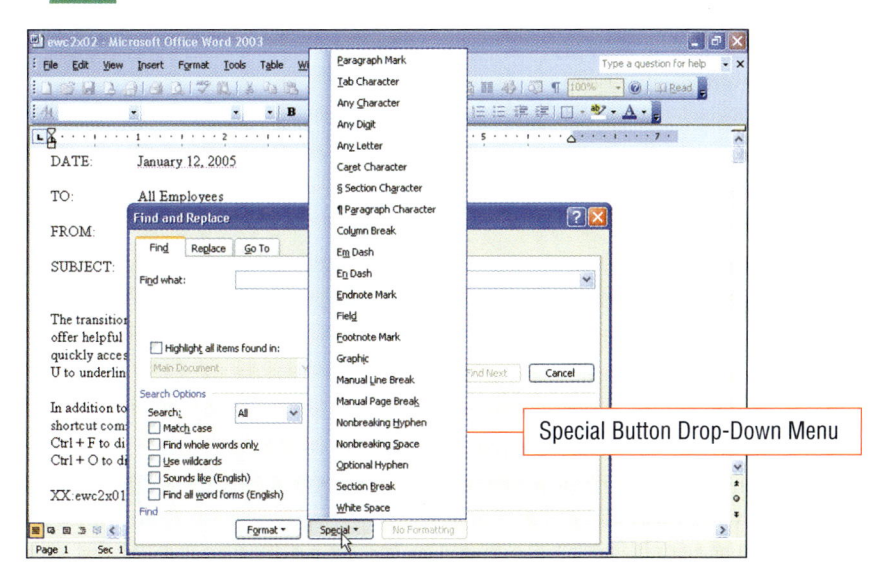

exercise 2

FINDING AND REPLACING A NONPRINTING ELEMENT

1. Open **ewc2x01**.
2. Save the document with Save As and name it **ewc2x02**.
3. Find all occurrences of the nonbreaking space and replace with a regular space by completing the following steps:
   a. Click Edit and then Replace.
   b. At the Find and Replace dialog box with the Replace tab selected, click the More button.
   c. With the insertion point positioned in the *Find what* text box (make sure the text box does not contain any text), click the No Formatting button that displays toward the bottom of the dialog box. (This removes any formatting.)

Formatting With Special Features E51

d. With the insertion point still positioned in the *Find what* text box, click the Special button that displays toward the bottom of the dialog box.
e. At the drop-down menu that displays, click *Nonbreaking Space*. (This inserts ^s in the *Find what* text box.
f. Click in the *Replace with* text box (make sure the text box does not contain any text) and then click the No Formatting button located toward the bottom of the dialog box. (This removes any formatting.)
g. With the insertion point still positioned in the *Replace with* text box, press the spacebar once. (This tells the Find and Replace feature to find a nonbreaking space and replace it with a regular space.)
h. Click the Replace All button.
i. At the message telling you that Word has completed the search and made the replacements, click OK.
j. Click the Less button.
k. Click the Close button to close the Find and Replace dialog box.
4. Save, print, and then close **ewc2x02**.

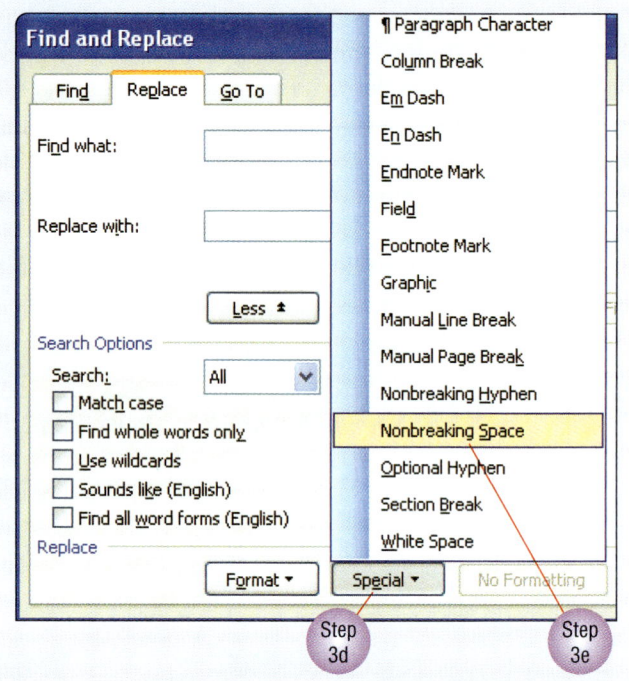

Inserting a Manual Line Break

When you press the Enter key, the insertion point is moved down to the next line and a paragraph mark is inserted in the document. Paragraph formatting is stored in this paragraph mark. For example, if your paragraph includes formatting such as spacing before and/or after the paragraph, pressing the Enter key continues this formatting to the next line. If you want to move the insertion point down to the next line without the before and/or after paragraph spacing, press Shift + Enter, which is the manual line break command. If you turn on the display of nonprinting symbols, a manual line break displays as the ↵ symbol.

exercise 3

INSERTING A MANUAL LINE BREAK IN A DOCUMENT

1. Open **WordDocument05**.
2. Save the document with Save As and name it **ewc2x03**.
3. Select the text from the beginning of the first paragraph to the end of the document.
4. Display the Paragraph dialog box by clicking Format and then Paragraph.
5. At the Paragraph dialog box with the Indents and Spacing tab selected, click the up-pointing arrow at the right side of the *After* text box until *12 pt* displays in the text box.
6. Click OK to close the dialog box.
7. Deselect the text.
8. Click the Show/Hide ¶ button on the Standard toolbar. (This turns on the display of nonprinting symbols.)
9. Insert manual line breaks by completing the following steps:

a. Move the insertion point to the end of the one-line second paragraph immediately left of the ¶ symbol (the line that begins *Research has centered...*).
b. Press the Enter key.
c. Press the Tab key and then type **Problem solving**.
d. Press Shift + Enter. (This moves the insertion point down to the next line without including the space after formatting.)
e. Press the Tab key and then type **Pattern recognition**.
f. Press Shift + Enter.
g. Press the Tab key and then type **Natural-language processing**.
h. Press Shift + Enter.
i. Press the Tab key and then type **Learning**.
j. Press Shift + Enter.
k. Press the Tab key and then type **Representation of real-world knowledge**.
l. Click the Show/Hide ¶ button to turn off the display of nonprinting symbols.

10. Save, print, and then close **ewc2x03**.

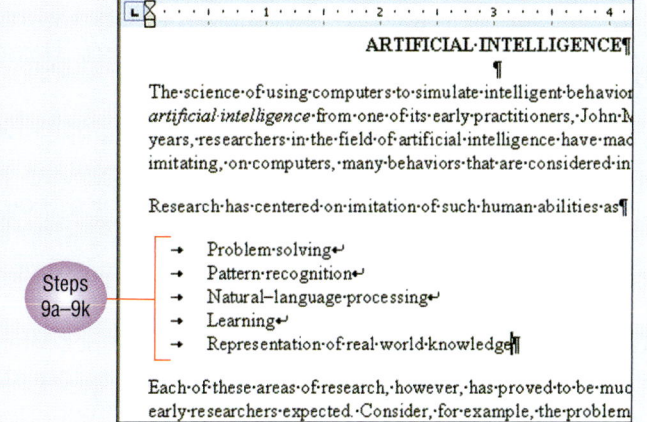

Controlling Pagination

Several options from the Paragraph dialog box with the Line and Page Breaks tab selected will affect the position of page breaks within a document. With the Line and Page Breaks tab selected, the Paragraph dialog box displays as shown in Figure 2.3.

FIGURE 2.3 *Paragraph Dialog Box with Line and Page Breaks Tab Selected*

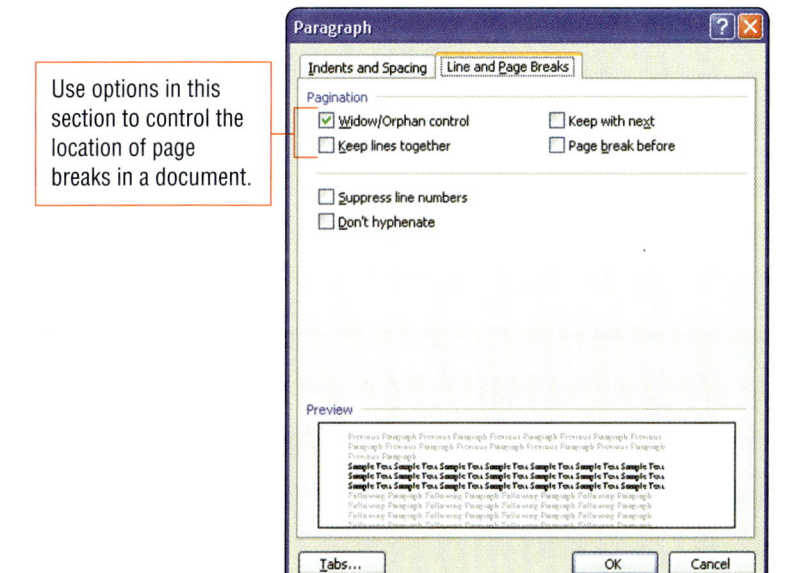

Use options in this section to control the location of page breaks in a document.

WORD — Formatting With Special Features — E53

QUICK STEPS

Turn On/Off Widow/Orphan Control
1. Click Format, Paragraph.
2. Click Line and Page Breaks tab.
3. Click *Widow/Orphan control*.
4. Click OK.

Turning On/Off Widow/Orphan Control

In a long document, you will want to avoid creating widows or orphans. A widow is the last line of a paragraph that appears at the top of a page. An orphan is the first line of a paragraph that appears at the bottom of a page. In Word, widows and orphans are automatically prevented from appearing in text. Word accomplishes this by adjusting the page breaks in a document. Because of this, the last line of text on various pages will not always occur at the same line measurement or count. If you wish to turn off the widow and orphan control, display the Paragraph dialog box with the Line and Page Breaks tab selected, and then click *Widow/Orphan control*. This removes the check mark from the option.

Keeping a Paragraph or Paragraphs Together

Even with widow/orphan control on, Word may insert a page break in a document between text in a paragraph or several paragraphs that should stay together as a unit. The Paragraph dialog box with the Line and Page Breaks tab selected contains options to keep a paragraph, a group of paragraphs, or a group of lines together.

QUICK STEPS

Keep Text Together
1. Click Format, Paragraph.
2. Click Line and Page Breaks tab.
3. Click *Keep lines together*, *Keep with next*, and/or *Page break before*.
4. Click OK.

To keep a paragraph together, you can instruct Word not to insert a page break within a paragraph. This format instruction is stored in the paragraph mark, so as the paragraph is moved within the document, the format instruction moves with it. To tell Word not to insert a page break within a paragraph, display the Paragraph dialog box with the Line and Page Breaks tab selected, and then click *Keep lines together*. The same steps can be used to keep a group of consecutive paragraphs together. To do this, select the paragraphs first, display the Paragraph dialog box, and then click *Keep lines together*.

With the *Keep with next* option at the Paragraph dialog box, you can tell Word to keep the paragraph where the insertion point is located together with the next paragraph (for example, to keep a heading together with the paragraph of text that follows it). If the page does not contain enough room for the paragraph and the next paragraph, Word moves both paragraphs to the next page. Use the *Page break before* option if you want a particular paragraph to print at the top of a page. Position the insertion point in the paragraph that you want to begin a new page, display the Paragraph dialog box with the Line and Page Breaks tab selected, and then click *Page break before*.

exercise 4 — KEEPING TEXT TOGETHER

(Note: Due to slight differences in how printers interpret line height, a page break may not display in the report after the heading Planning the Publication. *Before completing this exercise, check with your instructor to see if you need to make any minor changes to margins or font size for text and headings.)*

1. Open **WordReport01**.
2. Save the document with Save As and name it **ewc2x04**.
3. Make the following changes to the document:
   a. Change the top, left, and right margins to 1.5 inches.
   b. Select the title DESKTOP PUBLISHING and then change the font to 14-point Arial bold.

c. Select the heading *Defining Desktop Publishing* and then change the font to 14-point Arial bold.
d. Use Format Painter to apply 14-point Arial bold to the remaining headings: *Initiating the Desktop Publishing Process*, *Planning the Publication*, and *Creating the Content*.
4. Tell Word to keep the heading *Planning the Publication* and the paragraph that follows it together on the same page and turn off the widow/orphan control by completing the following steps:
   a. Position the insertion point on any character in the heading *Planning the Publication* (located at the bottom of page 2).
   b. Click Format and then Paragraph.
   c. At the Paragraph dialog box, click the Line and Page Breaks tab.
   d. Click in the *Keep with next* check box to insert a check mark.
   e. Click the *Widow/Orphan control* option to remove the check mark.
   f. Click OK or press Enter.
5. Save, print, and then close **ewc2x04**.

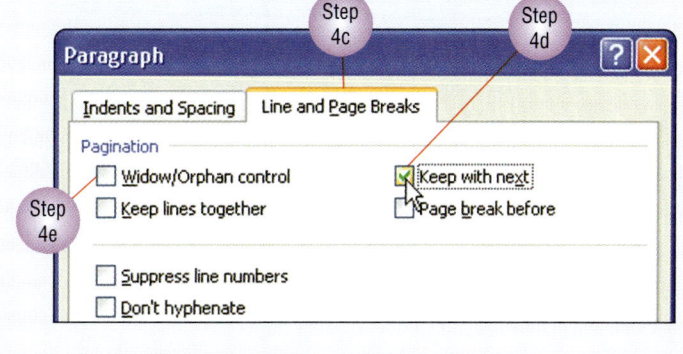

Creating Footnotes and Endnotes

A research paper or report contains information from a variety of sources. To give credit to those sources, a footnote can be inserted in the document. A ***footnote*** is an explanatory note or reference that is printed at the bottom of the page where it is referenced. An ***endnote*** is also an explanatory note or reference, but it prints at the end of the document.

Two steps are involved when creating a footnote or endnote. First, the note reference number is inserted in the document at the location where the note is referenced. The second step for creating a footnote or endnote is to type the note entry text. Footnotes and endnotes are created in a similar manner. To create a footnote in a document, position the insertion point at the location in the document where the reference number is to appear. Click Insert, point to Reference, and then click Footnote. At the Footnote and Endnote dialog box shown in Figure 2.4, make sure *Footnotes* is selected, and then click the Insert button. At the footnote pane shown in Figure 2.5, type the footnote entry text and then click the Close button.

QUICK STEPS

Insert Footnote
1. Click Insert, Reference, Footnote.
2. Click Insert.
3. Type footnote text.
4. Click Close.

HINT
Press Ctrl + Alt + F to display the footnote pane.

FIGURE 2.4 *Footnote and Endnote Dialog Box*

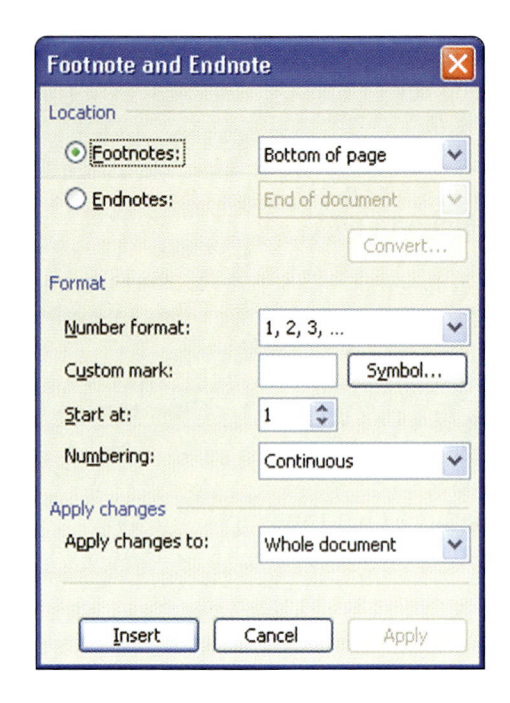

FIGURE 2.5 *Footnote Pane*

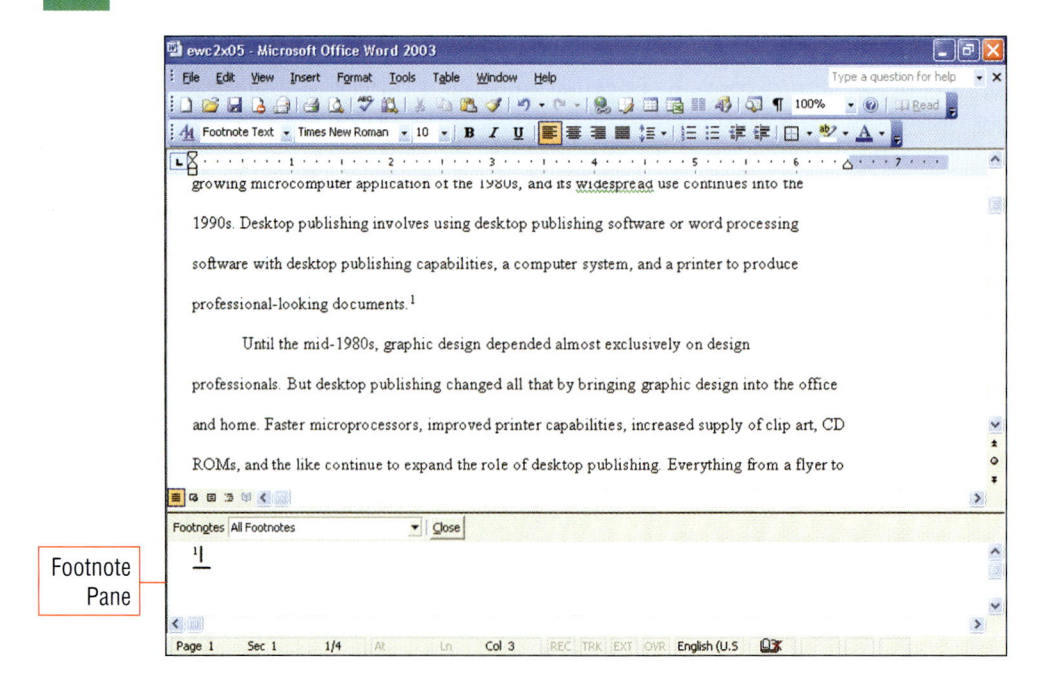

Footnote Pane

When creating footnotes, Word numbers footnotes with Arabic numbers (1, 2, 3, and so on.). If you press the Enter key after typing the footnote entry text, footnotes will be separated by a blank line (double space).

E56 Chapter Two

exercise 5

CREATING FOOTNOTES

1. Open **ewc2x04**.
2. Save the document with Save As and name it **ewc2x05**.
3. Change the top, left, and right margins to 1 inch.
4. Create the first footnote shown in Figure 2.6 at the end of the second paragraph in the *Defining Desktop Publishing* section by completing the following steps:
    a. Position the insertion point at the end of the second paragraph in the *Defining Desktop Publishing* section.
    b. Click Insert, point to Reference, and then click Footnote.
    c. At the Footnote and Endnote dialog box, make sure *Footnotes* is selected, and then click the Insert button.
    d. At the footnote pane, type the first footnote shown in Figure 2.6. Press the Enter key once after typing the footnote text (this will separate the first footnote from the second footnote by a blank line).
    e. Click the Close button to close the footnote pane.
5. Move the insertion point to the end of the fourth paragraph in the *Defining Desktop Publishing* section and then create the second footnote shown in Figure 2.6 by completing steps similar to those in Step 4.
6. Move the insertion point to the end of the only paragraph in the *Initiating the Desktop Publishing Process* section and then create the third footnote shown in Figure 2.6 by completing steps similar to those in Step 4.
7. Move the insertion point to the end of the last paragraph in the *Planning the Publication* section and then create the fourth footnote shown in Figure 2.6.
8. Move the insertion point to the end of the last paragraph in the *Creating the Content* section (the last paragraph in the document) and then create the fifth footnote shown in Figure 2.6.
9. Save, print, and then close **ewc2x05**.

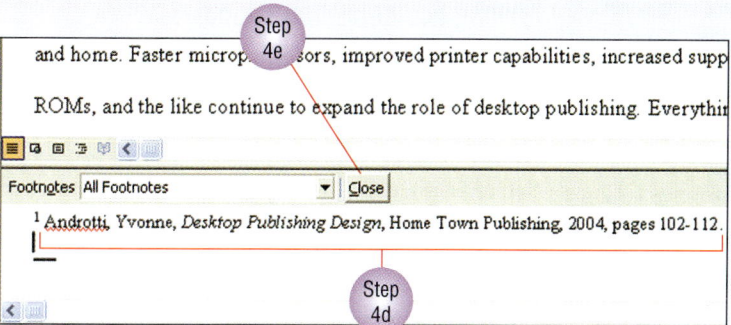

FIGURE 2.6 Exercise 5

Androtti, Yvonne, *Desktop Publishing Design*, Home Town Publishing, 2004, pages 102-112.

Bolle, Lynette and Jonathon Steadman, "Designing with Style," *Design Technologies*, January/February 2003, pages 22-24.

Doucette, Wayne, "Beginning the DTP Process," *Desktop Designs*, November 2004, pages 31-34.

Elstrom, Lisa, *Desktop Publishing Technologies*, Lilly-Harris Publishers, 2003, pages 88-94.

Busching, Wallace, "Designing a Newsletter," *Business Computing*, April 2005, pages 15-22.

QUICK STEPS

Insert Endnote
1. Click Insert, Reference, Footnote.
2. Click *Endnotes*.
3. Click Insert.
4. Type endnote text.
5. Click Close.

HINT
Press Ctrl + Alt + D to display the endnote pane.

HINT
Specify where you want footnotes or endnotes printed with options at the Footnote and Endnote dialog box.

Create an endnote in a similar manner as a footnote. At the Footnote and Endnote dialog box, click *Endnotes*, and then click the Insert button. At the endnote pane, type the endnote entry text, and then click the Close button. When creating endnotes, Word numbers endnotes with lowercase Roman numerals (i, ii, iii, and so on). The endnote numbering method will display after *AutoNumber* at the Footnote and Endnote dialog box. Press the Enter key after typing the endnote entry text if you want the endnote separated from the next endnote by a blank line (double space).

You can format footnotes and endnotes in the normal manner. The note reference number and the note entry number print in the default font at 8-point size. The note entry text prints in the default font size. You can format the note reference and the note entry text, if desired, to match the formatting of the document text.

Printing Footnotes and Endnotes

When a document containing footnotes is printed, Word automatically reduces the number of text lines on a page by the number of lines in the footnote plus two lines for spacing between the text and the footnote. If the page does not contain enough space, the footnote number and footnote entry text are taken to the next page. Word separates the footnotes from the text with a 2-inch separator line that begins at the left margin. When endnotes are created in a document, Word prints all endnote references at the end of the document separated from the text by a 2-inch separator line.

exercise 6 — CREATING ENDNOTES

1. Open **WordReport02**.
2. Save the document with Save As and name it **ewc2x06**.
3. Select the entire document and then change the font to 12-point Century (or a similar serif typeface).
4. Select the title *DESKTOP PUBLISHING DESIGN* and then change the font to 14-point Century bold.
5. Apply 14-point Century bold to the headings *Designing a Document* and *Creating Focus*.
6. Create the first endnote shown in Figure 2.7 at the end of the last paragraph in the *Designing a Document* section by completing the following steps:
   a. Position the insertion point at the end of the last paragraph in the *Designing a Document* section.
   b. Click Insert, point to Reference, and then click Footnote.
   c. At the Footnote and Endnote dialog box, click *Endnotes*.
   d. Click the Insert button.
   e. At the endnote pane, type the first endnote shown in Figure 2.7. Press the Enter key once after typing the endnote text.
   f. Click the Close button to close the endnote pane.

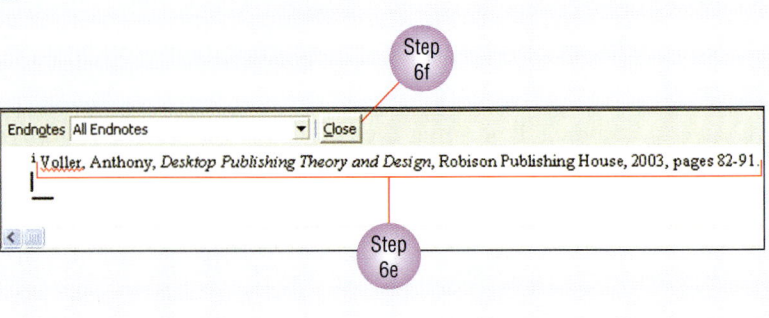

7. Move the insertion point to the end of the first paragraph below the two bulleted paragraphs in the *Creating Focus* section and then create the second endnote shown in Figure 2.7 by completing steps similar to those in Step 6.
8. Move the insertion point to the last paragraph in the document and then create the third endnote shown in Figure 2.7 by completing steps similar to those in Step 6.
9. Save, print, and then close **ewc2x06**. (You may want to preview the document before printing.)

FIGURE 2.7 Exercise 6

Voller, Anthony, *Desktop Publishing Theory and Design*, Robison Publishing House, 2005, pages 82-91.

Rubiano, Lee and Eleanor Bolton, "Choosing the Right Typeface," *Designing Publications*, December 2004, pages 20-23.

Klein, Leland, "Focusing in on Your Document," *System Technologies*, March/April 2004, pages 9-12.

Viewing and Editing Footnotes and Endnotes

To edit existing footnote or endnote entry text, display the footnote or endnote text or the pane. In the Normal view, the footnote or endnote text does not display. To display footnotes or endnotes, change to the Print Layout view. Footnotes will display at the bottom of the page where they are referenced and endnotes will display at the end of the document. Footnotes or endnotes can be edited in the normal manner in the Print Layout view.

Another method for displaying a footnote or endnote pane is to click View and then Footnotes. (The Footnotes option is dimmed unless an open document contains footnotes or endnotes.) If the document contains footnotes, the footnote pane is opened. If the document contains endnotes, the endnote pane is opened. If the document contains both footnotes and endnotes, you can switch between the panes by choosing *All Footnotes* or *All Endnotes* from the *Notes* option at the top of the footnote or endnote pane. To do this, click the down-pointing arrow at the right side of the option box at the top of the pane, and then click *All Footnotes* or *All Endnotes*. With the footnote or endnote pane visible, you can move the insertion point between the pane and the document by clicking in the document text or clicking in the footnote or endnote pane.

If you insert or delete footnotes or endnotes in a document, check the page breaks to determine if they are in a desirable position. You can adjust the soft page breaks in the document using the widow/orphan control, using options in the *Pagination* section of the Paragraph dialog box with the Line and Page Breaks tab selected, or by inserting a hard page break by pressing Ctrl + Enter.

> **HINT**
> Position the mouse pointer on a footnote or endnote reference mark, and the footnote or endnote text displays above the mark in a yellow box.

exercise 7

EDITING FOOTNOTES

1. Open **ewc2x05**.
2. Save the document with Save As and name it **ewc2x07**.
3. Edit the footnotes by completing the following steps:
   a. Change to the Print Layout view.
   b. Move the insertion point to the bottom of the second page until the second footnote is visible.
   c. Make the following changes to the second footnote:
      1) Change *January/February* to *May/June*.
      2) Change *22-24* to *31-33*.
   d. Move the insertion point to the bottom of the third page until the fourth footnote is visible and then make the following changes to the fourth footnote:
      1) Change *Lilly-Harris Publishers* to *Gray Mountain Press*.
      2) Change *2003* to *2005*.
   e. Change back to the Normal view.
4. Save, print, and then close **ewc2x07**.

Moving, Copying, and Deleting Footnotes or Endnotes

You can move, copy, or delete footnote or endnote reference numbers. If a footnote or endnote reference number is moved, copied, or deleted, all footnotes or endnotes remaining in the document are automatically renumbered. To move a footnote or endnote in a document, select the reference mark of the footnote or endnote you want moved, and then click the Cut button on the Standard toolbar. Position the insertion point at the location where you want the footnote or endnote reference inserted and then click the Paste button on the Standard toolbar. You can also move a reference number to a different location in the document by selecting the reference number and then dragging it to the desired location.

To copy a reference number, complete similar steps, except click the Copy button on the Standard toolbar. A reference number can also be copied to a different location in the document by selecting the reference number, holding down the Ctrl key, dragging the reference number to the desired location, then releasing the mouse key and then the Ctrl key.

To delete a footnote or endnote from a document, select the reference number, and then press the Delete key. When the reference number is deleted, the entry text is also deleted.

exercise 8

EDITING AND DELETING FOOTNOTES

1. Open **ewc2x05**.
2. Save the document with Save As and name it **ewc2x08**.
3. Select the entire document and then change the font to Century (or a similar serif typeface such as Bookman Old Style or Garamond).
4. Change the font for the footnotes by completing the following steps:
   a. Click View and then Footnotes.

b. At the footnote pane, press Ctrl + A to select all the footnote entry text and footnote numbers.
   c. Change the font to 12-point Century (or the typeface you chose in Step 3).
   d. Click the Close button to close the footnote pane.
5. Delete the fourth footnote by completing the following steps:
   a. Move the insertion point to the fourth footnote reference number in the document text.
   b. Select the fourth footnote reference number and then press the Delete key.
6. Move the third footnote reference number from the end of the only paragraph in *Initiating the Desktop Publishing Process* section to the end of the second paragraph in the *Planning the Publication* section by completing the following steps:
   a. Move the insertion point to the third footnote reference number.
   b. Select the third footnote reference number.
   c. Click the Cut button on the Standard toolbar.
   d. Position the insertion point at the end of the second paragraph in the *Planning the Publication* section.
   e. Click the Paste button on the Standard toolbar.
7. Save, print, and then close **ewc2x08**.

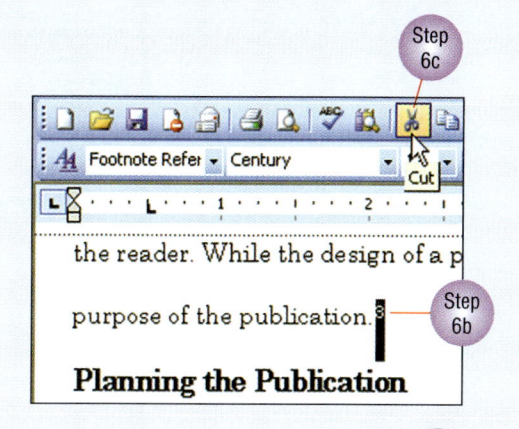

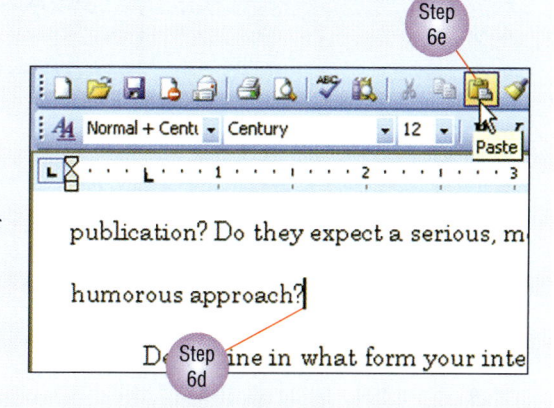

Automatically Summarizing a Document

Use the AutoSummarize feature to identify the key points in a document. AutoSummarize identifies key points by analyzing the text in the document and then assigning a score to each sentence. Sentences containing frequently used words in the document are assigned a higher score. By default, AutoSummarize chooses 25% of the highest scoring sentences. You can increase or decrease this default number. AutoSummarize operates most efficiently on well-structured documents such as reports and articles.

When using the AutoSummarize feature, you can choose to highlight key points, insert an executive summary or abstract at the top of the document, create a new document containing the summary, or hide everything but the summary. To use AutoSummarize, open the desired document, click Tools and then click AutoSummarize. This displays the AutoSummarize dialog box shown in Figure 2.8. At the AutoSummarize dialog box, specify the type of summary desired, the length of the summary (by number of sentences or percentage), and specify whether or not you want the document statistics updated. After making the desired selections, click OK.

QUICK STEPS

Summarize Document
1. Click Tools, AutoSummarize.
2. Choose type of summary.
3. Click OK.

HINT
Press the Esc key to cancel a summary in progress.

FIGURE 2.8 AutoSummarize Dialog Box

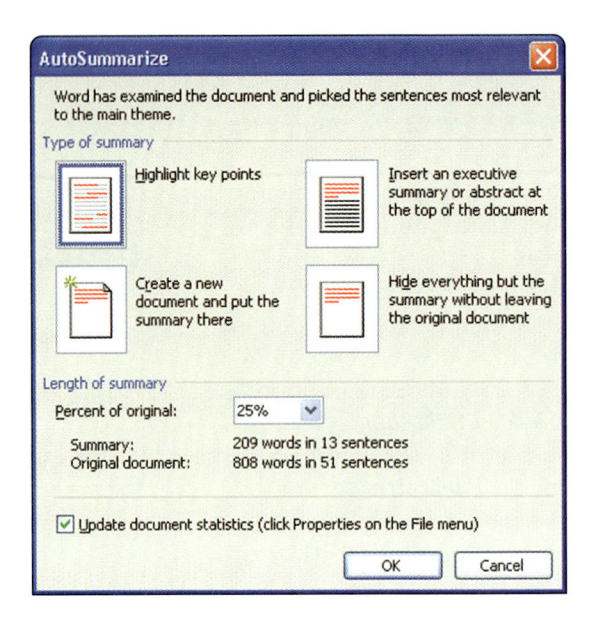

exercise 9

SUMMARIZING A DOCUMENT WITH AUTOSUMMARIZE

1. Open **WordReport02**.
2. Save the document with Save As and name it **ewc2x09**.
3. Summarize the document automatically by completing the following steps:
    a. Click Tools and then AutoSummarize.
    b. At the AutoSummarize dialog box, make sure *Highlight key points* is selected in the *Type of summary* section, and then click OK.
    c. At the document with the AutoSummarize toolbar displayed, click the left arrow on the Percent of Original button until *10%* displays.
    d. Click the Close button on the AutoSummarize toolbar.

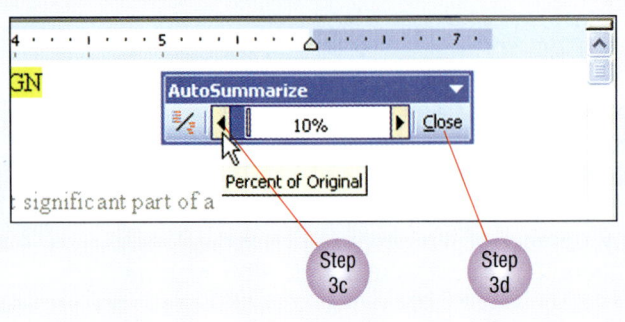

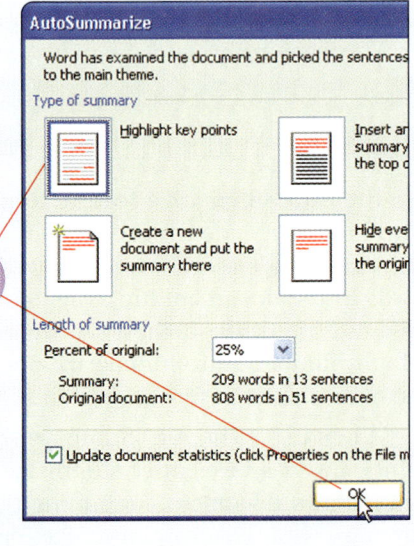

4. Summarize the document and insert the summary in a separate document by completing the following steps:
   a. Click Tools and then AutoSummarize.
   b. At the AutoSummarize dialog box, click the *Create a new document and put the summary there* option.
   c. Click the down-pointing arrow at the right side of the *Percent of original* option and then click *100 words or less* at the drop-down list.
   d. Click OK to close the dialog box.
5. Save the summary document and name it **ewc2Summary**.
6. Print and then close **ewc2Summary**.
7. Close **ewc2x09** without saving the changes.

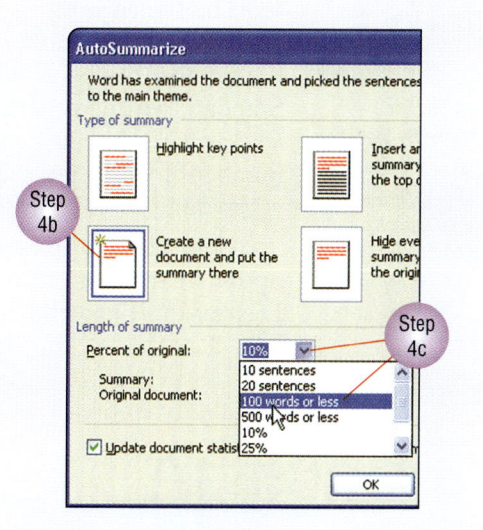

Analyzing a Document with Readability Statistics

When completing a spelling and grammar check, you can display readability statistics about the document. Figure 2.9 displays the readability statistics for ewc2x10. Statistics include word, character, paragraph, and sentence count; average number of sentences per paragraph, words per sentence, and characters per word; and readability information such as the percentage of passive sentences in the document, the Flesch reading ease, and the Flesch-Kincaid grade level.

FIGURE 2.9 **Readability Statistics**

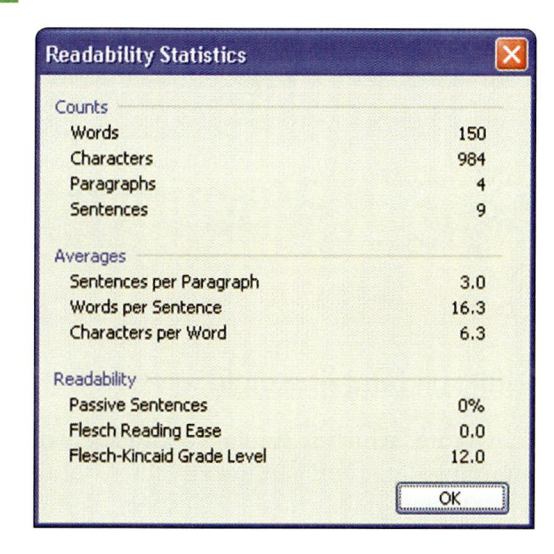

QUICK STEPS

Turn On/Off Readability Statistics
1. Click Tools, Options.
2. Click Spelling & Grammar tab.
3. Click *Show readability statistics* option.
4. Click OK.

The Flesch reading ease is based on the average number of syllables per word and the average number of words per sentence. The higher the score, the greater the number of people who will be able to understand the text in the document. Standard writing generally scores in the 60-70 range. The Flesch-Kincaid grade level is based on the average number of syllables per word and the average number of words per sentence. The score indicates a grade level. Standard writing is generally written at the seventh or eighth grade level.

Control the display of Readability statistics with the *Show readability statistics* option at the Options dialog box with the Spelling & Grammar tab selected. Display this dialog box by clicking Tools and then Options. At the Options dialog box, click the Spelling & Grammar tab. With options at the dialog box, you can control spell checking options, grammar checking options, turn on or off readability statistics, and specify grammar checking style.

exercise 10 — DISPLAYING READABILITY STATISTICS

1. Open **WordStatistics01**.
2. Save the document with Save As and name it **ewc2x10**.
3. Make sure the *Show readability statistics* option is selected by completing the following steps:
   a. Click Tools and then Options.
   b. At the Options dialog box, click the Spelling & Grammar tab.
   c. Make sure the *Show readability statistics* option contains a check mark. If it does not, click the option.
   d. Click OK.
4. Begin checking the spelling and grammar in the document by clicking the Spelling and Grammar button on the Standard toolbar. Make spelling and grammar corrections as needed. When the spelling and grammar check is completed, the readability statistics display. Check the readability statistics that display and compare them to the statistics shown in Figure 2.9. (They should be the same.) Click OK to close the Readability Statistics dialog box.
5. Save, print, and then close **ewc2x10**.

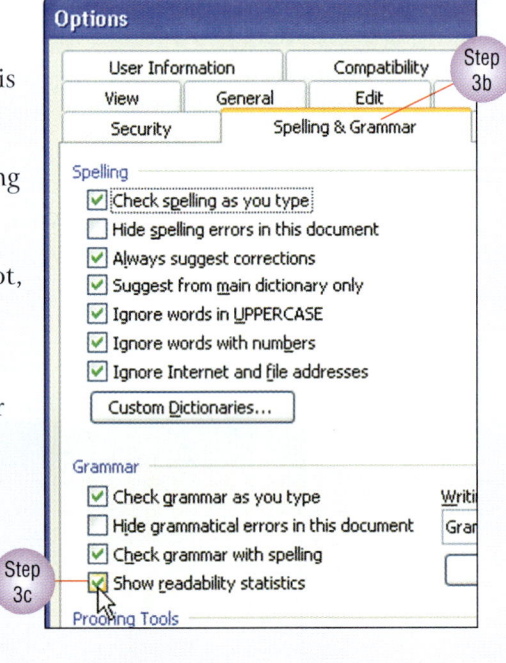

QUICK STEPS

Perform Calculation
1. Click in desired cell in table.
2. Click Table, Formula.
3. Type desired formula.
4. Click OK.

Performing Calculations on Data in a Table

You can create a table in Word, which is similar to an Excel spreadsheet, with columns and rows containing data. You can insert values, total numbers, and formulas in a table in a manner similar to a spreadsheet. Performing calculations on data in a table is an important aspect of manipulating data. Numbers in cells in a table can be added, subtracted, multiplied, and divided. In addition, you can calculate averages, percentages, and minimum and maximum values. Calculations can be performed in a Word table; however, for complex calculations, use a Microsoft Excel worksheet.

To perform a calculation in a table, position the insertion point in the cell where you want the result of the calculation to display, click Table, and then click Formula. This displays the Formula dialog box shown in Figure 2.10. At this dialog box, accept the default formula that displays in the *Formula* text box or type the desired calculation in the *Formula* text box, and then click OK.

> **HINT**
> Click the Insert Microsoft Excel Worksheet button to use Excel functions in Word.

FIGURE 2.10 Formula Dialog Box

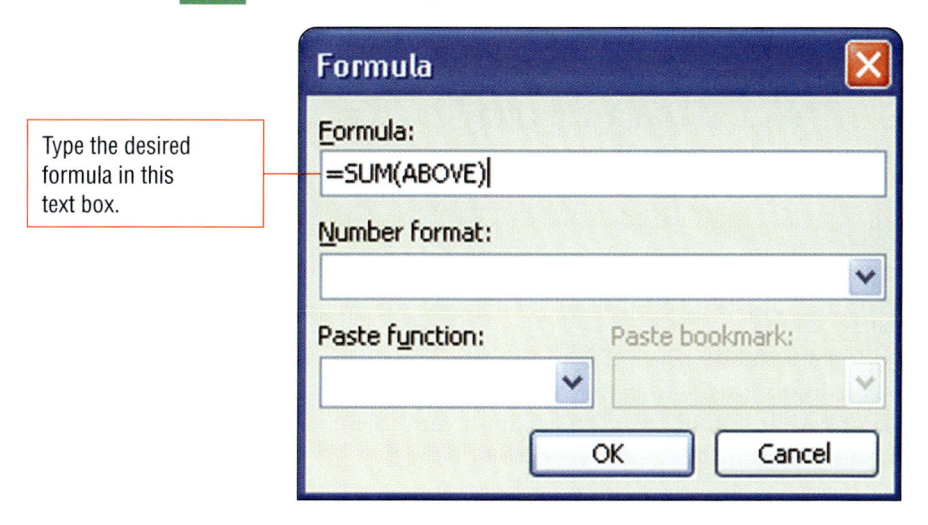

Type the desired formula in this text box. → `=SUM(ABOVE)`

Four basic operators can be used when writing formulas: the plus sign (+) for addition, the minus sign (hyphen) for subtraction, the asterisk (*) for multiplication, and the forward slash (/) for division. If a calculation contains two or more operators, Word calculates from left to right. If you want to change the order of calculation, use parentheses around the part of the calculation to be performed first.

In the default formula, the SUM part of the formula is called a *function*. Word provides other functions you can use to write a formula. These functions are available with the *Paste function* option at the Formula dialog box. For example, you can use the AVERAGE function to average numbers in cells. Examples of how formulas can be written are shown in Table 2.1.

The numbering format can be specified at the Formula dialog box. For example, if you are calculating money amounts, you can specify that the calculated numbers display with two numbers following the decimal point. To specify the numbering format, display the Formula dialog box, and then click the down-pointing arrow to the right of the *Number format* option. Click the desired formatting at the drop-down list that displays.

TABLE 2.1 Example Formulas

Cell E4 is the total price of items.
Cell B4 contains the quantity of items, and cell D4 contains the unit price. The formula for cell E4 is **=B4*D4**. (This formula multiplies the quantity of items in cell B4 by the unit price in cell D4.)

Cell D3 is the percentage of increase of sales from the previous year.
Cell B3 contains the amount of sales for the previous year, and cell C3 contains the amount of sales for the current year. The formula for cell D3 is **=(C3-B3)/C3*100**. (This formula subtracts the amount of sales last year from the amount of sales this year. The remaining amount is divided by the amount of sales this year and then multiplied by 100 to display the product as a percentage.)

Cell E1 is the average of test scores.
Cells A1 through D1 contain test scores. The formula to calculate the average score is **=(A1+B1+C1+D1)/4**. (This formula adds the scores from cells A1 through D1 and then divides that sum by 4.) You can also enter the formula as **=AVERAGE(LEFT)**. The AVERAGE function tells Word to average all entries left of cell E1.

Modifying Table Formats and Properties

Modify the table format with options from the Table drop-down menu. With the drop-down menu options, you can perform such functions as insert/delete rows and/or columns, split and/or merge cells, apply autoformats, and customize the table with options from the Table Properties dialog box.

Display the Table Properties dialog box by clicking Table and then Table Properties. The selected tab in the dialog box and the dialog box options vary depending on where the insertion point is positioned in the table and what is selected in the table. For example, if the entire table is selected, clicking Table and then Table Properties will display the Table Properties dialog box with the Table tab selected as shown in Figure 2.11. Use options at this dialog box to specify the size, alignment, and wrapping options for the table.

HINT
To split a table into two tables, click in the row that will be the first row of the new table, click Table, and then click Table Split.

FIGURE 2.11 Table Properties Dialog Box with Table Tab Selected

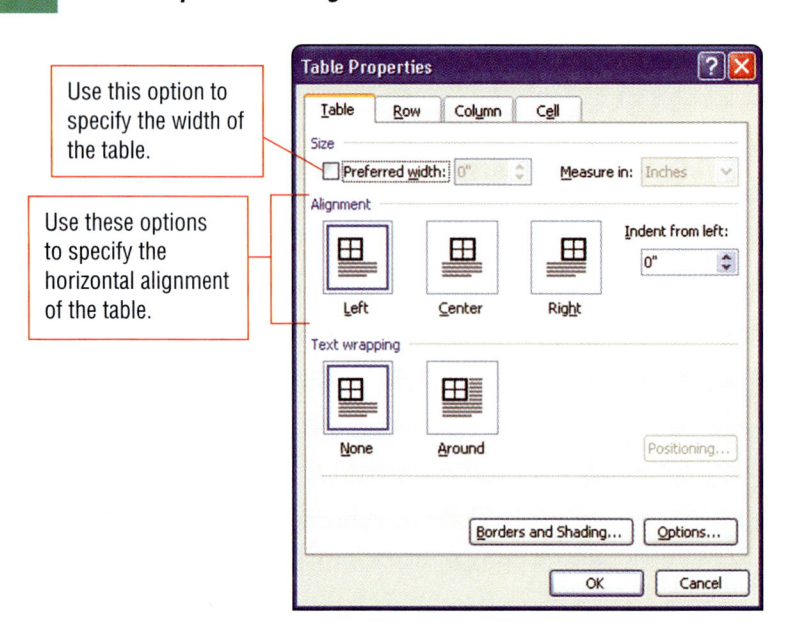

Changing Data Direction in Cell

Rotate text in a cell using the Change Text Direction button on the Tables and Borders toolbar. Display this toolbar by clicking the Tables and Borders button on the Standard toolbar. To rotate text, click in the desired cell and then click the Change Text Direction button until the text is in the desired position.

Change Text Direction

Tables and Borders

exercise 11

MODIFYING A TABLE AND CALCULATING SALES

1. Open **WordTable01**.
2. Save the document with Save As and name it **ewc2x11**.
3. Position the insertion point in any cell in the bottom row (row 6) and then insert a row below by clicking Table, pointing to Insert, and then clicking Rows Below.
4. Position the insertion point in cell A7 (in the new row), turn on bold, and then type **Total**.
5. Insert a formula in cell B7 that calculates first half total sales by completing the following steps:
   a. Position the insertion point in cell B7.
   b. Click Table and then Formula.
   c. At the Formula dialog box, make sure =SUM(ABOVE) displays in the *Formula* text box.
   d. Click the down-pointing arrow at the right side of the *Number format* text box, and then click the third option from the top of the drop-down list.
   e. Click OK to close the dialog box.
6. Move the insertion point to cell C7 and then insert a formula to calculate total sales for the second half by completing steps similar to those in Step 5.
7. Insert a new column and insert text and rotate the text by completing the following steps:
   a. Position the insertion point in any cell in the first column.
   b. Click Table, point to Insert, and then click Columns to the Left.
   c. With the column selected, merge the cells by clicking Table and then Merge Cells.
   d. Type **Rene Hebert** and then press Enter.
   e. Type **Top Sales, 2005**.
   f. Click the Tables and Borders button on the Standard toolbar.
   g. On the Tables and Borders toolbar, click the Change Text Direction button twice.
   h. Turn off the display of the Tables and Borders toolbar.

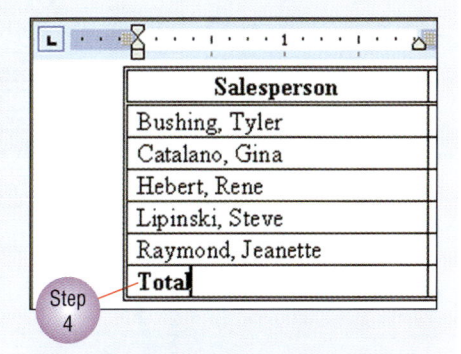

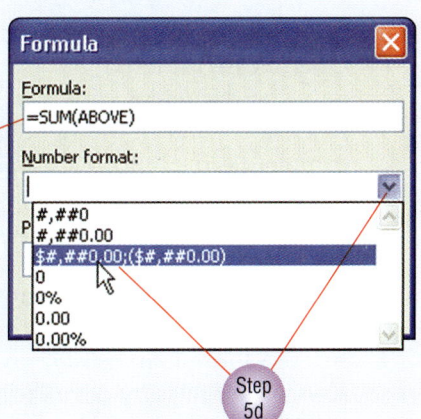

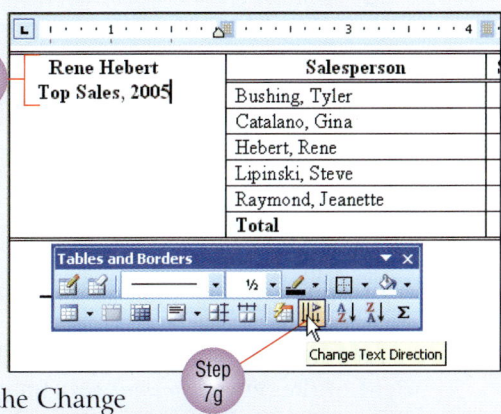

WORD Formatting With Special Features E67

i. Autofit the table contents by clicking Table, pointing to AutoFit, and then clicking AutoFit to Contents.
j. Compare your table with the table shown in Figure 2.12. Make any modifications to your table so it appears as shown in the figure.
8. Save, print, and then close **ewc2x11**.

FIGURE 2.12 Exercise 11

	Salesperson	Sales, First Half	Sales, Second Half
Rene Hebert Top Sales, 2005	Bushing, Tyler	543,241.70	651,438.45
	Catalano, Gina	431,668.55	486,876.50
	Hebert, Rene	612,348.25	684,245.10
	Lipinski, Steve	412,209.55	468,908.45
	Raymond, Jeanette	563,205.60	600,345.20
	Total	$2,562,673.65	$2,891,813.70

exercise 12

AVERAGING SALES

1. Open **WordTable01**.
2. Save the document with Save As and name it **ewc2x12**.
3. Insert a column to the right side of the table by completing the following steps:
   a. Position the insertion point in any cell in column C.
   b. Click Table, point to Insert, and then click Columns to the Right.
   c. Move the insertion point to cell D1 and then type **Average**.
4. Insert a formula in cell D2 to average first half and second half sales by completing the following steps:
   a. Position the insertion point in cell D2 (the cell below *Average*).
   b. Click Table and then Formula.
   c. Delete the formula in the *Formula* text box *except* the equals sign.
   d. With the insertion point positioned immediately after the equals sign, click the down-pointing arrow to the right of the *Paste function* text box.
   e. At the drop-down list that displays, click *AVERAGE*.
   f. With the insertion point positioned between the left and right parentheses, type **left**.
   g. Click the down-pointing arrow to the right of the *Number format* text box and then click the third option from the top at the drop-down list.
   h. Click OK or press Enter.

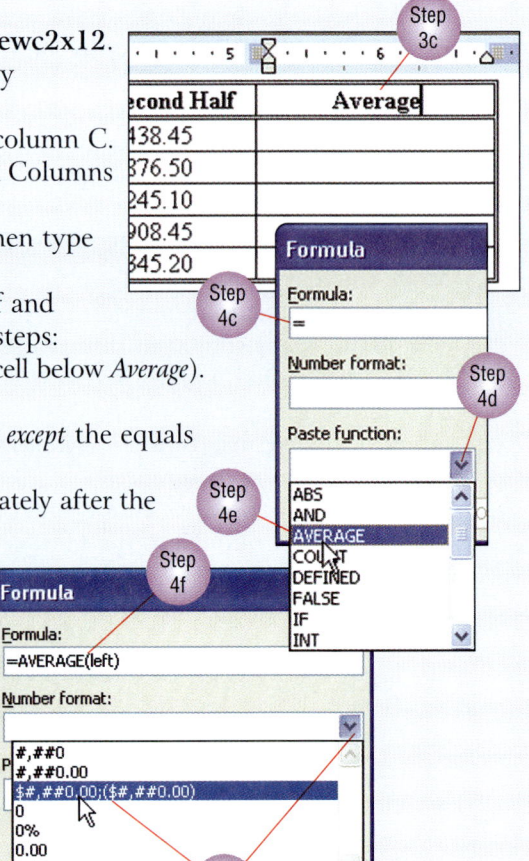

E68 Chapter Two

5. Position the insertion point in cell D3 and then press F4 (the Repeat command).
6. Position the insertion point in cell D4 and then press F4.
7. Position the insertion point in cell D5 and then press F4.
8. Position the insertion point in cell D6 and then press F4.
9. Fit the table to the contents by clicking Table, pointing to AutoFit, and then clicking AutoFit to Contents.
10. Save, print, and then close **ewc2x12**.

Recalculating a Formula

If changes are made to numbers in cells that are part of a formula, select the result of the calculation, and then press the F9 function key. This recalculates the formula and inserts the new result of the calculation in the cell. You can also recalculate by completing the following steps:

1. Select the number in the cell containing the formula.
2. Click Table and then Formula.
3. At the Formula dialog box, click OK or press Enter.

exercise 13

RECALCULATING AVERAGE SALES

1. Open **ewc2x12**.
2. Save the document with Save As and name it **ewc2x13**.
3. Make the following changes to the table:
    a. Change the number in cell C2 from *651,438.45* to *700,375.10*.
    b. Change the number in cell B5 from *412,209.55* to *395,960.50*.
    c. Position the mouse pointer in cell D2, click the left mouse button, and then press F9. (Pressing F9 recalculates the average.)
    d. Click the number in cell D5 and then press F9.
4. Save, print, and then close **ewc2x13**.

Inserting and Modifying Fields

Microsoft Word includes a number of fields you can insert in a document. In Chapter 1, you inserted fields in a main document when following the steps of the wizard and also with a button on the Mail Merge toolbar. You can also insert fields in a document with options at the Field dialog box. Display this dialog box, shown in Figure 2.13, by clicking Insert and then Field. Click an option in the *Field names* list box and the options change at the right side of the dialog box.

QUICK STEPS

Insert Fill-in Field
1. Click Insert, Field.
2. Click *Fill-in* in the *Field names* list box.
3. Click in *Prompt* text box.
4. Type prompt text.
5. Click OK.
6. Click OK.

HINT To display the field codes for a field, click the Field Codes button in the Field dialog box.

FIGURE

2.13 Field Dialog Box

Click a field in this list box and the options change in the *Field properties* section.

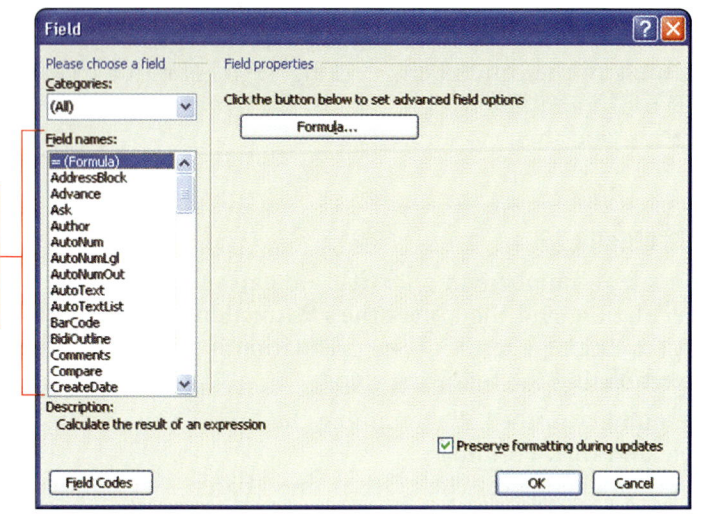

exercise 14

INSERTING AND MODIFYING FIELDS IN A TABLE

1. Open **WordTable02**.
2. Save the document with Save As and name it **ewc2x14**.
3. Evergreen Organics sells organic apples at a price determined by a consortium. The price fluctuates, so you want to include a Fill-in field in the table that asks for the price as of a specific day. Complete the following steps to insert Fill-in fields in the table:
   a. Position the insertion point in the cell B3 (the cell immediately below *Price*).
   b. Click Insert and then Field.
   c. At the Field dialog box, click *Fill-in* in the *Field names* list box. (You will need to scroll down the list to make this option visible.)
   d. Click in the *Prompt:* text box located in the *Field properties* section.
   e. Type **Enter price per pound on first day of current month**.
   f. Click OK.
   g. At the Microsoft Word prompt box, click OK.
   h. Complete steps similar to those in Steps 3b through 3g to insert the same Fill-in field in cell B4.
   i. Position the insertion point in cell B5 and then insert a Fill-in field and include the prompt **Enter price per pound as of last Friday**.
   j. Position the insertion point in cell B6 and then insert a Fill-in field and include the prompt **Enter price per pound as of last Friday**.
4. Save **ewc2x14**.
5. With the table document still open, insert prices by completing the following steps:
   a. Right-click in cell B3 and then click Update Field at the shortcut menu.

E70 Chapter Two

b. At the prompt box, type **$0.65** and then click OK.
c. Right-click in cell B4 and then click Update Field.
d. At the prompt box, type **$0.75** and then click OK.
e. Right-click in cell B5 and then click Update Field.
f. At the prompt box, type **$1.05** and then click OK.
g. Right-click in cell B6 and then click Update Field.
h. At the prompt box, type **$1.10** and then click OK.

6. Cells D3 through D6 contain a formula that multiplies the price by the pounds. Update the amounts in these cells by selecting cells D3 through D6 and then pressing F9.
7. Insert a field that inserts the date the document is printed by completing the following steps:
    a. Merge cells A7 and B7. To do this, select cells A7 and B7, click Table, and then click Merge Cells.
    b. Click the Align Left button on the Formatting toolbar.
    c. Type **Date Printed:** and then press the spacebar once.
    d. Click Insert and then Field.
    e. At the Field dialog box, click *PrintDate* in the *Field names* list box. (You will need to scroll down the list to display this option.)
    f. Click the date option in the *Date formats* list box that inserts the date and time as shown in the figure at the right. (The date and time will display as zeroes until printed.)
    g. Click OK.
8. Click the Print button on the Standard toolbar.
9. The consortium has changed the day on which some prices are posted so you need to edit the prompts for Fuji and Granny Smith apples. Complete the following steps to edit the prompts:
    a. Right-click in cell B5 and then click Edit Field.
    b. At the Field dialog box, click in the *Prompt*: text box and then change *Friday* to *Monday*. (The entire prompt should read *Enter price per pound as of last Monday*.)
    c. Click OK.
    d. At the prompt dialog box, type **$1.16** and then click OK.
    e. Right-click in cell B6 and then click in Edit Field.
    f. At the Field dialog box, click in the *Prompt*: text box and then change *Friday* to *Monday*.
    g. Click OK.
    h. At the prompt dialog box, type **$1.20** and then click OK.
10. Update the totals by selecting cells D5 and D6 and then pressing F9.
11. Center the table between the left and right margins by completing the following steps:
    a. With the insertion point positioned in any cell in the table, click Table and then Table Properties.

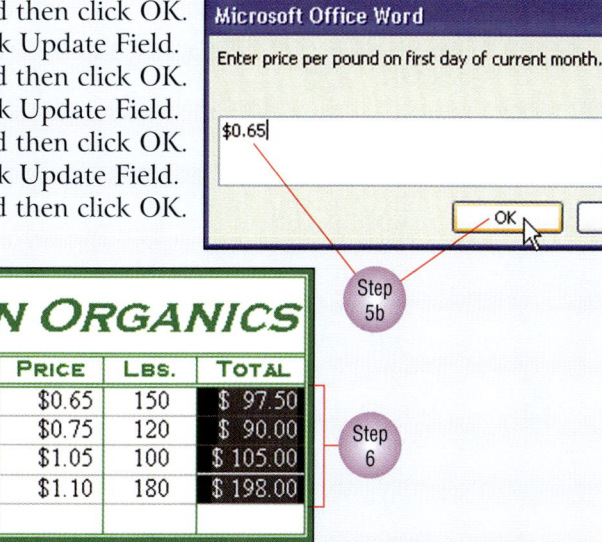

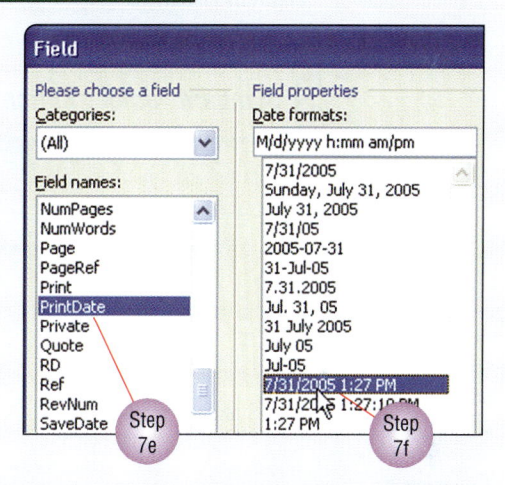

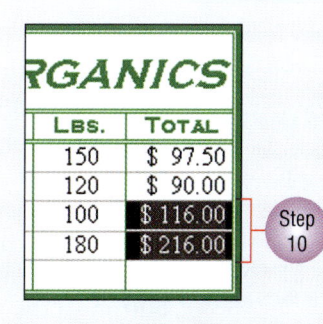

Formatting With Special Features E71

b. At the Table Properties dialog box, make sure the Table tab is selected.
c. Click the *Center* option in the *Alignment* section.
d. Click OK.
12. Save, print, and then close **ewc2x14**.

Customizing Toolbars

You can customize Word toolbars. For example, you can add buttons to a toolbar representing features you use on a consistent basis or remove buttons you do not need. You can also move buttons on a toolbar or reset the position of buttons.

Toolbar Options

To add a button to or remove a button from a toolbar, click the Toolbar Options button located at the right side of the toolbar, point to Add or Remove Buttons, and then click the name of the toolbar at the side menu. For example, click the Toolbar Options button at the right side of the Standard toolbar, point to Add or Remove Buttons, and then point to Standard and a drop-down list of button options displays as shown in Figure 2.14.

FIGURE 2.14 *Standard Toolbar Buttons Drop-Down List*

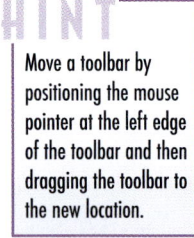

HINT
Move a toolbar by positioning the mouse pointer at the left edge of the toolbar and then dragging the toolbar to the new location.

HINT
If you add buttons to a full toolbar, some of the buttons may be hidden.

QUICK STEPS

Customize Toolbar
1. Click Toolbar Options button.
2. Point to Add or Remove Buttons option.
3. Point to desired toolbar name.
4. Click buttons to be added or removed.
5. Click in the document screen.

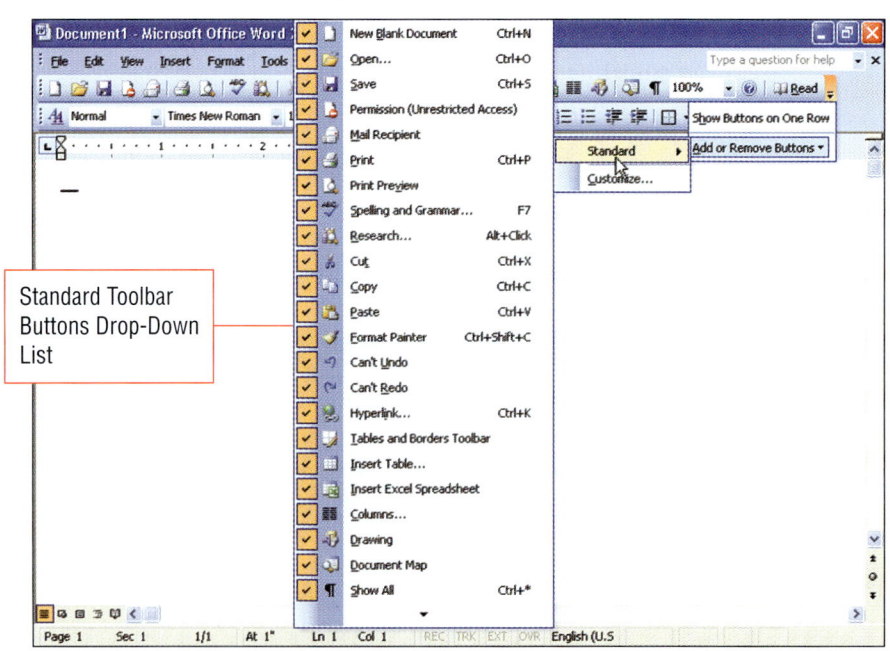

To add a button to the toolbar, click the desired option at the drop-down list. This inserts the button at the right side of the toolbar. To remove a button, click the desired option to remove the check mark. Another method for removing a button from a toolbar is to display the Customize dialog box and then drag the button off the toolbar.

Buttons you add to a toolbar are inserted at the right side of the toolbar. You may want to move buttons to different locations on a toolbar. To do this, click Tools and then Customize. With the Customize dialog box displayed, drag a button to the desired position. You can also move a button from one toolbar to another.

E72 Chapter Two

You can reset buttons on a toolbar back to their original positions. To do this, display the Customize dialog box with the Toolbars tab selected, and then click the Reset button. At the Reset Toolbar dialog box, click OK.

exercise 15

ADDING/REMOVING BUTTONS FROM THE STANDARD TOOLBAR

1. Add a Close button to the Standard toolbar and remove the Document Map button by completing the following steps:
    a. At a clear document screen, click the Toolbar Options button located at the right side of the Standard toolbar.
    b. Point to Add or Remove Buttons and then point to Standard.
    c. At the drop-down menu that displays, click Document Map. (This removes the check mark from the option.)
    d. Scroll down the drop-down menu until the Close button is visible and then click Close. (This inserts a check mark before the option.)
    e. Click outside the drop-down menu to remove it from the screen. (Check the Standard toolbar and notice the Close button that displays at the right side of the toolbar.)
2. Drag the Close button on the Standard toolbar so it is positioned between the Open button and the Save button by completing the following steps:
    a. Click Tools and then Customize.
    b. With the Customize dialog box displayed, position the mouse pointer on the Close button, hold down the left mouse button, drag the icon representing the button so it is positioned between the Open button and Save button, and then release the mouse button.
    c. Close the Customize dialog box by clicking the Close button in the dialog box.
3. Move the Change Text Direction button from the Tables and Borders toolbar to the Standard toolbar by completing the following steps:
    a. Click the Tables and Borders button on the Standard toolbar to display the Tables and Borders toolbar.
    b. Display the Customize dialog box by clicking Tools and then Customize.
    c. Position the arrow pointer on the Change Text Direction button on the Drawing toolbar, hold down the left mouse button, drag up so the button icon displays between the Insert Table button and the Insert Microsoft Excel Worksheet button on the Standard toolbar, and then release the mouse button.
    d. Close the Customize dialog box by clicking the Close button in the dialog box.
    e. Turn off the display of the Tables and Borders toolbar.

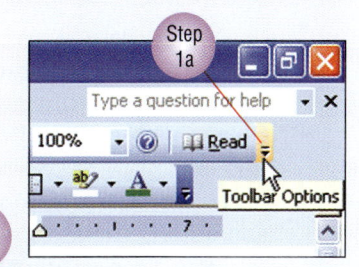

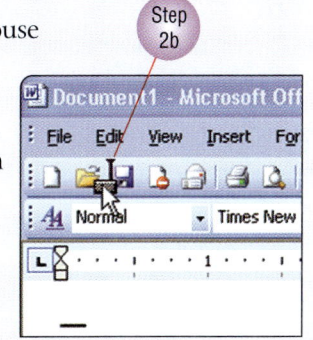

WORD   Formatting With Special Features   E73

4. Open **WordTable01**.
5. Save the document with Save As and name it **ewc2x15**.
6. Make the following changes to the document:
   a. Insert a new column at the left side of the table.
   b. Merge the cells of the new column.
   c. Click the Change Text Direction button twice.
   d. Type Yearly Sales.
   e. Select the text and then change the font size to 14 points.
   f. Autofit the contents of the table.
7. Save and then print **ewc2x15**.
8. Close the document by clicking the Close button on the Standard toolbar. (You added this button to the Standard toolbar.)
9. Reset the Standard toolbar (removing the Close button, Change Text Direction button, and adding the Document Map button) by completing the following steps:
   a. At a clear document screen, click Tools and then Customize.
   b. At the Customize dialog box, click the Toolbars tab.
   c. At the Customize dialog box with the Toolbars tab selected, make sure *Standard* is selected in the *Toolbars* list box.
   d. Click the Reset button.
   e. At the Reset Toolbar dialog box, click OK.
   f. Close the Customize dialog box by clicking the Close button in the dialog box.
10. Complete steps similar to those in Step 9 to reset the Tables and Borders toolbar. (At the Customize dialog box, click *Tables and Borders* in the *Toolbars* list box.)

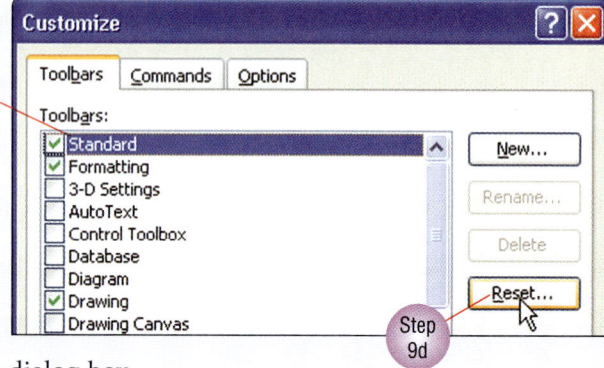

QUICK STEPS

Customizing Menus

Customize a Menu
1. Click Tools, Customize.
2. Click Commands tab.
3. Click desired menu category in *Categories* list box.
4. Drag and drop specific menu options on Menu bar.

Menus, like toolbars, can be customized. For example, you can add or remove commands from a menu and also create a custom menu. Customize an existing menu by displaying the Customize dialog box with the Commands tab selected and then clicking the desired menu category. In the *Commands* list box, drag and then drop the desired command to the specific menu option on the Menu bar. Remove a command from a menu by displaying the Customize dialog box, clicking the desired menu option on the Menu bar, and then dragging the command off the menu.

exercise 16

CUSTOMIZING AN EXISTING MENU

1. Add two commands to the Format menu by completing the following steps:
   a. At a clear document screen, click Tools and then Customize.
   b. At the Customize dialog box, click the Commands tab.

c. Click *Format* in the *Categories* list box.
d. Scroll down the *Commands* list box until the *Grow Font 1 Pt* and *Shrink Font 1 Pt* commands display.
e. Position the mouse pointer on the *Grow Font 1 Pt* command, hold down the left mouse button, drag to the Format menu option on the Menu bar, drag down below the Font option until a black line displays below Font, and then release the mouse button. (The Grow Font 1 Pt command now displays below Font on the Format drop-down menu.)
f. Drag the *Shrink Font 1 Pt* command below the Grow Font 1 Pt command on the Format drop-down menu.
g. Click the Close button in the Customize dialog box.
2. Open **WordNotice01**.
3. Save the document with Save As and name it **ewc2x16**.
4. Select the entire document and then change the font to 14-point Bookman Old Style bold (or a similar serif typeface).
5. Increase the font size for specific text by completing the following steps:
   a. Select *McCORMACK FUNDS* and *Annual Stockholders' Meeting*.
   b. Click Format and then Grow Font 1 Pt at the drop-down list.
   c. Click Format and then Grow Font 1 Pt. (The size of the selected text should now be 16 points.)
6. Reduce the font size for specific text by completing the following steps:
   a. Select *King Auditorium*, *Wednesday, September 21, 2005*, and *6:30 p.m.*
   b. Click Format and then Shrink Font 1 Pt.
   c. Click Format and then Shrink Font 1 Pt again. (The size of the selected text should now be 12 points.)
7. Save, print, and then close **ewc2x16**.
8. Remove the two font commands from the Format drop-down menu by completing the following steps:
   a. Click Tools and then Customize.
   b. Make sure the Commands tab is selected.
   c. Click Format on the Menu bar.
   d. Position the mouse pointer on Grow Font 1 Pt, hold down the left mouse button, drag onto the document screen, and then release the mouse button.
   e. Drag Shrink Font 1 Pt onto the document screen.
   f. Click the Close button in the Customize dialog box.

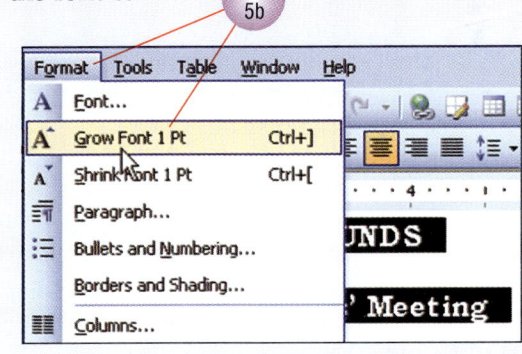

Along with customizing existing menu, you can create your own menu and then include it on the Menu bar. To create a custom menu, display the Customize dialog box with the Commands tab selected. Click *New Menu* in the *Categories* list box and then drag the *New Menu* command to the Menu bar. Rename the menu and then add commands to the menu.

exercise 17
CREATING A CUSTOM MENU

1. At a clear document screen, click Tools and then Customize.
2. At the Customize dialog box, make sure the Commands tab is selected.
3. Scroll down the *Categories* list box until *New Menu* is visible and then click *New Menu*.
4. Position the mouse pointer on *New Menu* in the *Commands* list box, hold down the left mouse button, drag to the right of the View option on the Menu bar, and then release the mouse button. (This inserts *New Menu* between View and Insert.)
5. Rename *New Menu* to *Go To* by completing the following steps:
    a. Right-click New Menu on the Menu bar.
    b. At the drop-down list that displays, select the text *New Menu* that displays in the *Name* text box, and then type **Go To**.
    c. Press Enter.
6. At the Customize dialog box, click *Edit* in the *Categories* list box. (You will need to scroll up this list box to display *Edit*.)
7. Scroll down the *Commands* list box until *Go To Next Page* is visible.
8. Drag *Go To Next Page* in the *Commands* list box to the Go To menu option on the Menu bar. (This displays a square, blue box below the Go To menu option.)
9. Drag down to the box below Go To and then release the mouse button.
10. Drag *Go To Previous Page* from the *Commands* list box in the Customize dialog box so it is positioned below the Go To Next Page command on the Go To menu.
11. Click the Close button in the Customize dialog box.
12. Open **WordReport03**.
13. Use options on the Go To menu by completing the following steps:
    a. Move the insertion point to page 2 by clicking Go To on the Menu bar and then clicking Go To Next Page at the drop-down list.
    b. Move the insertion point to page 3 by clicking Go To and then Go To Next Page.
    c. Move the insertion point to page 2 by clicking Go To and then Go To Previous Page.
14. Remove the Go To menu option from the Menu bar by completing the following steps:
    a. Click Tools and then Customize.
    b. With the Customize dialog box displayed, drag the Go To menu option onto the document screen.
    c. Close the Customize dialog box.
15. Close **WordReport03**.

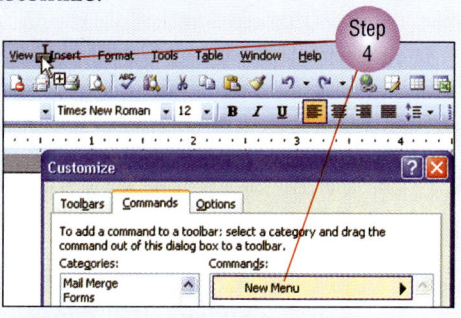

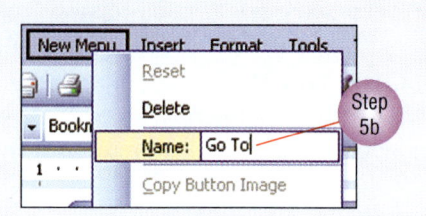

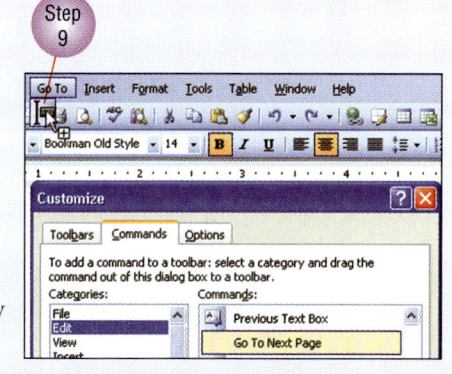

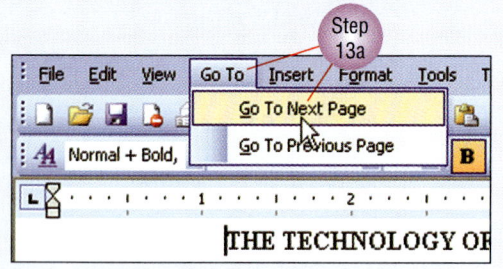

CHAPTER summary

- When a nonbreaking space is inserted between words, Word considers these words as one unit and will not divide them. Insert a nonbreaking space with the shortcut command, Ctrl + Shift + spacebar.
- Use the find and replace feature to find special formatting, characters, or nonprinting elements, and replace with other special text.
- Press Shift + Enter to move the insertion point down to the next line without applying paragraph formatting.
- In Word, widows and orphans are automatically prevented from appearing in text. Turn off this feature at the Paragraph dialog box with the Line and Page Breaks tab selected.
- The Paragraph dialog box with the Line and Page Breaks tab selected contains options to keep a paragraph, a group of paragraphs, or a group of lines together.
- Footnotes and endnotes are explanatory notes or references. Footnotes are printed at the bottom of the page and endnotes are printed at the end of the document. Type footnote/endnote text at the footnote or endnote pane.
- By default, footnotes are numbered with Arabic numbers and endnotes are numbered with lowercase Roman numerals.
- Move and/or copy a reference number in a document and all other footnotes/endnotes are automatically renumbered.
- Delete a footnote or endnote by selecting the reference number and then pressing the Delete key.
- Use the AutoSummarize feature to identify the key points in a document. AutoSummarize identifies key points by analyzing the text in the document and then assigning a score to each sentence.
- When a spelling and grammar check is completed, readability statistics display about the document. Turn on/off the display of readability statistics with the *Show readability statistics* option at the Options dialog box with the Grammar & Spelling tab selected.
- Calculate numbers in a table by inserting a formula in a cell at the Formula dialog box.
- Four basic operators are used when writing a formula: the plus sign for addition, the minus sign for subtraction, the asterisk for multiplication, and the forward slash for division.
- Modify the table format with options from the Table Properties dialog box.
- Rotate text in a cell using the Change Text Direction button on the Tables and Borders toolbar.
- Recalculate a formula by clicking in the cell in the table containing the formula and then pressing F9.
- Insert fields in a table with options at the Field dialog box. Edit a field by right-clicking in the cell containing the field and then clicking Edit Field at the shortcut menu.
- Customize toolbars by adding, removing, and/or moving buttons. Return toolbars to the default buttons with the Reset button at the Customize dialog box.
- Customize menus by adding and/or removing commands or create a custom menu.

FEATURES summary

FEATURE	BUTTON	MENU	KEYBOARD
Nonbreaking space			Ctrl + Shift + spacebar
Find and Replace dialog box		Edit, Replace	Ctrl + H
Manual line break			Shift + Enter
Footnote and Endnote dialog box		Insert, Reference, Footnote	
Footnote pane			Ctrl + Alt + F
Endnote pane			Ctrl + Alt + D
AutoSummarize dialog box		Tools, AutoSummarize	
Formula dialog box		Table, Formula	
Table Properties dialog box		Table, Table Properties	
Tables and Borders toolbar	🖉	View, Toolbars, Tables and Borders	
Recalculate numbers in table			F9
Field dialog box		Insert, Field	
Customize dialog box		Tools, Customize	

CONCEPTS check

Completion: On a blank sheet of paper, indicate the correct term, command, or number for each description.

1. This is the keyboard shortcut command to insert a nonbreaking space.
2. Click this button at the expanded Find and Replace dialog box to display a drop-down menu containing special characters and nonprinting elements.
3. Turn on/off the widow/orphan control at the Paragraph dialog box with this tab selected.
4. The footnote entry text is typed here.
5. Word numbers footnotes with this type of number.
6. Word numbers endnotes with this type of number.
7. Use this feature to identify the key points in a document.
8. This is the operator for multiplication that is used when writing a formula in a table.
9. This is the operator for division that is used when writing a formula in a table.
10. This is the formula to multiply A1 by B1.
11. Use this button on the Tables and Borders toolbar to rotate text within the cell.

12. Recalculate a formula by clicking in the cell in the table containing the formula and then pressing this key.
13. Insert this field in a table that will prompt the user to enter specific data in the cell.
14. To add a button to or remove a button from a toolbar, begin by clicking this button located at the right side of the toolbar.
15. Customize an existing menu by displaying the Customize dialog box with this tab selected.

SKILLS check

Assessment 1

1. At a clear document screen, create the memo shown in Figure 2.15. Insert nonbreaking spaces within the shortcut commands.
2. Save the document and name it **ewc2sc01**.
3. Print and then close **ewc2sc01**.

FIGURE 2.15 Assessment 1

DATE: (current date)

TO: All Employees

FROM: Cynthia Stophel

SUBJECT: SHORTCUT COMMANDS

Shortcut commands can be used to format text, display dialog boxes, and insert special characters. For example, insert a nonbreaking space in text with the command Ctrl + Shift + spacebar. You can also insert symbols in a document with shortcut commands. For example, insert a copyright symbol in a document by pressing Alt + Ctrl + C and insert a registered trademark symbol with the shortcut command Alt + Ctrl + R.

A Microsoft Word training session has been scheduled for next month. At this training, additional shortcut commands will be introduced.

XX:ewc2sc01

Assessment 2

1. Open **WordReport06**.
2. Save the document with Save As and name it **ewc2sc02**.
3. Insert a section break that begins a new page at the line containing the title *MODULE 4: CREATING A NEWSLETTER LAYOUT.*
4. Create the first footnote shown in Figure 2.16 at the end of the first paragraph in the *Applying Desktop Publishing Guidelines* section of the report.
5. Create the second footnote shown in Figure 2.16 at the end of the third paragraph in the *Applying Desktop Publishing Guidelines* section of the report.
6. Create the third footnote shown in Figure 2.16 at the end of the last paragraph in the *Applying Desktop Publishing Guidelines* section of the report.
7. Create the fourth footnote shown in Figure 2.16 at the end of the only paragraph in the *Choosing Paper Size and Type* section of the report.
8. Create the fifth footnote shown in Figure 2.16 at the end of the only paragraph in the *Choosing Paper Weight* section of the report.
9. Check page breaks in the document and, if necessary, adjust the page breaks.
10. Save, print, and then close **ewc2sc02**.

FIGURE 2.16 *Assessment 2*

Habermann, James, "Designing a Newsletter," *Desktop Designs*, January/February 2005, pages 23-29.

Pilante, Shirley G., "Adding Pizzazz to Your Newsletter," *Desktop Publisher*, September 2004, pages 32-39.

Maddock, Arlita G., "Guidelines for a Better Newsletter," *Business Computing*, June 2004, pages 9-14.

Alverso, Monica, "Paper Styles for Newsletters," *Design Technologies*, March 14, 2005, pages 45-51.

Alverso, Monica, "Paper Styles for Newsletters," *Design Technologies*, March 14, 2005, pages 52-53.

Assessment 3

1. Open **ewc2sc02**.
2. Save the document with Save As and name it **ewc2sc03**.
3. Select the entire document and then change the font to 12-point Century (or a similar serif typeface).
4. Display the footnote pane, select all of the footnotes, and then change the font to 12-point Century (or the serif typeface you chose in Step 3).
5. Move the first footnote (the one after the first paragraph in the *Applying Desktop Publishing Guidelines* section) to the end of the fourth paragraph in the *Applying Desktop Publishing Guidelines* section.
6. Delete the third footnote.
7. Save, print, and then close **ewc2sc03**.

Assessment 4

1. Open **WordTable03**.
2. Save the document with Save As and name it **ewc2sc04**.
3. Insert a formula in cells D3, D4, D4, D5, D6, D7, and D8 that totals the first and second half sales.
4. Save, print, and then close **ewc2sc04**.

Assessment 5

1. Open **WordTable04**.
2. Save the document with Save As and name it **ewc2sc05**.
3. Insert a new row at the top of the table.
4. Merge the cells in the new row.
5. Type FUND-RAISING EVENTS centered and bolded in the new cell.
6. Insert a formula in cells D3, D4, D5, and D6 that calculates the net profit. *(Hint: The Net Profit is Revenue minus Costs. At the Formula dialog box, change the Number format to the third option from the top of the drop-down list.)*
7. Save, print, and then close **ewc2sc05**.

Assessment 6

1. Open **WordTable05**.
2. Save the document with Save As and name it **ewc2sc06**.
3. Insert a new column at the left side of the table and then merge the cells in the new column.
4. Make sure bold and italics are on, and then type Regional Sales in the new cell. Rotate the text so it displays from the bottom to the top of the cell. (The text will display on two lines.)
5. Decrease the size of the new column so only a minimal amount of space displays between the edge of the column and the text.
6. Insert a new row at the bottom of the table and then merge the cells in the new row. (The new row will display below the new column as well as the remaining columns in the table.)
7. Turn on bold, click the Center button on the Formatting toolbar, type the text Top Regional Salesperson for 2005:, and then press the spacebar once.
8. Insert a Fill-in field in the cell with the following prompt: *Enter the name of the top salesperson from the 2005 Sales Report document.* At the Prompt dialog box, type the name Dana Powell.
9. Save, print, and then close **ewc2sc06**.

CHAPTER challenge

Case study

You work with the Sales Manager at Software and More, a computer store specializing in computer software. You plan to prepare a price list for various operating systems, such as Windows 2000, Windows ME, Windows XP, and so on. Use the Table feature to create a table displaying this information. If necessary use the Internet to research prices for the various operating systems. Format the table appropriately. This table, along with other tables and figures will be inserted in a report. Be sure that the table will stay together if it appears at the bottom of a page in the report. Save the table.

HELP?

Since there will be other tables in the report, you need to identify the table with a caption. Use the Help feature to learn how to add a caption to a table. Use the caption feature to automatically identify the table with a number. Position the caption below the table. Save and then print the file.

INTEGRATED

Copy the information in the table created in the first part of the Chapter Challenge to Excel. Create a column chart comparing the prices among the operating systems. Use appropriate titles to identify the chart. Save and then print the chart.

CHAPTER 3

ADDING VISUAL ELEMENTS

Performance Objectives

Upon successful completion of Chapter 3, you will be able to:
- Insert a page border
- Insert a horizontal line
- Insert and customize images
- Insert and align objects
- Create a watermark
- Create and modify text using WordArt
- Create and format Web pages
- Save Web pages and images

Microsoft Word contains a variety of features that help you enhance the visual appeal of a document. Some methods for adding visual appeal that you will learn in this chapter include inserting a page border and horizontal line, inserting, customizing, and aligning objects, images, creating a watermark, and creating and modifying WordArt. You will also learn how to create and format Web pages and save Web pages and images.

Inserting Page Borders

To improve the visual appeal of a document, consider inserting a page border. To insert a page border in a document, display the Borders and Shading dialog box with the Page Border tab selected as shown in Figure 3.1. To display this dialog box, click Format, and then Paragraph. At the Borders and Shading dialog box, click the Page Border tab. With options at the dialog box, you can specify the border style, color, and width.

> **HINT**
> Use graphic elements such as images, borders, and horizontal lines to break the monotony of regular text, emphasize text, and draw the reader's attention.

FIGURE 3.1 Borders and Shading Dialog Box with Page Border Tab Selected

QUICK STEPS

Insert Page Border
1. Click Format, Borders and Shading.
2. Click Page Border tab.
3. Click desired options.
4. Click OK.

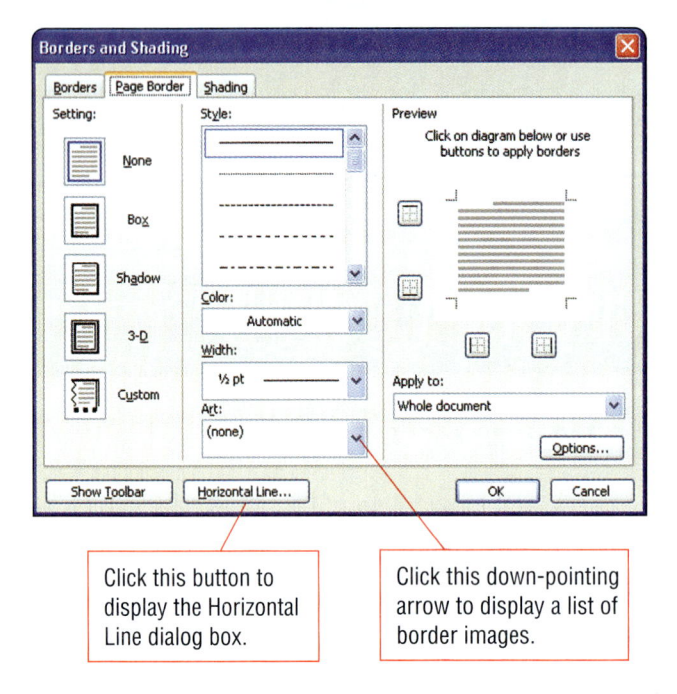

Click this button to display the Horizontal Line dialog box.

Click this down-pointing arrow to display a list of border images.

exercise 1

INSERTING A PAGE BORDER IN A DOCUMENT

1. Open **WordComputers**.
2. Save the document with Save As and name it **ewc3x01**.
3. Add a border to each page in the document by completing the following steps:
    a. With the insertion point positioned at the beginning of the document, click Format and then Borders and Shading.
    b. At the Borders and Shading dialog box, click the Page Border tab.
    c. Click the *Box* button in the *Setting* section.
    d. Scroll down the list of line styles in the *Style* list box until the end of the list displays and then click the third line from the end.

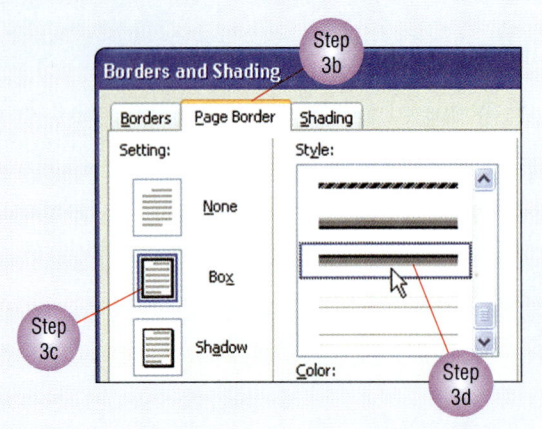

    Step 3b
    Step 3c
    Step 3d

    e. Click OK to close the dialog box.
4. Save, print, and then close **ewc3x01**.

E84 Chapter Three

The Borders and Shading dialog box with the Page Border tab selected offers an option for inserting a page border containing an image. To display the images available, click the down-pointing arrow at the right side of the *Art* option box. Scroll down the list and then click the desired image. (This feature will need to be installed the first time you use it.)

HINT
The first time you try to insert an art page border, you may be prompted to install the feature.

exercise 2

INSERTING A PAGE BORDER CONTAINING BALLOONS

1. Open **WordTravel**.
2. Save the document with Save As and name it **ewc3x02**.
3. Add a decorative border to the document by completing the following steps:
    a. Display the Borders and Shading dialog box.
    b. At the Borders and Shading dialog box, click the Page Border tab.
    c. Click the *Box* option in the *Setting* section.
    d. Click the down-pointing arrow at the right side of the *Art* option box, scroll down the drop-down list until the first globe images display, and then click the globe images.
    e. Click the down-pointing arrow at the right side of the *Width* text box until *25 pt* displays. 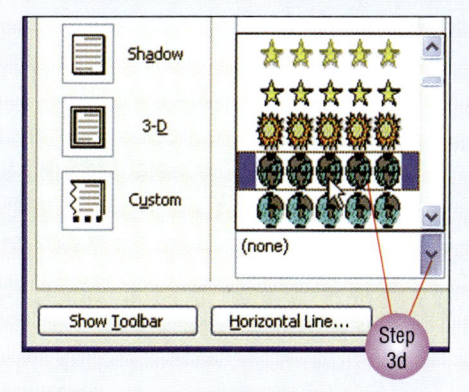 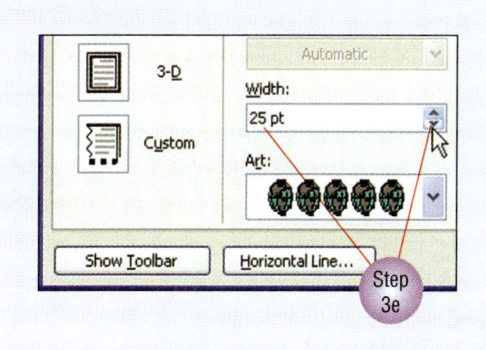
    f. Click OK to close the dialog box.
4. Save, print, and then close **ewc3x02**.

Inserting Horizontal Lines

Word includes a horizontal line feature that inserts a graphic horizontal line in a document. To display the Horizontal Line dialog box shown in Figure 3.2, display the Borders and Shading dialog box with any tab selected, and then click the Horizontal Line button located at the bottom of the dialog box. Insert a horizontal line into a document by clicking the desired line option and then clicking the OK button.

QUICK STEPS

Insert Horizontal Line
1. Click Format, Borders and Shading.
2. Click Horizontal Line button.
3. Click desired horizontal line option.
4. Click OK.

WORD
Adding Visual Elements E85

FIGURE 3.2 Horizontal Line Dialog Box

Click a horizontal line option in this list box or click in the *Search text* box, type a search topic, and then click the Go button.

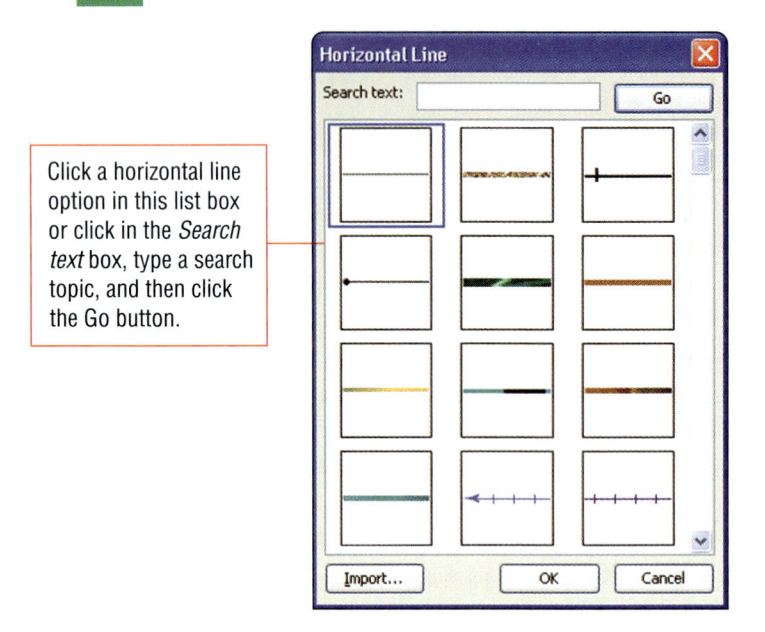

exercise 3

INSERTING HORIZONTAL LINES IN A DOCUMENT

1. Open **WordNotice01**.
2. Save the document with Save As and name it **ewc3x03**.
3. Select the entire document, change the font to 14-point Goudy Old Style bold, and then deselect the document.
4. Move the insertion point to the beginning of the document and then press Enter three times.
5. Move the insertion point back to the beginning of the document and then insert a graphic horizontal line by completing the following steps:
   a. Click Format and then Borders and Shading.
   b. At the Borders and Shading dialog box, click the Horizontal Line button located at the bottom of the dialog box.
   c. At the Horizontal Line dialog box, click the second horizontal line option in the second row.
   d. Click the OK button.
6. Move the insertion point a triple space below the last line of text in the document and then insert the same graphic horizontal line as the one inserted in Step 5c.
7. Save, print, and then close **ewc3x03**.

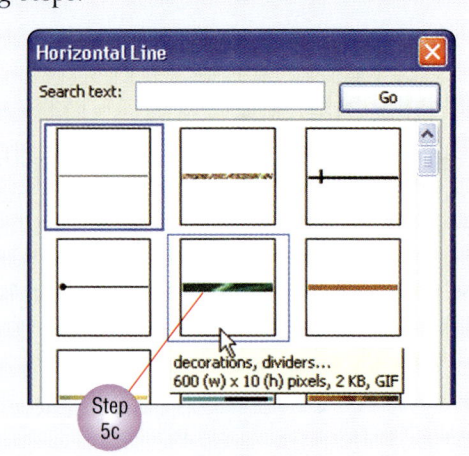

Step 5c

E86 Chapter Three   WORD

Inserting and Customizing Images

Word includes a gallery of media images you can insert in a document such as clip art images, photographs, and movie images, as well as sound clips. Insert images in a document using options at the Clip Art task pane shown in Figure 3.3. Display this task pane by clicking Insert, pointing to Picture, and then clicking Clip Art; or by clicking the Insert Clip Art button on the Drawing toolbar. To display the Drawing toolbar, click the Drawing button on the Standard toolbar. If you are searching for specific images, click in the *Search for* text box, type the desired topic, and then click the Go button.

Insert Clip Art

Drawing

FIGURE 3.3 Clip Art Task Pane

Type a search word or topic and then click the Go button.

Insert an Image
1. Click Insert Clip Art button.
2. Type desired topic in *Search for* text box.
3. Press Enter.
4. Click desired image in Clip Art task pane.

Formatting an Image with Buttons on the Picture Toolbar

The Picture toolbar, shown in Figure 3.4, offers a number of buttons you can use to format a selected image. Display this toolbar by clicking an image in a document. If the Picture toolbar does not display, position the mouse pointer on the image, click the *right* mouse button, and then click Show Picture Toolbar.

FIGURE 3.4 Picture Toolbar Buttons

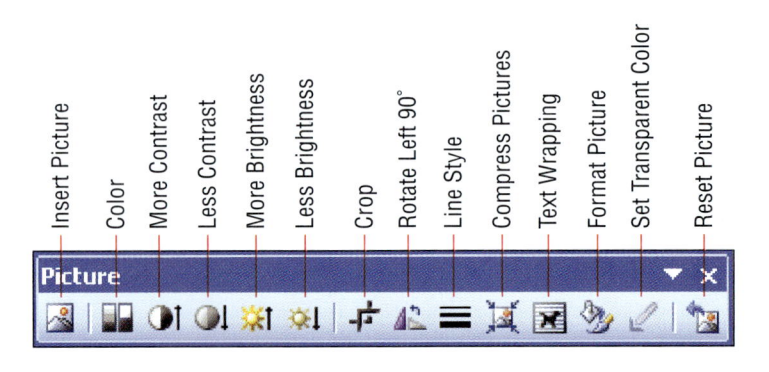

Buttons (left to right): Insert Picture, Color, More Contrast, Less Contrast, More Brightness, Less Brightness, Crop, Rotate Left 90°, Line Style, Compress Pictures, Text Wrapping, Format Picture, Set Transparent Color, Reset Picture.

Sizing and Moving an Image

Click an image in a document to select it and then use the sizing handles that display around the image to change the size. To move an image in a document you must first choose a text wrapping option. To do this, select the image, click the Text Wrapping button on the Picture toolbar, and then click a wrapping option. This changes the sizing handles that display around the selected image from squares to white circles and also inserts a green rotation handle. To move the image, position the mouse pointer inside the image until the pointer turns into a four-headed arrow. Hold down the left mouse button, drag the image to the desired position, and then release the mouse button. Rotate the image by positioning the mouse pointer on the round, green rotation handle until the pointer displays as a circular arrow. Hold down the left mouse button, drag in the desired direction, and then release the mouse button.

HINT Move an image up, down, left, or right in small increments with the Nudge option on the Draw button.

exercise 4 — INSERTING AND FORMATTING AN IMAGE

1. At a clear document screen, create the text and image shown in Figure 3.5. To begin, change to the Print Layout view.
2. Change font to 36-point Curlz MT bold (or a similar decorative typeface).
3. Type **Party Planners** and then press Enter.
4. Type **1-888-555-4444**.
5. Move the insertion point to the beginning of the document.
6. Click Insert, point to Picture, and then click Clip Art.
7. Click in the *Search for* text box, type **balloons**, and then press Enter.
8. Click the balloon image shown at the right. (If this image is not available, choose another image containing a balloon, a party hat, or party supplies.)
9. Close the Clip Art task pane.

10. Change the contrast and brightness of the image and then crop the image so just the party hat displays by completing the following steps:
    a. Click the image to select it. (Make sure the Picture toolbar displays.)
    b. Click the More Contrast button on the Picture toolbar five times.
    c. Click the More Brightness button on the Picture toolbar five times.
    d. Click the Crop button on the Picture toolbar.
    e. Position the mouse pointer on the upper left sizing handle (the mouse pointer turns into a crop tool, which is a black square with overlapping lines), hold down the left mouse button, drag into the image to isolate the party hat as shown below, and then release the mouse button.
    f. Drag the bottom middle sizing and the right middle sizing handle until the image displays as shown in Figure 3.5. (If you are not satisfied with the result, click the Reset Picture button on the Picture toolbar and then try again.)
    g. With the party hat isolated, click the Crop button on the Picture toolbar to turn it off.
11. Change the wrapping style by clicking the Text Wrapping button on the Picture toolbar and then clicking *Tight* at the drop-down list.
12. Rotate the image as shown in Figure 3.5 by completing the following steps:
    a. Position the mouse pointer on the round, green sizing handle until the pointer turns into a circular arrow.
    b. Hold down the left mouse button, drag to the left until the image is rotated as shown in Figure 3.5, and then release the mouse button.
13. Increase the size of the image and then drag it to the approximate location shown in Figure 3.5.
14. Click outside the image to deselect it.
15. Save the image and name it **ewc3x04**.
16. Print and then close **ewc3x04**.

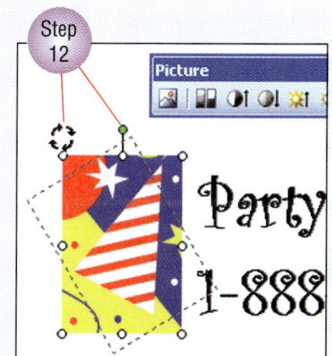

FIGURE
3.5 *Exercise 4*

[Party Planners
1-888-555-4444]

Format Picture

Formatting an Image at the Format Picture Dialog Box

With buttons on the Picture toolbar you can customize an image. The same options on the Picture toolbar are also available at the Format Picture dialog box along with some additional options. To display the Format Picture dialog box, select an image, and then click the Format Picture button on the Picture toolbar. You can also display the Format Picture dialog box by selecting an image, clicking Format on the Menu bar, and then clicking Picture.

The Format Picture dialog box displays with a variety of tabs. Click the Colors and Lines tab and options are available for choosing fill color; line color, style, and weight; and arrows. Click the Size tab and display options for specifying the height, width, and rotation degree of the image. Options at the Format Picture dialog box with the Layout tab selected include wrapping style and horizontal alignment. Click the Picture tab to display options for cropping the image and changing the color.

Applying Advanced Layout and Text Wrapping Options

Use options at the Advanced Layout dialog box to specify horizontal and vertical layout options as well as text wrapping options. Display the Advanced Layout dialog box by displaying the Format Picture dialog box with the Layout tab selected and then clicking the Advanced button. Choose options at the Advanced Layout dialog box with the Picture Position tab selected, as shown in Figure 3.6, to specify the horizontal and vertical position of the image.

In the *Horizontal* section, choose the *Alignment* option to specify whether you want the image horizontally left-, center-, or right-aligned relative to the margin, page, column, or character. Choose the *Book Layout* option if you want to align the image with inside or outside margins on the page. Use the *Absolute position* option to align the image horizontally with the specified amount of space between the left edge of the image and the left edge of the page, column, left margin, or character. In the *Vertical* section of the dialog box, use the *Alignment* option to align the image at the top, bottom, center, inside, or outside relative to the page, margin, or line.

In the *Options* section, you can attach (anchor) the image to a paragraph so that the image and paragraph move together. Choose the *Move object with text* option if you want the image to move up or down on the page with the paragraph to which it is anchored. Keep the image anchored in the same place on the page by choosing the *Lock anchor* option. Choose the *Allow overlap* option if you want images with the same wrapping style to overlap.

FIGURE 3.6 Advanced Layout Dialog Box with Picture Position Tab Selected

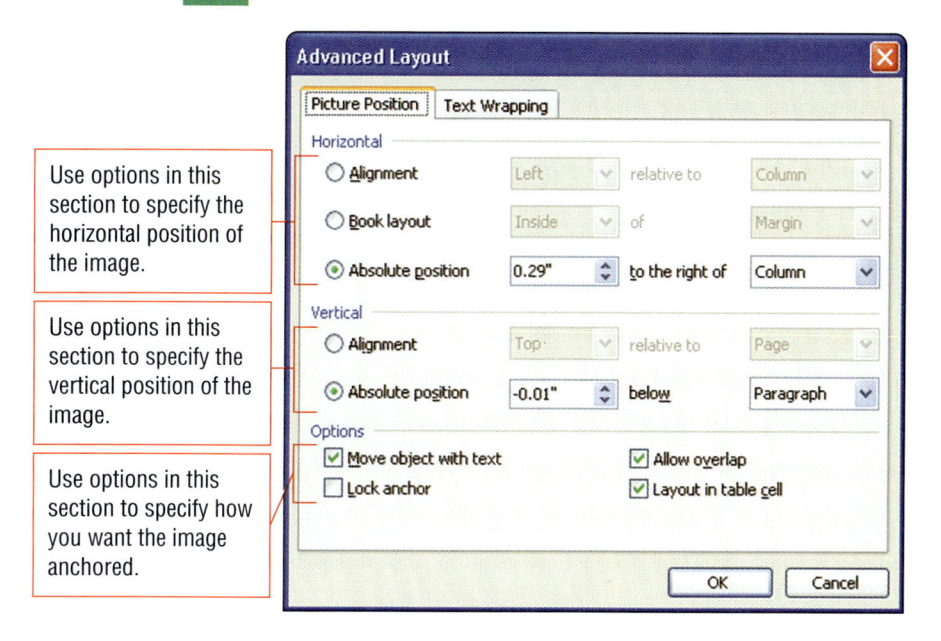

Use options in this section to specify the horizontal position of the image.

Use options in this section to specify the vertical position of the image.

Use options in this section to specify how you want the image anchored.

Use options at the Advanced Layout dialog box with the Text Wrapping tab selected, as shown in Figure 3.7, to specify the wrapping style for the image as well as the sides around which you want text to wrap, and the amount of space you want between the text and the top, bottom, left, and right edges of the image.

FIGURE 3.7 Advanced Layout Dialog Box with Text Wrapping Tab Selected

WORD
Adding Visual Elements   E91

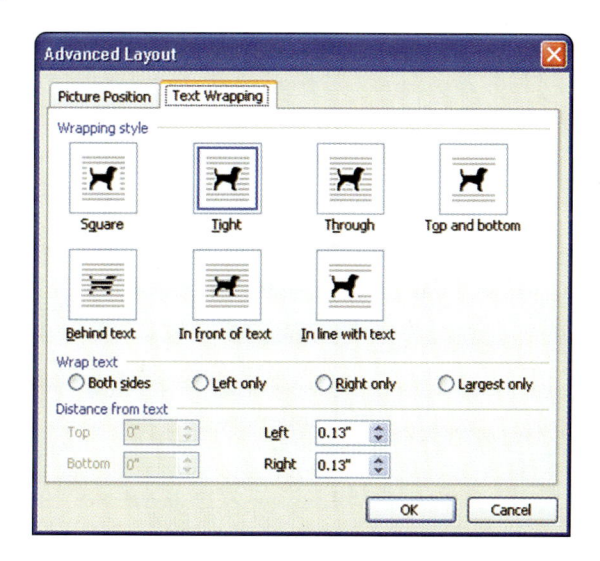

exercise 5
FORMATTING AN IMAGE AT THE FORMAT PICTURE AND ADVANCED LAYOUT DIALOG BOXES

1. Open **WordDTP**.
2. Save the document with Save As and name it **ewc3x05**.
3. Insert an image of a computer in the document as shown in Figure 3.8. To begin, change to the Print Layout view.
4. Click the Insert Clip Art button on the Drawing toolbar. (If the Drawing toolbar is not visible, click the Drawing button on the Standard toolbar.)
5. At the Clip Art task pane, click in the *Search for* text box, type computer, and then press Enter.
6. Click once on the computer image shown in Figure 3.8 (and at the right). (If this image is not available, choose another computer image.)
7. Close the Clip Art task pane.
8. Change the size, position, wrapping style, and brightness and contrast of the image by completing the following steps:
   a. Click once on the image to select it.
   b. Click the Format Picture button on the Picture toolbar.
   c. At the Format Picture dialog box, click the Size tab.
   d. Select the current measurement in the *Height* text box and then type 2.5.
   e. Click the Layout tab.
   f. Click the Advanced button located in the lower right corner of the dialog box.
   g. Click the Text Wrapping tab.
   h. Click the *Tight* option in the *Wrapping style* section.
   i. Click the up-pointing arrow at the right side of the *Left* option until *0.3"* displays in the text box.
   j. Click the up-pointing arrow at the right side of the *Right* option until *0.3"* displays in the text box.

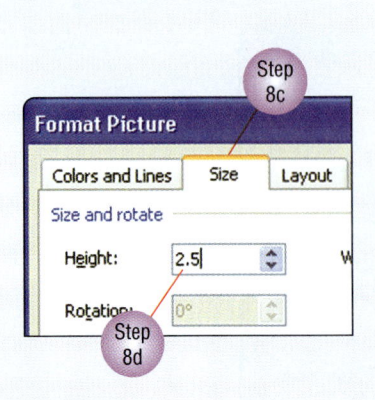

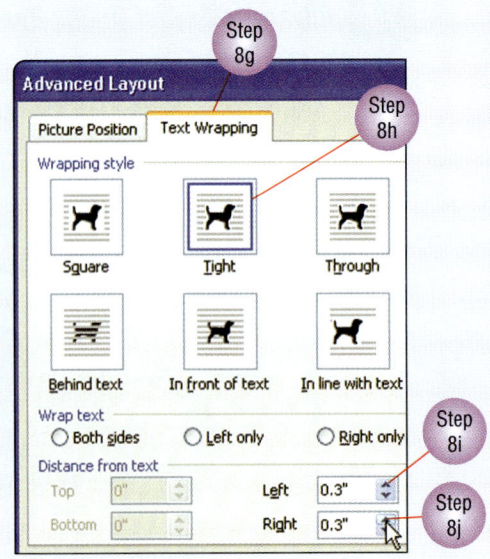

E92 Chapter Three

k. Click the Picture Position tab.
l. Click the *Alignment* option in the *Horizontal* section.
m. Click the down-pointing arrow at the right side of the *Alignment* box (in the *Horizontal* section) and then click *Centered* at the drop-down list.
n. Click the down-pointing arrow at the right side of the *relative to* box and then click *Page* at the drop-down list.
o. Click the *Absolute position* option in the *Vertical* section. (Skip this step if *Absolute position* is already selected.)
p. Select the current measurement in the box to the right side of the *Absolute position* option and then type 4.
q. Click the down-pointing arrow at the right side of the *below* option and then click *Page* at the drop-down list.
r. Click in the *Lock anchor* check box to insert a check mark.
s. Remove any check marks from the other options in the *Options* section.
t. Click OK to close the Advanced Layout dialog box.
u. At the Format Picture dialog box, click the Picture tab.
v. Select the *50 %* in the *Brightness* option and then type 40. (You can also drag the slider until *40 %* displays in the *Brightness* text box.)
w. Select the *50 %* in the *Contrast* option and then type 70. (You can also drag the slider until *70 %* displays in the *Contrast* text box.)

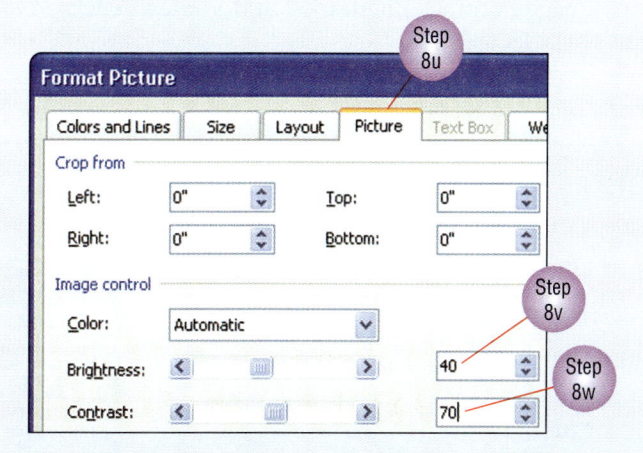

x. Click OK to close the Format Picture dialog box.
9. At the document screen, click outside the image to deselect it.
10. Save, print, and then close **ewc3x05**.

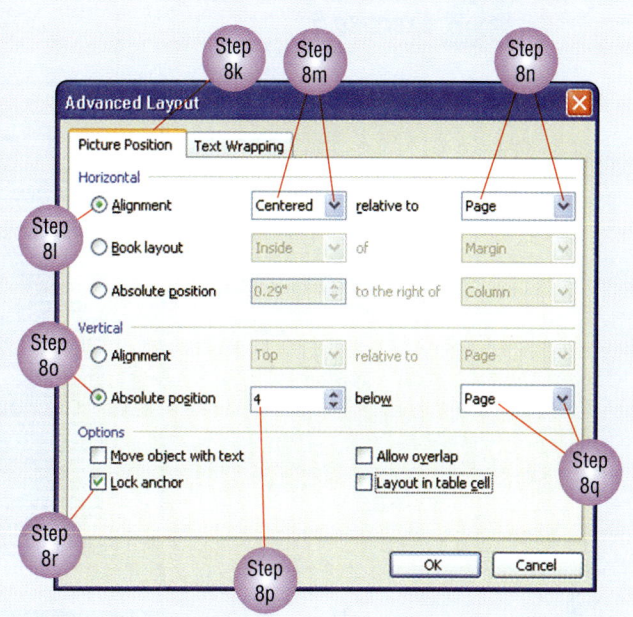

FIGURE
3.8 **Exercise 5**

Displaying Images in an Editable Format

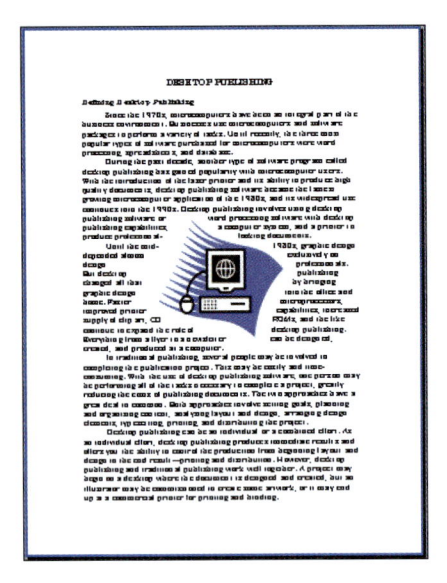

QUICK STEPS

Display Image in Editable Format
1. Right-click image.
2. Click Edit Picture at shortcut menu.

If you want to edit individual components of a clip art image, display the image in a graphic editor. By default, Word uses the Microsoft Word Picture graphic editor. (Determine the graphic editor at the Options dialog box with the Edit tab selected. The *Picture editor* option displays the current graphic editor.) To invoke the graphic editor, right-click the image, and then click Edit Picture at the shortcut menu. You can also invoke the graphic editor by selecting the image, clicking Edit, and then clicking Edit Picture. In the graphic editor, the selected image becomes a drawing object and the Drawing canvas surrounds the image. Also, the image becomes ungrouped and you can click on any part of the image and edit the selected part.

exercise 6

EDITING AN IMAGE

1. At a clear document screen, insert the image named *laptop*. To begin, change to the Print Layout view.
2. Insert the CD that accompanies this textbook into the CD drive.
3. Click Insert, point to Picture, and then click From File.
4. At the Insert Picture dialog box, change to the drive where the CD is located.
5. Double-click the *Word* folder.
6. Double-click the *Word2003Expert* folder.
7. Double-click the *Clipart* folder.
8. Double-click *laptop* in the list box.
9. Display the computer image in the graphic editor by right-clicking the image and then clicking Edit Picture at the shortcut menu.

10. Change the color behind the computer from yellow to blue by completing the following steps:
    a. Position the mouse pointer on the yellow color that displays behind the computer and then double-click the left mouse button. (This displays the Format AutoShape dialog box.)
    b. At the Format AutoShape dialog box, make sure the Colors and Lines tab is selected. (If not, click the Colors and Lines tab.)
    c. Click the down-pointing arrow at the right side of the *Color* option and then click Blue at the color palette (sixth color from the left in the second row).

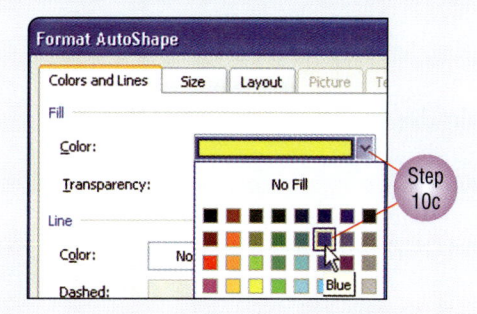

    d. Click OK to close the Format AutoShape dialog box.
11. Complete steps similar to those in Step 8 to change the color of the streak in the computer monitor from red to turquoise.
12. Complete steps similar to those in Step 8 to change the color behind the keys from light green to pale blue.
13. Click outside the image to remove the Drawing canvas.
14. Save the document and name it **ewc3x06**.
15. Print and then close **ewc3x06**.

Inserting and Aligning Objects

Objects, such as images, autoshapes, text boxes, and shapes can be inserted in a document. Insert images in a document with options at the Clip Art task pane or with options at the Insert Picture dialog box. You can also insert objects such as autoshapes and text boxes with buttons on the Drawing toolbar. Along with buttons for drawing objects, the Drawing toolbar contains options for aligning and distributing objects.

To align and distribute objects, select the objects, click the Draw button on the Drawing toolbar, and then point to Align or Distribute. This causes a side menu to display with alignment and distribution options. Choose the desired alignment and distribution option from this list.

To identify the objects you want to align and/or distribute, click the Select Objects button on the Drawing toolbar and then draw a border around the objects. Another method for selecting objects is to click the first object, hold down the Shift key, and then click any other object you want aligned.

QUICK STEPS

Align Objects
1. Select objects.
2. Click Draw, point to Align or Distribute, and then click desired option.

HINT
Select at least two objects to make alignment options available and at least three objects to make distribution options available.

exercise 7
CREATING A CERTIFICATE WITH ALIGNED AUTOSHAPES

1. Create the certificate shown in Figure 3.9. To begin, change the page margins and orientation by completing the following steps:
   a. Click File and then Page Setup.
   b. At the Page Setup dialog box with the Margins tab selected, change the top, bottom, left, and right margins to .75 inch.
   c. Click *Landscape* in the *Orientation* section.
   d. Click OK.
2. Insert the page border shown in Figure 3.9 by completing the following steps:
   a. Click Format and then Borders and Shading.
   b. At the Borders and Shading dialog box, click the Page Border tab.
   c. Click the down-pointing arrow at the right side of the *Art* option box and then click the third star option shown at the right (and in Figure 3.9) at the drop-down list.
   d. Click the up-pointing arrow at the right side of the *Width* text box until *20 pt* displays in the text box.
   e. Click OK to close the dialog box.
3. Create the text in the certificate as shown in Figure 3.9 with the following specifications:
   a. Set *Gold Star Service Award* centered and in 42-point Lucida Calligraphy bold with a Shadow effect. (Add the shadow effect by clicking the *Shadow* check box at the Font dialog box. If the Lucida Calligraphy typeface is not available, choose a similar decorative typeface.)
   b. Set *Awarded to* in 18-point Lucida Calligraphy bold.
   c. Set *Presented by* in 18-point Lucida Calligraphy bold.
   d. Set *King County Outreach* in 22-point Lucida Calligraphy bold.
   e. Set *June 2005* in 18-point Lucida Calligraphy bold.
4. Create the star in the middle of the certificate by completing the following steps:
   a. Click the AutoShapes button on the Drawing toolbar, point to Stars and Banners, and then click 5-Point Star in the side menu (last option from the left in the top row).
   b. Press the Delete key to delete the drawing canvas.
   c. Draw the star in the middle of the certificate as shown in Figure 3.9.

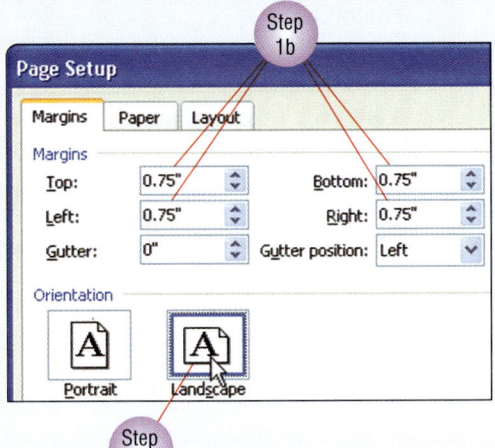

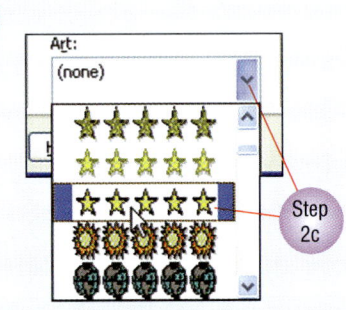

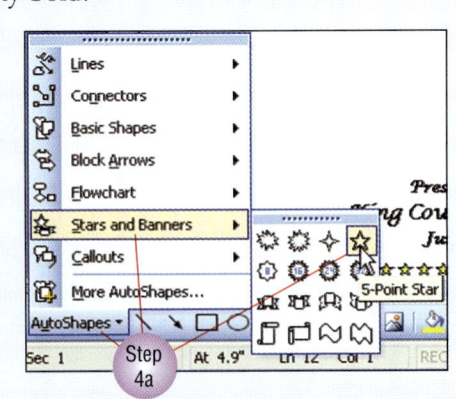

E96 Chapter Three

d. Add light yellow fill to the star by clicking the down-pointing arrow at the right side of the Fill Color button on the Drawing toolbar, and then clicking the light yellow color (third color option from the left in the bottom row of the color palette).
e. Click the Text Box button on the Drawing toolbar and then draw a text box inside the star.
f. Type **Chad Jeffries** inside the text box. Set *Chad Jeffries* in 22-point Lucida Calligraphy bold.
g. Click the Fill Color button to add light yellow fill to the text box.
h. Remove the line around the text box by clicking the down-pointing arrow at the right side of the Line Color button and then clicking *No Line* at the color palette.

5. Create the small stars toward the bottom of the certificate by completing the following steps:
   a. Click the AutoShapes button on the Drawing toolbar, point to Stars and Banners, and then click 5-Point Star at the side menu.
   b. Press the Delete key to delete the drawing canvas.
   c. Hold down the Shift key and then drag to create the first star. (If you are not happy with the size of the star, delete it, and then draw it again.)
   d. Add light yellow fill to the star.
   e. Copy the star by holding down the Ctrl key, using the mouse to drag the star to the right, and then releasing the Ctrl key.
   f. Copy the star four more times so the six stars are positioned as shown in Figure 3.9.

6. Align the stars at the bottom by completing the following steps:
   a. Click the Select Objects button on the Drawing toolbar.
   b. Draw a border around all six stars.
   c. Click the Draw button on the Drawing toolbar, point to Align or Distribute, and then click Align Bottom.
   d. Select the three stars at the left side of the certificate and then distribute the stars horizontally. (To do this, click the Draw button, point to Align or Distribute, and then click Distribute Horizontally.)
   e. Select the three stars at the right side of the certificate and then align and distribute the stars horizontally.

7. Save the completed certificate and name it **ewc3x07**.
8. Print and then close **ewc3x07**.

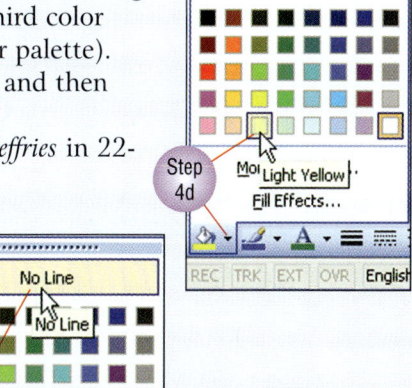

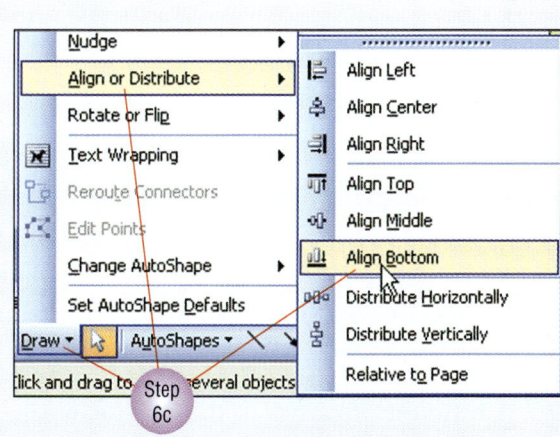

FIGURE 3.9 Exercise 7

Gold Star Service Award
Awarded to

Chad Jeffries

Presented by
King County Outreach
June 2005

Quick Steps

Flip or Rotate Object
1. Select object.
2. Click Draw, point to Rotate or Flip, and then click desired option.

Flipping and Rotating an Object

A selected object can be rotated and flipped horizontally or vertically. To rotate or flip an object, select the object, click the Draw button on the Drawing toolbar, point to Rotate or Flip, and then click the desired rotation or flip option at the side menu. A drawn object can be rotated but a text box cannot.

exercise 8

CREATING A LETTERHEAD AND ROTATING AN ARROW

1. At a clear document screen, create the letterhead shown in Figure 3.10. To begin, press the Enter key four times.
2. Click the Center button on the Formatting toolbar.
3. Change the font to 36-point Impact. (If Impact is not available, choose a similar typeface.)
4. Type **Quick Time Printing**.
5. Create the red arrow at the left side of the text by completing the following steps:
   a. Click the AutoShapes button on the Drawing toolbar, point to Block Arrows, and then click the Bent Arrow option (first arrow from the left in the third row).
   b. Press the Delete key to delete the drawing canvas.

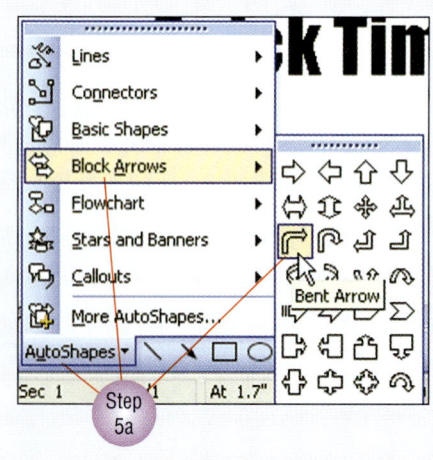

E98 Chapter Three

c. Draw the arrow at the left side of the text as shown in Figure 3.10. If you are not satisfied with the location of the arrow, drag it to the desired location. If you are not satisfied with the size of the arrow, use the sizing handles to increase or decrease the size.
d. With the arrow still selected, add red fill. To do this, click the down-pointing arrow at the right side of the Fill Color button on the Drawing toolbar. At the palette of color choices that displays, click the Red color (first color from the left in the third row from the bottom).
6. With the red arrow still selected, copy it to the right side of the text. To do this, position the mouse pointer inside the arrow (displays with a four-headed arrow attached), hold down the Ctrl key, and then the left mouse button. Drag the arrow to the right side of the text, release the mouse button, and then release the Ctrl key.
7. Flip the arrow horizontally by clicking Draw, pointing to Rotate or Flip, and then clicking Flip Horizontal.
8. If necessary, reposition the arrow so it displays as shown in Figure 3.10.
9. Save the document and name it **ewc3x08**.
10. Print and then close **ewc3x08**.

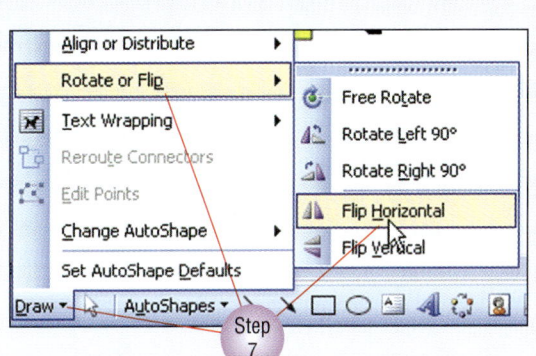

FIGURE

3.10 *Exercise 8*

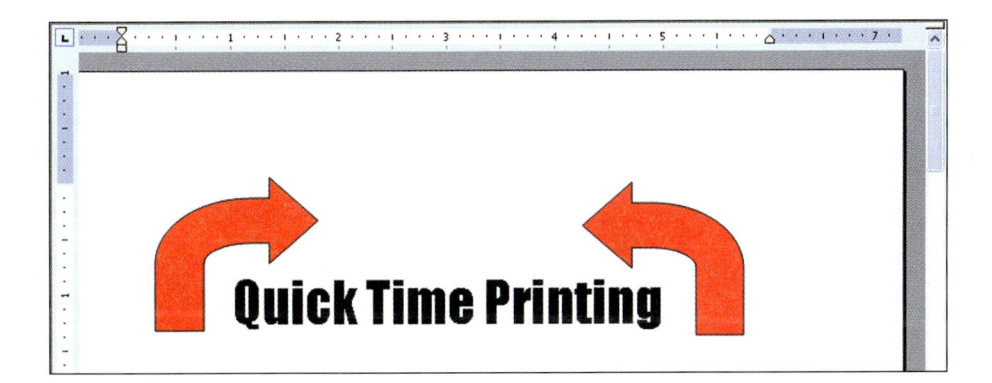

HINT
Use a watermark to add visual appeal to a document.

Creating a Watermark

An interesting effect can be created in a document with a watermark. A **watermark** is a lightened image that displays in a document. Text can be inserted in front of the watermark creating a document with a foreground and a background. The foreground is the text and the background is the watermark image. Figure 3.12 shows an example of a watermark you will be creating in Exercise 9. The image of the computer is the watermark and creates the background, and the text of the notice displays in front of the watermark and creates the foreground. Create a watermark with options from the Printed Watermark dialog box or with buttons on the Picture toolbar.

With options at the Printed Watermark dialog box shown in Figure 3.11, you can create a picture watermark or a text watermark. Display the Printed Watermark dialog box by clicking Format, pointing to Background, and then clicking Printed Watermark. If you are creating a picture watermark, click *Picture watermark*, and then click the Select Picture button. This displays the Insert Picture dialog box. At this dialog box, specify the drive or folder where the picture is located, and then double-click the desired picture image. To create a text watermark, click the *Text watermark* option and then customize the watermark by choosing the font, size, color, and layout of the watermark.

QUICK STEPS

Create Picture Watermark
1. Click Format, Background, Printed Watermark.
2. Click *Picture watermark* option.
3. Navigate to desired folder.
4. Double-click desired image.
5. Click OK.

FIGURE 3.11 *Printed Watermark Dialog Box*

QUICK STEPS

Create Text Watermark
1. Click Format, Background, Printed Watermark.
2. Click *Text watermark* option.
3. Select current text in *Text* box and then type desired text.
4. Click OK.

Click this option to create a picture watermark.

Click this option to create a text watermark.

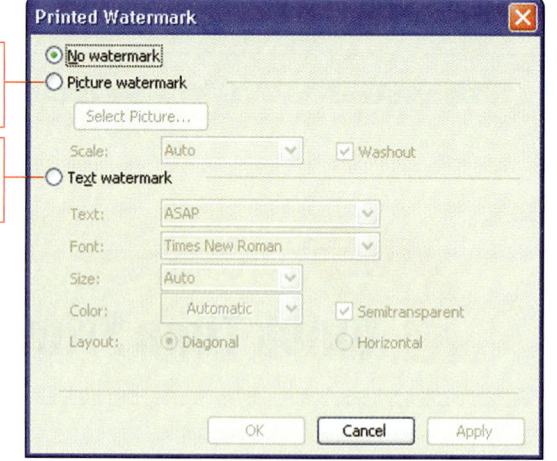

E100
Chapter Three
WORD

exercise 9

CREATING A PICTURE WATERMARK

1. Insert the CD that accompanies this textbook in the CD drive.
2. Create the watermark image shown in Figure 3.12. To begin, open **WordNotice03** from the WordChapter03E folder on your disk in drive A.
3. Save the document with Save As and name it **ewc3x09**.
4. Insert from the CD an image of a computer by completing the following steps:
    a. Click Format, point to Background, and then click Printed Watermark.
    b. At the Printed Watermark dialog box, click the *Picture watermark* option.
    c. Click the Select Picture button.
    d. At the Insert Picture dialog box, click the down-pointing arrow at the right side of the *Look in* option.
    e. At the drop-down list, click the drive where the CD is located.
    f. Double-click the *Word* folder.
    g. Double-click the *Word2003Expert* folder.
    h. Double-click the *ClipArt* folder.
    i. Double-click the image named *pc* in the list box.
    j. At the Printed Watermark dialog box, click OK.
5. Save, print, and then close **ewc3x09**.

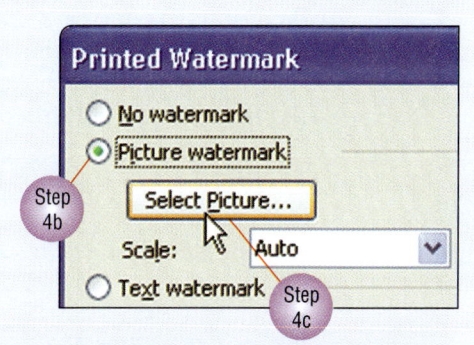

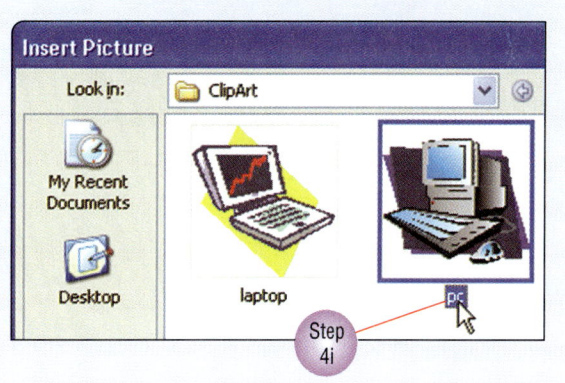

FIGURE 3.12 Exercise 9

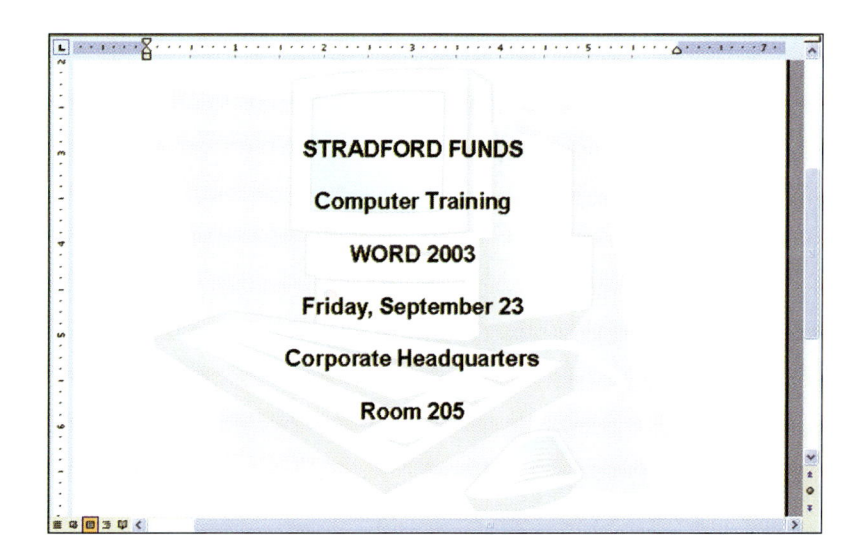

exercise 10

CREATING A TEXT WATERMARK

1. Open **WordContract01**.
2. Save the document with Save As and name it **ewc3x10**.
3. Insert a text watermark by completing the following steps:
    a. Click Format, point to Background, and then click Printed Watermark.
    b. At the Printed Watermark dialog box, click *Text watermark*.
    c. Select the text *ASAP* in the *Text* box and then type **Sample Agreement**.
    d. Change the *Font* option to Arial.
    e. Click OK to close the Printed Watermark dialog box.

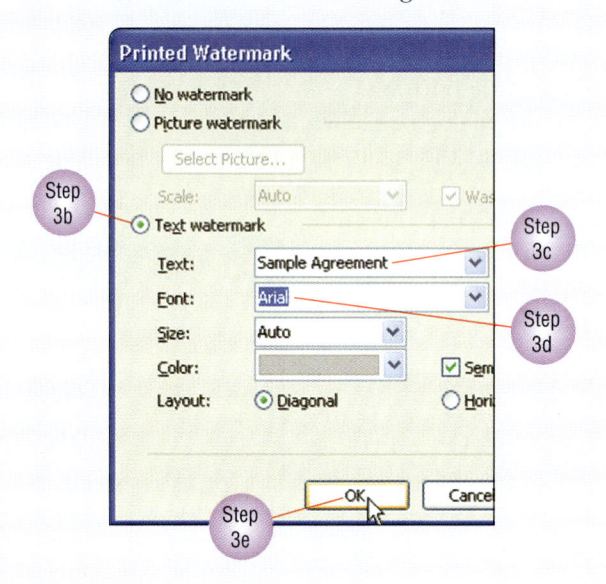

4. Save, print, and then close **ewc3x10**.

Using WordArt

Insert Word Art

QUICK STEPS

Create a Watermark
1. Click Insert WordArt button on Drawing toolbar.
2. At WordArt gallery, double-click desired option.
3. At Edit WordArt Text dialog box, type desired text.
4. Click OK.

With the WordArt application, you can distort or modify text to conform to a variety of shapes. This is useful for creating company logos and headings. With WordArt, you can change the font, style, and alignment of text. You can also use different fill patterns and colors, customize border lines, and add shadow and three-dimensional effects. Display the WordArt Gallery shown in Figure 3.13 by clicking the Insert WordArt button on the Drawing toolbar. Double-click a WordArt style at the WordArt Gallery and the Edit WordArt Text dialog box displays. At this dialog box, type the desired WordArt text, and then click the OK button.

FIGURE

3.13 *WordArt Gallery*

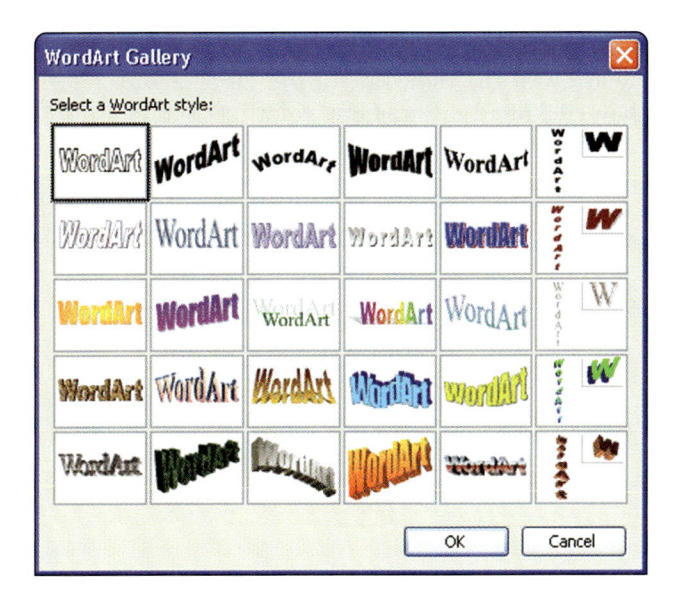

exercise 11

CREATING A HEADING WITH WORDART

1. At a clear document screen, create the heading shown in Figure 3.14. To begin, press Enter seven times, and then move the insertion point back up to the first line.
2. Display the Drawing toolbar. (Skip this step if the Drawing toolbar is already displayed.)
3. Click the Insert WordArt button on the Drawing toolbar.
4. At the WordArt Gallery, double-click the second option from the left in the fourth row.
5. At the Edit WordArt Text dialog box, type **Retirement Investment Funds**.
6. Click OK to close the dialog box.
7. Create the line below the report name by completing the following steps:
    a. Click the Arrow button on the Drawing toolbar.
    b. Press the Delete key to delete the drawing canvas.
    c. Draw a horizontal line as shown in Figure 3.14.
    d. With the horizontal line selected, change the arrow style by clicking the Arrow Style button on the Drawing toolbar, and then clicking the second option from the bottom (Arrow Style 10).

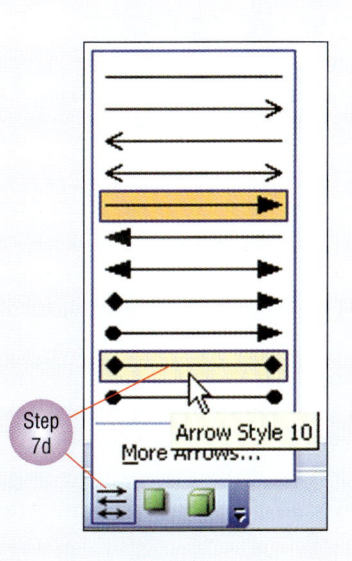

WORD

Adding Visual Elements   E103

e. Increase the width of the line by clicking the Line Style button on the Drawing toolbar and then clicking the first *3 pt* line at the pop-up menu.
f. Change the color of the horizontal line by clicking the down-pointing arrow at the right side of the Line Color button and then clicking the Blue-Gray color (second color option from the *right* in the second row from the top).
8. Deselect the line.
9. Save the document and name it **ewc3x11**.
10. Print and then close **ewc3x11**.

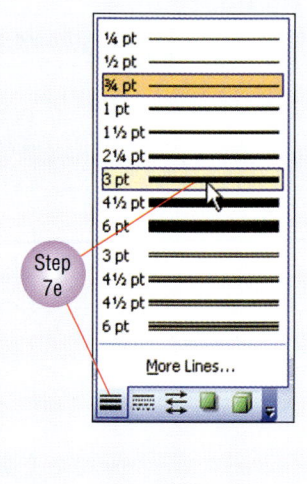

FIGURE

3.14 Exercise 11

Sizing and Moving WordArt

WordArt text displays in the document with the formatting you selected at the WordArt Gallery. Click the WordArt text to select it and black, square sizing handles display around the text. Use these handles to increase or decrease the WordArt size.

If you want to move and/or format the WordArt text, choose a wrapping style and the sizing handles change to white circles along with a green rotation handle and a yellow adjustment diamond. Use the green rotation handle to rotate the WordArt text and use the yellow adjustment diamond to change the slant of the text.

To move WordArt text, position the mouse pointer on any letter of the text until the mouse pointer displays with a four-headed arrow attached. Hold down the left mouse button, drag the outline of the WordArt text box to the desired position, and then release the mouse button. When all changes have been made to the WordArt text, click outside the WordArt text box to remove the sizing handles.

exercise 12

CREATING, MOVING, AND SIZING WORDART TEXT

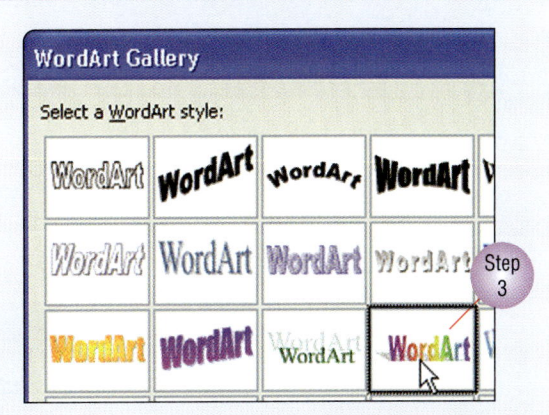

1. At a clear document screen, change to the Print Layout view.
2. Click the Insert WordArt button on the Drawing toolbar.
3. At the WordArt Gallery, double-click the fourth option from the left in the third row.
4. At the Edit WordArt Text dialog box, type **Lincoln Jazz Festival**.
5. Click OK to close the dialog box.
6. Change the wrapping style and increase the size of the WordArt text by completing the following steps:
    a. Click the Zoom button on the Standard toolbar and then click *Whole Page* at the drop-down list.
    b. Click the WordArt text to select it.
    c. Click the Text Wrapping button on the WordArt toolbar and then click *Through* at the drop-down list.
    d. Make the WordArt text twice as big by positioning the mouse pointer on the middle sizing handle at the bottom of the WordArt text box, dragging down until the height of the box is approximately doubled, and then releasing the mouse button. 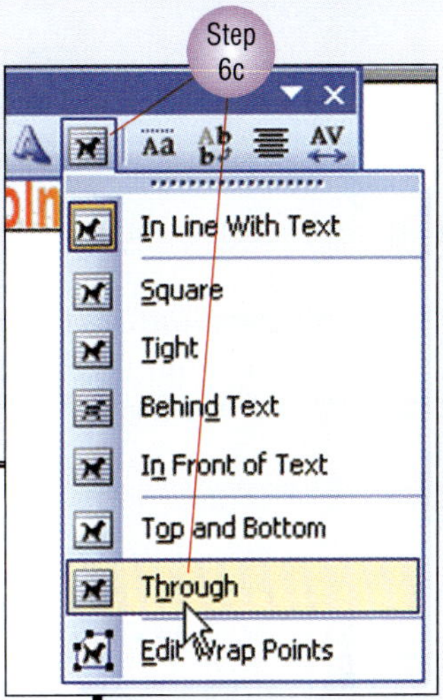 
7. Position the mouse pointer (turns into a four-headed arrow) inside the WordArt text box, hold down the left mouse button, drag the text box so it is centered horizontally and vertically on the page, and then release the mouse button.
8. Click outside the WordArt text box to deselect it.
9. Change the Zoom back to 100%.
10. Save the document and name it **ewc3x12**.
11. Print and then close **ewc3x12**.

Customizing WordArt

The WordArt toolbar, shown in Figure 3.15, contains buttons for customizing WordArt text. Using buttons on the WordArt toolbar, you can perform such actions as changing size and shape, rotating WordArt text, changing wrapping style, changing the letter height and alignment of text, and changing character spacing.

HINT Double-click WordArt text and the Edit WordArt Text dialog box displays.

WORD
Adding Visual Elements E105

F I G U R E

3.15 *WordArt Toolbar Buttons*

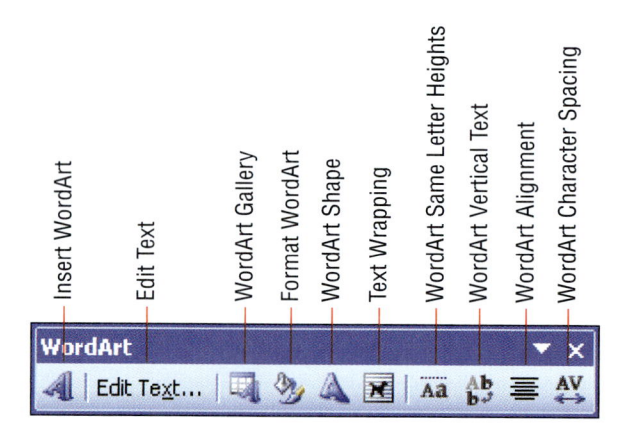

Insert WordArt | Edit Text | WordArt Gallery | Format WordArt | WordArt Shape | Text Wrapping | WordArt Same Letter Heights | WordArt Vertical Text | WordArt Alignment | WordArt Character Spacing

exercise 13

CREATING AND THEN CUSTOMIZING WORDART TEXT

1. At a clear document screen, change to the Print Layout view.
2. Click the Insert WordArt button on the Drawing toolbar.
3. At the WordArt Gallery, double-click the second option from the left in the second row. 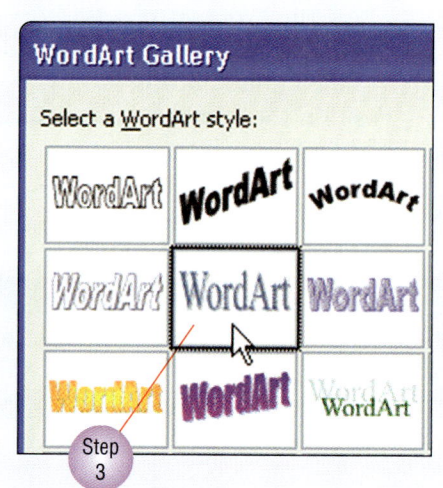
4. At the Edit WordArt Text dialog box, make the following changes:
   a. Type **Now is the time**.
   b. Press Enter and then type **to get out and**.
   c. Press Enter and then type **vote!**.
   d. Change the font to Braggadocio. To do this, click the down-pointing arrow at the right side of the *Font* option box, and then click *Braggadocio* at the drop-down list. (You will need to scroll up the list to display *Braggadocio*.)
   e. Click the OK button to close the dialog box.
5. Change the alignment, size, and position of the WordArt text by completing the following steps:
   a. Click the WordArt text to select it.
   b. Click the Text Wrapping button on the WordArt toolbar and then click *Through* at the drop-down list.
   c. Click the WordArt Alignment button on the WordArt toolbar and then click *Letter Justify* at the drop-down list.
   d. Change the size and position of the WordArt by completing the following steps:
      1) Click the Format WordArt button on the WordArt toolbar.

Step 3

Step 5c

E106 Chapter Three

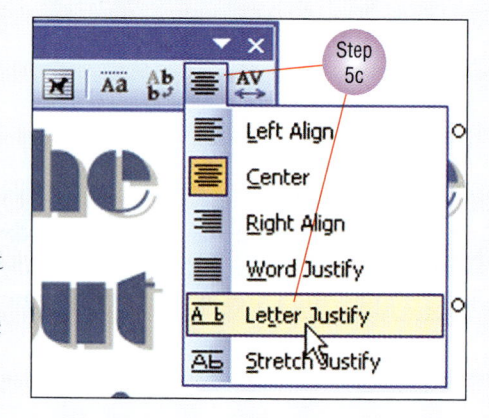

2) At the Format WordArt dialog box, click the Size tab.
3) At the Format WordArt dialog box with the Size tab selected, select the current measurement in the *Height* text box (in the *Size and rotate* section), and then type 2.5.
4) Select the current measurement in the *Width* text box (in the *Size and rotate* section), and then type 5.

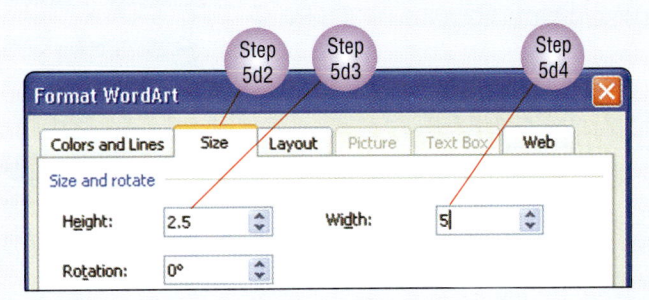

5) Click the Layout tab.
6) At the Format WordArt dialog box with the Layout tab selected, click the Advanced button (located at the bottom of the dialog box).
7) At the Advanced Layout dialog box, click the Picture Position tab.
8) At the Advanced Layout dialog box with the Picture Position tab selected, click the down-pointing arrow at the right side of the *to the right of* option box (in the *Horizontal* section—contains the word *Column*) and then click *Margin* at the drop-down list.
9) Select the current measurement in the *Absolute position* text box in the *Horizontal* section and then type 0.5. (Be sure to type a zero and not the letter *O*.)
10) Select the current measurement in the *Absolute position* text box in the *Vertical* section and then type 3.
11) Click OK to close the Advanced Layout dialog box.
12) Click OK to close the Format WordArt dialog box.
6. Click outside the WordArt text box to deselect it.
7. Save the document and name it **ewc3x13**.
8. Print and then close **ewc3x13**.

Customizing WordArt with Buttons on the Drawing Toolbar

You can use buttons on the Drawing toolbar to customize WordArt text. For example, with buttons on the Drawing toolbar, you can change the letter color, line color, and line style, add a shadow, and add a three-dimensional effect.

exercise 14
CREATING AND THEN APPLYING PATTERN, COLOR, AND SHADING TO WORDART TEXT

1. Create the WordArt text shown in Figure 3.16. To begin, change to the Print Layout view.
2. Click the Insert WordArt button on the Drawing toolbar.
3. At the WordArt Gallery, double-click the third option from the left in the top row.
4. At the Edit WordArt Text dialog box, type **Exploring Office 2003**, and then click OK to close the dialog box.
5. Click the WordArt text to select it.
6. Click the Text Wrapping button on the WordArt toolbar and then click *Through* at the drop-down list.
7. Click the WordArt Shape button on the WordArt toolbar and then click the second shape from the left in the fourth row (Deflate).
8. Change the size and position of the WordArt by completing the following steps:
    a. Click the Format WordArt button on the WordArt toolbar.
    b. At the Format WordArt dialog box, click the Size tab.
    c. At the Format WordArt dialog box with the Size tab selected, select the current measurement in the *Height* text box (in the *Size and rotate* section), and then type 2.
    d. Select the current measurement in *Width* text box (in the *Size and rotate* section) and then type 6.
    e. Click the Layout tab.
    f. At the Format WordArt dialog box with the Layout tab selected, click the Advanced button (located at the bottom of the dialog box).
    g. At the Advanced Layout dialog box, click the Picture Position tab.
    h. Select the current measurement in the *Absolute position* text box (in the *Vertical* section of the dialog box) and then type 3.5.
    i. Click OK to close the Advanced Layout dialog box.
    j. Click OK to close the Format WordArt dialog box.
9. Add a pattern and change colors by completing the following steps:
    a. Click the down-pointing arrow at the right side of the Fill Color button on the Drawing toolbar.
    b. At the palette of color choices that displays, click Fill Effects located at the bottom of the palette.

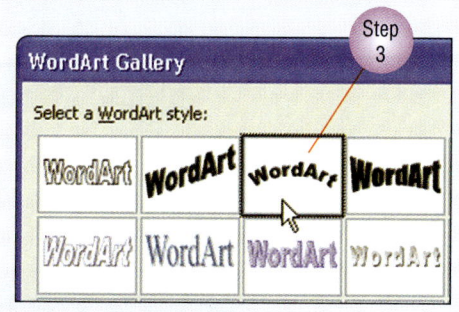

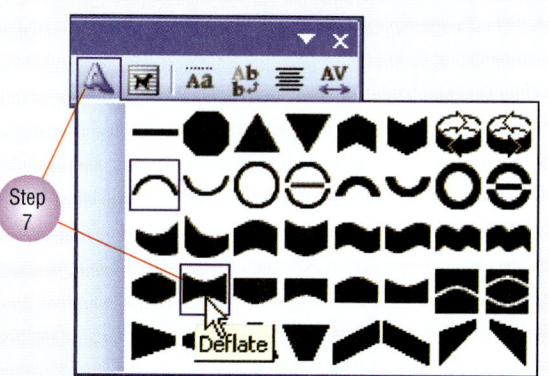

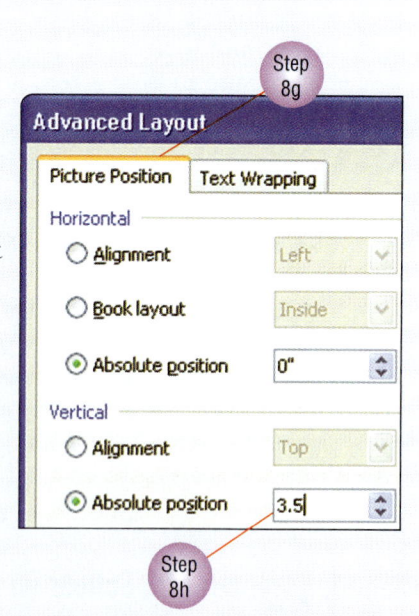

E108 Chapter Three

c. At the Fill Effects dialog box, click the Pattern tab.
d. At the Fill Effects dialog box with the Pattern tab selected, click the fourth pattern option from the left in the second row (Light horizontal).
e. Click the down-pointing arrow at the right side of the *Foreground* box.
f. At the color palette that displays, click the Turquoise color (fifth color from the left in the fourth row).
g. Click the down-pointing arrow at the right side of the *Background* box.
h. At the color palette that displays, click the Pink color (first color from the left in the fourth row).
i. Click OK to close the Fill Effects dialog box.
10. Add a shadow to the text by clicking the Shadow Style button on the Drawing toolbar and then clicking the second shadow option from the left in the fourth row (Shadow Style 14).
11. Click outside the WordArt text to deselect the WordArt box.
12. Save the document and name it **ewc3x14**.
13. Print and then close **ewc3x14**.

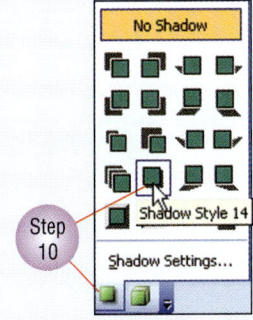

FIGURE 3.16 *Exercise 14*

Creating and Formatting Web Pages

You can save a Word document as a Web page by clicking File and then Save as Web Page. When you save a document as a Web page, Word automatically changes to the Web Layout view. The Web Layout view displays a page as it will appear when published to the Web or an intranet. You can also change to the Web Layout view by clicking the Web Layout View button located at the left side of the horizontal scroll bar or by clicking View and then Web Layout.

Word provides a number of features you can use to format a Web page. Some features include themes, backgrounds and frames. Themes and backgrounds are designed for viewing in a Word document, in an e-mail message, or on the Web. Backgrounds and some theme formatting do not print.

When creating a Web page, you may want to preview it in your default Web browser. To do this, click File and then Web Page Preview. This displays the currently open document in the default Web browser and displays formatting supported by the browser.

Web Layout View

QUICK STEPS

Apply a Theme
1. Click Format, Theme.
2. Double-click desired theme in *Choose a Theme* list box.

HINT

Remove a theme by displaying the Theme dialog box and then double-clicking *(No Theme)*.

Applying a Theme

Some interesting and colorful formatting can be applied to a document with options at the Theme dialog box shown in Figure 3.17. Display this dialog box by clicking Format and then Theme. Click a theme in the *Choose a Theme* list box and a preview displays at the right side. When a theme is applied to a document, Word automatically changes to the Web Layout view. Theme formatting is designed for documents that will be published on the Web, on an intranet, or sent as an e-mail. Not all of the formatting applied by a theme will print.

FIGURE 3.17 *Theme Dialog Box*

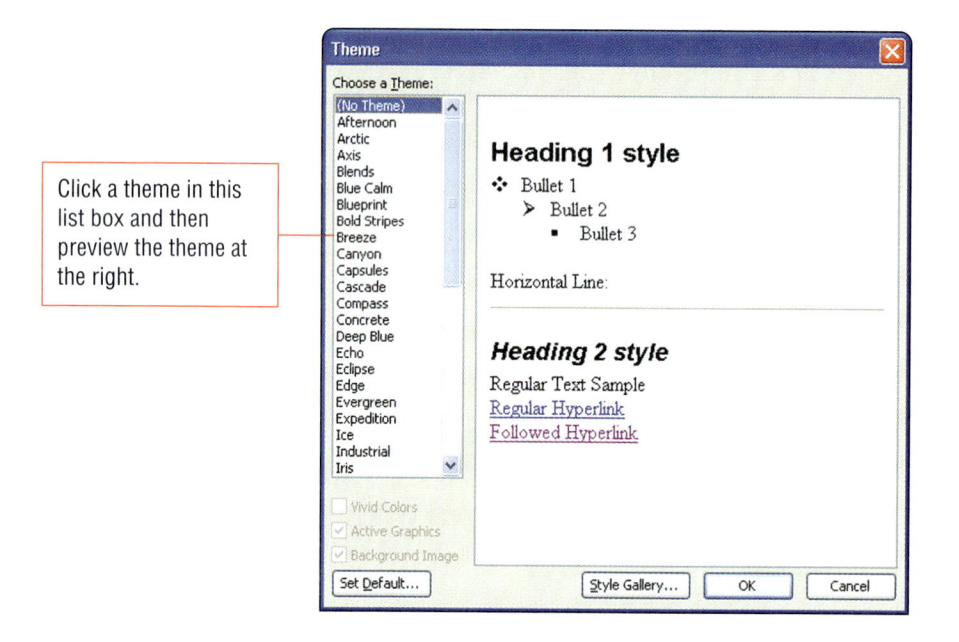

Click a theme in this list box and then preview the theme at the right.

Formatting with Buttons on the Web Tools Toolbar

A Web page designer uses a variety of tools to prepare an appealing and successful Web page. Tools are available for formatting a Web page with buttons on the Web Tools toolbar shown in Figure 3.18. Display the Web Tools toolbar by clicking View, pointing to Toolbars, and then clicking Web Tools. You can also display the Web Tools toolbar by right-clicking a currently displayed toolbar and then clicking Web Tools at the drop-down menu. The shape of the toolbar shown in Figure 3.18 has been changed to easily identify the buttons. The shape of your Web Tools toolbar may vary.

An interactive Web page, a page in which the viewer will provide input or answer questions, might include check boxes and option buttons. A Web page with a variety of options and choices might include drop-down boxes and list boxes. In Exercise 15 you will be using two of the buttons on the Web Tools toolbar. As you continue to create and design Web pages, consider experimenting with other buttons on the toolbar.

FIGURE 3.18 Web Tools Toolbar Buttons

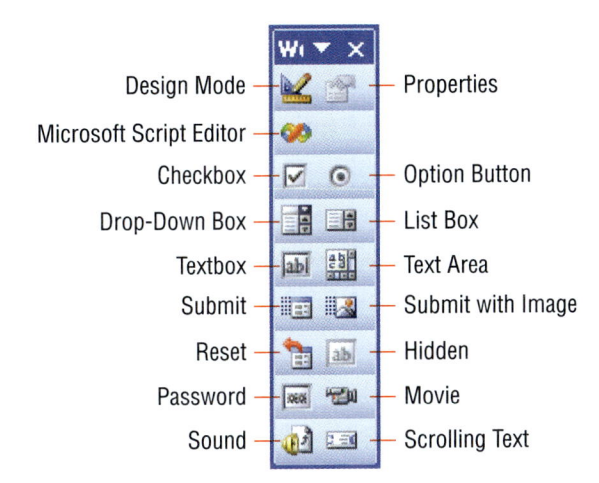

- Design Mode
- Microsoft Script Editor
- Checkbox
- Drop-Down Box
- Textbox
- Submit
- Reset
- Password
- Sound
- Properties
- Option Button
- List Box
- Text Area
- Submit with Image
- Hidden
- Movie
- Scrolling Text

exercise 15 — CREATING AND FORMATTING A WEB PAGE

1. Open **BeltwayHomePage**.
2. Save the document as a Web page by completing the following steps:
   a. Click File and then Save as Web Page.
   b. At the Save As dialog box, type **BeltwayWebPage** and then press Enter. (If a message displays telling you that some features are not supported by certain versions of browsers, click the Continue button.)
3. Apply the Sumi Painting theme by completing the following steps:
   a. Click Format and then Theme.
   b. At the Theme dialog box, scroll through the list of themes in the *Choose a Theme* list box until *Sumi Painting* is visible and then click *Sumi Painting*.
   c. Insert a check mark in the *Vivid Colors* option and the *Active Graphics* check box located towards the bottom left side of the dialog box. (One or both of these check boxes may already contain a check mark.)
   d. Remove the check mark from the *Background Image* check box.
   e. Click OK to close the Theme dialog box.
4. Preview the document in Web Page Preview by clicking File and then Web Page Preview. (If the Internet Explorer window display is small, click the Maximize button to enlarge the display.)
5. After viewing the document in the Web browser, click File and then Close.
6. Save and then print **BeltwayWebPage**. (Not all of the theme formatting will print.)
7. Insert scrolling text in the Web page by completing the following steps:
   a. Display the Web Tools toolbar by clicking View, pointing to Toolbars, and then clicking Web Tools.

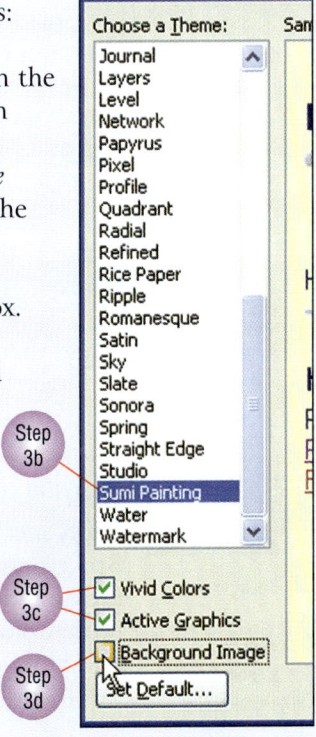

b. Position the insertion point at the left margin on the blank line below the company Web address, press the Enter key once, and then click the Center button on the Formatting toolbar.
c. Click the Scrolling Text button on the Web Tools toolbar.
d. At the Scrolling Text dialog box, select *Scrolling Text* that displays in the *Type the scrolling text here* text box and then type **Let Beltway Transportation take care of all your moving needs!**.
e. Click the down-pointing arrow at the right side of the *Background color* text box and then click *Gray-25%* at the drop-down list.
f. Click OK to close the Scrolling Text dialog box.
8. Add a sound clip to the Web page by completing the following steps:
a. Click the Sound button on the Web Tools toolbar.
b. At the Background Sound dialog box, click the Browse button.
c. At the Open dialog box (with the Media folder displayed), double-click *TOWN* in the list box. (If the media folder does not display, you will need to navigate to the folder, which should be in the WINDOWS folder.)
d. At the Background Sound dialog box, click the down-pointing arrow at the right side of the *Loop* text box, and then click *Infinite* at the drop-down list.
e. Click OK to close the Background Sound dialog box.
9. Close the Web Tools toolbar.
10. Save, print, and then close **BeltwayWebPage**.

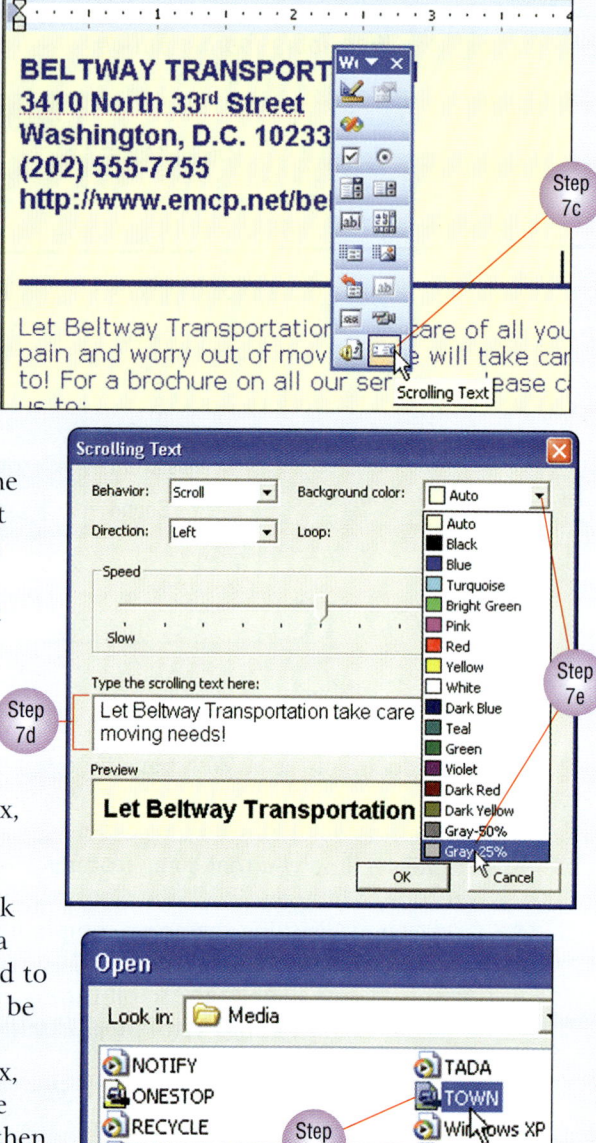

QUICK STEPS

Apply Background Color
1. Click Format, Background.
2. Click desired color.

Applying a Background to a Document

Apply a colorful background to a document by clicking Format and then Background. This causes a palette of color choices to display at the right side of the drop-down menu as shown in Figure 3.19. Click the desired color or click More Colors to display the Colors dialog box. Click Fill Effects from the Background side menu and the Fill Effects dialog box displays. Use options from this dialog box to apply formatting such as a gradient, texture, and pattern.

Apply a background and the view automatically changes to Web Layout. A background color does not display in the Normal or Print Layout views and will not print. Like a theme, background color is designed for formatting documents such as Web pages or e-mail messages that are viewed in the screen.

FIGURE
3.19 **Background Side Menu**

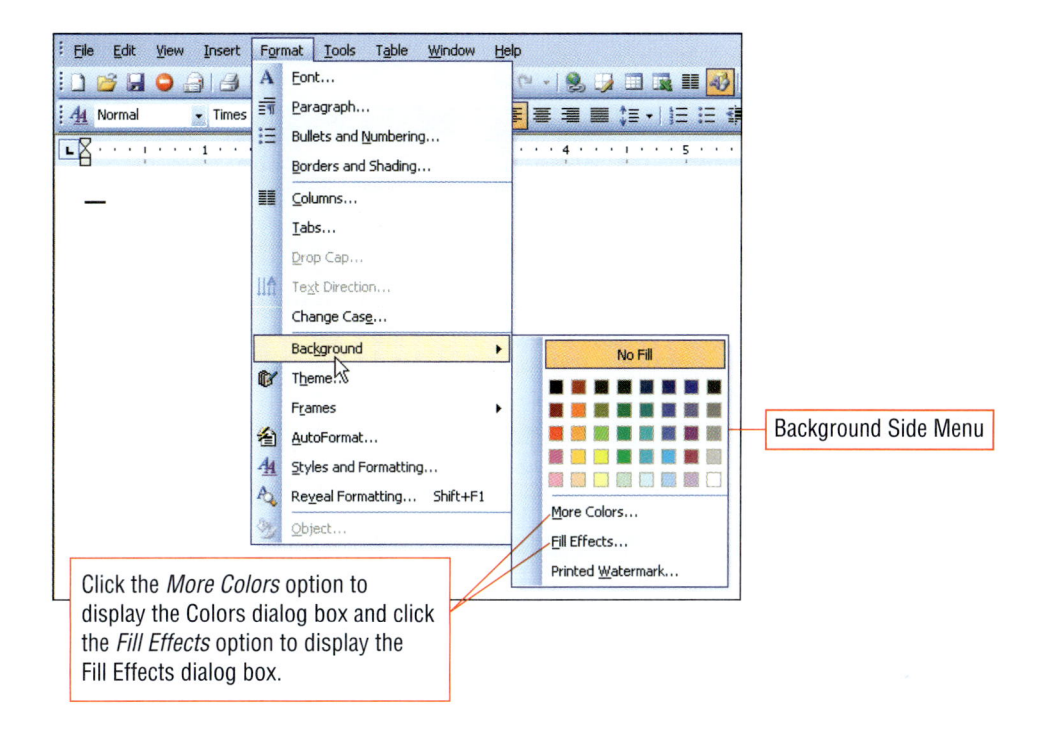

Background Side Menu

Click the *More Colors* option to display the Colors dialog box and click the *Fill Effects* option to display the Fill Effects dialog box.

Inserting Frames in a Document

Many Web pages that you visit on the World Wide Web are divided into *frames*. A frame is an adjustable pane within the window that is separate from other panes in the window. Using a frame, you can position elements on the page. Insert a frame in a document with options on the Frames toolbar. Display this toolbar, shown in Figure 3.20, by clicking Format, pointing to Frames, and then clicking New Frames Page. This changes the display to Web Layout and inserts the Frames toolbar. You can also display the Frames toolbar by clicking View, pointing to Toolbars, and then clicking Frames. This method does not change the view to Web Layout.

HINT
If you want a top or bottom frame to span the full width of the document, insert the top or bottom frame first before inserting other frames.

QUICK STEPS

Insert Frame
1. Click Format, Frames, New Frames Page.
2. Click button on Frames toolbar representing desired frame.

WORD
Adding Visual Elements   E113

FIGURE 3.20 Frames Toolbar

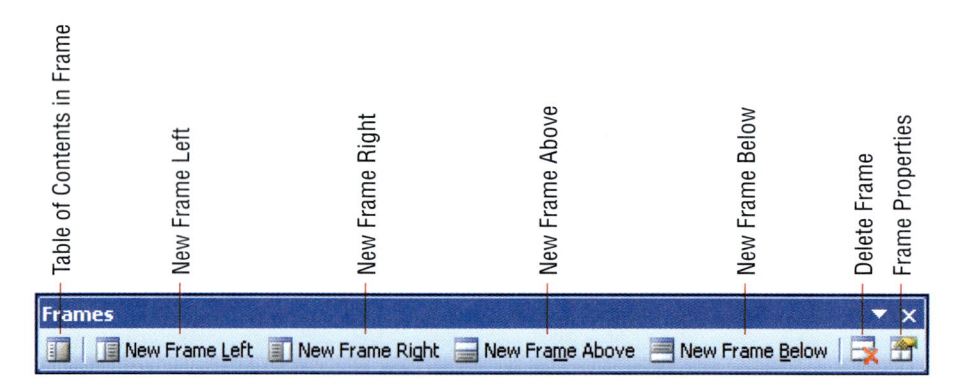

Labels (left to right): Table of Contents in Frame | New Frame Left | New Frame Right | New Frame Above | New Frame Below | Delete Frame | Frame Properties

Click a button on the toolbar representing the location where you want to insert the frame. For example, click the New Frame Left button to insert a frame at the left side of the screen. You can change the size of the frame by dragging the frame border. Remove a frame from a window by clicking the Delete Frame button on the Frames toolbar.

New Frame Left

Delete Frame

exercise 16 — APPLYING BACKGROUND FORMATTING AND INSERTING FRAMES IN A DOCUMENT

1. Open **PremiumProduce**.
2. Apply a background color by clicking Format, pointing to Background, and then clicking the Light Green color on the side menu (fourth color option from the left in the bottom row).
3. Add a fill effect to the background by completing the following steps:
   a. Click Format, point to Background, and then click Fill Effects.
   b. At the Fill Effects dialog box with the Gradient tab selected, click the *Two colors* option in the *Colors* section.
   c. Click the down-pointing arrow at the right of the *Color 2* option and then click Light Yellow at the color palette (third color from the left in the bottom row).
   d. Click the *From center* option in the *Shading styles* section.
   e. Click OK.
4. Insert a frame by completing the following steps:
   a. Click Format, point to Frames, and then click New Frames Page. (This changes the view to Web Layout and also displays the Frames toolbar.)

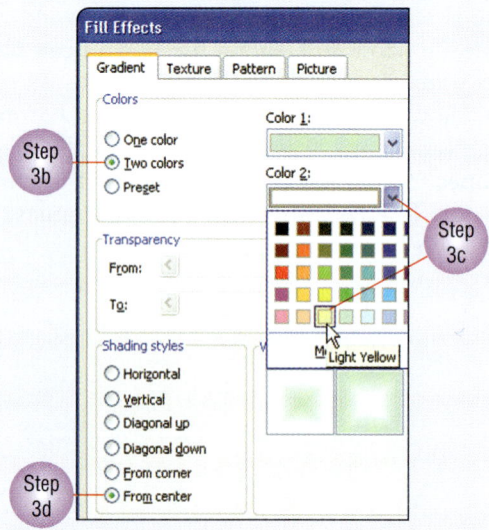

E114 Chapter Three

b. Click the New Frame Left button on the Frames toolbar.
c. With the insertion point positioned in the new frame located at the left side of the screen, type **Pricing**.
d. Select *Pricing* and then change the font to 10-point Trebuchet MS. (If this font is not available, choose a similar sans serif typeface.)
e. Decrease the size of the left frame to about 1 inch by dragging the right border of the frame.
f. Change the background color by clicking Format, pointing to Background, and then clicking the Light Green color at the side menu (fourth color option from the left in the bottom row).

5. Create a hyperlink by completing the following steps:
   a. Select *Pricing* in the left frame.
   b. Click the Insert Hyperlink button on the Standard toolbar.
   c. At the Insert Hyperlink dialog box, navigate to the WordChapter03E folder on your disk and then double-click **PremProPricing**.

6. Insert a frame along the bottom that contains scrolling text by completing the following steps:
   a. Click in the frame containing the document text (the right frame).
   b. Click the New Frame Below button on the Frames toolbar.
   c. Click the Close button (contains an X) located in the upper right corner of the Frames toolbar to close the toolbar.
   d. Decrease the size of the bottom frame to approximately .75 inch.
   e. Display the Web Tools toolbar by clicking View, pointing to Toolbars, and then clicking Web Tools.
   f. With the insertion point positioned in the bottom frame, click the Center button on the Formatting toolbar.
   g. Click the Scrolling Text button on the Web Tools toolbar.
   h. At the Scrolling Text dialog box, select *Scrolling Text* that displays in the *Type the scrolling text here* text box and then type **Order today and receive FREE two pounds of organically-grown strawberries!**.
   i. Click OK to close the Scrolling Text dialog box.
   j. Turn off the display of the Web Tools toolbar.
   k. Apply a background by clicking Format, pointing to Background, and then clicking the Light Yellow color (third color from the left in the bottom row).

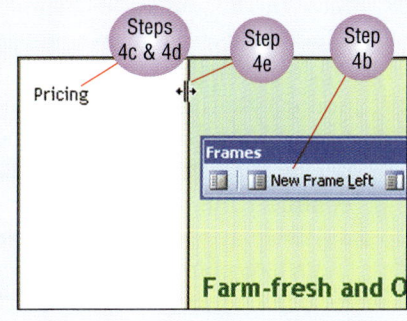

7. Save the document and name it **ewc3x16**.
8. View the document in your default browser by clicking File and then Web page Preview.
9. After viewing the document, close the browser by clicking File and then Close.
10. You decide that you do not like the scrolling text at the bottom of the screen so you decide to delete the frame. To do this, complete the following steps:
    a. Display the Frames toolbar by clicking View, pointing to Toolbars, and then clicking Frames.
    b. Click anywhere in the bottom frame. (This makes the frame active.)
    c. Click the Delete Frame button on the Frames toolbar (second button from the *right*).
    d. Close the Frames toolbar.
11. Display the **PremProPricing** document by completing the following steps:
    a. Click in the left frame to make the frame active.
    b. Position the mouse pointer on the Pricing hyperlink, hold down the Ctrl key, and then click the left mouse button.
    c. After viewing the **PremProPricing** document, close the document.
12. Save and then print **ewc3x16**. (The frame, background color, and fill effect will not print.)

Downloading and Saving Web Pages and Images

QUICK STEPS

Save Web Page
1. Open Web page in Internet Explorer.
2. Click File, Save As.
3. Specify folder.
4. Type desired name in *File name* text box.
5. Click Save button.

QUICK STEPS

Save Web Image
1. Display Web page with image.
2. Right-click image.
3. Click Save Picture As.
4. Type name for image.
5. Press Enter.

The image(s) and/or text that displays when you open a Web page as well as the Web page itself can be saved as a separate file. This separate file can be viewed, printed, or inserted in another file. The information you want to save in a separate file is downloaded from the Internet by Internet Explorer and saved in a folder of your choosing with the name you specify. Copyright laws protect much of the information on the Internet. Before using information downloaded from the Internet, check the site for restrictions. If you do use information, make sure you properly cite the source.

To save a Web page as a file, display the desired page, click File on the Internet Explorer Menu bar, and then click Save As at the drop-down menu. At the Save Web Page dialog box, specify the folder where you want to save the Web page. Select the text in the *File name* text box, type a name for the page, and then press Enter or click the Save button. A Web page is saved as an HTML file. A folder is automatically created when the Web page is saved. All images in the Web page are saved as separate files and inserted in the folder.

Save a specific Web image by right-clicking the image and then clicking Save Picture As at the shortcut menu. At the Save Picture dialog box, type a name for the image in the *File name* text box and then press Enter.

exercise 17
SAVING A WEB PAGE AND IMAGE AS SEPARATE FILES

1. Make sure you are connected to the Internet and then use Internet Explorer (or your default browser) to search for Web sites related to Yellowstone National Park.
2. When the search engine displays a list of Yellowstone National Park sites, choose a site that contains information about the park and also contains at least one image of the park.
3. Save the Web page as a file by completing the following steps:
   a. Click File on the Internet Explorer Menu bar and then click Save As at the drop-down menu. (These steps may vary if you are using a different browser.)
   b. At the Save Web Page dialog box, navigate (using the *Save in* option) to the WordChapter03E folder on your disk.
   c. Select the text in the *File name* text box, type **YellowstoneWebPage** and then press Enter. 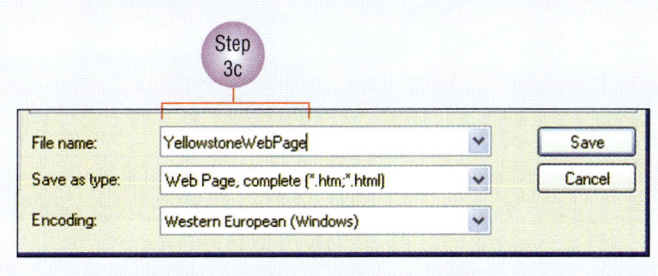
4. Save the image as a separate file by completing the following steps:
   a. Right-click the image of the park.
   b. At the shortcut menu that displays, click Save Picture As.
   c. At the Save Picture dialog box, change the location to the WordChapter03E folder on your disk.
   d. Select the text in the *File name* text box, type **YellowstoneImage**, and then press Enter.
5. Close Internet Explorer (or your default browser).

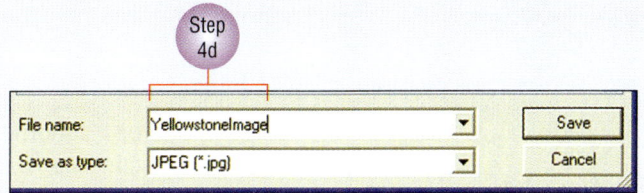

Opening and Editing a Saved Web Page

A Web page is saved as an HTML file. To open a Web page in Word, display the drive and/or folder where the page is located and then click the Open button on the Standard toolbar. At the Open dialog box, change the *Files of type* option to *All Files*, and then double-click the desired Web page file in the list box. Edit and save a Web page file in the normal manner.

exercise 18

OPENING AND EDITING A SAVED WEB PAGE

1. At a clear document Word screen, open the **YellowstoneWebPage** file by completing the following steps:
   a. Click the Open button on the Standard toolbar.
   b. At the Open dialog box, click the down-pointing arrow at the right side of the *Files of type* option box, and then click *All Files* at the drop-down list.

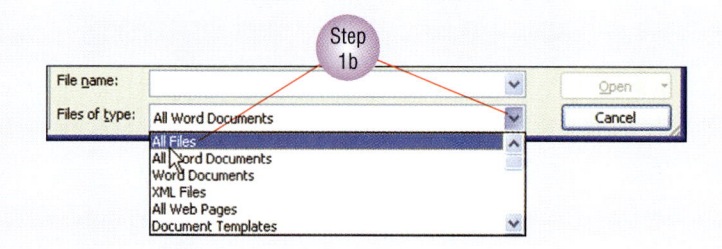

   Step 1b

   c. Change to the WordChapter03E folder on your disk.
   d. Double-click *YellowstoneWebPage* in the list box. (Make sure you double-click the **YellowstoneWebPage** file and *not* the folder.)
2. Move the insertion point to the end of the **YellowstoneWebPage** file.
3. Type your first and last name, press Enter, and then insert the current date.
4. Save the Web page file with Save As and name it **ewc3x18**.
5. Print and then close **ewc3x18**.

Inserting a Saved Image

Insert a Web image in a Word document by clicking the Insert Picture button on the Drawing toolbar or by clicking Insert, pointing to Picture, and then clicking From File. At the Insert Picture dialog box, specify the drive and/or folder where the image is located, and then double-click the image in the list box.

exercise 19

INSERTING A SAVED WEB IMAGE

1. At a clear document screen, click the Center button on the Formatting toolbar.
2. Click the Bold button.
3. Change the font size to 14 points.
4. Type Yellowstone National Park Image.
5. Press the Enter key twice.
6. Insert the Yellowstone image by completing the following steps:
   a. Click Insert on the Menu bar, point to Picture, and then click From File.
   b. At the Insert Picture dialog box, change the *Look in* option to the WordChapter03E folder on your disk, and then double-click *YellowstoneImage*.
7. Save the document and name it **ewc3x19**.
8. Print and then close **ewc3x19**.

E118 Chapter Three

CHAPTER summary

- Insert a page border with options at the Borders and Shading dialog box with the Page Border tab selected. Use the *Art* option at the dialog box to insert a page border consisting of images.
- Insert a graphic horizontal line with options at the Horizontal Line dialog box. Display this dialog box by clicking the Horizontal Line button at the Borders and Shading dialog box.
- Insert clip art images, photographs, movie images, and sound clips with options at the Clip Art task pane.
- Click an image in the Clip Art task pane, and the image is inserted in the current document.
- Format a selected image using buttons on the Picture toolbar. This toolbar displays when an image is selected.
- Click an image in the document to select it, and sizing handles display around the image. Use these handles to increase or decrease the image size.
- To move a selected image, choose a text wrapping option, and then drag the image to the desired location.
- Format a selected image with options at the Format Picture dialog box. Display this dialog box by clicking the Format Picture button on the Picture toolbar.
- With options at the Advanced Layout dialog box, you can specify the horizontal and vertical position of an image, choose a text wrapping style, and specify where the image is anchored. Display the Advanced Layout dialog box by clicking the Advanced button at the Format Picture dialog box with the Layout tab selected.
- To edit individual components of a clip art image, display the image in a graphic editor. The default Word graphic editor is Microsoft Word Picture. To invoke the editor, right-click an image and then click Edit Picture at the shortcut menu or select the image, click Edit, and then click Edit Picture.
- Insert objects such as autoshapes and text boxes with buttons on the Drawing toolbar. The Drawing toolbar also contains buttons for aligning, distributing, rotating, and flipping objects.
- Use the Select Objects button on the Drawing toolbar to draw a border around objects to be selected.
- A watermark is a lightened image that displays in a document. Create a watermark with an image or with text using options at the Printed Watermark dialog box.
- Use the WordArt application to distort or modify text to conform to a variety of shapes. Create WordArt text using the WordArt Gallery. Display the WordArt Gallery by clicking the Insert WordArt button on the Drawing toolbar.
- Click WordArt text and sizing handles display around the text. Use these sizing handles to increase or decrease the size. To move selected WordArt, choose a text wrapping style and then drag the text to the desired position.
- Customize WordArt using buttons on the WordArt toolbar or with buttons on the Drawing toolbar.
- Some features for formatting Web pages include themes, backgrounds, and frames.
- Apply a theme with options at the Theme dialog box. Display this dialog box by clicking Format and then Theme.

- Apply a background color to a document by clicking Format, pointing to Background, and then clicking the desired color. Click the *More Colors* option to display the Colors dialog box or click the *Fill Effects* option to display the Fill Effects dialog box.
- Insert a frame in a document using buttons on the Frames toolbar. Display this toolbar by clicking Format, pointing to Frames, and then clicking New Frames Page.
- Format Web pages with buttons on the Web Tools toolbar.
- You can save a Web page and/or text and images in a Web page as separate files. Save a Web page by clicking File on the Internet Explorer Menu bar and then clicking Save As.
- Save an image as a separate picture file by right-clicking the image and then clicking Save Picture As at the shortcut menu.

FEATURES summary

FEATURE	BUTTON	MENU	KEYBOARD
Borders and Shading dialog box		Format, Borders and Shading	
Horizontal Line dialog box		Format, Borders and Shading, Horizontal Line	
Clip Art task pane	🖼	Insert, Picture, Clip Art	
Format Picture dialog box	🖌	Format, Picture	
Microsoft Word Picture editor		Edit, Edit Picture	
Drawing toolbar	🖉	View, Toolbars, Drawing	
Printed Watermark dialog box		Format, Background, Printed Watermark	
WordArt Gallery	🅰	Insert, Picture, WordArt	
Theme dialog box		Format, Theme	
Web Tools toolbar		View, Toolbars, Web Tools	
Background color		Format, Background	
Frames toolbar		Format, Frames, New Frames Page	

CONCEPTS check

Completion: On a separate sheet of paper, indicate the correct term, command, or number for each description.

1. Use this option at the Borders and Shading dialog box with the Page Border tab selected to insert a page border containing an image.
2. Display the Horizontal Line dialog box by clicking the Horizontal Line button at this dialog box.
3. Use buttons on this toolbar to format a selected image.
4. Display the Advanced Layout dialog box by clicking the Advanced button at this dialog box with the Layout tab selected.
5. To invoke the graphic editor, right-click an image, and then click this option at the shortcut menu.
6. Insert autoshapes and text boxes with buttons on this toolbar.
7. Create a picture or text watermark with options at this dialog box.
8. Display the WordArt Gallery by clicking this button on the Drawing toolbar.
9. Save a Word document as a Web page by clicking File and then clicking this option at the drop-down menu.
10. Format a Web page with buttons on this toolbar.
11. This term refers to an adjustable pane within the window that is separate from other panes in the window.

SKILLS check

Assessment 1

1. Open **PremiumProduce**.
2. Save the document with Save As and name it **ewc3sc01**.
3. Vertically center the text on the page. *(Hint: To do this, display the Page Setup dialog box with the Layout tab selected and then change the* **Vertical alignment** *option to* **Center**.*)*
4. Insert an apple art border around the page.
5. Save, print, and then close **ewc3sc01**.

Assessment 2

1. Open **WordTravel**.
2. Save the document with Save As and name it **ewc3sc02**.
3. Insert a graphic horizontal line of your choosing between the Web address and the first paragraph of text (below the centered lines of text).
4. Save, print, and then close **ewc3sc02**.

Assessment 3

1. Open **WordComputers**.
2. Save the document with Save As and name it **ewc3sc03**.
3. Change the line spacing for the entire document to single spacing.
4. Delete the text in the document from the title COMPUTER OUTPUT DEVICES to the end of the document.
5. Insert a clip art image with the following specifications:
   a. Insert a clip art image related to "computer."
   b. Change the height of the image to 2.5 inches.
   c. Change the wrapping style to *Tight*.
   d. Change the horizontal alignment of the image to *Centered* relative to the *Margin*.
   e. Change the vertical alignment of the image to *Centered* relative to *Page*.
6. Make sure the text and image display on one page. (If text flows to a second page, change the top and/or bottom margins until the document is only one page in length.)
7. Save, print, and then close **ewc3sc03**.

Assessment 4

1. At a clear document screen, create the letterhead shown in Figure 3.21 with the following specifications:
   a. Change the paragraph alignment to center.
   b. Set *FRONT STREET* in 18-point Arial bold and set *Moving Company* in 14-point Arial bold.
   c. Draw the arrow at the left using the Striped Right Arrow autoshape. (Display this autoshape by clicking AutoShapes, pointing to Block Arrows, and then clicking Striped Right Arrow.)
   d. Add red fill to the arrow.
   e. Copy the arrow to the right and then flip the arrow as shown in Figure 3.21.
2. Save the completed document and name it **ewc3sc04**.
3. Print and then close **ewc3sc04**.

FIGURE 3.21 Assessment 4

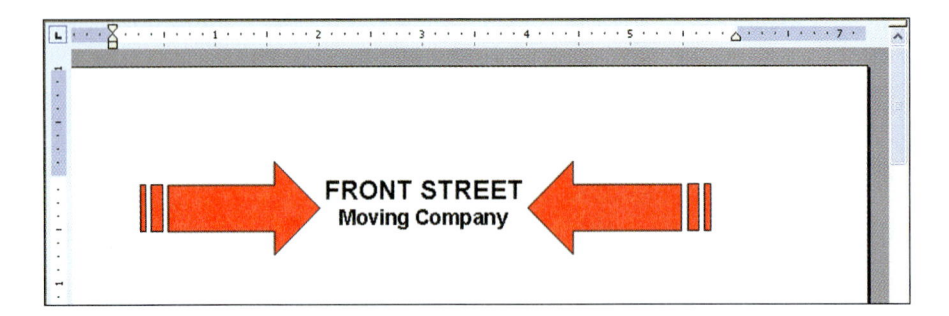

Assessment 5

1. Open **WordNotice02**.
2. Save the document with Save As and name it **ewc3sc05**.
3. Insert as a watermark the image named *laptop* that is located in the ClipArt folder on the CD that accompanies this textbook. ***(Hint: Use the Printed Watermark dialog box to insert the image as a watermark.)***
4. Save, print, and then close **ewc3sc05**.

Assessment 6

1. At a clear document screen, create the WordArt text shown in Figure 3.22 by completing the following steps:
    a. Display the WordArt Gallery.
    b. Double-click the third option from the left in the top row.
    c. At the Edit WordArt Text dialog box, type **Mountain**, press Enter, type **Ski Resort**, and then close the dialog box.
    d. Click the WordArt text to select it and then change the text wrapping to *Through*.
    e. Change the shape of the text to Triangle Up. *(Hint: Click the WordArt Shape button on the WordArt toolbar.)*
    f. Display the Format WordArt dialog box with the Size tab selected, change the height to *1.2* and the width to *2*, and then close the dialog box.
    g. Display the Format WordArt dialog box with the Layout tab selected, click *Left* in the *Horizontal alignment* section, and then close the dialog box.
    h. Change the fill color and line color to Blue. *(Hint: Do this with the Fill Color and Line Color buttons on the Drawing toolbar.)*
    i. Deselect the WordArt text.
2. Create the line below the company name with the following specifications:
    a. Use the Arrow button on the Drawing toolbar to draw the line. *(Hint: After clicking the Arrow button, press the Delete key to delete the drawing canvas.)*
    b. With the horizontal line selected, change the arrow style by clicking the Arrow Style and then clicking the second option from the bottom (Arrow Style 10).
    c. Increase the width of the line by clicking the Line Style button on the Drawing toolbar and then clicking the 4½ pt line at the pop-up menu.
    d. Change the color of the horizontal line to blue.
3. Save the document and name it **ewc3sc06**.
4. Print and then close **ewc3sc06**.

FIGURE 3.22 Assessment 6

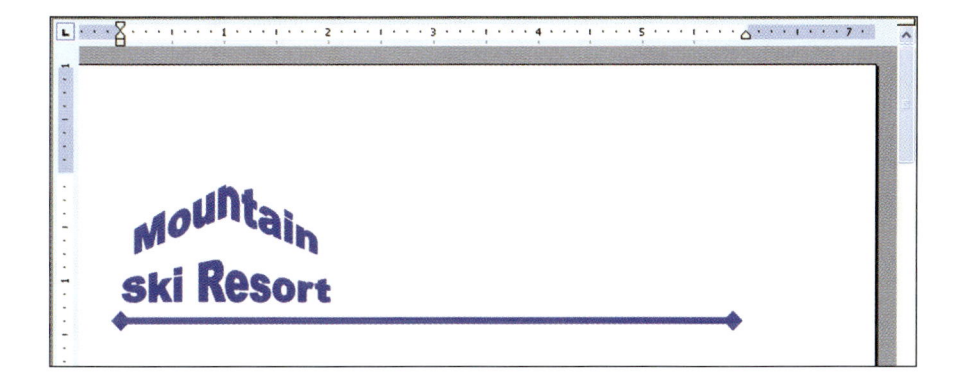

Assessment 7

1. At a clear document screen, create the WordArt text shown in Figure 3.23 with the following specifications. (Figure 3.23 displays the WordArt on the full page. Your text will appear much larger than what you see in the figure.)
    a. Change to the Print Layout view.
    b. Display the WordArt Gallery.
    c. Double-click the fifth option from the left in the top row.
    d. At the Edit WordArt Text dialog box, complete the following steps:
        1) Type **Coleman Development Corporation** and then press Enter.
        2) Type **Forest Renovation** and then press Enter.
        3) Type **and Revitalization Project**.
        4) Close the Edit WordArt Text dialog box.
    e. Click the WordArt text to select it and then change the text wrapping to *Through*.
    f. Change the shape of the text to a Button (Curve). *(Hint: Click the WordArt Shape button on the WordArt toolbar and then click the fourth option from the left in the second row.)*
    g. Display the Format WordArt dialog box with the Size tab selected, change the height and width to 6 inches, and then close the dialog box.
    h. Change the fill color to green.
    i. Change the Zoom to *Whole Page* and then drag the WordArt text so it is centered horizontally and vertically on the page.
2. Save the document and name it **ewc3sc07**.
3. Print and then close **ewc3sc07**.

FIGURE 3.23 Assessment 7

Assessment 8

1. Open **PremiumProduce**.
2. Save the document as a Web page and name it **ewc3sc08**.
3. Apply the Network theme and insert a check mark in the three check boxes located in the lower left corner of the Theme dialog box.
4. Preview the document in Web Page Preview. (If the Internet Explorer window display is small, click the Maximize button to enlarge the display.)
5. After viewing the document in the Web browser, close the browser.
6. Move the insertion point on the line immediately above the heading *Farm-fresh and Organic Produce*, press the Enter key twice, and then press the Up Arrow key once.
7. Click the Center button on the Formatting toolbar, turn on the Web Tools toolbar and then insert the following scrolling text: Order today and receive FREE two pounds of organically-grown strawberries!.
8. Add the ONESTOP sound clip to the Web page that is set on an *Infinite* loop.
9. Close the Web Tools toolbar.
10. Select *Pricing* located in the paragraph below the heading *Ordering from Premium Produce* and then insert a hyperlink to the document **PremProPricing** located in the WordChapter03E folder on your disk.
11. Save, print, and then close **ewc3sc08**.

Assessment 9

1. Open **WordTravel**.
2. Apply a background color and fill effect of your choosing.
3. Insert the following frame:
    a. Display the Frames toolbar.
    b. Insert a frame at the right side of the screen.
    c. Insert the text *Weekly Specials* in the frame and set the text in 10-point Arial. Decrease the size of the frame to fit the text.
    d. Apply a background color to the frame.
4. Select *Weekly Specials* and then insert a hyperlink to the document **TravelSpecials** located in the WordChapter03E folder on your disk.
5. Save the document and name it **ewc3sc09**.
6. Print and then close **ewc3sc09**. (The background color, fill effects, and frame will not print.)

Assessment 10

1. Make sure you are connected to the Internet and then search for information on mountain climbing.
2. Find a site that interests you and that contains at least one image (picture).
3. Save the Web page as a file named **ClimbingWebPage**.
4. Save the image as a picture and name it **ClimbingImage**. *(Hint: Right-click the image and then click Save Picture As at the pop-up menu.)*
5. Close Internet Explorer.
6. At a clear document Word screen, open the **ClimbingWebPage** file.
7. Move the insertion point to the end of the Web page and then insert your first and last name, the current date, and the current time.
8. Save, print, and then close **ClimbingWebPage**.
9. At a clear document screen, type a heading that is centered, bolded, and set in 14-point size and describes the climbing image.
10. Insert the climbing image into the document below the heading. *(Hint: Click Insert, Picture, and then From File to insert the image.)*
11. Save the document and name it **ewc3sc10**.
12. Print and then close **ewc3sc10**.

Assessment 11

1. Word includes a ***dropped caps*** feature. You can apply dropped caps to text in a document to add visual interest and appeal. Use Word's Help feature to learn about dropped caps and how to apply dropped caps formatting to text.
2. Open **WordDocument04**.
3. Save the document with Save As and name it **ewc3sc11**.
4. Create a dropped cap with the first letter of each of the three paragraphs of text.
5. Save and then print **ewc3sc11**.
6. Remove the dropped caps from the three paragraphs of text.
7. Create a dropped cap with the word *The* that begins the first paragraph of text.
8. Save, print, and then close **ewc3sc11**.

CHAPTER challenge

Case study

You are the Promotions Manager for a golf discount store, Golf-N-Go. Annual sidewalk sale days are approaching, and a flyer needs to be created to promote various golf items that will be further discounted. Create a flyer for this purpose. Include page borders, clip art, WordArt, and any other enhancements you desire. Save and then print the flyer.

HELP?

When searching for just the right picture to insert into a document, clip art has its limitations. There are other resources available. Use the Help feature to learn how to insert a graphic from the Internet. Locate an appropriate graphic from the Internet and insert it into the flyer created in the first part of the Chapter Challenge. Save and then print the flyer.

INTEGRATED

In addition to using the Internet and clip art to locate pictures, it is possible to insert a picture from a scanner or a digital camera. Scan a picture of a golf item or use a digital camera to take a picture of a golf item. Use the picture as a watermark or simply a graphic for the flyer created in the first part of the Chapter Challenge. Save and then print the flyer.

CHAPTER 4

FORMATTING WITH MACROS AND STYLES

PERFORMANCE OBJECTIVES

Upon successful completion of Chapter 4, you will be able to:
- Record, run, edit, and delete macros
- Assign a macro to a keyboard command and a toolbar
- Format a document with the AutoFormat feature
- Create, apply, modify, remove, and delete styles
- Assign a shortcut key combination to a style
- Create a cross-reference
- Navigate in documents

Word includes a number of time-saving features you can use to format documents, such as macros and styles. With macros, you can automate the formatting of a document. With styles, you can apply formatting and maintain formatting consistency in a document. In this chapter, you will also learn techniques for navigating in lengthy documents.

Creating Macros

The word *macro* was coined by computer programmers for a collection of commands used to make a large programming job easier and save time. Like a macro created for a programming job, a Word macro is a document containing recorded commands that can accomplish a task automatically and save time.

In Word, creating a macro is referred to as ***recording***. As a macro is being recorded, all of the keys pressed and the menus and dialog boxes displayed are recorded and become part of the macro. For example, you can record a macro to change the left or right margins or insert page numbering in a document. Two steps are involved in working with macros: recording a macro and running a macro. Word's macro feature can also be used to write macros. For more information on writing macros, please refer to Microsoft Word documentation.

Recording a Macro

Recording a macro involves turning on the macro recorder, performing the steps to be recorded, and then turning off the recorder. To record a macro, click Tools, point to Macro, and then click Record New Macro. You can also double-click the REC button that displays on the Status bar. This displays the Record Macro dialog box shown in Figure 4.1.

REC

Stop Recording

FIGURE 4.1   *Record Macro Dialog Box*

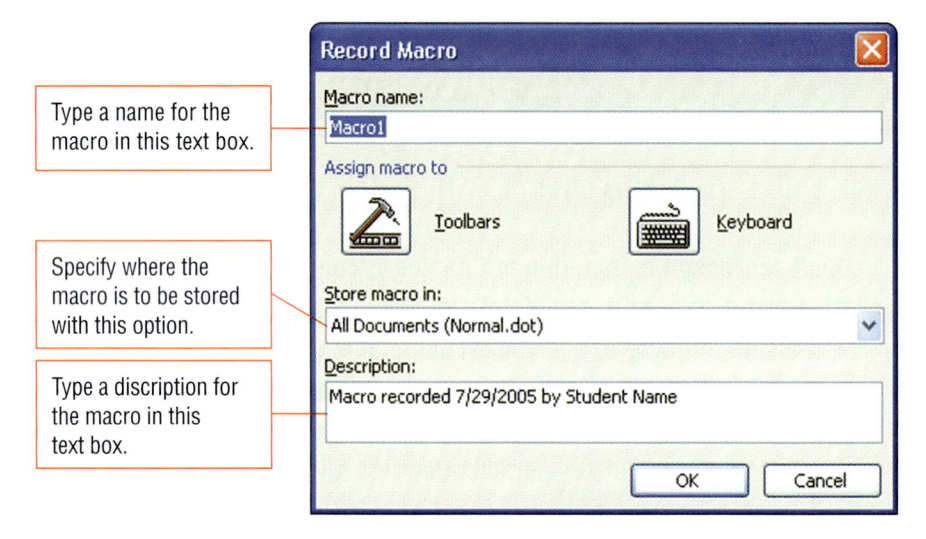

- Type a name for the macro in this text box.
- Specify where the macro is to be stored with this option.
- Type a discription for the macro in this text box.

At the Record Macro dialog box, type a name for the macro in the *Macro name* text box. A macro name must begin with a letter and can contain only letters and numbers. Type a description for the macro in the *Description* text box located at the bottom of the dialog box. A macro description can contain a maximum of 255 characters and may include spaces.

By default, Word stores a macro in the Normal template document. Macros stored in this template are available for any document based on the Normal template. In a company or school setting where computers may be networked, consider storing macros in personalized documents or templates. Specify the location for macros with the *Store macro in* option at the Record Macro dialog box (refer to Figure 4.1).

After typing the macro name, specifying where the macro is to be stored, and typing a description, click OK or press Enter to close the Record Macro dialog box. This displays the document screen with the Macro Record toolbar displayed as shown in Figure 4.2. At this screen, perform the actions to be recorded. After all steps to be recorded have been performed, stop the recording of the macro by clicking the Stop Recording button on the Macro Record toolbar, or by double-clicking the REC button on the Status bar.

HINT
Some reasons for recording a macro:
- Speed up formatting and editing
- Combine multiple commands
- Make an option in a dialog box more accessible
- Automate a series of tasks

HINT
Before recording a macro, plan the steps and commands.

HINT
When recording a macro, you can use the mouse to click commands and options, but the macro recorder does not record mouse movements on the document screen.

FIGURE 4.2 Macro Record Toolbar

Stop Recording

Pause Recording

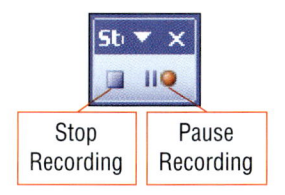

When you record macros in exercises in this chapter, you will be instructed to name the macros beginning with your initials. An exercise step may instruct you, for example, to "record a macro named XXXInd01." Insert your initials in the macro name instead of the *XXX*. Recorded macros are stored in the Normal template document by default and display at the Macros dialog box. If the computer you are using is networked, macros recorded by other students will also display at the Macros dialog box. Naming a macro with your initials will enable you to distinguish your macros from the macros of other users.

QUICK STEPS

Record a Macro
1. Click Tools, Macro, Record New Macro.
2. Type name and description for macro.
3. Click OK.
4. Complete steps to apply desired formatting.
5. Click Stop Recording button.

exercise 1

RECORDING MACROS

1. Record a macro named XXXInd01 (where your initials are used instead of *XXX*) that indents text in a paragraph .5 inch and hang indents second and subsequent lines of the paragraph by completing the following steps:
   a. At a clear document screen, double-click the REC button on the Status bar.
   b. At the Record Macro dialog box, type **XXXInd01** in the *Macro name* text box.
   c. Click inside the *Description* text box and then type **Indent and hang text in paragraph..** (If the *Description* text box contains any text, select the text first, and then type **Indent and hang text in paragraph..**)
   d. Click OK.
   e. At the document screen with the Macro Record toolbar displayed, complete the following steps:
      1) Click Format and then Paragraph.
      2) At the Paragraph dialog box, click the up-pointing arrow at the right side of the *Left* option until *0.5"* displays in the *Left* text box.
      3) Click the down-pointing arrow at the right side of the *Special* text box and then click *Hanging* at the drop-down list.
      4) Click OK or press Enter.
   f. Double-click the REC button on the Status bar.
2. Complete steps similar to those in Step 1 to create a macro named XXXInd02 that indents text in a paragraph 1 inch and hang indents second and subsequent lines of the paragraph.

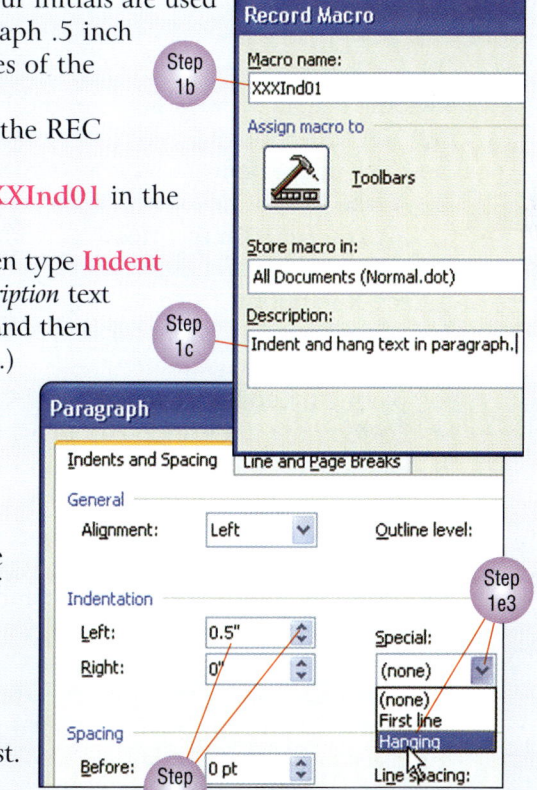

WORD Formatting with Macros and Styles E129

3. Record a macro named XXXFormat01 that changes the top margin to 1.5 inches and the left and right margins to 1 inch by completing the following steps:
   a. At a clear document screen, click Tools, point to Macro, and then click Record New Macro.
   b. At the Record Macro dialog box, type **XXXFormat01** in the *Macro name* text box.
   c. Click in the *Description* text box (or select existing text in the *Description* text box) and then type **Change top, left, and right margins.**.
   d. Click OK.
   e. At the document screen with the Macro Record toolbar displayed, change the top margin to 1.5 inches and the left and right margins to 1 inch. (Do this at the Page Setup dialog box with the Margins tab selected.)
   f. Click the Stop Recording button on the Macro Record toolbar.
4. Close the document without saving it.

QUICK STEPS

Run a Macro
1. Click Tools, Macro, Macros.
2. Click desired macro.
3. Click Run button.

Running a Macro

After a macro has been recorded, it can be run in a document. To run a macro, click Tools, point to Macro, and then click Macros. At the Macros dialog box, click the desired macro name in the list box, and then click the Run button. You can also just double-click the desired macro name in the list box.

exercise 2

RUNNING MACROS

1. Open **WordSurvey**.
2. Save the document with Save As and name it **ewc4x02**.
3. Run the XXXFormat01 macro by completing the following steps:
   a. Click Tools, point to Macro, and then click Macros.
   b. At the Macros dialog box, click *XXXFormat01* in the *Macro name* list box, and then click the Run button. 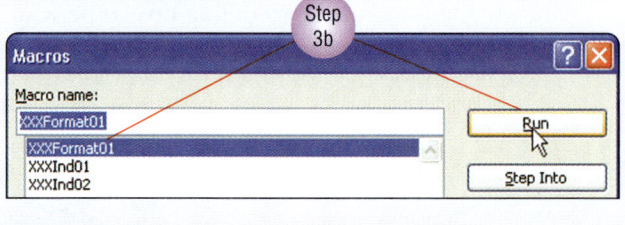
4. Run the XXXInd01 macro for the first numbered paragraph by completing the following steps:
   a. Position the insertion point anywhere in the paragraph that begins with *1*.
   b. Click Tools, point to Macro, and then click Macros.
   c. At the Macros dialog box, double-click *XXXInd01* in the list box.
5. Complete steps similar to those in Step 4 to run the XXXInd01 macro for each of the numbered paragraphs (just the numbered paragraphs, not the lettered paragraphs).
6. Run the XXXInd02 macro for the lettered paragraphs (a through d) after the first numbered paragraph by completing the following steps:
   a. Select paragraphs a through d below the first numbered paragraph.
   b. Click Tools, point to Macro, and then click Macros.
   c. At the Macros dialog box, double-click *XXXInd02* in the list box.

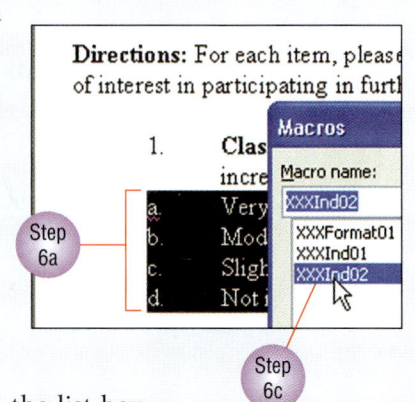

7. Complete steps similar to those in Step 6 to run the macro for the lettered paragraphs below each of the numbered paragraphs.
8. Save, print, and then close **ewc4x02**.

Pausing and then Resuming a Macro

When recording a macro, you can temporarily suspend the recording, perform actions that are not recorded, and then resume recording the macro. To pause the recording of a macro, click the Pause Recording button on the Macro Record toolbar. To resume recording the macro, click the Resume Recorder button (previously the Pause Recording button).

Pause Recording

Deleting a Macro

If you no longer need a macro, delete it at the Macros dialog box. At the Macros dialog box, click the macro name in the list box, and then click the Delete button. At the message asking if you want to delete the macro, click Yes. Click the Close button to close the Macros dialog box.

QUICK STEPS

Delete a Macro
1. Click Tools, Macro, Macros.
2. Click desired macro.
3. Click Delete button.
4. Click Yes.
5. Click Close button.

exercise 3

DELETING MACROS

1. At a clear document screen, delete the XXXFormat01 (where your initials display instead of the *XXX*) macro by completing the following steps:
   a. Click Tools, point to Macro, and then click Macros.
   b. At the Macros dialog box, click *XXXFormat01* in the list box.
   c. Click the Delete button.
   d. At the message asking if you want to delete XXXFormat01, click Yes.
   e. Click the Close button to close the Macros dialog box.
2. Close the document.

Assigning a Macro a Keyboard Command

If you use a macro on a regular basis, you may want to assign it a keyboard command. To run a macro that has been assigned a keyboard command, all you do is press the keys assigned to the macro. A macro can be assigned a keyboard command with a letter plus Alt + Ctrl, Ctrl + Shift, or Alt + Shift. Word has already used many combinations for Word functions. For example, pressing Ctrl + Shift + A changes selected text to all capital letters.

Assign a keyboard command to a macro at the Record Macro dialog box. In Exercise 4 you will record a macro and then assign the macro to a keyboard command. If you delete the macro, the keyboard command is also deleted. This allows you to use the key combination again.

QUICK STEPS

Assign Macro a Keyboard Command
1. Click Tools, Macro, Record New Macro.
2. Type name and description for macro.
3. Click Keyboard button.
4. Press shortcut keys.
5. Click Assign button.
6. Click Close button.

HINT
If you use a macro on a consistent basis, assign it to a toolbar or assign shortcut keys to the macro.

WORD

Formatting with Macros and Styles

exercise 4
RECORDING AND ASSIGNING A KEYBOARD COMMAND TO A MACRO

1. Record a macro named XXXLtrhd01 (where your initials are used instead of the *XXX*) that contains the letterhead text shown in Figure 4.3 and assign it the keyboard command, Alt + Shift + S by completing the following steps:
    a. At a clear document screen, double-click the REC button on the Status bar.
    b. At the Record Macro dialog box, type **XXXLtrhd01** in the *Macro name* text box.
    c. Click in the *Description* text box (or select existing text in the *Description* text box) and then type **St. Francis Letterhead**.
    d. Click the Keyboard button.
    e. At the Customize Keyboard dialog box with the insertion point positioned in the *Press new shortcut key* text box, press Alt + Shift + S.
    f. Click the Assign button.
    g. Click the Close button.
    h. At the document screen with the Macro Record toolbar displayed, create the letterhead shown in Figure 4.3 by completing the following steps:
        1) Press Ctrl + E.
        2) Type **ST. FRANCIS MEDICAL CENTER**.
        3) Press Enter and then type **300 Blue Ridge Boulevard**.
        4) Press Enter and then type **Kansas City, MO 63009**.
        5) Press Enter and then type **(816) 555-2000**.
        6) Press Enter.
        7) Press Ctrl + L to return the paragraph alignment to left.
        8) Press Enter.
        9) Select (using the keyboard) the hospital name, address, and telephone number and then change the font to 18-point Goudy Old Style bold (or a similar serif typeface).
        10) Deselect the text (using the keyboard).
        11) Move the insertion point to the end of the document.
    i. Click the Stop Recording button on the Macro Record toolbar.
2. Close the document without saving changes.
3. At a clear document screen, run the XXXLtrhd01 macro by pressing Alt + Shift + S.
4. With the insertion point a double space below the letterhead, insert the document named **WordLetter01** by completing the following steps:
    a. Click Insert and then File.
    b. At the Insert File dialog box, navigate to the WordChapter04E folder on your disk and then double-click **WordLetter01**.

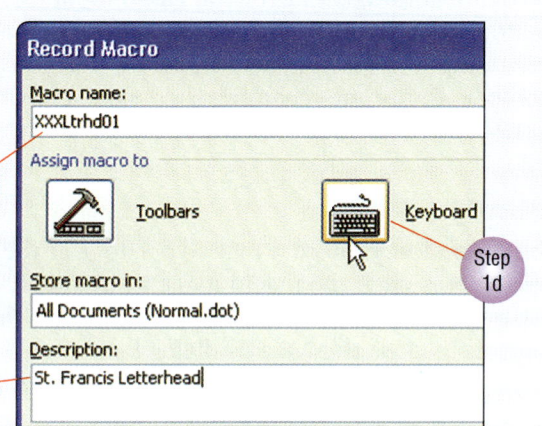

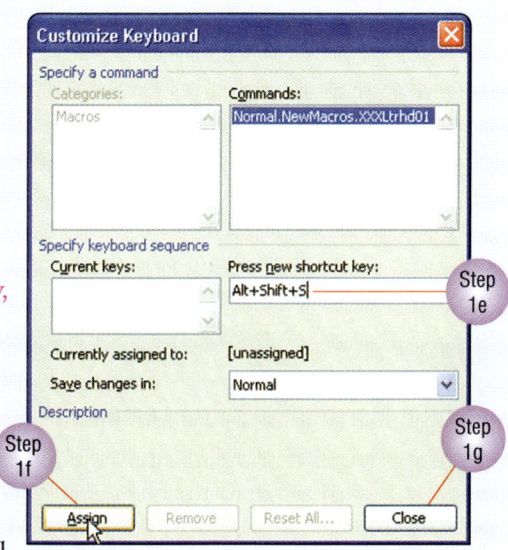

5. Make the following changes to the document:
    a. Change the left and right margins to 1 inch.
    b. Run the XXXInd01 macro for the numbered paragraphs.
    c. Run the XXXInd02 macro for the lettered paragraphs.
6. Save the document and name it **ewc4x04**.
7. Print and then close **ewc4x04**.

FIGURE 4.3 *Exercise 4*

> ### ST. FRANCIS MEDICAL CENTER
> 300 Blue Ridge Boulevard
> Kansas City, MO 63009
> (816) 555-2000

Assigning a Macro to the Toolbar

Add a macro that you use on a regular basis to a toolbar. To run a macro from a toolbar, just click the button. In Exercise 5, you will assign a macro to the Standard toolbar. A macro can be assigned to any toolbar that is displayed. For example, a macro can be assigned to the Formatting toolbar if that toolbar is displayed on the document screen.

An existing macro can also be assigned to a toolbar. To do this, display the Customize dialog box with the Commands tab selected as shown in Figure 4.4. Display this dialog box by clicking the Toolbars button at the Record Macro dialog box. You can also display this dialog box by clicking Tools, clicking Customize, and then clicking the Commands tab.

QUICK STEPS

Assign Macro to a Toolbar
1. Click Tools, Macro, Record New Macro.
2. Type name and description for macro.
3. Click Toolbars button.
4. Drag macro to desired toolbar.
5. Click Close button.

FIGURE 4.4 *Customize Dialog Box with Commands Tab Selected*

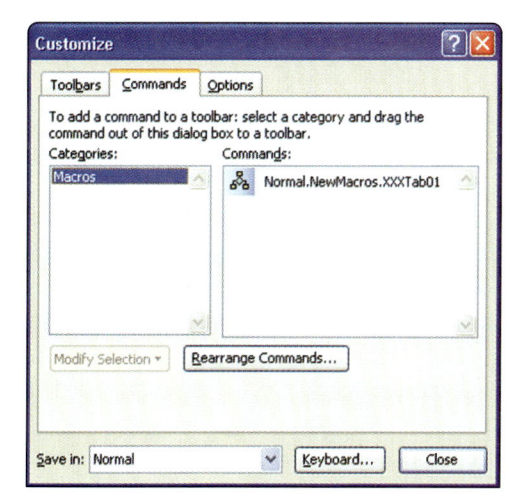

WORD — Formatting with Macros and Styles — E133

At the Customize dialog box with the Commands tab selected, click *Macros* in the *Categories* list box. Position the arrow pointer on the desired macro in the *Commands* list box, hold down the left mouse button, drag the outline of the button to the desired location on the desired toolbar, and then release the mouse button. Click the Close button to close the Customize dialog box.

A macro button can be removed from a toolbar with the Customize dialog box open. To do this, display the Customize dialog box. Position the arrow pointer on the button to be removed, hold down the left mouse button, drag the outline of the button off the toolbar, and then release the mouse button. Click Close to close the Customize dialog box. When a macro button is removed from a toolbar, the macro is not deleted. Delete the macro at the Macros dialog box.

exercise 5

ASSIGNING A MACRO TO THE STANDARD TOOLBAR

1. At a clear document screen, create a macro named XXXTab01 (where your initials are used instead of the *XXX*) and assign it to the Standard toolbar by completing the following steps:
    a. Double-click the REC button on the Status bar.
    b. At the Record Macro dialog box, type **XXXTab01** in the *Macro name* text box.
    c. Click in the *Description* text box (or select text) and then type **Set left tab at .5 and right tab with leaders at 5.5.**.
    d. Click the Toolbars button.
    e. At the Customize dialog box with the Commands tab selected, position the arrow pointer on the XXXTab01 macro in the *Commands* list box. (This macro name may display as *Normal.NewMacros.XXXTab01*.) Hold down the left mouse button, drag the mouse pointer with the button attached between the Spelling and Grammar button and the Research button on the Standard toolbar, and then release the mouse button.
    f. Shorten the name of the macro by completing the following steps:
        1) With the Customize dialog box still displayed, position the arrow pointer on the XXXTab01 button on the Standard toolbar, and then click the *right* mouse button.

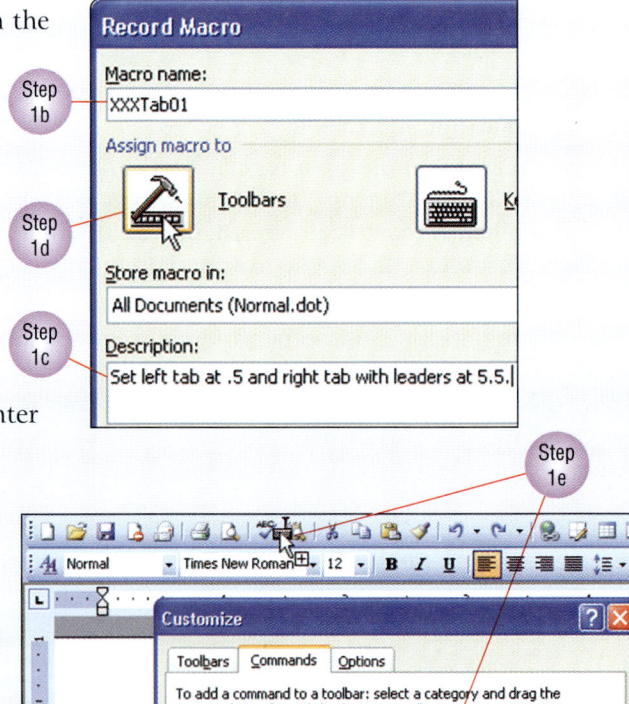

2) At the shortcut menu that displays, click the *Name* option.
3) Type **T01** in the *Name* text box, and then press Enter.
g. Click the Close button to close the Customize dialog box.
h. At the document screen with the Macro Record toolbar displayed, complete the necessary steps to set a left tab at the .5-inch mark and a right tab with preceding dot leaders at the 5.5-inch mark. (You must do this at the Tabs dialog box, not on the Ruler.)
i. After setting the tabs, click the Stop Recording button on the Macro Record toolbar.
2. Close the document without saving it.
3. At a clear document screen, create the document shown in Figure 4.5 by completing the following steps:
a. Click the T01 button on the Standard toolbar.
b. Type the text as shown in Figure 4.5. (Type the first column of text at the first tab stop, not the left margin.)
4. Save the document and name it **ewc4x05**.
5. Print and then close **ewc4x05**.
6. Remove the T01 button from the Standard toolbar by completing the following steps:
a. At a clear document screen, click Tools and then Customize.
b. At the Customize dialog box, position the arrow pointer on the T01 button on the Standard toolbar, hold down the left mouse button, drag the outline of the button off the toolbar, and then release the mouse button.
c. Click the Close button to close the Customize dialog box.
7. Close the clear document screen.

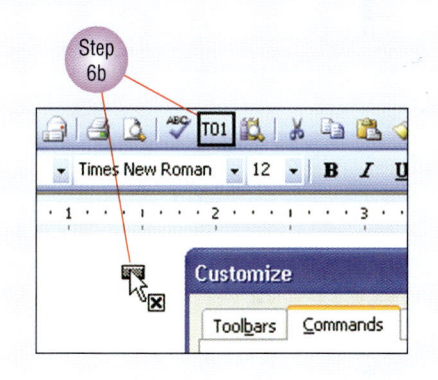

FIGURE 4.5 Exercise 5

STRADFORD FUNDS CORPORATION

Kelly Millerton .... Chief Executive Officer

Lyle Harmstead .... President

Alicia Wyatt .... Vice President

Alexander Li .... Vice President

Danielle Cohen .... Vice President

Recording a Macro with Fill-in Fields

In Chapter 1, you inserted a Fill-in field in a document that prompted the operator to insert information at the keyboard during a merge. A Fill-in field can also be inserted in a macro that requires input from the keyboard. To insert a Fill-in field in a macro, begin the recording of the macro. At the point where the Fill-in field is to be inserted, click Insert and then Field. At the Field dialog box with *(All)* selected in the *Categories* list box as shown in Figure 4.6, scroll down the *Field names* list box until *Fill-in* is visible and then click it. Add information telling the operator what text to enter at the keyboard by clicking in the *Description* text box and then typing the prompt message surrounded by parentheses. When the macro is run, type the desired text specified by the prompt message.

FIGURE 4.6 *Field Dialog Box*

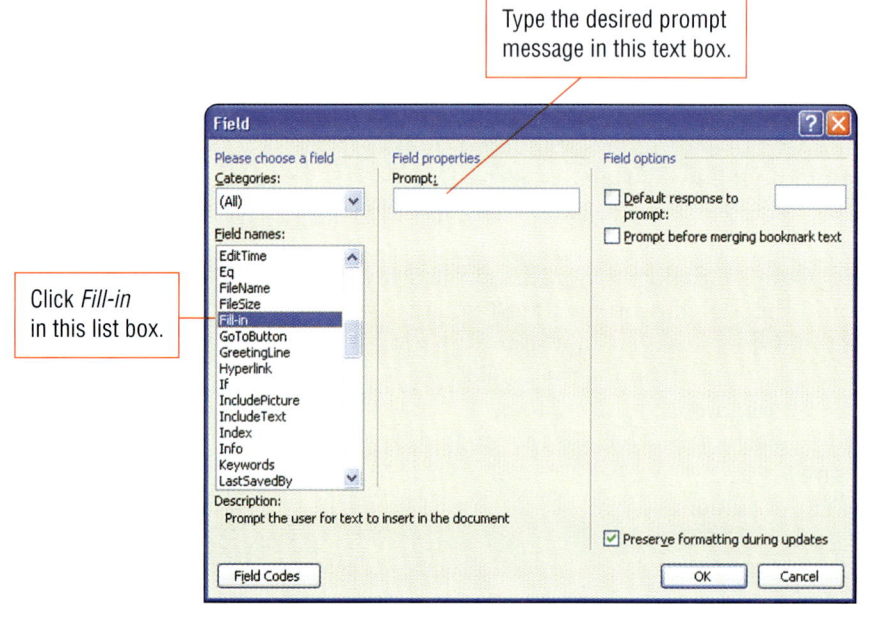

Type the desired prompt message in this text box.

Click *Fill-in* in this list box.

exercise 6

RECORDING A MACRO WITH FILL-IN FIELDS

1. At a clear document screen, record a macro for inserting notary signature information by completing the following steps:
   a. Double-click the REC button on the Status bar.
   b. At the Record Macro dialog box, type **XXXNotary** (where your initials are used instead of the *XXX*) in the *Macro name* text box.
   c. Click in the *Description* text box (or select existing text) and then type **Notary signature information.**.
   d. Click the Keyboard button.
   e. At the Customize Keyboard dialog box with the insertion point positioned in the *Press new shortcut key* text box, press Alt + Ctrl + A.
   f. Click the Assign button.
   g. Click the Close button.

h. At the document screen with the Macro Record toolbar displayed, type the text shown in Figure 4.7 up to the text *(name of person)*. (Do not type the text *(name of person)*.)
i. Insert a Fill-in field by completing the following steps:
   1) Click Insert and then Field.
   2) At the Field dialog box with *(All)* displayed in the *Categories* option box, scroll down the *Field names* list box until *Fill-in* is visible and then click it.
   3) Click in the *Prompt* text box (below *Field properties*) and then type **Type name of person signing**.
   4) Click the OK button.
   5) At the Microsoft Office Word dialog box, type **(name of person)** in the text box, and then click OK.
j. Continue typing the notary signature information shown in Figure 4.7 up to the text *(day)* and then insert a Fill-in field by completing steps similar to those in Step 1i that tells the operator to type the current day.
k. Continue typing the notary signature information shown in Figure 4.7 up to the text *(month)* and then insert a Fill-in field by completing steps similar to those in Step 1i that tells the operator to type the current month.
l. Continue typing the notary signature information shown in Figure 4.7 up to the text *(expiration date)* and then insert a Fill-in field by completing steps similar to those in Step 1i that tells the operator to type the expiration date.
m. When all of the notary signature information is typed, end the recording of the macro by double-clicking the REC button on the Status bar.
2. Close the document without saving it.

FIGURE

4.7 **Exercise 6**

STATE OF CALIFORNIA   )
) ss.
COUNTY OF LOS ANGELES   )

On this day personally appeared before me (name of person), known to me to be the individual described in and who executed the aforesaid instrument, and acknowledged that he/she signed as his/her free and voluntary act and deed for the uses and purposes therein mentioned.
   Given under my hand and official seal this (day) of (month), 2005.

_____
NOTARY PUBLIC in and for the State of California
My appointment expires (expiration date)

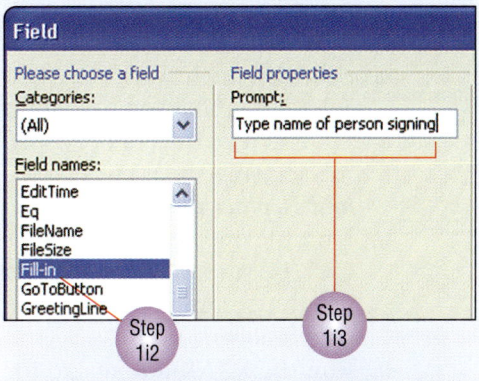

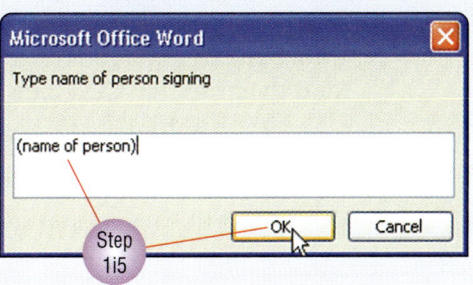

exercise 7

RUNNING A MACRO WITH FILL-IN FIELDS

1. Open **WordLegal01**.
2. Save the document with Save As and name it **ewc4x07**.
3. Complete the following find and replaces:
   a. Find all occurrences of *NAME* and replace with *LOREN HOUSTON*. (Be sure to replace only the occurrences of *NAME* in all uppercase letters. **Hint: Expand the Find and Replace dialog box and insert a check mark in the** Match case **option.**)
   b. Find the one occurrence of *ADDRESS* and replace with *102 Marine Drive, Los Angeles, CA*. (Be sure to replace only the occurrence of *ADDRESS* in all uppercase letters and not the occurrence of *address* in all lowercase letters.)
4. Run the following macros:
   a. Run the XXXInd01 macro for the numbered paragraphs and the XXXInd02 macro for the lettered paragraphs.
   b. Move the insertion point to the end of the document a double space below the text and then run the XXXNotary macro by completing the following steps:
      1) Press Alt + Ctrl + A.
      2) When the macro stops and prompts you for the name of person signing, type **SYLVIA WHITT**, and then click OK.
      3) When the macro stops and prompts you for the day, type **12th**, and then click OK.
      4) When the macro stops and prompts you for the month, type **March**, and then click OK.
      5) When the macro stops and prompts you for the expiration date, type **12/31/05**, and then click OK.
5. Save, print, and then close **ewc4x07**.

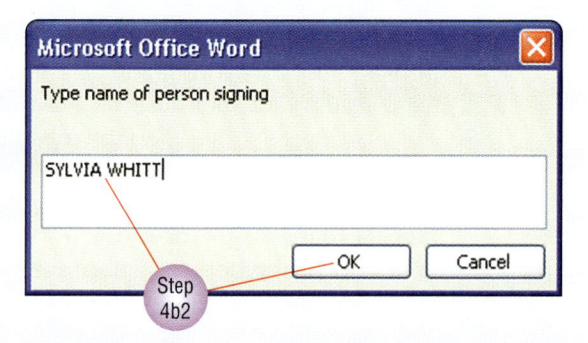

Editing a Macro

HINT
Word records a macro as a series of commands in Visual Basic for Applications (VBA).

In Word, a macro is created with Visual Basic and can be edited using the Visual Basic Editor. To edit a macro, display the Macros dialog box, select the macro to be edited, and then click the Edit button. This displays the macro in the Visual Basic Editor as shown in Figure 4.8. (The macro displayed in Figure 4.8 is the one you will be creating and then editing in Exercise 8.)

FIGURE

4.8 Visual Basic Editor

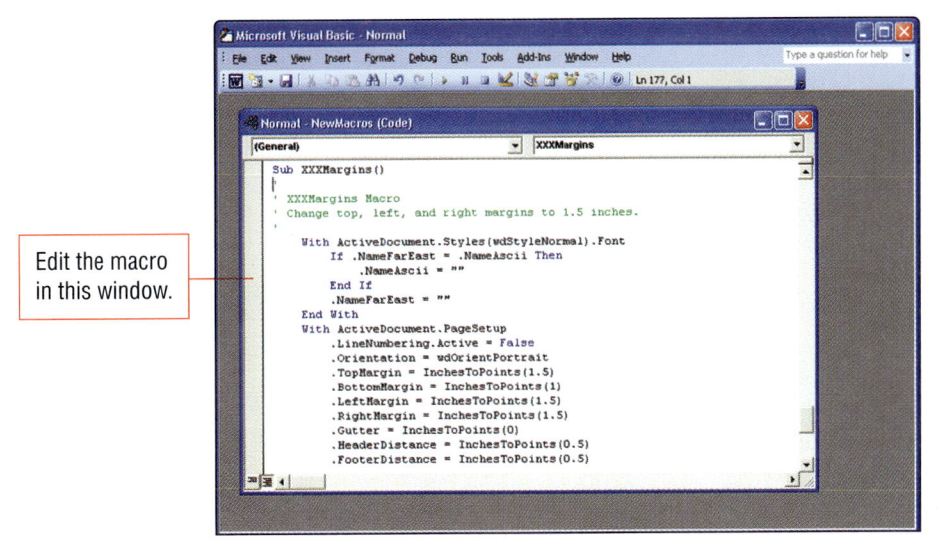

Edit the macro in this window.

```
Sub XXXMargins()
'
' XXXMargins Macro
' Change top, left, and right margins to 1.5 inches.
'
    With ActiveDocument.Styles(wdStyleNormal).Font
        If .NameFarEast = .NameAscii Then
            .NameAscii = ""
        End If
        .NameFarEast = ""
    End With
    With ActiveDocument.PageSetup
        .LineNumbering.Active = False
        .Orientation = wdOrientPortrait
        .TopMargin = InchesToPoints(1.5)
        .BottomMargin = InchesToPoints(1)
        .LeftMargin = InchesToPoints(1.5)
        .RightMargin = InchesToPoints(1.5)
        .Gutter = InchesToPoints(0)
        .HeaderDistance = InchesToPoints(0.5)
        .FooterDistance = InchesToPoints(0.5)
```

HINT
If you make a mistake while recording a macro, the corrections you make will also be recorded.

QUICK STEPS

Edit a Macro
1. Click Tools, Macro, Macros.
2. Click desired macro.
3. Click Edit button.
4. Make desired changes in Visual Basic Editor.
5. Click Save Normal button.
6. Click File, Close and Return to Microsoft Word.

When you edit a macro, you can remove unwanted steps from the list box, add steps, or change existing steps. When all changes are made, click the Save Normal button on the Visual Basic Editor Standard toolbar (third button from the left) or click File and then Save Normal. Close the Visual Basic Editor by clicking File and then Close and Return to Microsoft Word.

exercise 8

RECORDING, RUNNING, AND EDITING A MACRO

1. At a clear document screen, record a macro that changes the top, left, and right margins by completing the following steps:
    a. Double-click the REC button on the Status bar.
    b. At the Record Macro dialog box, type **XXXMargins** (where your initials are used instead of the *XXX*) in the *Macro name* text box.
    c. Click in the *Description* text box (or select existing text) and then type **Change margins in document.**.
    d. Click OK.
    e. At the document screen with the Macro Record toolbar displayed, complete the following steps:
        1) Click File and then Page Setup.
        2) At the Page Setup dialog box with the Margins tab selected, change the top, left, and right margins to 1.5 inches.
        3) Click OK to close the dialog box.
    f. Turn off recording by double-clicking the REC button on the Status bar.
2. Close the document without saving it.
3. Open **WordReport03**.
4. Save the document with Save As and name it **ewc4x08**.
5. Run the XXXMargins macro by completing the following steps:
    a. Display the Macros dialog box.
    b. At the Macros dialog box, double-click *XXXMargins* in the list box.
6. Save and then print **ewc4x08**.

Formatting with Macros and Styles

7. With **ewc4x08** still open, edit the XXXMargins macro so it changes the left and right margins to 1 inch by completing the following steps:
   a. Display the Macros dialog box.
   b. At the Macros dialog box, click *XXXMargins* in the list box, and then click the Edit button.
   c. At the Visual Basic Editor, make the following changes:
      1) Edit the step *.LeftMargin = InchesToPoints(1.5)* so it displays as *.LeftMargin = InchesToPoints(1)*.
      2) Edit the step *.RightMargin = InchesToPoints(1.5)* so it displays as *.RightMargin = InchesToPoints(1)*.
   d. Click the Save Normal button on the Visual Basic Editor Standard toolbar (third button from the left).
   e. Close the Visual Basic Editor by clicking File and then Close and Return to Microsoft Word.
8. Run the XXXMargins macro.
9. Save, print, and then close **ewc4x08**.

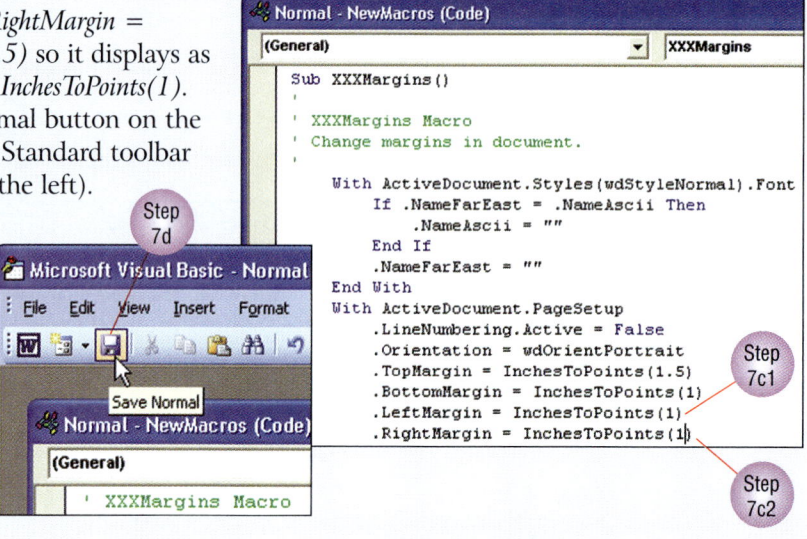

Formatting Text with Styles

A Word document, by default, is based on the Normal template document. Within a Normal template document, a Normal style is applied to text by default. This Normal style sets text in the default font (this may vary depending on what you have selected or what printer you are using), uses left alignment and single spacing, and turns on the Widow/Orphan control. In addition to this Normal style, other predesigned styles are available in a document based on the Normal template document. These styles can be displayed by clicking the down-pointing arrow to the right of the Style button on the Formatting toolbar.

Other template documents also contain predesigned styles. If you choose a different template document from the Templates dialog box, click the down-pointing arrow to the right of the Style button on the Formatting toolbar to display the names of styles available for that particular template document.

Styles can be changed and/or applied to text in three ways. The quickest way to apply styles to text in a document is with Word's AutoFormat feature. The advantage to using AutoFormat is that Word automatically applies the styles without you having to select them. The disadvantage is that you have less control over the styles that are applied.

Another method you can use to apply styles is to select a new template at the Style Gallery dialog box. The advantage to this is that you can preview your document as it will appear if formatted with various templates, and then apply

HINT Use a style to apply a group of formats at one time.

the desired template. The disadvantage is that you have less control over the selection of styles.

A third method for applying styles to text is to make changes to those styles available in the template upon which your document is based. The advantage to this method is that you can format a document any way you want by creating and selecting styles. The disadvantage is that you have to create and/or select a style for each element in the document that you want formatted.

Formatting with AutoFormat

Word provides a variety of predesigned styles in the Normal template document that can be applied to text in a document. With this feature, called AutoFormat, Word goes through a document paragraph by paragraph and applies appropriate styles. For example, Word changes the font and size for heading text and adds bullets to listed items. The formatting is done automatically; all you do is sit back and watch Word do the work.

Format a document by displaying the AutoFormat dialog box shown in Figure 4.9. To display this dialog box, click Format and then AutoFormat. At the AutoFormat dialog box with the *AutoFormat now* option selected, click OK. This applies formatting to the open document.

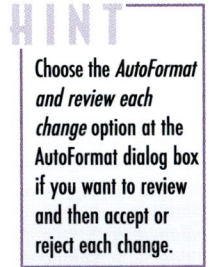

HINT
Choose the *AutoFormat and review each change* option at the AutoFormat dialog box if you want to review and then accept or reject each change.

FIGURE 4.9 AutoFormat Dialog Box

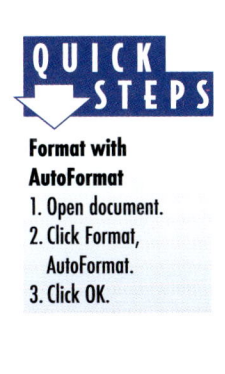

QUICK STEPS

Format with AutoFormat
1. Open document.
2. Click Format, AutoFormat.
3. Click OK.

exercise 9

FORMATTING A DOCUMENT WITH AUTOFORMAT

1. Open **WordReport01**.
2. Save the document with Save As and name it **ewc4x09**.
3. Automatically format the document by completing the following steps:
   a. Click Format and then AutoFormat.
   b. At the AutoFormat dialog box, make sure the *AutoFormat now* option is selected (if not, click this option), and then click OK.
4. Save, print, and then close **ewc4x09**.

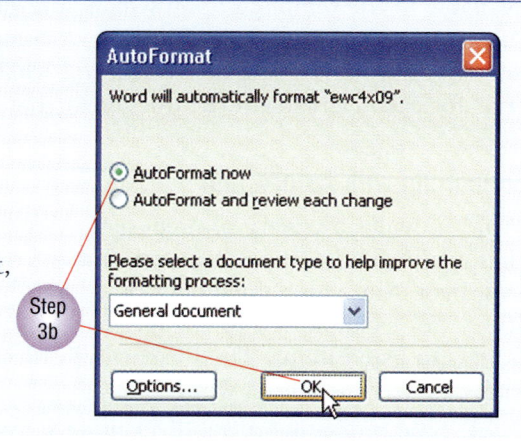

Step 3b

Creating Styles

If all of the styles predesigned by Word do not contain the formatting you desire, you can create your own style. A style can be created in two ways: You can either apply the desired formatting instructions to a paragraph and then save those instructions in a style, or you can specify the formatting instructions for a particular style without applying them to text. The first method is useful if you want to see how text appears with certain formatting instructions applied. The second method is often used when you know the particular format that you want to use for certain paragraphs.

When you create your own style, you must give the style a name. When naming a style, avoid using the names already used by Word. The list of style names will display in the *Styles* list box at the Style dialog box if *All styles* is selected in the *List* text box. When naming a style, try to name it something that gives you an idea what the style will accomplish. Consider the following when naming a style:

- A style name can contain a maximum of 213 characters.
- A style name can contain spaces and commas.
- A style name is case-sensitive. Uppercase and lowercase letters can be used.
- Do not use the backslash (\), braces ({}), or a semicolon (;) when naming a style.

Creating a Style by Example

QUICK STEPS

Create Style by Example
1. Position insertion point in text containing desired formatting.
2. Click down-pointing arrow at right of Style button.
3. Type style name.
4. Press Enter.

Create a style by formatting text first and then using the Style button on the Formatting toolbar or the New Style dialog box to create the style. To do this, position the insertion point in a paragraph of text containing the formatting you wish to include in the style, and then click the down-pointing arrow to the right of the Style button on the Formatting toolbar. Type a unique name for the style and then press Enter. This creates the style and also displays the style in the Style button. The new style will be visible in the Style drop-down list from the Formatting toolbar as well as the Style dialog box.

You can also create a style by example using the New Style dialog box. To do this, position the insertion point in a paragraph of text containing the formatting you wish to include in the style and then click the Styles and Formatting button on the Formatting toolbar (or click Format and then Styles and Formatting). At the Styles and Formatting task pane, click the New Style button. At the New Style dialog box, type a name for the style in the *Name* text box, and then click OK.

Styles and Formatting

exercise 10 — CREATING STYLES BY EXAMPLE

1. Open **WordStyle**.
2. Save the document with Save As and name it **Sty01**.
3. Create a style by example named Title1 by completing the following steps:
    a. Position the insertion point anywhere in the title *TITLE OF DOCUMENT*.
    b. Click the down-pointing arrow to the right of the Style button on the Formatting toolbar.
    c. Type **Title1** and then press Enter.
4. Create a style by example named Subtitle1 using the *Subtitle of Document* text by completing steps similar to those in Step 3.
5. Select all of the text in the document and then delete it. (This removes the text but keeps the styles you created.)
6. Save and then close **Sty01**.

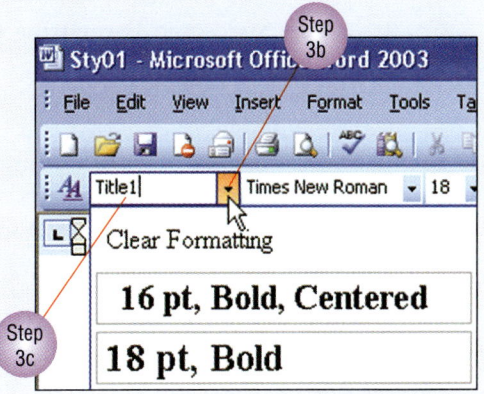

Creating a Style Using the New Style Dialog Box

You can create a style before using it rather than creating it by example. To do this, use options from the New Style dialog box shown in Figure 4.10. To display the New Style dialog box, click the New Style button in the Styles and Formatting task pane. At the New Style dialog box, type a name for the style in the *Name* text box, and specify whether you are creating a paragraph or character style at the *Style type* option. Click the Format button and then click the desired formatting options.

QUICK STEPS

Create Style Using New Style Dialog Box
1. Display Styles and Formatting task pane.
2. Click New Style button.
3. Use options at New Style dialog box to select desired formatting.
4. Click OK.

FIGURE
4.10   **New Style Dialog Box**

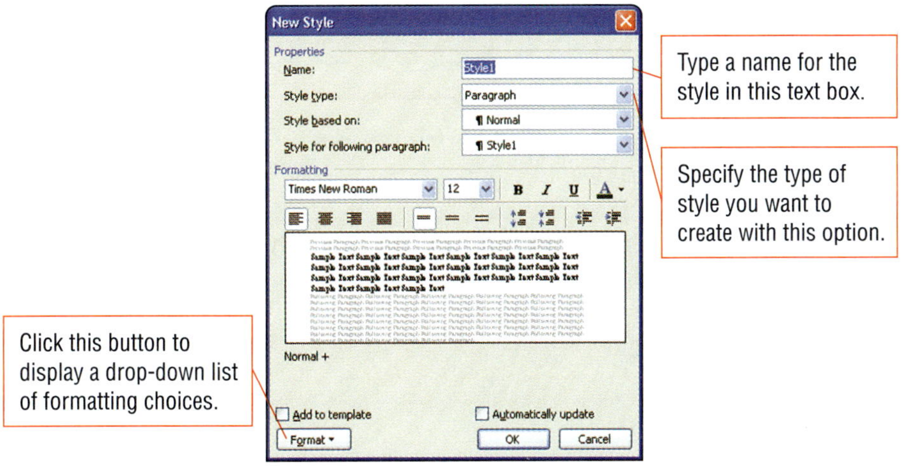

Click this button to display a drop-down list of formatting choices.

Type a name for the style in this text box.

Specify the type of style you want to create with this option.

WORD
Formatting with Macros and Styles   E143

exercise 11
CREATING STYLES AT THE NEW STYLES DIALOG BOX

1. Open **Sty01**.
2. Using the New Style dialog box, create a style named Indent1 that indents text .5 inch and adds 12 points of space after the paragraph by completing the following steps:
    a. Click the Styles and Formatting button on the Formatting toolbar.
    b. At the Styles and Formatting task pane, click the New Style button.
    c. At the New Style dialog box, type **Indent1** in the *Name* text box.
    d. Click the Format button that displays toward the bottom of the dialog box and then click Paragraph at the drop-down menu.
    e. At the Paragraph dialog box, click the up-pointing arrow to the right of the *Left* text box until *0.5"* displays in the text box.
    f. Click the up-pointing arrow to the right of the *After* text box until *12 pt* displays in the text box.
    g. Click OK to close the Paragraph dialog box.
    h. Click OK to close the New Style dialog box. 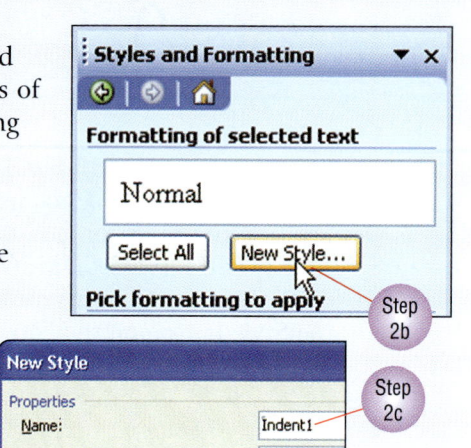 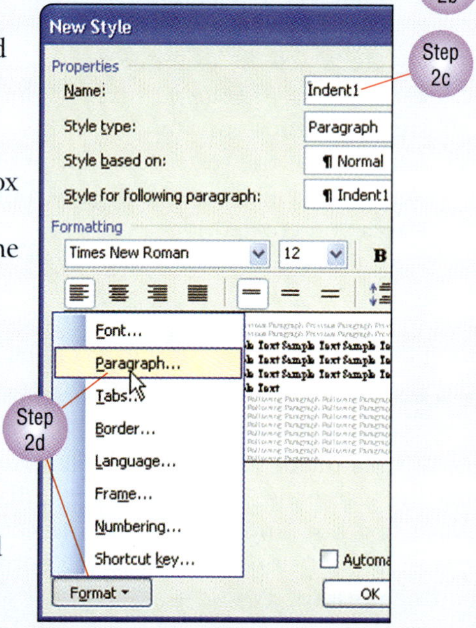
3. Using the New Style dialog box, create a style named Font1 that changes the font to Bookman Old Style by completing the following steps:
    a. Click the New Style button in the Styles and Formatting task pane.
    b. At the New Style dialog box, type **Font1** in the *Name* text box.
    c. Click the down-pointing arrow at the right side of the *Style type* text box and then click *Character* at the drop-down list.
    d. Click the Format button that displays toward the bottom of the dialog box and then click Font at the drop-down menu.
    e. At the Font dialog box, click *Bookman Old Style* (or a similar serif typeface) in the *Font* list box, *Regular* in the *Font style* list box, and *12* in the *Size* list box.
    f. Click OK to close the Font dialog box.
    g. Click OK to close the New Style dialog box.
    h. Close the Styles and Formatting task pane. 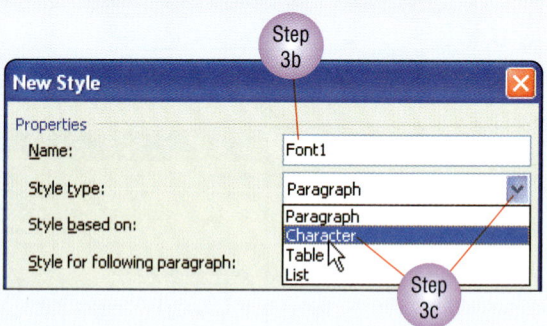
4. Save and then close **Sty01**.

E144 Chapter Four WORD

Applying a Style

A style can be applied to the paragraph where the insertion point is positioned. You can also select several paragraphs and then apply a paragraph style. If you are applying a style that contains character formatting, you must select the text first, and then apply the style. A style can be applied using the Style button on the Formatting toolbar or the Styles and Formatting task pane.

To apply a style using the Style button, position the insertion point in the paragraph to which you want the style applied, or select the text, and then click the down-pointing arrow to the right of the Style button. At the drop-down list of styles, click the desired style. To apply a style using the Styles and Formatting task pane, display the task pane, and then click the desired style in the *Pick formatting to apply* list box.

QUICK STEPS

Apply a Style
1. Position insertion point at desired location.
2. Click down-pointing arrow at right of Style button.
3. Click desired style at drop-down list.

OR
1. Position insertion point at desired location.
2. Display Styles and Formatting task pane.
3. Click desired style in *Pick formatting to apply* list box.

exercise 12

APPLYING STYLES IN A DOCUMENT

1. Open **Sty01**.
2. Save the document with Save As and name it **ewc4x12**.
3. Insert the document named **WordQuiz01** into the **ewc4x12** document. *(Hint: Use the File option from the Insert drop-down menu to do this.)*
4. Apply a style to the title by completing the following steps:
   a. Position the insertion point on any character in the title *CHAPTER QUIZ*.
   b. Click the down-pointing arrow at the right side of the Style button on the Formatting toolbar and then click *Title1* at the drop-down list.
5. Apply styles to text in the document by completing the following steps:
   a. Click the Styles and Formatting button on the Formatting toolbar.
   b. Select the text in the document (except the title).
   c. Click *Font1* in the *Pick formatting to apply* list box in the Styles and Formatting task pane.
   d. Click *Indent1* in the *Pick formatting to apply* list box in the Styles and Formatting task pane.
   e. Deselect the text.
   f. Click the Styles and Formatting button to turn off the display of the Styles and Formatting task pane.
6. Save, print, and then close **ewc4x12**.

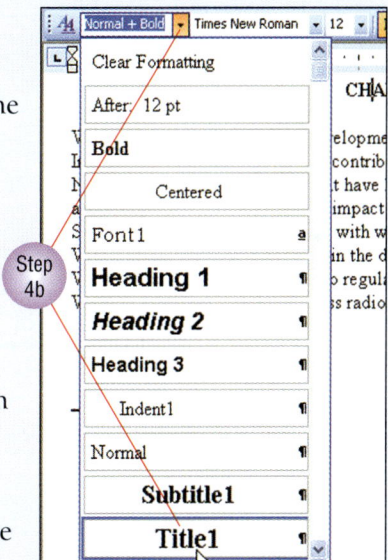

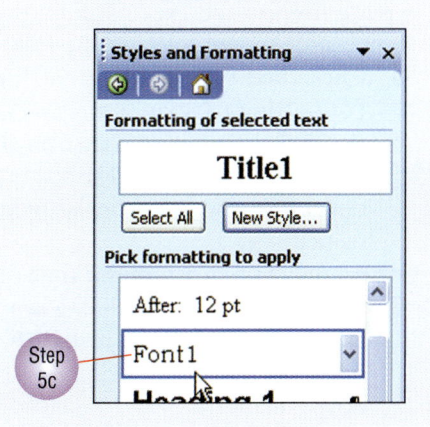

Assigning a Shortcut Key Combination to a Style

HINT
When you insert the shortcut key combination, make sure the combination has not already been assigned to another function.

A style can be applied quickly in a document if a shortcut key has been assigned to the style. You can use the letters A through Z, numbers 0 through 9, the Delete and Insert keys, combined with the Ctrl, Alt, and Shift keys to create a shortcut key combination. Word has already assigned shortcut key combinations to many features. If you assign a shortcut key combination to a style that is already used by Word, the message *Currently assigned to (name of feature)* displays. When this happens, choose another shortcut key combination. Create a shortcut key combination for a style with options at the Customize Keyboard dialog box shown in Figure 4.11.

FIGURE 4.11 *Customize Keyboard*

The shortcut keys you press display in this text box.

QUICK STEPS

Assign Shortcut Key Combination to Style
1. Display Styles and Formatting task pane.
2. Right-click style in *Pick formatting to apply* list box.
3. Click Modify.
4. Click Format, Shortcut keys.
5. Press desired shortcut keys.
6. Click Assign button.
7. Click Close button.
8. Click OK.

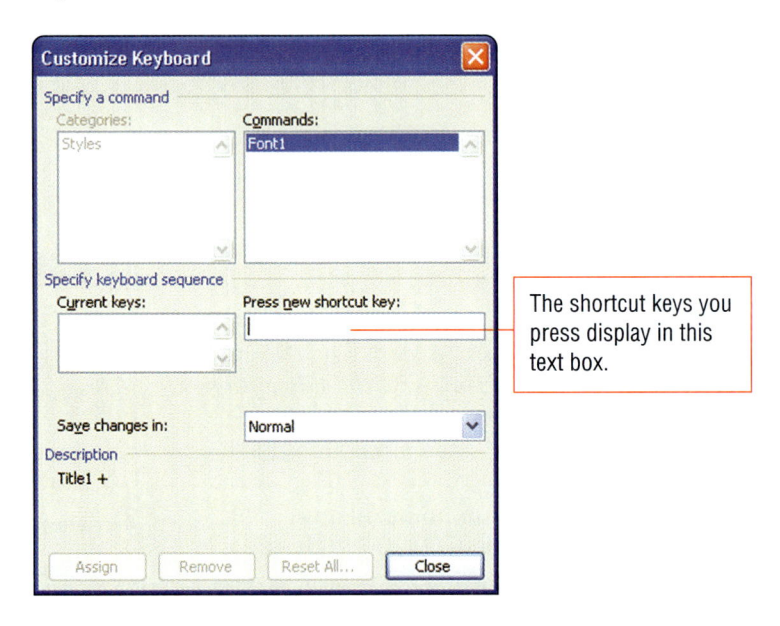

exercise 13

ASSIGNING SHORTCUT KEY COMBINATIONS TO STYLES

1. Open **Sty01**.
2. Save the document with Save As and name it **Sty02**.
3. Create the shortcut key combination, Alt + F, for the Font1 style by completing the following steps:
    a. Click the Styles and Formatting button on the Formatting toolbar.
    b. Position the mouse pointer on the *Font1* style in the *Pick formatting to apply* list box and then click the down-pointing arrow at the right side of the style name.
    c. At the drop-down menu that displays, click Modify.
    d. At the Modify Style dialog box, click the Format button that displays toward the bottom of the dialog box, and then click Shortcut key at the drop-down menu.

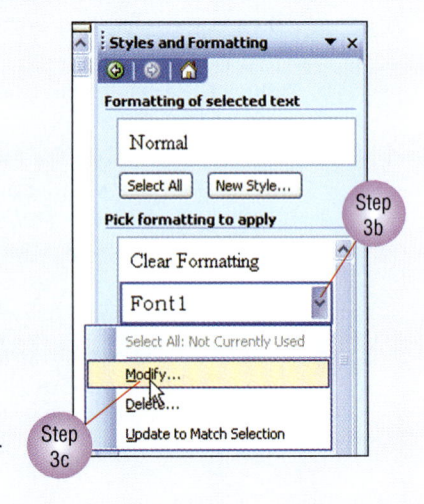

E146 *Chapter Four*

e. At the Customize Keyboard dialog box, press Alt + F. (This inserts *Alt+F* in the *Press new shortcut key* text box.)
f. Click the Assign button.
g. Click the Close button to close the Customize Keyboard dialog box.
h. Click OK to close the Modify Style dialog box.
4. Create the shortcut key combination, Alt + I, for the *Indent1* style by completing steps similar to those in Step 3.
5. Create the shortcut key combination, Alt + S, for the *Subtitle1* style by completing steps similar to those in Step 3.
6. Create the shortcut key combination, Alt + T, for the *Title1* style by completing steps similar to those in Step 3.
7. Close the Styles and Formatting task pane.
8. Save and then close **Sty02**.

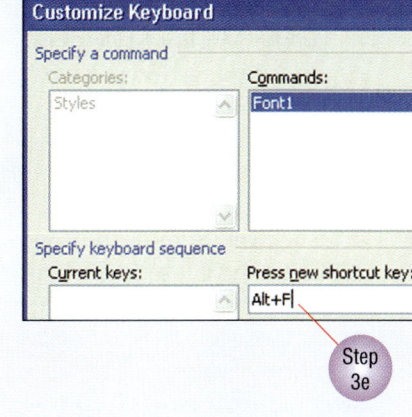

exercise 14 — APPLYING STYLES IN A DOCUMENT WITH SHORTCUT KEY COMBINATIONS

1. Open **Sty02**.
2. Save the document with Save As and name it **ewc4x14**.
3. Insert the document **WordReport01** into the **ewc4x14** document.
4. Select the entire document and then change line spacing to single.
5. Position the insertion point on any character in the title *DESKTOP PUBLISHING* and then apply the Title1 style by pressing Alt + T.
6. Position the insertion point on any character in the subtitle *Defining Desktop Publishing* and then apply the Subtitle1 style by pressing Alt + S.
7. Apply the Subtitle1 style to the following headings:
    Initiating the Desktop Publishing Process
    Planning the Publication
    Creating the Content
8. Save, print, and then close **ewc4x14**.

To remove a shortcut key combination from a style, display the Customize Keyboard dialog box for the specific style and then click the Remove button.

exercise 15 — REMOVING A SHORTCUT KEY COMBINATION

1. Open **Sty02**.
2. Save the document with Save As and name it **Sty03**.
3. Remove the shortcut key combination, Alt + I, by completing the following steps:
    a. Click the Styles and Formatting button on the Formatting toolbar.
    b. At the Styles and Formatting task pane, position the mouse pointer on the *Indent1* style in the *Pick formatting to apply* list box, and then click the down-pointing arrow at the right side of the style name.

c. At the drop-down menu that displays, click Modify.
d. At the Modify Style dialog box, click the Format button that displays toward the bottom of the dialog box, and then click Shortcut key at the drop-down menu.
e. At the Customize Keyboard dialog box, click *Alt+I* in the *Current keys* list box.
f. Click the Remove button.
g. Click the Close button to close the Customize Keyboard dialog box.
h. At the Modify Style dialog box, click OK.
4. Close the Styles and Formatting task pane.
5. Save and then close **Sty03**.

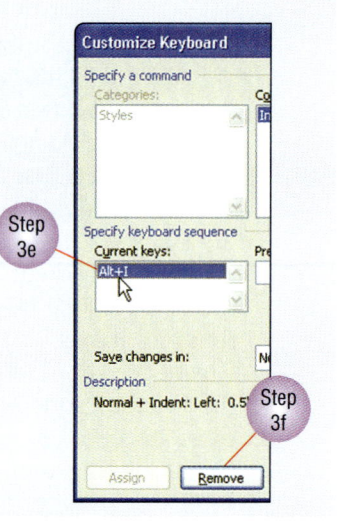

QUICK STEPS

Modifying a Style

Modify a Style
1. Display Styles and Formatting task pane.
2. Right-click style in *Pick formatting to apply* list box.
3. Click Modify.
4. Make desired changes.
5. Click OK.

Once a style has been created, you can modify the style by changing the formatting instructions that it contains. When you modify a style by changing the formatting instructions, all text to which that style has been applied is changed accordingly. To modify a style, you would click the down-pointing arrow at the right side of the style name in the Styles and Formatting task pane, and then click Modify at the drop-down menu. At the Modify Style dialog box shown in Figure 4.12, you would add or delete formatting options.

TABLE 4.12 Modify Style Dialog Box

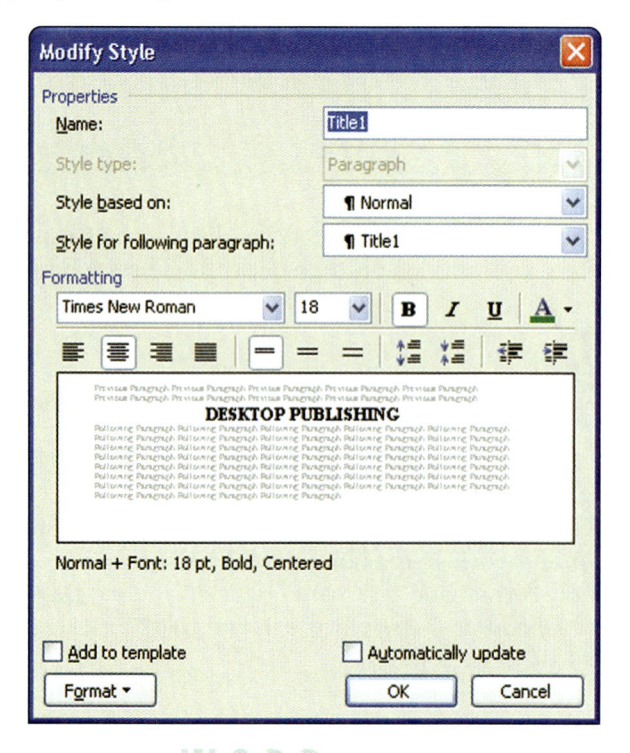

exercise 16

MODIFYING STYLES

1. Open **ewc4x14**.
2. Save the document with Save As and name it **ewc4x16**.
3. Modify the Title1 style by completing the following steps:
    a. Click the Styles and Formatting button on the Formatting toolbar.
    b. At the Styles and Formatting task pane, position the mouse pointer on the *Title1* style in the *Pick formatting to apply* list box, and then click the down-pointing arrow at the right side of the style name.
    c. At the drop-down menu that displays, click Modify.
    d. At the Modify Style dialog box, change the font to 18-point Arial bold by completing the following steps:
        1) Click the Format button located toward the bottom of the dialog box.
        2) At the drop-down menu that displays, click Font.
        3) At the Font dialog box, click *Arial* in the *Font* list box. Make sure *Bold* is selected in the *Font style* list box and *18* is selected in the *Size* list box.
        4) Click OK or press Enter to close the Font dialog box.
    e. At the Modify Style dialog box, change the spacing after the paragraph to 6 points by completing the following steps:
        1) Click the Format button located toward the bottom of the dialog box.
        2) Click Paragraph at the drop-down menu.
        3) At the Paragraph dialog box, click once on the up-pointing arrow to the right of the *After* text box. (This inserts *6 pt* in the text box.)
        4) Click OK or press Enter.
    f. At the Modify Style dialog box, click OK.
4. Complete steps similar to those in Step 3 to modify the Subtitle1 style so that it applies 14-point Arial bold and 6 points of spacing before and after the paragraph.
5. Close the Styles and Formatting task pane.
6. Save, print, and then close **ewc4x16**. (The title should print in 18-point Arial bold and the four headings should print in 14-point Arial bold.)

Creating a Style by Modifying an Existing Style

Predesigned styles can be used as the basis for a custom style. Use the formatting in a predesigned style as a beginning point for creating a custom style. One method for creating a style based on a predesigned style is to display the Styles and Formatting task pane, hover the mouse over the desired style, click the down-pointing arrow that displays at the right side of the style, and then click Modify at the drop-down menu. At the Modify Style dialog box, type a new name for the style in the *Name* text box, choose the desired formatting, and then click OK. In Exercise 17, you will use the predesigned Table Grid style to create a new style with additional formatting.

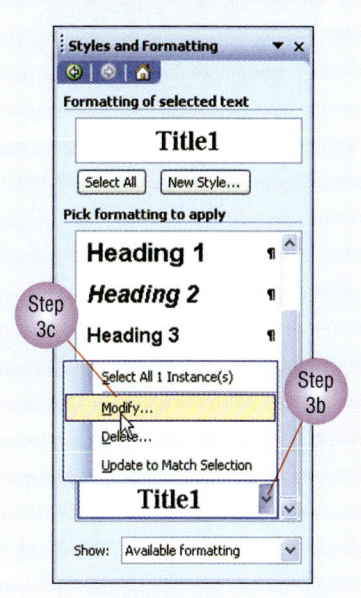

exercise 17

CREATING AND MODIFYING A TABLE STYLE

1. Open **WordTable06**.
2. Save the document with Save As and name it **ewc4x17**.
3. Create a custom table style named SNTableStyle (for *Student Name Table Style*) by completing the following steps:
   a. Click the Styles and Formatting button on the Formatting toolbar.
   b. At the Styles and Formatting task pane, position the mouse pointer on the *Table Grid* style in the *Pick formatting to apply* list box, and then click the down-pointing arrow at the right side of the style name.
   c. At the drop-down menu that displays, click Modify.
   d. At the Modify Style dialog box, type **SNTableStyle** in the *Name* text box.
   e. Click the down-pointing arrow at the right side of the *Font* option box (located immediately below the *Apply formatting to* option) and then click *Bookman Old Style* at the drop-down list.
   f. Click the down-pointing arrow at the right side of the Font Color button and then click the Indigo color (second color from the *right* in the top row).
   g. Click the down-pointing arrow at the right side of the Shading Color button and then click Light Green at the color palette (fourth color from the left in the bottom row).
   h. Click the down-pointing arrow at the right of the *Apply formatting to* option and then click *Header row* at the drop-down list.
   i. Click the Bold button.
   j. Click the down-pointing arrow at the right of the Alignment button and then click *Align Center* at the alignment palette (second choice from the left in the second row).
   k. Click the down-pointing arrow at the right of the *Apply formatting to* option and then click *Left column*.
   l. Click the Bold button.
   m. Click OK to close the Modify Style dialog box. (This closes the dialog box and also applies the new style to the table in the document.)
4. At the document, make the following changes to the table:
   a. Close the Styles and Formatting task pane.
   b. Select the cells containing the money amounts and then click the Align Right button.
   c. Autofit the contents by clicking Table, pointing to AutoFit, and then click AutoFit to Contents.
5. Save, print, and then close **ewc4x17**.

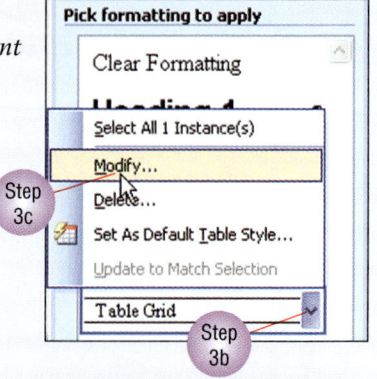

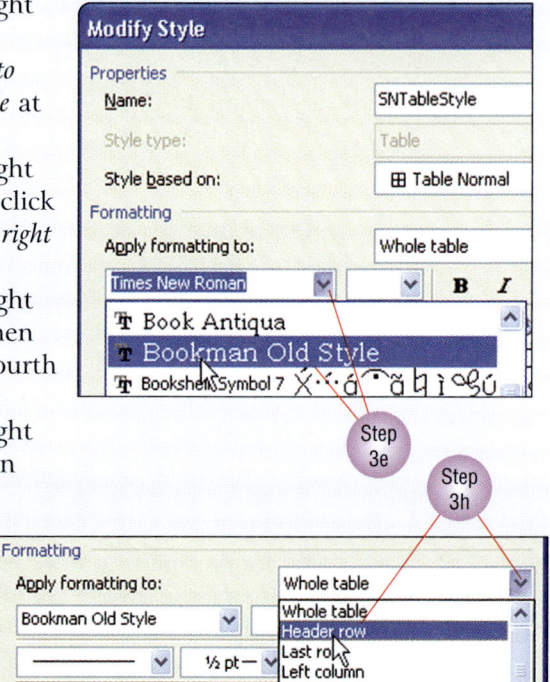

The style you created based on the Table Grid style displays in the Styles and Formatting task pane as *Table Grid,SNTableStyle*. The name of the style identifies the predesigned style (*Table Grid*) upon which the new style was based.

Creating and Modifying a List Style

You can create a custom list style in a document that will be available any time that document is open. You can apply a custom list style to text and then modify the style, if needed, and any occurrence of that style in the document is automatically modified. Create a new list style by basing it on an existing list style or create a new list style at the New Style dialog box. To create a new list style based on an existing list style, display the Styles and Formatting task pane, point to the desired list style, and then click the Modify option. At the Modify Style dialog box, type the new name for the style, make the desired formatting changes, and then click OK. You can also create a new list style by clicking the Add button at the Bullets and Numbering dialog box with the List Styles tab selected.

The new list style is saved with the current document. If you want to modify the list style, open the document containing the style. Display the Bullets and Numbering dialog box with the List Styles tab selected, click the desired style in the *List styles* list box, and then click the Modify button. At the Modify Style dialog box (contains the same options as the New Style dialog box), make the desired changes, and then click OK.

exercise 18

CREATING AND MODIFYING A LIST STYLE

1. Open **WordList01**.
2. Save the document with Save As and name it **ewc4x18**.
3. Create a custom list style named SNListStyle (for *Student Name List Style*) by completing the following steps:
   a. Click Format and then Bullets and Numbering.
   b. At the Bullets and Numbering dialog box, click the List Styles tab.
   c. Click the Add button.
   d. At the New Style dialog box, type **SNListStyle**.
   e. Make sure the *Apply formatting to* option is set at *1st level* (look for this text in the box to the right of the option).
   f. Click the Insert Symbol button.
   g. At the Symbol dialog box, change the *Font* to (normal text). (The *(normal text)* option is the first option in the drop-down list.)
   h. Double-click the dollar sign symbol (fifth symbol box from the left in the top row).

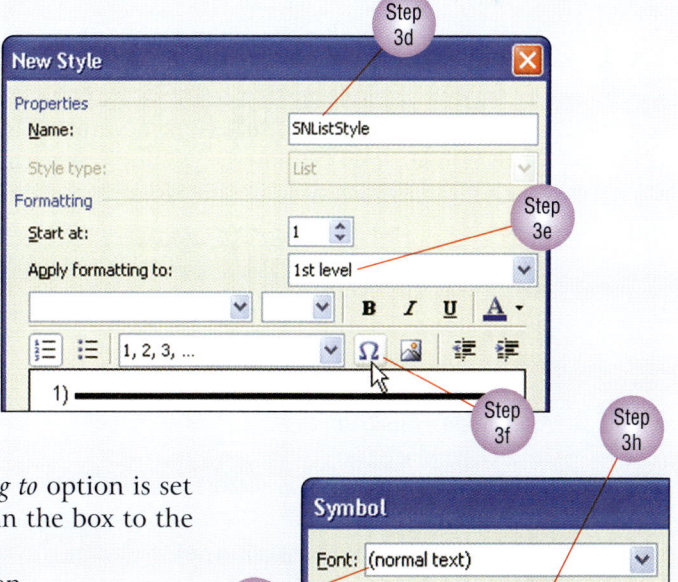

Formatting with Macros and Styles — E151

i. Click the down-pointing arrow at the right side of the *Font* option box (located immediately below the *Apply formatting to* option) and then click *Bookman Old Style* at the drop-down list.
j. Click the down-pointing arrow at the right of the option box immediately right of the *Bookman Old Style* option box and then click *18* at the drop-down list.
k. Click the Bold button.
l. Click the down-pointing arrow at the right of the Font Color button at then click the Red color (first color from the left in the third row).
m. Click the OK button.
n. At the Bullets and Numbering dialog box, click the Close button.
4. Apply the SNListStyle by completing the following steps:
    a. Select the text from *The First Mortgage Account* through *Expense Deductions*.
    b. Click Format and then Bullets and Numbering.
    c. At the Bullets and Numbering dialog box, click the List Styles tab.
    d. Double-click *SNListStyle* in the *List styles* list box.
    e. At the document, deselect the text.
5. Save and then print **ewc4x18**.
6. Modify the SNListStyle custom list style by completing the following steps:
    a. Click Format and then Bullets and Numbering.
    b. At the Bullets and Numbering dialog box with the List Styles tab selected, click once on the *SNListStyle* style in the *List styles* list box.
    c. Click the Modify button.
    d. At the Modify Style dialog box, click the down-pointing arrow at the right of the Font Color button and then click the Green color at the palette (fourth color from the left in the second row).
    e. Click the down-pointing arrow at the right of the font size list box (contains *18*) and then click *14* at the drop-down list.
    f. Click OK to close the Modify Style dialog box.
    g. At the Bullets and Numbering dialog box, click OK.
7. Save, print, and then close **ewc4x18**.

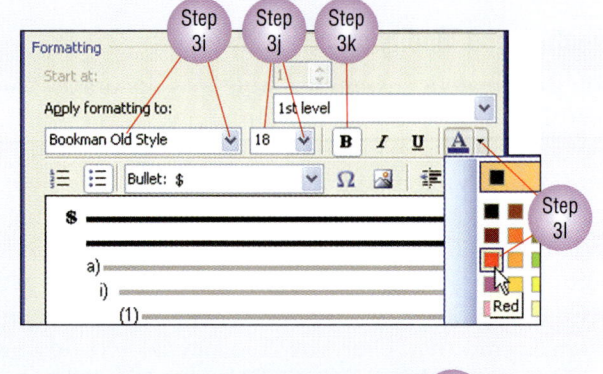

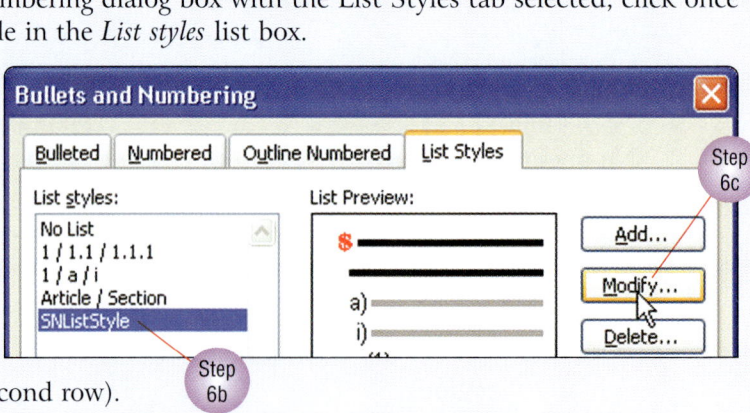

Removing a Style from Text

You may apply a style to text in a document and then change your mind and wish to remove the style. If you decide to remove the style immediately after applying it (before performing some other action), click the Undo button on the Standard toolbar. You can also click Edit and then Undo Style. When a style is removed, the style that was previously applied to the text is applied once again (usually this is the Normal style).

You can also remove a style from text by applying a new style. Only one style can be applied at a time to the same text. For example, if you applied the Heading 1 style to text and then later decide you want to remove it, position the insertion point in the text containing the Heading 1 style, and then apply the Normal style.

Word contains a Clear Formatting style you can use to remove all formatting from selected text. To use this style, position the insertion point in the paragraph of text or select specific text, click the down-pointing arrow at the right side of the Style button on the Formatting toolbar, and then click *Clear Formatting* at the drop-down list. The Styles and Formatting task pane also contains a Clear Formatting style in the *Pick formatting to apply* list box. You can also clear formatting by clicking Edit, pointing to Clear, and then clicking Formats.

Renaming a Style

As you create more and more styles in a particular document, you may find that you need to rename existing styles to avoid duplicating style names. When a style is renamed, the formatting instructions contained within the style remain the same. Any text to which the style has been applied reflects the new name. You can rename styles that you create as often as needed, but you cannot rename Word's standard styles. To rename a style, click the down-pointing arrow at the right side of the style name in the Styles and Formatting task pane and then click Modify at the drop-down menu. At the Modify Style dialog box, type the new name for the style, and then click OK.

Deleting a Style

A style can be deleted in a document and any text to which that style is applied is returned to the Normal style. To delete a style, display the Styles and Formatting task pane. Position the mouse pointer on the style name to be deleted and then click the down-pointing arrow at the right side of the style name. At the drop-down menu that displays, click Delete. At the message asking if you want to delete the style, click Yes. You can delete styles that you create but you cannot delete Word's standard styles.

exercise 19

DELETING A STYLE

1. Open **Sty03**.
2. Insert the document named **WordReport02** into the **Sty03** document.
3. Save the document with Save As and name it **ewc4x19**.
4. Select the entire document and then change the line spacing to single.

5. Delete the Indent1 style by completing the following steps:
   a. Click the Styles and Formatting button on the Formatting toolbar.
   b. At the Styles and Formatting task pane, position the mouse pointer on the Indent1 style in the *Pick formatting to apply* list box, and then click the down-pointing arrow at the right side of the style name.
   c. At the drop-down menu that displays, click Delete.
   d. At the message asking if you want to delete the style, click Yes.
6. Select the entire document and then apply the Font1 style.
7. Apply the Title1 style to the title, *DESKTOP PUBLISHING DESIGN*.
8. Apply the Subtitle1 style to the headings *Designing a Document* and *Creating Focus*.
9. Close the Styles and Formatting task pane.
10. Save, print, and then close **ewc4x19**.

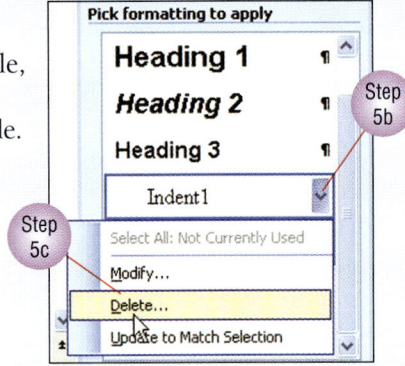

QUICK STEPS

Copy Style to a Template
1. Click Tools, Templates and Add-Ins.
2. Click Organizer button.
3. In left list box, click style to be copied.
4. Click Copy button.
5. Click Close button.

Copying a Style to a Template

If you create a style that you want available for other documents, copy the style to the template. One method for copying a style to a template is to use the Organizer. At the Organizer, you can copy a style to a template, copy a style from a template into a document, and delete styles. Display the Organizer by clicking Tools and then Templates and Add-Ins. At the Templates and Add-ins dialog box, click the Organizer button. This displays the Organizer dialog box with the Styles tab selected similar to what you see in Figure 4.13. At the Organizer dialog box with the Styles tab selected, click the style in the list box at the left that you want to copy, and then click the Copy button.

The styles you copy to a template are available for any future documents you create based on the template. The copied styles will not be available if you open a document created with the template before the styles were copied.

FIGURE 4.13 *Organizer Dialog Box with Styles Tab Selected*

Copy a style to the Normal template by clicking the style in this list box and then clicking the Copy button.

Deleting a Style from a Template

If you copy a style to a template, you can delete the style at the Organizer dialog box. To delete a style from the template, display the Organizer dialog box with the Styles tab selected, click the style in the list box at the left that you want to delete and then click the Delete button. At the message asking if you are sure you want to delete the style, click Yes.

exercise 20 — COPYING/DELETING A STYLE TO/FROM THE NORMAL TEMPLATE

1. Open **Sty01**.
2. Copy the Title1 and the Subtitle1 styles to the Normal template by completing the following steps:
   a. Click Tools and then Templates and Add-Ins.
   b. At the Templates and Add-ins dialog box, click the Organizer button.
   c. At the Organizer dialog box, click *Title1* in the left list box (you will need to scroll down the list box to display this style), and then click the Copy button. (This inserts *Title1* in the right list box.)
   d. Click *Subtitle1* in the left list box, and then click the Copy button.
   e. Click the Close button to close the Organizer dialog box.
   f. Close **Sty01**.
3. Click the New Blank Document button on the Standard toolbar.
4. Insert **WordReport06** in the current blank document. (Do this with the File option from the Insert drop-down menu.)
5. Save the document with Save As and name it **ewc4x20**.
6. Select the entire document, change the line spacing to single, and then deselect the document.
7. Apply the Title1 style to the two titles in the document (*MODULE 3: DESIGNING A NEWSLETTER* and *MODULE 4: CREATING NEWSLETTER LAYOUT*).
8. Apply the Subtitle1 style to the four headings (*Applying Desktop Publishing Guidelines*, *Choosing Paper Size and Type*, *Choosing Paper Weight*, and *Creating Margins for Newsletter*).
9. Save, print, and then close **ewc4x20**.
10. Delete the Title1 and Subtitle1 styles from the Normal template by completing the following steps:
    a. Click the New Blank Document button on the Standard toolbar to display a clear document screen.
    b. Click Tools and then Templates and Add-Ins.
    c. At the Templates and Add-ins dialog box, click the Organizer button.
    d. At the Organizer dialog box with the Styles tab selected, click *Subtitle1* in the right list box, and then click the Delete button.

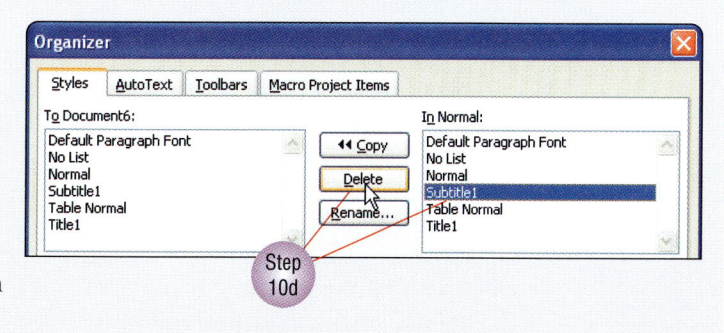

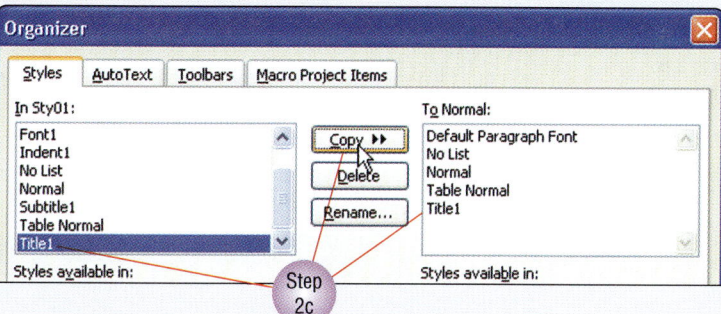

WORD — Formatting with Macros and Styles — E155

e. At the message asking if you want to delete the style, click Yes.
f. Click *Title1* in the right list box and then click the Delete button.
g. At the message asking if you want to delete the style, click Yes.
h. Click the Close button to close the Organizer dialog box.
11. Close the clear document screen.

Navigating in a Document

Word offers a number of methods you can use to navigate to specific locations in a document. Navigating is particularly useful in lengthy, multiple-paged documents. Some navigating methods include using thumbnails, Document Map, bookmarks, and cross-references.

Navigating Using the Thumbnails Pane

> **QUICK STEPS**
> **Display Thumbnails Pane**
> Click View, Thumbnails.

Display a miniature of pages in a document by turning on the display of the Thumbnails pane. To do this, click View and then Thumbnails, and the Thumbnails pane displays at the left side of the screen similar to what you see in Figure 4.14. In a multiple-page document, the first three pages of the document display as miniatures in the Thumbnails pane. Scroll through the pages in the Thumbnails pane by using the vertical scroll bar at the right side of the Thumbnails pane.

FIGURE 4.14 *Document with Thumbnails Pane Displayed*

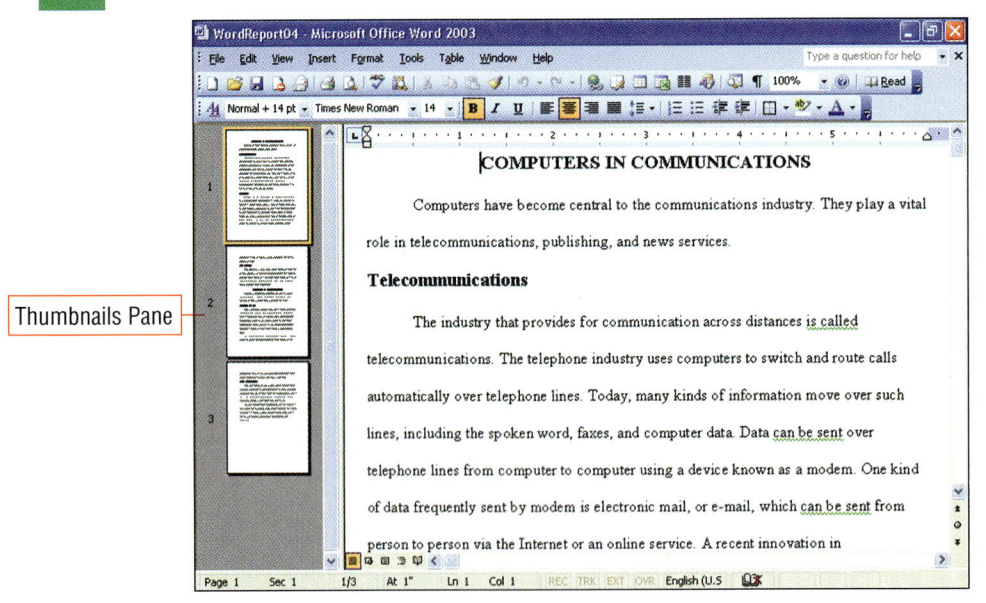

> **HINT**
> Increase or decrease the size of the Thumbnails or Document Map pane by dragging the right pane border.

Navigate to a particular page in the document by clicking the page miniatures representing the desired page. The page number displays at the left side of the page miniature in the Thumbnails pane. The first three pages display in the Thumbnails pane. Click the down-pointing arrow at the bottom of the vertical scroll bar located at the right side of the Thumbnails pane to display the next three pages in the document. Click the up-pointing arrow on the scroll bar to display the previous three pages. You can increase or decrease the size of the Thumbnails pane by dragging the right border of the pane.

Navigating Using the Document Map Pane

Display the Document Map pane to navigate easily in a document and keep track of your location within the document. The Document Map pane displays any headings that are formatted with heading styles or outline-level paragraph format. If no headings are formatted with heading styles or outline levels, Document Map searches for paragraphs that look like headings, such as short lines set in a larger type size. If no headings are found, the Document Map pane is blank.

To display the Document Map pane, click the Document Map button on the Standard toolbar or click View, and then Document Map. This displays the Document Map pane at the left side of the screen similar to what you see in Figure 4.15. Like the Thumbnails pane, you can increase and/or decrease the size of the Document Map pane by dragging the right border of the pane.

QUICK STEPS

Display Document Map Pane
Click Document Map button.
OR
Click View, Document Map.

Document Map

FIGURE 4.15 Document Map Pane

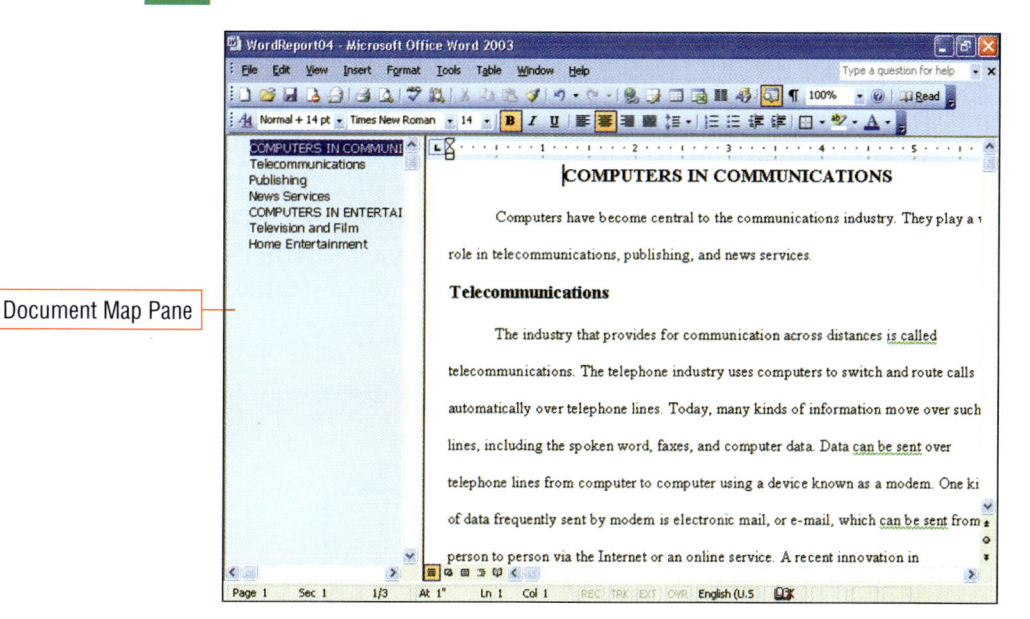

exercise 21

DISPLAYING THE THUMBNAILS AND DOCUMENT MAP PANES IN A DOCUMENT

1. Open **WordReport04**.
2. Navigate in the document using the Thumbnails pane by completing the following steps:
    a. Display the Thumbnails pane by clicking View and then Thumbnails.
    b. Click the page 3 miniature in the Thumbnails pane.
    c. Click the page 2 miniature in the Thumbnails pane.
    d. Click View and then Thumbnails to remove the Thumbnails pane.
3. Navigate using the Document Map pane by completing the following steps:
    a. Click the Document Map button on the Standard toolbar.

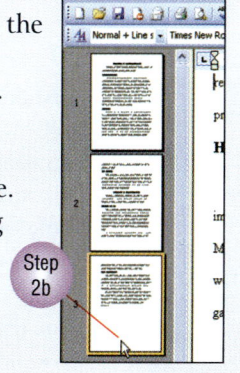

Step 2b

WORD Formatting with Macros and Styles E157

b. Click the *Television and Film* heading in the Document Map pane to navigate to that heading in the document.
   c. Click the *Telecommunications* heading to navigate to that heading in the document.
   d. Close **WordReport04**.
   e. Open **WordReport06**.
   f. Click the heading *Choosing Paper Size and Type* to navigate to that heading in the document.
   g. Click the title *MODULE 3: DESIGNING A NEWSLETTER* to navigate to that title in the document.
   h. Remove the Document Map pane by clicking the Document Map button on the Standard toolbar.
4. Close **WordReport06**.

Using Bookmarks

> **HINT**
> Consider inserting a bookmark in a document to identify text for future revisions.

In long documents, you may find marking a location in the document useful so you can quickly move the insertion point to the location. Create bookmarks for locations in a document at the Bookmark dialog box. When you create bookmarks, you can insert as many as needed in a document. To create a bookmark, position the insertion point at the location in the document where the bookmark is to appear, click Insert and then Bookmark. At the Bookmark dialog box shown in Figure 4.16, type a name for the bookmark in the *Bookmark name* text box, and then click the Add button. Repeat these steps as many times as needed in a document to insert bookmarks.

FIGURE 4.16 Bookmark Dialog Box

> **QUICK STEPS**
>
> **Insert a Bookmark**
> 1. Position insertion point at desired location.
> 2. Click Insert, Bookmark.
> 3. Type bookmark name.
> 4. Click Add button.

Make sure you give each bookmark a unique name. A bookmark name can contain a maximum of 40 characters and can include letters, numbers, and the underscore character (_). You cannot use spaces in a bookmark name. When you insert a bookmark in a document, by default the bookmark is not visible. To make a bookmark visible, click Tools and then Options. At the Options dialog box, click the View tab. At the Options dialog box with the View tab selected, click *Bookmarks* in the *Show* section of the dialog box. (This inserts a check mark in the *Bookmarks* check box.) Complete similar steps to turn off the display of bookmarks. A bookmark displays as an I-beam marker.

You can also create a bookmark for selected text. To do this, select the text first and then complete the steps to create a bookmark. When you create a bookmark for selected text, a left bracket ([) indicates the beginning of the selected text and a right bracket (]) indicates the end of the selected text.

After bookmarks have been inserted in a document, you can move the insertion point to a specific bookmark. To do this, click Insert and then Bookmark. At the Bookmark dialog box, double-click the bookmark name in the list box. You can also click once on the bookmark name and then click the Go To button. When Word stops at the location of the bookmark, click the Close button to close the Bookmark dialog box. If you move the insertion point to a bookmark created with selected text, Word moves the insertion to the bookmark and selects the text.

Bookmarks in a document are deleted at the Bookmark dialog box (not the document). To delete a bookmark, display the Bookmark dialog box, select the bookmark to be deleted in the list box, and then click the Delete button.

exercise 22

INSERTING BOOKMARKS IN A DOCUMENT

1. Open **WordReport01**.
2. Turn on the display of bookmarks by completing the following steps:
    a. Click Tools and then Options.
    b. At the Options dialog box, click the View tab.
    c. Click *Bookmarks* in the *Show* section. (This inserts a check mark in the *Bookmarks* check box.)
    d. Click OK.
3. Insert a bookmark at the beginning of the heading *Defining Desktop Publishing* by completing the following steps:
    a. Position the insertion point at the beginning of the line containing the heading *Defining Desktop Publishing*.
    b. Click Insert and then Bookmark.
    c. At the Bookmark dialog box, type **Define** in the *Bookmark name* text box.
    d. Click the Add button.
4. Insert a bookmark at the beginning of the following headings with the names listed by following steps similar to those in Step 3.
    Initiating the Desktop Publishing Process = **Initiate**
    Planning the Publication = **Plan**
    Creating the Content = **Create**
5. Position the insertion point at the *Define* bookmark by completing the following steps:
    a. Click Insert and then Bookmark.
    b. At the Bookmark dialog box, double-click *Define* in the list box.
    c. When Word stops at the heading *Defining Desktop Publishing*, click the Close button to close the Bookmark dialog box.
6. Complete steps similar to those in Step 5 to move the insertion point to the *Initiate*, *Plan*, and *Create* bookmarks.
7. Turn off the display of bookmarks by completing steps similar to those in Step 2.
8. Close the report without saving the changes.

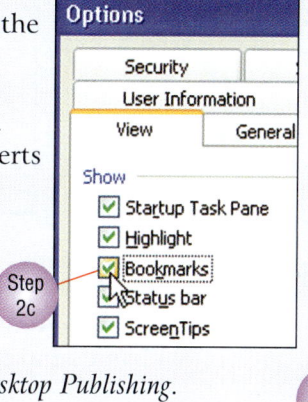

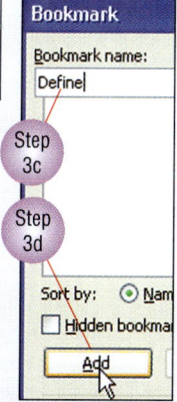

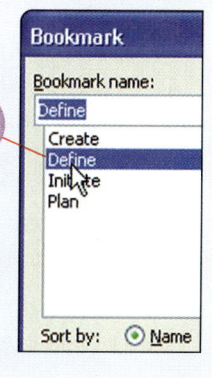

HINT
Create a cross-reference to other locations or text in a document such as a figure, caption, footnote, bookmark, or heading.

Creating a Cross-Reference

A cross-reference in a Word document refers the reader to another location within the document. This feature is useful in a long document or a document containing related information. Insert a cross-reference to move to a specific location within the document. Type introductory text and then click Insert, point to Reference, and then click Cross-reference. At the Cross-reference dialog box shown in Figure 4.17, identify the reference type, where to refer, and the specific text, and then click the Insert button and then the Close button.

FIGURE 4.17 *Cross-Reference Dialog Box*

QUICK STEPS

Insert a Cross-reference
1. Position insertion point at desired location.
2. Click Insert, Reference, Cross-reference.
3. Specify *Reference type* at the Cross-reference dialog box.
4. Click desired option in list box.
5. Click Insert button.
6. Click Close button.

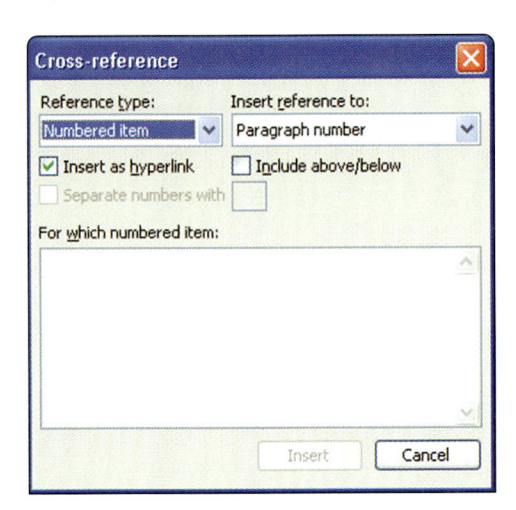

The reference identified in the Cross-reference dialog box displays immediately after the introductory text. To move to the specified reference, hold down the Ctrl key, position the mouse pointer over the introductory text (pointer turns into a hand), and then click the left mouse button.

exercise 23 — INSERTING A CROSS-REFERENCE IN A DOCUMENT

1. Open **WordReport03**.
2. Save the document with Save As and name it **ewc4x23**.
3. Apply the specified styles to the following headings:
   THE TECHNOLOGY OF DESKTOP PUBLISHING   =   Heading 1
   WHAT IS DESKTOP PUBLISHING?   =   Heading 2
   BASIC HARDWARE   =   Heading 2
4. Insert a cross-reference by completing the following steps:
   a. Position the insertion point immediately following the period at the end of the last sentence in the document.
   b. Press the spacebar once and then type **(For more information, refer to**.
   c. Press the spacebar once.
   d. Click Insert, point to Reference, and then click Cross-reference.
   e. At the Cross-reference dialog box, click the down-pointing arrow at the right side of the *Reference type* list box, and then click *Heading* at the drop-down list.
   f. Click *BASIC HARDWARE* in the *For which heading* list box.

g. Click the Insert button.
h. Click the Close button to close the dialog box.
i. At the document, type a period followed by the right parenthesis.
5. Move to the reference text by holding down the Ctrl key, positioning the mouse pointer over *BASIC HARDWARE* until the mouse pointer turns into a hand, and then clicking the left mouse button.
6. Save, print, and then close **ewc4x23**.

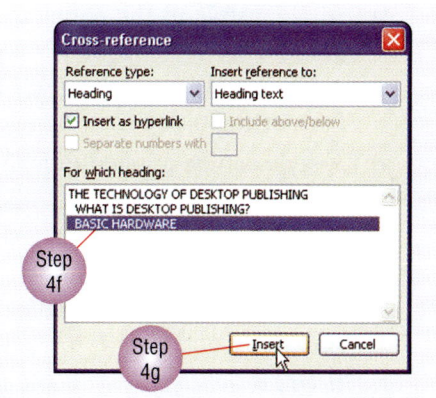

CHAPTER summary

- Use the Macro feature to execute a series of commands or apply formatting.
- Recording a macro involves turning on the macro recorder, performing the steps to be recorded, and then turning off the recorder.
- Run a macro by displaying the Macros dialog box and double-clicking the desired macro name.
- Temporarily suspend the recording of a macro by clicking the Pause Recording button on the Macro Record toolbar.
- Delete a macro by displaying the Macros dialog box, clicking the macro name to be deleted, and then clicking the Delete button.
- Assign a keyboard command to a macro at the Record Macro dialog box. To run a macro that has been assigned a keyboard command, press the keys assigned to the macro.
- A macro can be added to a toolbar. To run a macro assigned to a toolbar, just click the button.
- Insert a Fill-in field in a macro that requires keyboard entry during the running of the macro.
- A macro is created with Visual Basic and can be edited using the Visual Basic Editor. To display a macro in the Visual Basic Editor, display the Macros dialog box, click the macro to be edited, and then click the Edit button.
- Formatting that is applied to a variety of documents on a regular basis or that maintains a consistency within a publication can be applied to text using a style. A style is a set of formatting instructions saved with a specific name in order to use the formatting over and over.
- When the formatting instructions contained within a style are changed, all of the text to which the style has been applied is automatically updated.
- Styles are created for a particular document and are saved with the document.
- In addition to the Normal style that is applied to text by default, other predesigned styles are available in a document based on the Normal template document. Other template documents also contain predesigned styles.
- Styles can be changed and/or applied to text in three ways: 1) use Word's AutoFormat feature; 2) select a new template at the Style Gallery dialog box; or 3) make changes to styles available in the template upon which your document is based.
- The AutoFormat feature automatically applies styles to text in the document.
- A new style can be created in two ways: apply the desired formatting instructions to a paragraph and then save those instructions in a style, or specify the formatting instructions for a style without applying the formatting to text.

- Apply a style to the paragraph where the insertion point is positioned, or select several paragraphs and then apply a paragraph style.
- Apply a style using the Style button on the Formatting toolbar or at the Styles and Formatting task pane.
- A style can be applied quickly in a document if a shortcut key combination has been assigned to the style.
- Modify a style by changing the formatting instructions that it contains with options at the Modify Style dialog box.
- A style can be deleted and/or renamed. Remove a style from text by applying a new style, since only one style can be applied at a time to the same text.
- If you want a style available for other documents, copy the style to the Normal template. Use the Organizer to copy a style to a template.
- Display a miniature of pages in a document by turning on the Thumbnails pane. Display the outline of a document in the Document Map pane.
- Insert a bookmark to mark a location in a document so you can later move the insertion point quickly to that location. Create or delete bookmarks at the Bookmark dialog box.
- Create a cross-reference in a document to refer the reader to another location within the document.

FEATURES summary

FEATURE	BUTTON	MENU	KEYBOARD
Macros dialog box		Tools, Macro, Macros	Alt + F8
Record Macro dialog	REC	Tools, Macro, Record New Macro	
Customize dialog box		Tools, Customize	
Field dialog box		Insert, Field	
Visual Basic Editor		Tools, Macro, Macros, Edit	
AutoFormat dialog box		Format, AutoFormat	Alt + Ctrl + K
Styles and Formatting task pane	A4	Format, Styles and Formatting	
Organizer dialog box		Tools, Templates and Add-ins, Organizer	
Thumbnails pane		View, Thumbnails	
Document Map pane		View, Document Map	
Bookmark dialog box		Insert, Bookmark	Ctrl + Shift + F5
Cross-reference dialog box		Insert, Reference, Cross-reference	

CONCEPTS check

Completion: On a blank sheet of paper indicate the correct term, command, or number for each description.

1. Double-click this button on the Status bar to display the Record Macro dialog box.
2. To run a macro, double-click the macro name at this dialog box.
3. Assign a keyboard command to a macro at this dialog box.
4. Assign a macro to a toolbar with options from this dialog box.
5. Insert this field in a macro that requires keyboard entry during the running of the macro.
6. Edit a macro using this editor.
7. By default, a Word document is based on this template document.
8. The predesigned styles based on the default template document are displayed by clicking this button on the Formatting toolbar.
9. Create a new style at this dialog box.
10. Use options at this dialog box to copy a style to a template.
11. This is the name of a separate pane that displays the outline of a document at the left side of the screen.
12. Insert this in a document to mark a specific location.
13. Insert this in a document to refer the reader to another location within the document.

SKILLS check

Assessment 1

1. At a clear document screen, record a macro named XXXLtrhd02 (where your initials are used instead of the *XXX*) that contains the letterhead text shown in Figure 4.18 and assign it the keyboard command Alt + Ctrl + G. (The text in Figure 4.18 is set in 18-point Goudy Old Style bold.)
2. Close the document without saving it.
3. At a clear window, run the XXXLtrhd02 macro.
4. With the insertion point a double space below the letterhead, insert the document named **WordLetter02** into the current document. *(Hint: Do this by clicking Insert and then File.)*
5. Save the letter and name it **ewc4sc01**.
6. Print and then close **ewc4sc01**.

FIGURE 4.18 Assessment 1

GOOD SAMARITAN HOSPITAL
1201 James Street
St. Louis, MO 62033
(314) 555-1201

Assessment 2

1. At a clear document screen, run the XXXTab01 macro and then create the document shown in Figure 4.19. (Type the text in the first column at the first tab stop, not the left margin.)
2. After creating the document, save it and name it **ewc4sc02**.
3. Print and then close **ewc4sc02**.

FIGURE 4.19 Assessment 2

STRADFORD FUNDS CORPORATION

Public Relations Department, Extension Numbers

Roger Maldon 129

Kimberly Holland 143

Richard Perez 317

Sharon Rawlins 211

Earl Warnberg 339

Susan Fanning 122

Assessment 3

1. At a clear document screen, record a macro named XXXNotSig that includes the information shown in Figure 4.20. Include Fill-in fields in the macro where you see the text in parentheses.
2. After recording the macro, close the document without saving it.

3. Open **WordContract01**.
4. Save the document with Save As and name it **ewc4sc03**.
5. Make the following changes to the document:
   a. Move the insertion point to the end of the document, press the Enter key twice and then insert the following information at the left margin:

   _____
   LLOYD KOVICH, President
   Reinberg Manufacturing

   _____
   JOANNE MILNER, President
   Labor Worker's Union

   b. Move the insertion point to the end of the document, press the Enter key three times, and then run the XXXNotSig macro and type the following information when prompted:

(name1)	=	LLOYD KOVICH
(name2)	=	JOANNE MILNER
(county)	=	Ramsey County

6. Save, print, and then close **ewc4sc03**.

FIGURE 4.20 Assessment 3

STATE OF MINNESOTA   )
) ss.
COUNTY OF RAMSEY   )

   I certify that I know or have satisfactory evidence that (name1) and (name2) are the persons who appeared before me, and said persons acknowledge that they signed the foregoing Contract and acknowledged it to be their free and voluntary act for the uses and purposes therein mentioned.

_____
NOTARY PUBLIC in and for the State of
Minnesota residing in (county)

Assessment 4

1. At a clear document screen, record a macro named XXXQuizFormat that does the following:
    a. Changes the font to 12-point Bookman Old Style (or a similar serif typeface).
    b. Changes the left paragraph indent to .3 inch.
    c. Adds 12 points of spacing before paragraphs.
2. Close the document without saving it.
3. Open **WordQuiz01**.
4. Save the document with Save As and name it **ewc4sc04**.
5. Select the entire document and then run the XXXQuizFormat macro.
6. Save and then print **ewc4sc04**.
7. With **ewc4sc04** still open, edit the XXXQuizFormat macro as follows:
    a. At the Visual Basic Editor, edit the step *.LeftIndent = InchesToPoints(0.3)* so it displays as *.LeftIndent = InchesToPoints(0.5)*. (You may need to scroll down the macro to display this macro line.)
    b. Edit the step *.RightIndent = InchesToPoints(0)* so it displays as *.RightIndent = InchesToPoints(0.5)*.
    c. Edit the step *.SpaceBefore = 12* so it displays as *.SpaceBefore = 24*.
8. After closing the Visual Basic Editor, select the entire document, and then run the XXXQuizFormat macro.
9. Center and bold the title *CHAPTER QUIZ*.
10. Save, print, and then close **ewc4sc04**.
11. At a clear document screen, display the Macros dialog box, delete all macros that begin with your initials, and then close the dialog box.

Assessment 5

1. Open **WordReport05**.
2. Save the document with Save As and name it **ewc4sc05**.
3. Automatically format the document at the AutoFormat dialog box.
4. Save, print, and then close **ewc4sc05**.

Assessment 6

1. At a clear document screen, create the following styles:
    a. Create a style named DocumentTitle that applies 16-point Tahoma bold.
    b. Create a style named ParagraphSpacing that applies 24 points of spacing after the paragraph.
2. Save the document and name it **ewc4sc06**.
3. With the document still open, insert the document named **WordDocument02**.
4. Apply the following styles:
    a. Apply the DocumentTitle style to the text *ARE YOU PREPARING FOR RETIREMENT?*.
    b. Select the paragraphs of text (excluding the title and the blank line below the title) and then apply the ParagraphSpacing style.
5. Save, print, and then close **ewc4sc06**.

Assessment 7

1. Open **ewc4sc06**.
2. Save the document with Save As and name it **ewc4sc07**.
3. Make the following changes to the styles:

a. Modify the DocumentTitle style so it applies 16-point Times New Roman bold and also center aligns the text.
b. Modify the ParagraphSpacing style so the space after is 18 points rather than 24 points.
4. Save, print, and then close **ewc4sc07**.

Assessment 8

1. Open **WordReport05**.
2. Save the document with Save As and name it **ewc4sc08**.
3. Select the entire document and then change to single line spacing.
4. Apply the specified styles to the following headings:

MODULE 1: DEFINING NEWSLETTER ELEMENTS	=	Heading 1
Designing a Newsletter	=	Heading 2
Defining Basic Newsletter Elements	=	Heading 2
MODULE 2: PLANNING A NEWSLETTER	=	Heading 1
Defining the Purpose of a Newsletter	=	Heading 2

5. Insert a cross-reference following the period at the end of the first paragraph that contains the text *For more information, refer to* and refers readers to the *Defining the Purpose of a Newsletter* heading.
6. Move to the reference text using the cross-reference.
7. Save, print, and then close **ewc4sc08**.

CHAPTER challenge

You work with the marketing director for The Best of Both Worlds: Land and Water, which is a company specializing in recreational vehicles and boats. You are responsible for much of the correspondence that occurs among customers and distributors. To save time when writing letters and memos, create a macro for the company name. Also, create a macro that can be used for a closing in letters. Choose an appropriate closing (Best Wishes, Sincerely, and so on.) and use your name as the typed signature. Save the document in which these macros have been created.

Instead of using the macro names to run the macros, you would like to create a customized toolbar that includes both of these macros, as well as a few of your favorite or most frequently used buttons. Use the Help feature to learn about creating a new toolbar and adding buttons to it. Open the document created in the first part of the Chapter Challenge. Create a new toolbar, titled *(your first name)* **Shortcuts**. Be sure that the new toolbar is made available and saved in the existing document. Add the two macros created in the first part of the Chapter Challenge as well as two of your favorite or most frequently used buttons to the toolbar. Shorten the names of macro buttons. Save the document.

INTEGRATED

The marketing director has brainstormed ideas for an upcoming presentation and typed some ideas into a Word document titled, Summer Extravaganza. She has asked you to take these ideas and put them into a PowerPoint presentation. You know that a Word outline based on styles can be imported into PowerPoint presentation. Open the file, **Summer Extravaganza**. Apply Heading 1 style to the lines aligned at the left margin. Apply Heading 2 style to the lines that have been indented. Save and close the file. Open the revised Word file in PowerPoint. Make the first slide a title slide. Add the text, **Presented by** *your marketing director's name* in the subtitle textbox. Save and print (on one page) the three slides in the PowerPoint presentation.

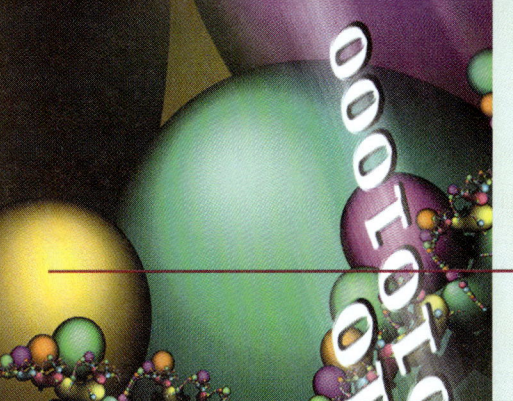

WORK IN Progress

Unit 1: Formatting and Enhancing Documents

ASSESSING proficiencies

In this unit, you learned to format Word documents with features such as mail merge, sorting and selecting, footnotes and endnotes, bookmarks, and cross-references; to add visual appear with features such as borders, images, watermarks, and WordArt; and to automate formatting with features such as macros and styles.

Assessment 1

1. Look at the information shown in Figure U1.1 and Figure U1.2. Use the Mail Merge Wizard to prepare six letters using the information shown in the figures. When completing the steps, consider the following:
   a. At Step 3, create a data source document using the information shown in Figure U1.1. Save the data source document in the WordUnit01E folder on your disk and name it **SoundMedDS**.
   b. At Step 6, complete the following steps:
      1) Click the Edit individual letters hyperlink in the task pane.
      2) At the Merge to New Document dialog box, make sure *All* is selected, and then click the OK button.
      3) Save the merged letters in the normal manner in the WordUnit01E folder on your disk and name the document **SoundMedLetters**.
      4) Print **SoundMedLetters**. (This document will print six letters.)
      5) Close **SoundMedLetters**.
      6) Save the main document in the normal manner on your disk in drive A and name it **SoundMedMD**.

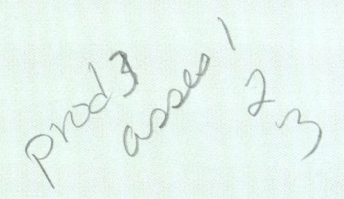

WORD — Performance Assessment — E169

Mrs. Antonio Mercado
3241 Court G
Tampa, FL 33623

Ms. Kristina Vukovich
1120 South Monroe
Tampa, FL 33655

Ms. Alexandria Remick
909 Wheeler South
Tampa, FL 33620

Mr. Minh Vu
9302 Lawndale Southwest
Tampa, FL 33623

Mr. Curtis Iverson
10139 93rd Court South
Tampa, FL 33654

Mrs. Holly Bernard
8904 Emerson Road
Tampa, FL 33620

Figure U1.1 • Assessment 1

December 12, 2004

«AddressBlock»

«GreetingLine»

Sound Medical is switching hospital care in Tampa to St. Jude's Hospital beginning January 1, 2005. As mentioned in last month's letter, St. Jude's Hospital was selected because it meets our requirements for high-quality, customer-pleasing care that is also affordable and accessible. Our physicians look forward to caring for you in this new environment.

Over the past month, staff members at Sound Medical have been working to make this transition as smooth as possible. Surgeries planned after January 1 are being scheduled at St. Jude's Hospital. Mothers delivering babies any time after January 1 are receiving information about delivery room tours and prenatal classes available at St. Jude's. Your Sound Medical doctor will have privileges at St. Jude's and will continue to care for you if you need to be hospitalized.

You are a very important part of our patient family, «Title» «Last_Name», and we hope this information is helpful. If you have any additional questions or concerns, please call our hospital transition manager, Jeff Greenswald, at (813) 555-9886, between 8:00 a.m. and 4:30 p.m.

Sincerely,

Jody Tiemann
District Administrator

XX: SoundMedMD

Figure U1.2 • Assessment 1

Assessment 2

1. Use the Mail Merge Wizard to prepare envelopes for the letters created in Assessment 1.
2. Specify **SoundMedDS** as the data source document.
3. Save the merged envelope document on your disk and name the document **SoundMedEnvs**.
4. Print the **SoundMedEnvs** document.
5. Do not save the envelope main document.

Assessment 3

1. Open **WordTab01**.
2. Save the document with Save As and name it **ewu1pa03**.
3. Sort the columns of text alphabetically by last name in the first column. (Display the Sort Options dialog box and make sure *Tabs* is selected in the *Separate fields at* section.)
4. Print **ewu1pa03**.
5. Sort the second column of text alphabetically by the title in the second column and then alphabetically by last name in the first column. (This is one sort.)
6. Print and then close **ewu1pa03**.

Assessment 4

1. Open **WordTable07**.
2. Save the document with Save As and name it **ewu1pa04**.
3. Sort the text alphabetically in the first column (except the header row).
4. Use the AutoFit feature to make the columns in the table automatically fit the contents.
5. Apply the Table Contemporary table formatting to the table.
6. Save, print, and then close **ewu1pa04**.

Assessment 5

1. Open **WordReport06**.
2. Save the document with Save As and name it **ewu1pa05**.
3. Make the following changes to the document:
    a. Bold the titles and headings in the document.
    b. Change the left and right margins to 1 inch.
    c. Insert a page break that begins a new page at the line containing the title *MODULE 4: CREATING NEWSLETTER LAYOUT*.
    d. Make sure the widow/orphan control is turned on.
    e. Create the first footnote shown in Figure U1.3 at the end of the first paragraph in the *Applying Desktop Publishing Guidelines* section of the document.
    f. Create the second footnote shown in Figure U1.3 at the end of the third paragraph in the *Applying Desktop Publishing Guidelines* section of the document.
    g. Create the third footnote shown in Figure U1.3 at the end of the last paragraph in the *Applying Desktop Publishing Guidelines* section of the document.

h. Create the fourth footnote shown in Figure U1.3 at the end of the only paragraph in the *Choosing Paper Weight* section of the document.
4. Save, print, and then close **ewu1pa05**.

Fellers, Laurie, *Desktop Publishing Design*, Cornwall & Lewis Publishing, 2003, pages 67-72.

Moriarity, Joel, "Adding Emphasis to Documents," *Desktop Publishing*, August 2004, pages 3-6.

Wong, Chun Man, *Desktop Publishing with Style*, Monroe-Ackerman Publishing, 2003, pages 87-93.

Jaquez, Andre, *Desktop Publishing Tips and Tricks*, Aurora Publishing House, 2004, pages 103-106.

Figure U1.3 • Assessment 5

Assessment 6

1. Open **ewu1pa05**.
2. Save the document with Save As and name it **ewu1pa06**.
3. Make the following changes to the document:
   a. Edit the third footnote and change the publication year from *2003* to *2004* and change the pages from *87-93* to *61-68*.
   b. Move the first footnote to the end of the only paragraph in the *Choosing Paper Size and Type* section of the document.
   c. Delete the fourth footnote.
4. Save, print, and then close **ewu1pa06**.

Assessment 7

1. Open **WordReport04**.
2. Save the document with Save As and name it **ewu1pa07**.
3. Make the following changes to the document:
   a. Delete text in the document from the beginning of the title COMPUTERS IN ENTERTAINMENT (located on page 2) to the end of the document.
   b. Select the entire document, change the line spacing to 1.5, change the font size to 13 points, and then deselect the text.
   c. Move the insertion point immediately past the title COMPUTERS IN COMMUNICATIONS and then press the Enter key once.
   d. Set the title in 14-point Arial bold.
   e. Set the headings *Telecommunications*, *Publishing*, and *News Services* in 14-point Arial bold.
   f. Move the insertion point to the beginning of the document and then insert a clip art image of a computer (you choose the image) with the following specifications:
      1) Change the wrapping style to *Tight*.
      2) Change the width of the image to 1 inch.
      3) Change the horizontal alignment of the image to *Left* relative to the *Column*.

4) Change the vertical absolute position to *1.6" below Page*.
4. Save, print, and then close **ewu1pa07**.

Assessment 8

1. At a clear document screen, create the document shown in Figure U1.4 with the following specifications:
   a. Set the title *CORPORATE COMMITMENT* in 24-point Times New Roman bold.
   b. Create the top box with the following specifications:
      1) Use the Rectangle tool to draw the box.
      2) Add light green fill to the box.
      3) Click the 3-D Style button on the Drawing toolbar and then click the 3-D Style 11 option (third option from the left in the third row).
      4) Click the Text Box button and then draw a text box inside the first box.
      5) Set the text inside the text box center-aligned in 20-point Times New Roman bold.
      6) Add light green fill to the text box.
      7) Remove the line around the text box. (Do this with the Line Color button on the Drawing toolbar.)
   c. After creating the top box, copy the box two times so a total of three boxes appear in the document as shown in Figure U1.4. ***(Hint: To select the box, click the Select Objects button on the Drawing toolbar and then draw a border around the box. This selects the box and all objects inside the box.)***
   d. Make sure the text appears in the boxes as shown in Figure U1.4.
   e. Make sure the boxes are center-aligned. To do this, select all three boxes, click the Draw button on the Drawing toolbar, point to Align or Distribute, and then click Align Center.
2. Save the completed document and name it **ewu1pa08**.
3. Print and then close **ewu1pa08**.

Figure U1.4 • Assessment 8

Assessment 9

1. Create a certificate with the following specifications:
   a. Change the page orientation to Landscape.
   b. Change the top, bottom, left, and right margins to .75 inch.
   c. Insert a page border of your choosing.
   d. Insert the following text (you determine the typeface, typestyle, and type size of the text):

   > Volunteer of the Year Award
   > Presented to Simone Moore
   > Sun Valley School District
   > June 2005

   e. Insert either an appropriate clip art image in the certificate or an appropriate autoshape.
   f. Include at least four small sun autoshapes that are aligned and distributed. (Find the sun shape by clicking the AutoShapes button on the Drawing toolbar and then pointing to Basic Shapes. The Sun shape is the third shape from the left in the sixth row.)
2. Save the completed certificate and name it **ewu1pa09**.
3. Print and then close **ewu1pa09**.

Assessment 10

1. At a clear document screen, use WordArt to create the flyer letterhead shown in Figure U1.5 by completing the following steps:
   a. Press the Enter key seven times and then move the insertion point back to the beginning of the document.
   b. Display the WordArt Gallery and then double-click the second option from the left in the third row (from the top).
   c. At the Edit WordArt Text dialog box, type Newbury News, and then click OK.
   d. Make the following changes to the WordArt text:
      1) Click the WordArt text to select it.
      2) Change the text wrapping to *Through*.
      3) Change the shape to Arch Up (Curve).
      4) Change the height and width to 2 inches.
      5) Change the horizontal alignment to left.
   e. Deselect the WordArt text.
   f. Move the insertion point to the end of the document and then insert the border line shown in Figure U1.5. *(Hint: Do this at the Borders and Shading dialog box. Choose the fourth option from the end of the Style list box and change the color to Lavender.)*
2. Save the document and name it **ewu1pa10**.
3. Print and then close **ewu1pa10**.

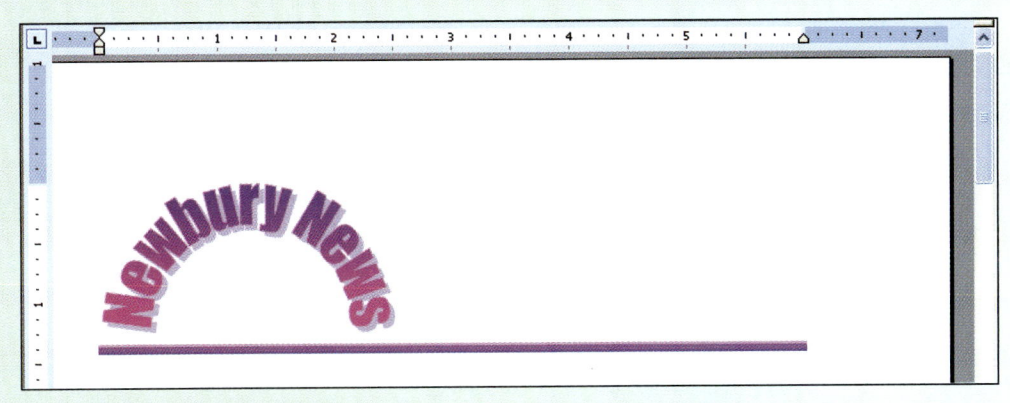

Figure U1.5 • Assessment 10

Assessment 11

1. At a clear document screen, record a macro named CInfo that includes the copyright information shown in Figure U1.6. Include Fill-in fields in the macro where you see the text in parentheses.
2. After recording the macro, close the document without saving it.
3. Open **WordContract01**.
4. Save the document with Save As and name it **ewu1pa11**.
5. Change the top, bottom, left, and right margins to .8 inch.
6. Move the insertion point to the end of the document, press the Enter key once, and then run the CInfo macro and insert the following information when prompted:
   (name) = Oliver Middleton
   (date) = March 22, 2005
7. Save, print, and then close **ewu1pa11**.

This document is the sole property of Reinberg Manufacturing and may not be reproduced, copied, or sold without express written consent of a legal representative of Reinberg Manufacturing.

Prepared by: (name)
Date: (date)

Figure U1.6 • Assessment 11

Assessment 12

1. At a clear document screen, create a style named TitleFormatting that applies the following formatting:
   a. 16-point Arial bold
   b. 6 points of spacing before and after paragraph
2. Create a style named HeadingFormatting that applies the following:
   a. 12-point Arial bold
   b. 6 points of spacing before and after paragraph
3. Save the document and name it **ewu1pa12**.

4. With **ewu1pa12** open, insert the document named **WordReport05** into **ewu1pa12**.
5. Make the following changes to the document:
    a. Select the entire document and change the line spacing to single.
    b. Apply the TitleFormatting style to the following titles:
        MODULE 1: DEFINING NEWSLETTER ELEMENTS
        MODULE 2: PLANNING A NEWSLETTER
    c. Apply the HeadingFormatting style to the following headings:
        Designing a Newsletter
        Defining Basic Newsletter Elements
        Defining the Purpose of a Newsletter
6. Save and then print **ewu1pa12**.
7. With **ewu1pa12** still open, save the document with Save As and name it **ewu1pa12Second**.
8. Edit the TitleFormatting style so it applies the following formatting:
    a. 14-point Times New Roman bold
    b. 12 points of spacing before and after paragraph
    c. Center alignment
9. Edit the HeadingFormatting style so it applies 12-point Times New Roman bold (leave the 6 points before and after spacing).
10. Save, print, and then close **ewu1pa12Second**.

WRITING activity

Activity 1

Situation: You are an employee for the City of Greenwater and are responsible for coordinating volunteers for the city's Safe Night program. Compose a letter to the volunteers listed in Figure U1.7 and include the following information:
- Safe Night event scheduled for Saturday, June 25, 2005.
- Volunteer orientation scheduled for Thursday, May 19, 2005, at 7:30 p.m. At the orientation, participants will learn about the types of volunteer positions available and the work schedule.

Include any additional information in the letter, including a thank you to the volunteers. Use the Mail Merge Wizard to create a data source with the names and addresses in Figure U1.7 that is attached to the main document, which is the letter to the volunteers. You determine the names for the data source and main documents. Save the merged letters as **ewu1act01** and then print the letters.

Mrs. Laura Reston 376 Thompson Avenue Greenwater, OR 99034	Mr. Matthew Klein 7408 Ryan Road Greenwater, OR 99034
Ms. Cecilia Sykes 1430 Canyon Road Greenwater, OR 99034	Ms. Brian McDonald 890 Union Street Greenwater, OR 99034
Mr. Ralph Emerson 1103 Highlands Avenue Greenwater, OR 99034	Mrs. Nola Alverez 598 McBride Street Greenwater, OR 99034

Figure U1.7 • Activity 1

Activity 2

Situation: You have just opened a new mailing and shipping business and need letterhead stationery. Create a letterhead for your company that includes *at least* one of the following: a drawn shape, an autoshape, a line, and/or a 3-D object. Include the following information in the letterhead:

> Global Mailing
> 4300 Jackson Avenue
> Toronto, Ontario M4C 3X4
> (416) 555-0095
> www.emcp.net/gmail

Save the completed letterhead and name it **ewu1act02**. Print and then close **ewu1act02**.

INTERNET project

Make sure you are connected to the Internet and then use a search engine (you choose the search engine) to search for companies on the Web that provide information, services, and/or products for designing documents. Key words you might consider using to search the Web include:

> desktop publishing   typeface
> document design   electronic design

Find at least three Web sites that interest you and then create a report in Word about the sites that includes the following:
- Type of site (company, personal, magazine, etc.)
- Site name, address, and URL
- A brief description of the site
- Products, services, and/or information available at the site

Include any other additional information pertinent to the sites. Apply formatting to enhance the document. When the document is completed, save it and name it **ewu1IntAct**. Print and then close **ewu1IntAct**.

JOB Study

Preparing Guidelines for E-mail Communications

With the daily use of e-mail in the corporate environment, employees must know the rules of electronic communication. You have prepared the Pacific Northwest Technology corporate guidelines for e-mail communications. You will distribute the guidelines to all departments in a report via e-mail. In addition, in keeping with Pacific's marketing strategy, you will use the same information to prepare a newsletter to be mailed to a select list of clients.

Using the concepts and techniques you learned in Unit 1, complete the following tasks:

1. Open **WordNetiquette** and then format the information in an appropriate report form. Use the special features you learned in Chapter 2 to enhance the format of the document. Save the formatted document with Save As and name it **ewu1JobStudy**. Print **ewu1JobStudy**.
2. Create a newsletter based on the report you formatted in Step 1. Add visual appeal to the newsletter by incorporating the graphic and drawing techniques presented in Chapter 3. Save and print the document.
3. Use the Mail Merge Wizard to prepare six letters enclosing the newsletter you created in Step 2. Create the data source with the names and addresses shown in Figure U1.8. Use the same data source to create mailing labels. Utilize the concepts and techniques you learned in Unit 1 to design a custom letterhead for the main document. Save and print the main document and data source.
4. Create a macro that will open, print, and close the merged letters and labels you created in Step 3. Assign the macro to the toolbar.

Kathleen Richardson, President
Widden Communications
566 Longview Avenue
Bluestone, NY 12345

Raymond Lopez, CEO
United Freight, Inc.
887 Woodhaven Road
Garwood, NY 22355

Leonard Gothez, Chairman
Gothez Engineering
334 Bonhampton Avenue
Union Plains, NJ 12335

Cynthia Hu, Director
Hu Industrial Graphics, Inc.
908 Pinelawn Road
West Orange, NY 33425

Barbara Garwood, Dean
Information Technology
Fairfield Community College
Fairfield, IN 12445

Peter Young, President
On-line Now
664 West 57th Street
New York, NY 22335

Figure U1.8 • Job Study Addresses

EXPERT

MICROSOFT® WORD

Unit 2: Sharing and Publishing Information

- ➤ Working with Shared Documents
- ➤ Sharing Data
- ➤ Creating Specialized Tables and Indexes
- ➤ Using XML in Word 2003

BENCHMARK MICROSOFT® WORD 2003

MICROSOFT OFFICE SPECIALIST EXPERT SKILLS—UNIT 2

Reference No.	Skill	Pages
WW03E-1	**Formatting Content**	
WW03E-1-5	Create and modify diagrams and charts using data from other sources	
	Import data into a chart	E222-E223
	Import, embed and link an Excel worksheet into a table	E224-E230
	Copy a diagram from PowerPoint to Word	E230-E231
WW03E-2	**Organizing Content**	
WW03E-2-8	Structure documents using XML	
	Attach an XML schema to a Word document	E298-E305
	Load XML data into an Excel worksheet	E305-E307
	Enforce validation rules	E310-E314
	Display XML Options	E310-E314
	Enhance a schema	E314-E316
	Transform XML with style sheets	E319-E321
	Add a solution	E322-E324
	Delete schemas and solutions	E324-E325
WW03E-3	**Formatting Documents**	
WW03E-3-1	Create and modify forms	
	Create and fill in forms	E231-E237
	Edit and customize a form	E237-E247
WW03E-3-3	Create and modify document indexes and tables	
	Create and modify a table of contents	E263-E272
	Create and modify an index	E272-E281
	Create and modify a table of figures	E281-E284
	Create and modify a table of authorities	E284-E288
WW03E-3-4	Insert and modify endnotes, footnotes, captions, and cross-references	
	Create captions	E281-E283
WW03E-3-5	Create and manage master documents and subdocuments	E247-E254
WW03E-4	**Collaborating**	
WW03E-4-1	Modify track changes options	E181-E186
WW03E-4-3	Manage document versions	E186-E189
WW03E-4-4	Protect and restrict forms and documents	
	Protect documents	E189-E202
	Restrict formatting and editing, allow exceptions, enforce protection, add users	E190-E196
WW03E-4-5	Attach digital signatures to documents	E198-E199
WW03E-4-6	Customize document properties	E200-E202
WW03E-5	**Customizing Word**	
WW03E-5-3	Modify Word default settings	
	Change default file location for workgroup templates	E210-E213
	Create a custom dictionary and change the default dictionary	E208-E210
	Change the default font	E202-E205

CHAPTER 5

WORKING WITH SHARED DOCUMENTS

PERFORMANCE OBJECTIVES

Upon successful completion of Chapter 5, you will be able to:
- Track changes to a document and customize tracking
- Create multiple versions of a document
- Restrict formatting and editing in a document and allow exceptions to restrictions
- Protect a document with a password
- Save a document as read-only
- Create and apply a digital signature
- Insert summary and custom document properties
- Change the default font
- Search for specific documents
- Create a custom dictionary and change the default dictionary
- Set the file location for Workgroup templates
- Create a template

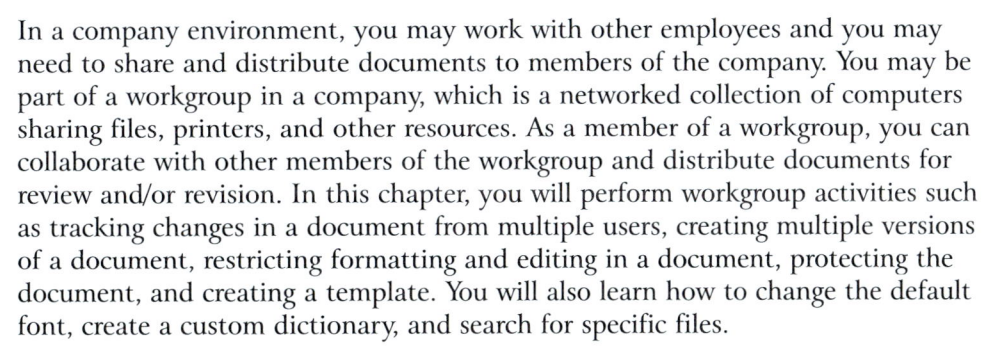

In a company environment, you may work with other employees and you may need to share and distribute documents to members of the company. You may be part of a workgroup in a company, which is a networked collection of computers sharing files, printers, and other resources. As a member of a workgroup, you can collaborate with other members of the workgroup and distribute documents for review and/or revision. In this chapter, you will perform workgroup activities such as tracking changes in a document from multiple users, creating multiple versions of a document, restricting formatting and editing in a document, protecting the document, and creating a template. You will also learn how to change the default font, create a custom dictionary, and search for specific files.

Tracking Changes to a Document

If more than one person in a workgroup needs to review and edit a document, consider using the tracking feature. When tracking is turned on, each deletion, insertion, or formatting change made to the document is tracked. For example,

QUICK STEPS

Turn on Tracking
Click Track Changes button on Reviewing toolbar.
OR
Click Tools, Track Changes.

Track Changes

Display for Review

HINT
Use the balloons to easily view and respond to reviewer changes.

Show

deleted text is not removed from the document but instead displays with a line through it and in a different color. Word uses a different color (up to eight) for each person in the workgroup making changes to the document. In this way, the person looking at the document can identify which author made what change.

Turn on tracking by clicking the Track Changes button on the Reviewing toolbar, clicking Tools and then Track Changes, or by pressing Ctrl + Shift + E. When tracking is on, the letters TRK display in black on the Status bar (located toward the bottom of the screen).

Controlling the Display of Editing Markings

Control how editing markings display in the document with the Display for Review button on the Reviewing toolbar. Click the down-pointing arrow at the right side of the Display for Review button and a drop-down list displays with the options *Final Showing Markup*, *Final*, *Original Showing Markup*, and *Original*.

Choose one of the first two options to specify how you want changes marked in the document. Choose the *Final Showing Markup* option if you want Word to mark all changes when you edit the document. If you choose *Final*, the changes you make to the document will be recorded but you will not see the editing markings.

Select the *Original Showing Markup* to view the unmodified version of the document with changes marked. Deleted text remains in the document and inserted text displays in the margin balloon, which is the opposite of how changed text displays with the *Final Showing Markup* option selected. If you want to display the document as it will appear if you accepted all changes, choose the *Final* option from the drop-down menu.

Control the marking changes that Word displays in a document with the options at the Show button drop-down menu shown in Figure 5.1. Insert a check mark before those options that you want Word to display in the document and remove the check mark from those options you do not want visible. You can show or hide markings by a specific reviewer by clicking the Show button and then pointing to the All Reviewers option. This displays a side menu with reviewer names. If you want all reviewer markings visible or hidden, insert a check mark before the All Reviewers option. If you want to show or hide reviewer markings for specific reviewers, insert a check mark before each of the desired reviewers.

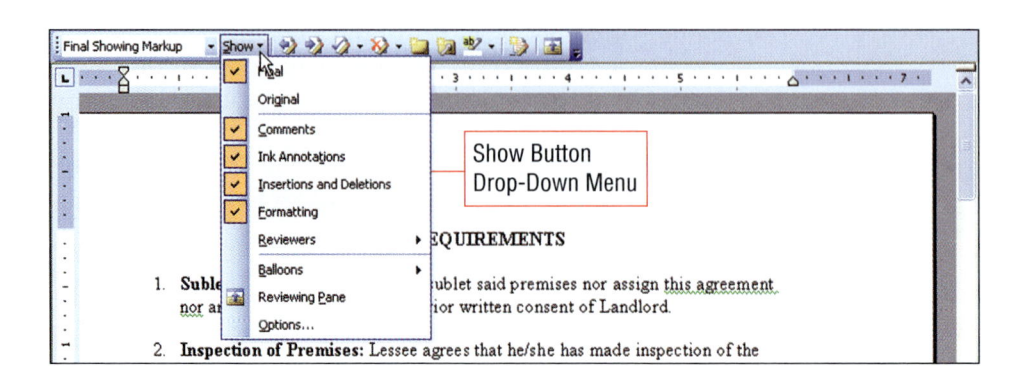

FIGURE 5.1 *Show Button Drop-Down Menu*

Customizing Track Changes Options

The track changes feature uses default settings when displaying inserted and deleted text in a document. For example, in Normal view, inserted text displays with an underline below the text and deleted text displays with strikethrough characters. In Print Layout and Web Layout views, inserted text displays with an underline and deleted text displays in a balloon at the right margin. (These defaults may vary.) Word uses the default settings as well as default colors, balloon location and width, and paper orientation. Change these settings with options at the Track Changes dialog box shown in Figure 5.2. Display this dialog box by clicking the Show button on the Reviewing toolbar and then clicking Options at the drop-down menu. You can also display this dialog box by clicking Tools on the Menu bar and then clicking Options at the drop-down menu. At the Options dialog box, click the Track Changes tab.

QUICK STEPS

Display Track Changes Dialog Box
1. Click Show button on Reviewing toolbar.
2. Click Options.

HINT
By default, Word chooses the zoom level and page orientation to best display the marked changes in the printed document.

FIGURE 5.2 Track Changes Dialog Box

Change the display of markup changes with options in this section.

Use options in this section to change the display of balloons.

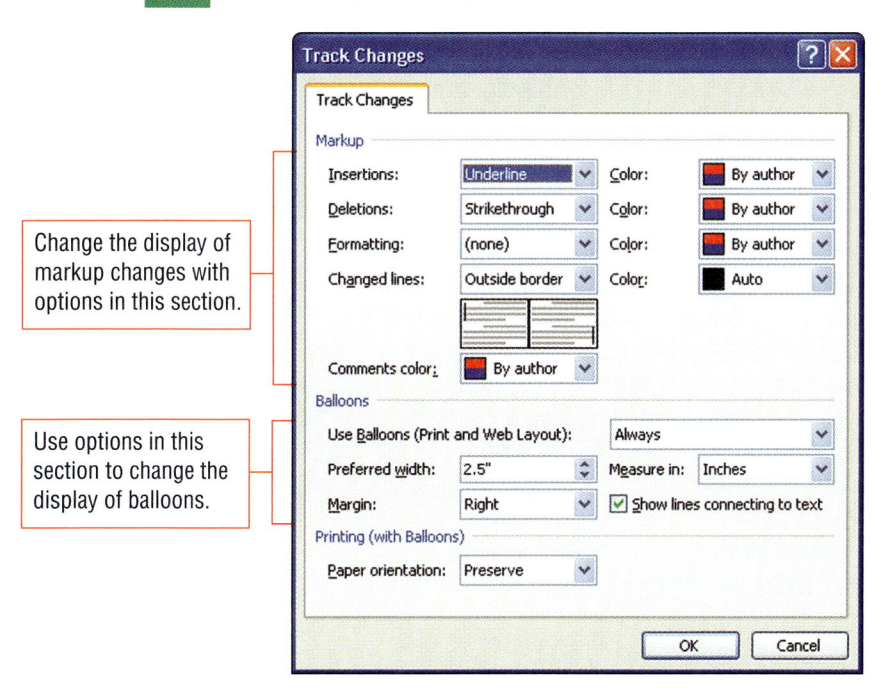

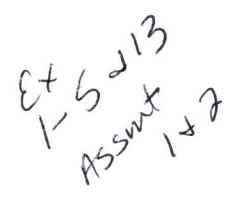

exercise 1

TRACKING AND CONTROLLING CHANGES IN A DOCUMENT

(Note: Check with your instructor before completing this exercise to determine if you can change User Information.)

1. Open **WordContract02**.
2. Save the document with Save As and name it **ewc5x01**.
3. Change to the Print Layout view.
4. Turn on the display of the Reviewing toolbar by right-clicking the Standard toolbar and then clicking Reviewing at the pop-up menu. (Skip this step if the Reviewing toolbar is already displayed.)

5. Make changes to the contract and track the changes by completing the following steps:
   a. Click the Track Changes button on the Reviewing toolbar.
   b. Delete *there are* in paragraph number 2. (Deleted text will display in a balloon at the right margin.)
   c. Insert the word *need* between *premises* and *to* in paragraph number 2. (The inserted word displays underlined and in a different color.) 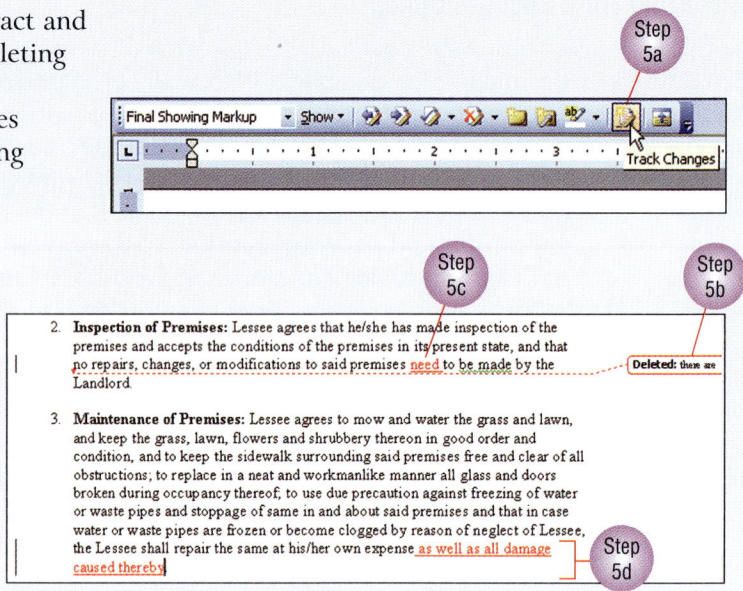
   d. Insert the text *as well as all damage caused thereby* immediately before the period that ends the last sentence in paragraph number 3.
   e. Click the Track Changes button to turn off tracking.
6. Change user information by completing the following steps:
   a. Click Tools and then Options.
   b. At the Options dialog box, click the User Information tab.
   c. At the Options dialog box with the User Information tab selected, make a note of the current name, initials, and mailing address. (You will reenter this information later in this exercise.)
   d. Type **Janelle Truman** in the *Name* text box.
   e. Press the Tab key. (This moves the insertion point to the *Initials* text box.)
   f. Type **JT**.
   g. Click OK to close the Options dialog box. 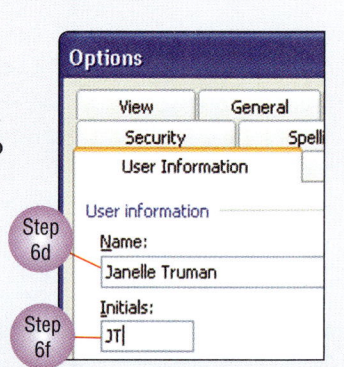
7. Make additional changes to the contract and track the changes by completing the following steps:
   a. Make sure the Reviewing toolbar is displayed.
   b. Click the Track Changes button to turn on tracking.
   c. Press Ctrl + End to move the insertion point to the end of the document, press the Enter key (this inserts *7.* in the document), and then type the following text: **Utilities: Lessee shall pay for service and utilities supplied to the premise.** (The text *Utilities* should be typed in bold.)
   d. Select and then delete paragraph 1. (You will not be able to select the number 1. When the paragraph is deleted, the other paragraphs are automatically renumbered.)
   e. Turn off tracking by clicking the Track Changes button on the Reviewing toolbar.
8. Customize tracking options by completing the following steps:
   a. Click the Show button on the Reviewing toolbar and then click Options at the drop-down menu.

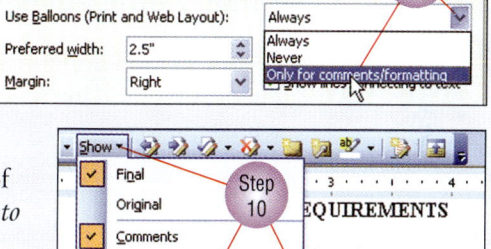

b. At the Track Changes dialog box, click the down-pointing arrow to the right of the *Insertions* option and then click *Double underline* at the drop-down list. 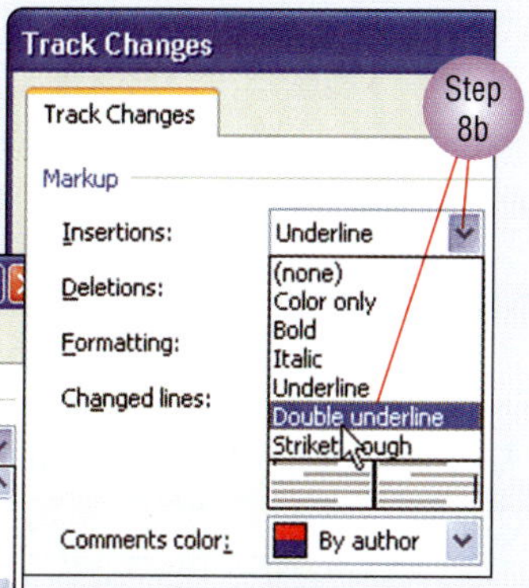
c. Click the down-pointing arrow at the right of the insertions *Color* option and then click *Green* at the drop-down list. (You will need to scroll down the list to display the *Green* option.) 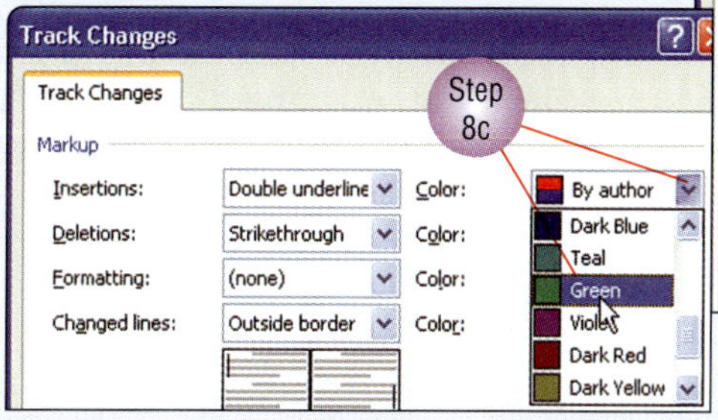
d. Click the down-pointing arrow at the right side of the *Use Balloons (Print and Web Layout)* option and then click *Only for comments/formatting* at the drop-down list.
e. Click the down-pointing arrow at the right of the *Preferred width* option until *2"* displays in the text box.
f. Click the down-pointing arrow to the right of the *Paper orientation* option and then click *Auto* at the drop-down list.
g. Click OK to close the dialog box.
9. Click the Print button on the Standard toolbar to print the documents with the insertions and deletions marked. 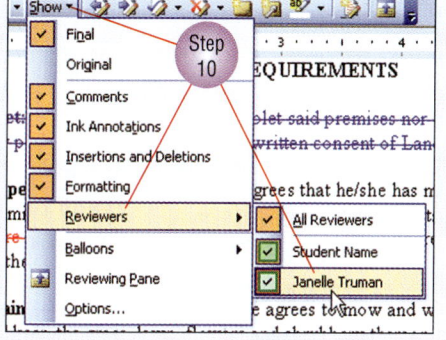
10. Do not display changes made by Janelle Truman by clicking the Show button on the Reviewing toolbar, pointing to Reviewers, and then clicking Janelle Truman. (This removes the check mark before her name.)
11. Click the Print button to print the document with the remaining changes.
12. Click the Display for Review button on the Reviewing toolbar and then click *Original* at the drop-down list. 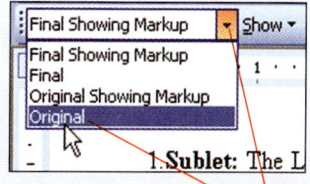
13. Click the Print button.
14. Click the Display for Review button and then click *Final* at the drop-down list. (This displays the document with all the changes accepted.)
15. Click the Print button. (Compare the original version of the document with the edited document.)
16. Click the Display for Review button and then click *Final Showing Markup* at the drop-down list.
17. Display all reviewers by clicking the Show button, pointing to Reviewers, and then clicking All Reviewers.
18. Click the down-pointing arrow at the right of the Accept Change button on the Reviewing toolbar and then click *Accept All Changes in Document* at the drop-down list.
19. Change the User Information back to the information that displayed before you typed *Janelle Truman* and the initials *JT*.
20. Return the tracking options back to the default by completing the following steps:
    a. Click the Show button on the Reviewing toolbar and then click Options at the drop-down menu.

b. At the Track Changes dialog box, click the down-pointing arrow to the right of the *Insertions* option and then click *Underline* at the drop-down list.
c. Click the down-pointing arrow at the right of the insertions *Color* option and then click *By author* at the drop-down list. (You will need to scroll up the list to display the *By author* option.)
d. Click the down-pointing arrow at the right side of the *Use Balloons (Print and Web Layout)* option and then click *Always* at the drop-down list.
e. Click the up-pointing arrow at the right of the *Preferred width* option until *2.5"* displays in the text box.
f. Click the down-pointing arrow to the right of the *Paper orientation* option and then click *Preserve* at the drop-down list.
g. Click OK to close the dialog box.
21. Save and then close **ewc5x01**.

Creating Multiple Versions of a Document

> **QUICK STEPS**
>
> **Save a Version of a Document**
> 1. Click File, Versions.
> 2. Click Save Now button.
> 3. Type a comment about the version.
> 4. Click OK.

Use Word's versioning feature to save multiple versions of a document in the same document. This saves disk space because only the differences between the versions are saved, not the entire document. You can create, review, open, and delete versions of a document. Creating versions is useful in a situation where you want to maintain the original document and use it as a "baseline" to compare with future versions of the document.

Saving a Version of a Document

To save a version of a document, click File and then Versions. This displays the Versions in (Document Name) dialog box shown in Figure 5.3.

FIGURE 5.3 *Versions in (Document Name) Dialog Box*

Click this button to save a version of the document.

> **HINT**
> If you want to keep a record of who makes changes to a document, insert a check mark in the *Automatically save a version on close* check box of the Versions in (Document Name) dialog box.

At the Versions in (Document Name) dialog box, click the Save Now button. This displays the Save Version dialog box shown in Figure 5.4. At this dialog box, type a comment about the version in the *Comments on version* text box, and then click OK. This removes the dialog box and returns you to the document. When a version is saved, a *File Versions* icon displays at the right side of the Status bar. To review the version information, display the Versions in (Document Name) dialog box.

FIGURE

5.4 Save Version Dialog Box

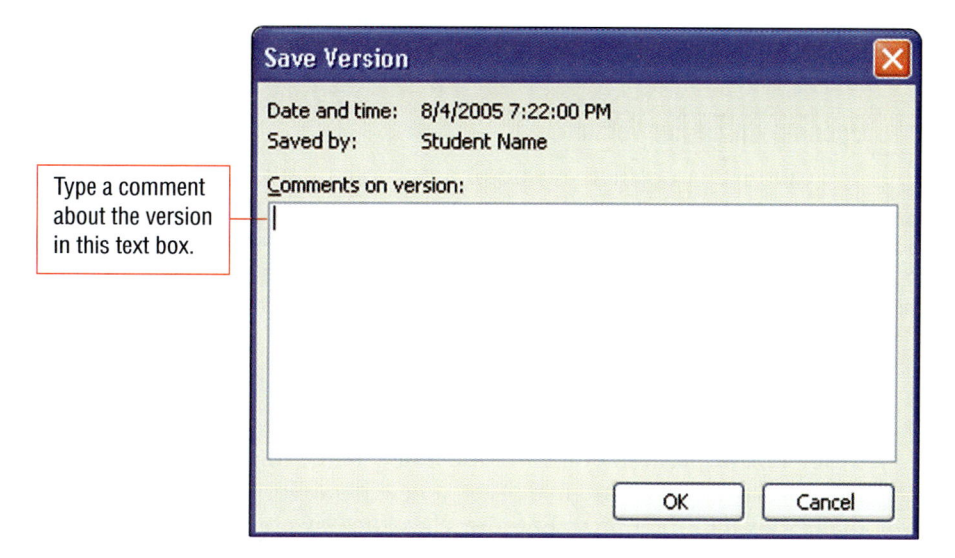

Type a comment about the version in this text box.

exercise 2

SAVING VERSIONS OF A DOCUMENT

1. Open **WordContract01**.
2. Save the document with Save As and name it **ewc5x02**.
3. Create a version of the original document by completing the following steps:
    a. Click File and then Versions.
    b. At the Versions in ewc5x02 dialog box, click the Save Now button.
    c. At the Save Version dialog box, type **First draft of contract** in the *Comments on version* text box.
    d. Click OK.
4. Make the following editing changes to the contract:
    a. Delete paragraph number 5 in the *Transfers and Moving Expenses* section.
    b. Type the text **and ten (10) hours of sick leave after ten (10) years of employment with RM** at the end of the sentence in paragraph number 1 in the *Sick Leave* section. (The text *RM* should be set in bold.)
5. Create another version of the document that contains the edits by completing the following steps:
    a. Click File and then Versions.
    b. At the Versions in ewc5x02 dialog box, click the Save Now button.
    c. At the Save Version dialog box, type **Second draft of contract** in the *Comments on version* text box.
    d. Click OK.
6. Make the following editing changes to the contract:
    a. Change *4,000* to *8,000* in paragraph number 3 in the *Transfers and Moving Expenses* section.

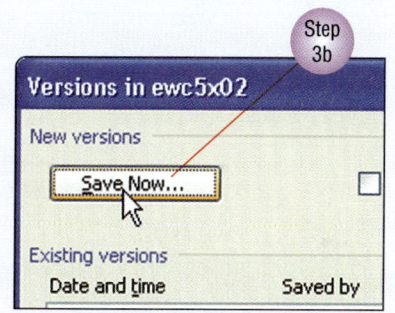

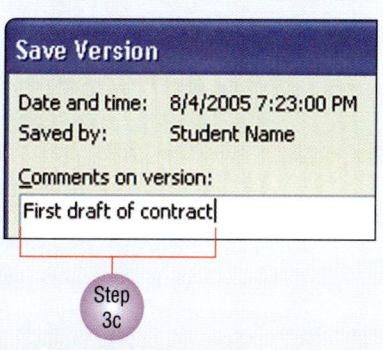

b. Delete paragraph number 2 in the *Sick Leave* section. (When you delete paragraph number 2, the remaining paragraphs are automatically renumbered.)
7. Create another version of the document with the comment *Third draft of contract*.
8. Close **ewc5x02**.

HINT
When saving multiple versions of a document, you are archiving the document. You cannot modify a saved version of the document. To make changes to an earlier version, open the version, then save it with File and then Save As.

Opening an Earlier Version

You can open an earlier version of a document and view it next to the current version. To do this, open the document containing the versions, and then display the Versions in (Document Name) dialog box. Click the desired earlier version in the *Existing versions* list box and then click the Open button. This opens the earlier version in a new window and tiles the two documents.

Saving a Version as a Separate Document

If you try to save an earlier version, the Save As dialog box will display. This dialog box displays so you will type a new name for the version document rather than overwriting the original. Type a new name for the version at the Save As dialog box and then press Enter or click the Save button.

Deleting a Version

Delete a version of a document at the Versions in (Document Name) dialog box. To delete a version, display the dialog box, click the version name in the *Existing versions* list box, and then click the Delete button. At the Confirm Version Delete message, click Yes.

exercise 3

OPENING, SAVING, DELETING, AND COMPARING VERSIONS

1. Open **ewc5x02**.
2. Open an earlier version by completing the following steps:
   a. Click File and then Versions.
   b. At the Versions in ewc5x02 dialog box, click the *First draft of contract* version in the *Existing versions* list box.
   c. Click the Open button. (This opens the earlier version in a new window and tiles the two documents.) 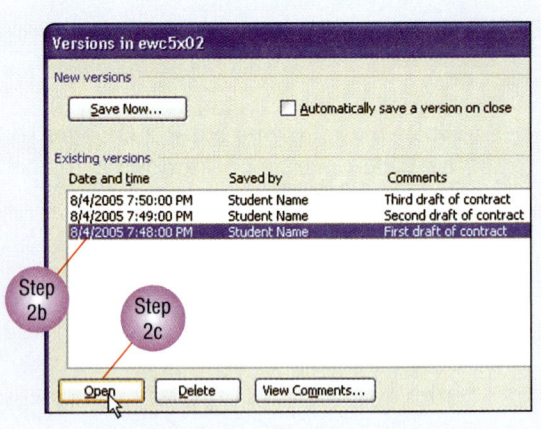
3. After viewing the documents, save the earlier version as a separate document by completing the following steps:
   a. Make sure the earlier version document window is active (and no text is selected). (The earlier version will probably display in the bottom window and will contain the word *version* somewhere in the Title bar.)
   b. Click File and then Save As.
   c. At the Save As dialog box, type **ContractFirstDraft**.
   d. Press Enter or click the Save button.
4. Close the **ContractFirstDraft** document.
5. Maximize the **ewc5x02** window.

6. Delete the second draft version of the document by completing the following steps:
   a. Click File and then Versions.
   b. At the Versions in ewc5x02 dialog box, click the *Second draft of contract* version in the *Existing versions* list box.
   c. Click the Delete button.
   d. At the Confirm Version Delete message, click Yes.
   e. At the Versions in ewc5x02 dialog box, click the Close button.
7. Save and then close **ewc5x02**.
8. Compare the first draft document with the latest version by completing the following steps:
   a. Open the document named **ContractFirstDraft**.
   b. Click Tools and then Compare and Merge Documents.
   c. At the Compare and Merge Documents dialog box, click once on **ewc5x02**.
   d. Click the down-pointing arrow at the right side of the Merge button and then click *Merge into new document* at the drop-down list.
9. Change to the Print Layout view. (Notice the results of the compare and merge.)
10. Print the document with the marked changes.
11. Make sure the Reviewing toolbar is displayed and then accept all of the changes.
12. Save the document and name it **ewc5x03**.
13. Print and then close **ewc5x03**.
14. Close **ContractFirstDraft**.

Protecting Documents

In a workgroup, you may want to distribute copies of a document to other members of the group. In some situations, you may want to protect your document and limit the changes that can be made to the document. If you create a document containing sensitive, restricted, or private information, consider protecting the document by saving it as a read-only document or securing it with a password. Also, consider adding a digital signature to a document to ensure that the document is not altered by someone else.

With options at the Protect Document task pane, you can limit what formatting and editing users can perform on text in a document. Limiting formatting and editing is especially useful in a workgroup environment where a number of people in an organization will be reviewing and editing the same document. For example, suppose you are responsible for preparing the yearly corporate report for your company. This corporate report contains information from a variety of departments such as Financial, Human Resources, and Sales and Marketing. You can prepare the report and then specify what portion of the report document an individual is allowed to edit. For example, you can specify that a person in the Financial Department would only be able to edit that portion of the report containing information on finances and someone in Human Resources would only be able to edit data pertinent to the Human Resources Department. In this way, you can protect the integrity of the document.

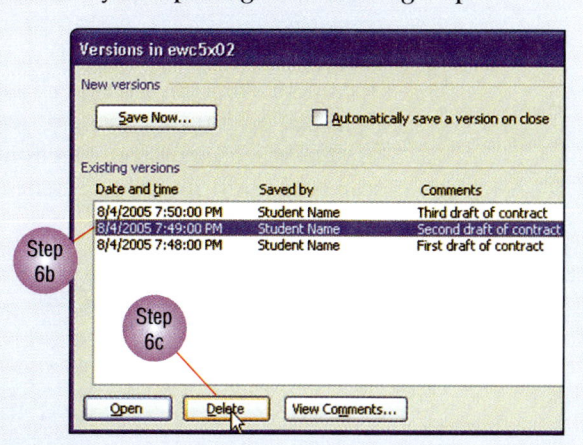

To protect a document, display the Protect Document task pane shown in Figure 5.5 by clicking Tools and then Protect Document. Use options in the *Formatting restrictions* section to limit formatting to specific styles and use options in the *Editing restrictions* section to specify the type of editing allowed in the document. You can also specify exceptions to the restrictions with the *Exceptions (optional)* option that displays when certain options are selected in the *Editing restrictions* section. After specifying formatting and editing restrictions, the next step is to start the enforcement of the restrictions.

FIGURE 5.5 **Protect Document Task Pane**

Use options in this section to limit formatting to specific styles.

Use options in this section to specify the type of editing allowed in the document.

After specifying formatting and editing restrictions, click this button to display the Start enforcing protection dialog box with protection options.

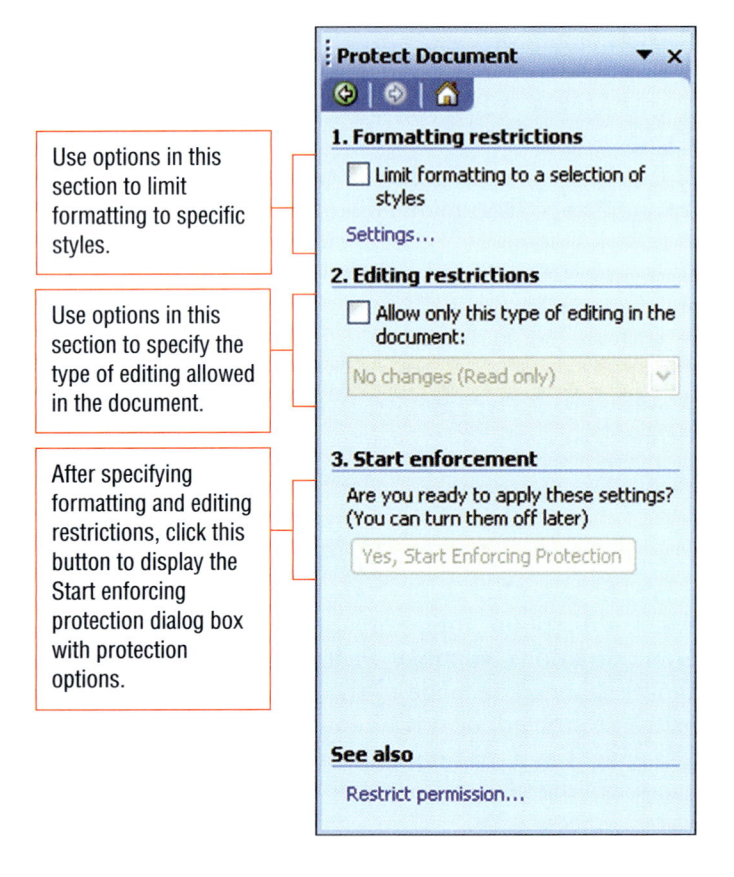

QUICK STEPS

Display Formatting Restrictions Dialog Box
1. Click Tools, Protect Document.
2. Click the Settings hyperlink.

Restricting Formatting

With options in the *Formatting restrictions* section of the Protect Document task pane, you can limit what formatting users can perform on text in a document. You can lock specific styles used in the document, allowing users the use of only specific styles, and prohibiting a user from adding formatting changes. Click the Settings hyperlink in the *Formatting restrictions* section and the Formatting Restrictions dialog box displays as shown in Figure 5.6.

FIGURE

5.6 Formatting Restrictions Dialog Box

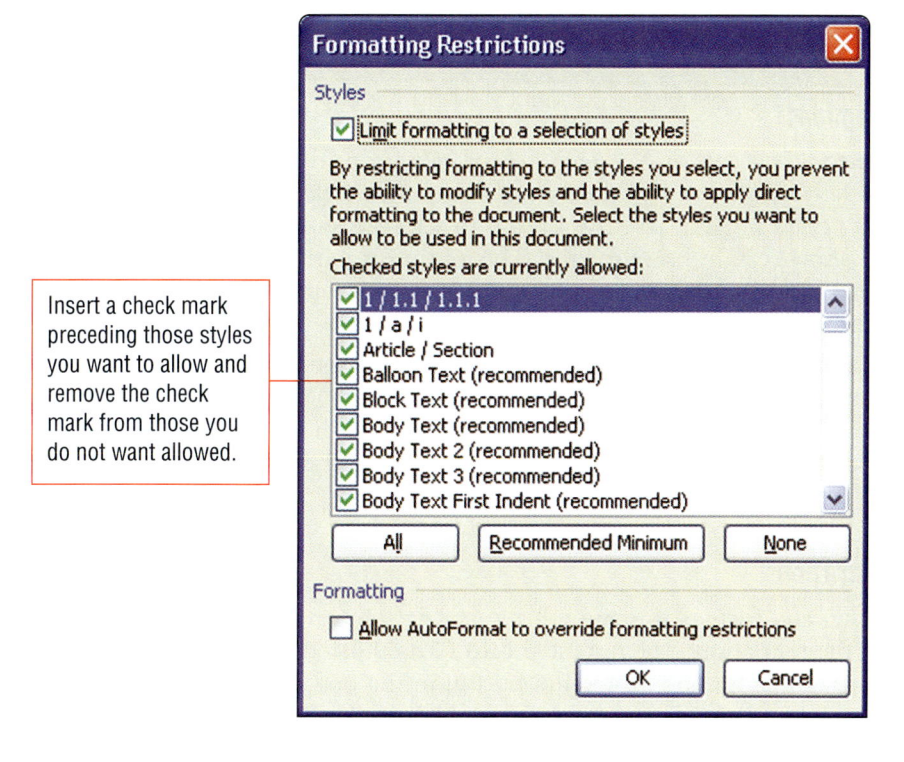

Insert a check mark preceding those styles you want to allow and remove the check mark from those you do not want allowed.

Insert a check mark in the *Limit formatting to a selection of styles* check box and the styles become available in the *Checked styles are currently allowed* list box. In this list box, insert a check mark in the check boxes preceding the styles you want to allow and remove the check mark in the check boxes preceding the styles you do not want allowed. Limit formatting to a minimum number of styles by clicking the Recommended Minimum button. This allows formatting with styles that Word uses for certain features such as bulleted or numbered lists. Click the None button to remove all check marks and allow no styles to be used in the document. Click the All button to insert a check mark in all the check boxes and allow all styles to be used in the document.

The AutoFormat feature automatically makes changes to a document such as changing and replacing straight quotes with smart quotes and changing ordinals to superscript. Insert a check mark in the Allow AutoFormat to override formatting restrictions check box to retain the AutoFormat features.

Restricting Editing

Use the *Editing restrictions* option at the Protect Document task pane to limit the types of changes a user can make to a document. Insert a check mark in the *Allow only this type of editing in the document* option and the drop-down list below the option becomes active. Click the down-pointing arrow at the right of the option box and these options are available: *No change (Read only)*, *Tracked changes*, *Comments*, and *Filling in form*. If you do not want a user to be able to make any changes to a document, choose the *No changes (Read only)* option. If you want the user to be able to make tracked changes in a document, choose the *Tracked changes*

> **QUICK STEPS**
>
> **Display More Users Dialog Box**
> 1. Click Tools, Protect Document.
> 2. Click the *Allow only this type of editing in the document* option.
> 3. Click the More users hyperlink.

option, and choose the *Comments* option if you want the user to be able to make comments in a document. These two options are useful in a workgroup environment where a document for review is routed to various members of the group. Choose the *Filling in form* option and a user will be able to fill in fields in a form but will not be able to make any other editing changes.

Allowing Exceptions

When you select *Comments* or *No changes (Read only)* from the option box below *Allow only this type of editing in the document*, the *Exceptions (optional)* option displays in the *Editing restrictions* section. Use this option to select specific parts of a document that you will allow certain users to edit. This option is particularly useful in a workgroup environment where you, along with other individuals, will be creating, editing, and/or formatting the same document.

To allow an exception to the restrictions, first select the part of the document that you want the chosen users to be able to freely edit. With the part of the document selected, insert a check mark in the *Everyone* check box and anyone opening the document will be able to make changes to the selected part of the document.

> **QUICK STEPS**
>
> **Display Start Enforcing Protection Dialog Box**
> 1. Click Tools, Protect Document.
> 2. Specify formatting and/or editing options.
> 3. Click Yes, Start Enforcing Protection button.

Enforcing Restrictions

After specifying any formatting and editing restrictions and specifying any exceptions to the restrictions, the next step is to start enforcement of the restrictions. Click the Yes, Start Enforcing Protection button in the task pane and the Start Enforcing Protection dialog box show in Figure 5.7 displays.

FIGURE 5.7 *Start Enforcing Protection Dialog Box*

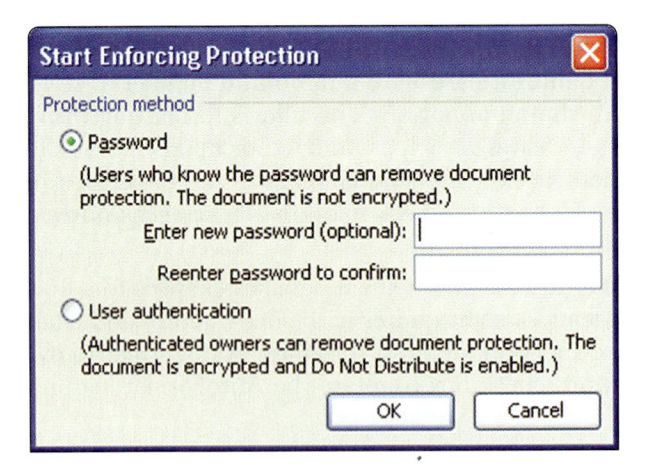

> **HINT**
> If Word does not recognize the password you type when opening a password-protected document, check to make sure Caps Lock is off, and then try typing the password again and remember that passwords are case sensitive.

At the Start Enforcing Protection dialog box, the *Password* option is automatically selected. At this setting, users will not be able to accidentally change any parts of the document they are not allowed to change. To further protect the document, you can add a password. To do this, click in the *Enter new password (optional)* text box, and then type the desired password. Click in the *Reenter password to confirm* text box and then type the same password again. Choose the *User authentication* option if you want to use encryption and SSL-secured authentication to prevent any unauthorized changes.

exercise 4
RESTRICTING FORMATTING OF A DOCUMENT AND PROTECTING A DOCUMENT

1. Open **WordAnnualReport**.
2. Save the document with Save As and name it **ewc5x04**.
3. Restrict formatting to recommended styles and the *Heading 1* and *Heading 2* styles by completing the following steps:
   a. Click Tools and then Protect Document.
   b. At the Protect Document task pane, click the *Limit formatting to a selection of styles* check box to insert a check mark. (Skip this step if the check box already contains a check mark.)
   c. Click the Settings hyperlink. 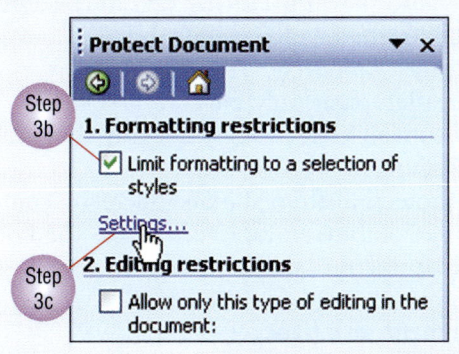
   d. At the Settings dialog box, click the None button.
   e. Scroll down the list box and then insert a check mark in the *Heading 1* check box and also the *Heading 2* check box.
   f. Click OK.
   g. At the message telling you that the document may contain direct formatting or styles that are not allowed and asking if you want to remove them, click Yes.
4. Click the Yes, Start Enforcing Protection button (located towards the bottom of the task pane).
5. At the Start Enforcing protection dialog box, click in the *Enter new password (optional)* text box and then type **formatting**. (Black circles will display in the text box rather than the letters you type.)
6. Press the Tab key (this moves the insertion point to the *Reenter password to confirm* text box) and then type **formatting**. (Black circles will display in the text box rather than the letters you type.)

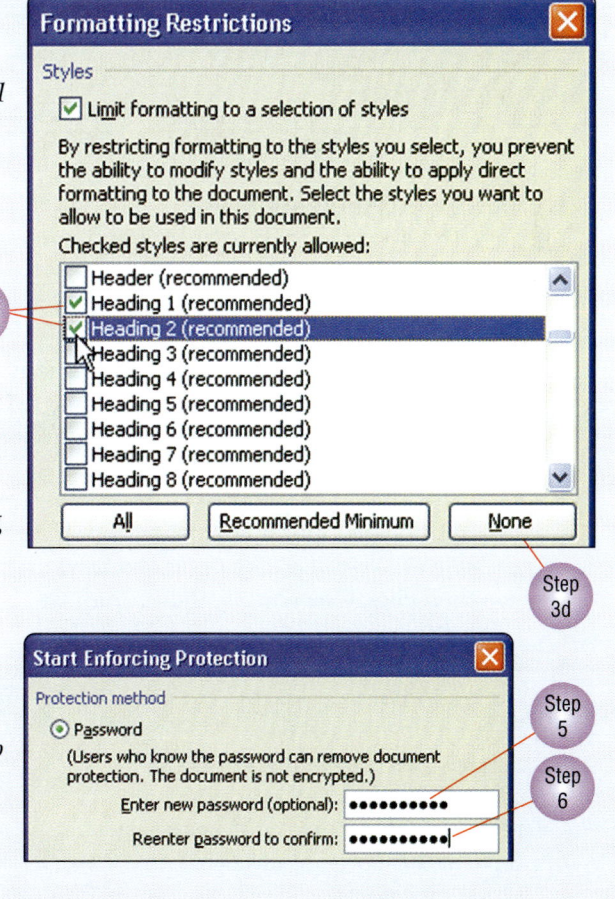

7. Click OK to close the dialog box.
8. Save and then close **ewc5x04**.
9. Open **ewc5x04**.
10. If necessary, display the Protect Document task pane by clicking View and then Task Pane. (If another task pane displays, click the Other Task Panes button [located towards the upper right corner of the task pane] and then click Protect Document).
11. Read the information in the task pane telling you that the document is password protected and special restrictions are in effect and that you may format text only with certain styles. Click the Available styles hyperlink. (This displays the Styles and Formatting task pane with only four styles in the *Pick formatting to apply* list box—*Clear Formatting, Heading 1, Heading 2,* and *Normal*.)
12. Apply the *Heading 1* style to the title TERRA ENERGY CORPORATION and apply the *Heading 2* style to the following headings: *Overview, Research and Development, Manufacturing,* and *Sales and Marketing*.
13. Save the document and then print only page 1.
14. Display the Protect Document task pane by clicking the Other Task Panes button and then clicking Protect Document.
15. Remove the password protection from the document by completing the following steps:
    a. Click the Stop Protection button located towards the bottom of the task pane.
    b. At the Unprotect Document dialog box, type **formatting** in the text box, and then click OK.
16. Close the Protect Document task pane.
17. Save and then close **ewc5x04**.

exercise 5 — RESTRICTING EDITING OF A DOCUMENT

1. Open **WordAnnualReport**.
2. Save the document with Save As and name it **ewc5x05**.
3. Restrict editing to only comments by completing the following steps:
   a. Click Tools and then Protect Document.
   b. Click the *Allow only this type of editing in the document* check box to insert a check mark.
   c. Click the down-pointing arrow at the right of the option box below the *Allow only this type of editing in the document* and then click *Comments* at the drop-down list.
4. Click the Yes, Start Enforcing Protection button located towards the bottom of the task pane.
5. At the Start Enforcing Protection dialog box, click OK. (Adding a password is optional, not necessary.)
6. Save and then close **ewc5x05**.
7. Open **ewc5x05**.

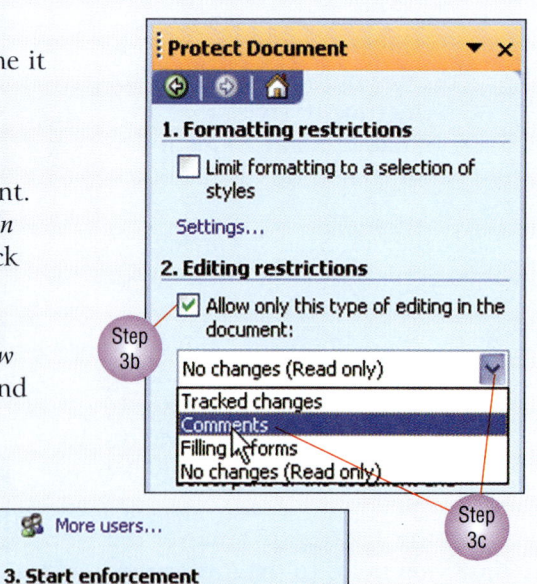

8. If necessary, display the Protect Document task pane by clicking View and then Task Pane. (If another task pane displays, click the Other Task Panes button [located towards the upper right corner of the task pane] and then click Protect Document.)
9. Read the information in the task pane telling you that the document is password protected and that you may only insert comments.
10. Scroll through the menu options on the Menu bar and notice the options that are dimmed and unavailable.
11. Insert a comment by completing the following steps:
    a. Change to the Print Layout view.
    b. Move the insertion point immediately after the period that ends the last sentence in the second paragraph of the *Overview* section.
    c. Click Insert and then Comment.
    d. Type the following in the comment balloon: **Include additional information on the impact of this purchase.**
12. Print only the comment. (To do this, display the Print dialog box, change the *Print what* option to *List of markup*, and then click OK.)
13. Close the Protect Document task pane.
14. Save and then close **ewc5x05**.

Step 11d

Microsoft Office 2003 includes a new feature, Information Rights Management, you can use to restrict permission or give limited access for personnel to specific data. Before using this feature, it must be downloaded (check the Microsoft Office Web site). If the Information Rights Management (IRM) feature is downloaded, you can allow an exception to the restrictions to an individual or individuals. To do this, click the More users hyperlink in the task pane. At the Add Users dialog box shown in Figure 5.8, type the name (or e-mail address) for the individual you want added to the exceptions list. You can type more than one name (e-mail address) at the dialog box by separating the name with a semicolon. When all names have been entered, click the OK button. The individual names you entered will display in a list box below the *Individuals* option (which displays below the *Groups* option). Insert a check mark in the check boxes preceding the names of those individuals for whom you want to make restriction exceptions. If you select more than one name, the names are added as an item to the *Groups* list box and can be selected more easily in the future.

FIGURE 5.8 **Add Users Dialog Box**

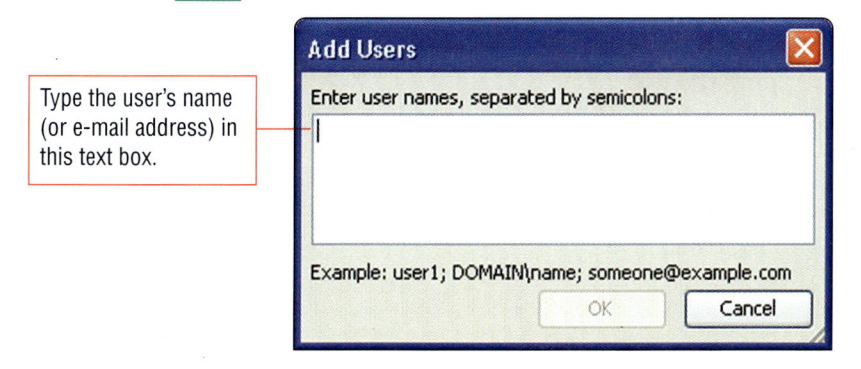

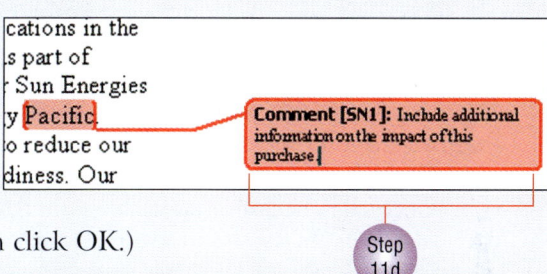

Type the user's name (or e-mail address) in this text box.

In the following optional exercise, you will add two fictitious users that will be excepted from the restrictions. The basic steps to except a user are presented in the exercise but you will not do any editing since the user names you will add are fictitious. Before completing the optional exercise, check with your instructor to determine if you should do all, none, or selected steps in the exercise.

exercise 6

(OPTIONAL) ADDING USERS

1. Open **WordAnnualReport**.
2. Save the document with Save As and name it **ewc5x06**.
3. Assume that you are sending the annual report document to several people for viewing and/or editing. You decide to restrict the document to read-only (no changes can be made) and then make specific portions available to individuals for editing. To do this, complete the following steps:
    a. Click Tools and then Protect Document.
    b. Click the check box preceding the *Allow only this type of editing in the document* option. (Make sure the option box below displays with *No changes (Read only)*.)
    c. Click the More users hyperlink located towards the bottom of the task pane.
    d. At the Add Users dialog box, type the following in the text box (insert your initials where you see the *XXX*):
       StudentAXXX@emcp.net;StudentBXXX@emcp.net
    e. Click OK. (This adds an *Individual* section below the *Groups* section and the *Individual* section contains the two new users [e-mail addresses].)
4. You want to allow StudentA to be able to edit the *Research and Development* section of the document. To do this, complete the following steps:
    a. Select the heading *Research and Development* and the paragraph of text that follows it.
    b. Click the check box preceding the user name *StudentAXXX@emcp.net* (where your initials display instead of the *XXX*).
    c. Deselect the text and notice that the text displays with a color background.
5. You want to allow StudentB to be able to edit the *Sales and Marketing* section of the document. To do this, complete the following steps:
    a. Select the heading *Sales and Marketing* and the two paragraphs of text that follow it.
    b. Click the check box preceding the user name *StudentBXXX@emcp.net* (where your initials display instead of the *XXX*).
    c. Deselect the text and notice that the text displays with a color background that is different from the color in the *Research and Development* section.
6. Close the Protect Document task pane.
7. Save and then close **ewc5x06**.

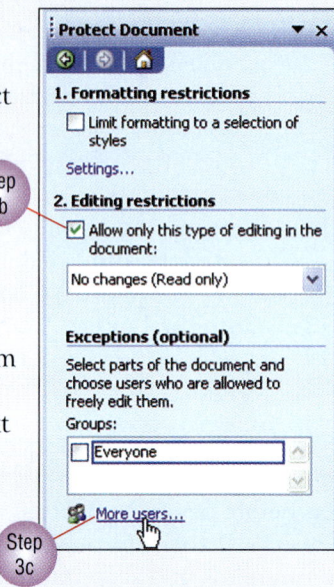

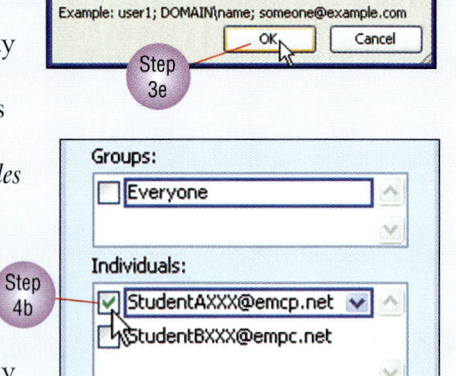

Protecting a Document with a Password

In the previous section of this chapter, you learned how to protect a document with a password using options at the Start Enforcing Protection dialog box. You can also protect a document with a password using options at the Options dialog box with the Security tab selected. To do this, display the Options dialog box by clicking Tools and then Options. At the Options dialog box, click the Security tab. Type a password in the *Password to modify* text box and then press Enter. At the Confirm Password dialog box, type the same password again and then press Enter. Follow the same basic steps to protect a document from being opened, except type a password in the *Password to open* text box. A password can contain up to 15 characters, can include spaces, and is case sensitive.

> **QUICK STEPS**
>
> **Add a Password to a Document**
> 1. Click Tools, Options.
> 2. Click the Security tab.
> 3. Type a password in the *Password to modify* text box.
> 4. Press Enter.
> 5. Type the same password again.
> 6. Press Enter.

exercise 7

PROTECTING A DOCUMENT WITH A PASSWORD

1. Open **WordContract01**.
2. Save the document with Save As and name it **ewc5x07**.
3. Protect the document with a password by completing the following steps:
    a. Click Tools and then Options.
    b. At the Options dialog box, click the Security tab.
    c. Type your first name in the *Password to open* text box. (If it is longer than 15 characters, abbreviate it. You will not see your name—instead Word inserts black circles.)
    d. After typing your name, press Enter.
    e. At the Confirm Password dialog box, type your name again (be sure to type it exactly as you did at the Save dialog box—including upper or lowercase letters), and then press Enter.
4. Save and then close **ewc5x07**.
5. Open **ewc5x07**, typing your password when prompted.
6. Close **ewc5x07**.

Identifying a Document as Read-Only

A document can be opened that is read-only. With a read-only document, you can make changes to the document but you cannot save those changes with the same name. Word protects the original document and does not allow you to save the changes to the document with the same name. You can, however, open a document as read-only, make changes to it, and then save the document with a different name. The documents in the folders you copy from the CD are read-only documents.

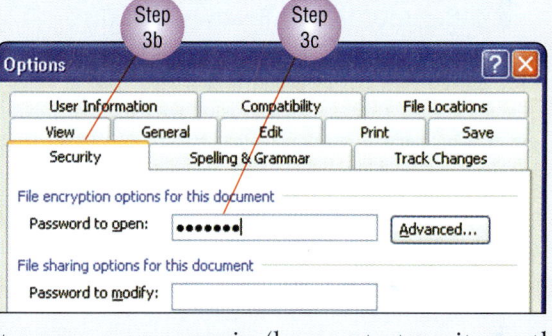

> **QUICK STEPS**
>
> **Identify Document as Read-Only**
> 1. Click Tools, Options.
> 2. Click the Security tab.
> 3. Click the *Read-only recommended* check box.
> 4. Click OK.

WORD Working with Shared Documents E197

To indicate the document is a read-only document, display the Options dialog box with the Security tab selected, click the *Read-only recommended* check box, and then click OK. When you open a read-only document, clicking the Save button, or clicking File and then Save causes the Save As dialog box to display, where you can type a new name for the document.

exercise 8

IDENTIFYING A DOCUMENT AS READ-ONLY

1. Open a document, identify it as read-only, and then save it with a new name by completing the following steps:
   a. Display the Open dialog box with WordChapter05E the active folder.
   b. Open **WordNotice04**.
   c. Click Tools and then Options.
   d. At the Options dialog box, click the Security tab. (Skip this step if the Security tab is already selected.)
   e. Click the *Read-only recommended* check box to insert a check mark.
   f. Click OK to close the Options dialog box.
   g. Save the document with Save As and name it **Training**.
2. Close the **Training** document.
3. Open the **Training** document. (When the message displays asking if you want to open the document as read-only, click the Yes button.)
4. Make the following changes to the document:
   a. Change *WORD* to *EXCEL*.
   b. Change *Friday, September 23* to *Thursday, September 29*.
5. Save the document by completing the following steps:
   a. Click the Save button on the Standard toolbar.
   b. At the Save As dialog box, type **ewc5x08** and then press Enter.
6. Print and then close **ewc5x08**.

Creating and Applying a Digital Signature

With Microsoft Authenticode technology offered by Microsoft Office you can apply a digital signature to a document. A digital signature is an encryption-based electronic stamp you can apply to a macro or a document that vouches for its authenticity. Before applying a digital signature, you must obtain a signature. You can obtain a digital signature from a commercial certification authority or you can create your own digital signature using the Selfcert.exe tool. A certificate you create is considered unauthenticated and will generate a security warning.

Before creating and applying a digital signature, you or your system administrator must set up the Microsoft Exchange Server security features on your computer and you must obtain a keyword to your security file to digitally sign a document. Depending on how your system is set up, you might be prevented from using a certificate. Check with your instructor to determine if you should complete the optional Exercise 9.

HINT Certificates you create yourself are considered unauthenticated and will generate a warning.

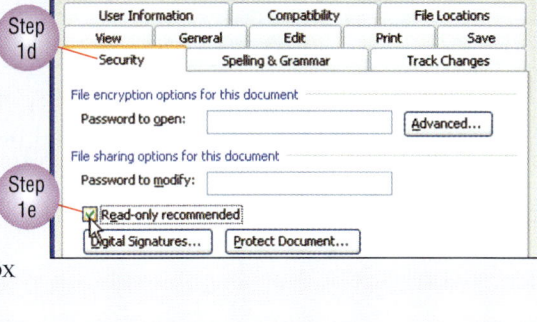

In the optional Exercise 9, you will use the Selfcert.exe tool to create a digital signature and then apply that signature to a Word document. When a person opens the document, he or she will be able to view the certificate to identify who has authenticated the document.

exercise 9

(OPTIONAL) CREATING, APPLYING, AND VIEWING A DIGITAL SIGNATURE

(Note: Check with your instructor before completing this exercise. You may not be able to create a digital signature.)

1. Open Internet Explorer.
2. At the Internet Explorer window, click File and then Open.
3. At the Open dialog box, click the Browse button.
4. At the Microsoft Internet Explorer dialog box, change the *Files of type* option to *All Files*, and then navigate to the folder containing the SELFCERT.EXE tool. (This tool is probably located in the *C:|Program Files|Microsoft Office|Office* folder.)
5. Double-click the *SELFCERT.EXE* tool.
6. At the Open dialog box, click OK.
7. At the Create Digital Certificate dialog box, type your first and last names in the *Your certificate's name* text box, and then click OK.
8. Close the Internet Explorer window.
9. With Word open, open the document named **WordLegal01**.
10. Save the document with Save As and name it **ewc5x09**.
11. Apply a digital signature to the document by completing the following steps:
    a. Click Tools and then Options.
    b. At the Options dialog box, click the Security tab.
    c. Click the Digital Signatures button.
    d. At the Digital Signature dialog box, click the Add button. (If a message appears asking if you want to continue signing without reviewing the document, click the Yes button.)
    e. At the Select Certificate dialog box, click the certificate in list the box containing your first and last name, and then click OK.
    f. At the Digital Signature dialog box, view the certificate by clicking the View Certificate button.
    g. At the Certificate dialog box, look at the certificate information, and then click the OK button.
    h. At the Digital Signature dialog box, click OK.
    i. At the Options dialog box, click OK.
    j. Click the Save button. (Notice that the document name in the Title bar is now followed by *(Signed)*.)
12. Close **ewc5x09**.

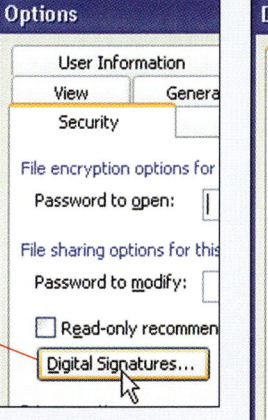

WORD
Working with Shared Documents E199

HINT
As a privacy issue, you can tell Word to remove personal information from the document properties when the document is saved. Do this at the Options dialog box with the Security tab selected.

Customizing Document Properties

The Properties dialog box displays information about a document and contains options you can use to further describe or identify the document. The Properties dialog box contains a number of tabs. Figure 5.9 displays the Properties dialog box with the General tab selected. Display the Properties dialog box by clicking File and then Properties. You can also display the Open (or Save As) dialog box, select the desired document, click the Tools button and then click Properties. Another method for displaying the Properties dialog box is to display the Open (or Save As) dialog box, right-click the desired document and then click Properties at the shortcut menu.

FIGURE 5.9 *Properties Dialog Box with General Tab Selected*

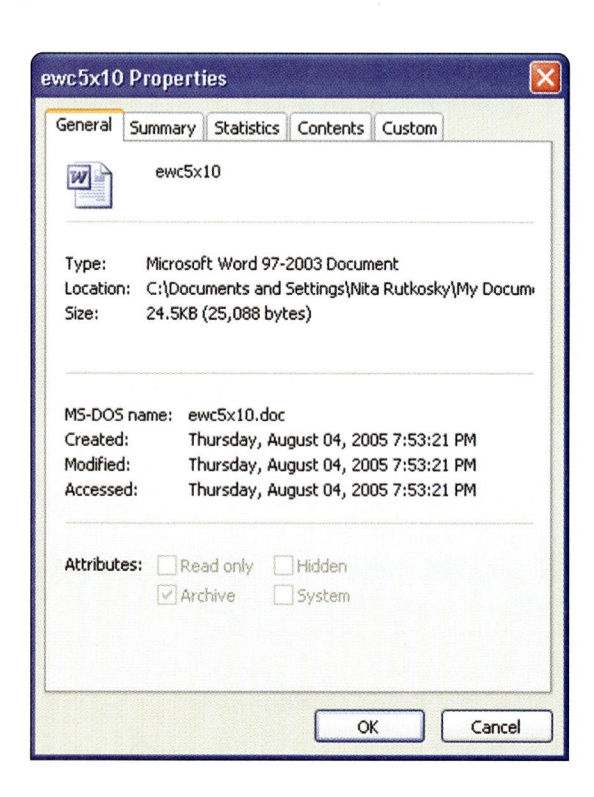

The Properties dialog box with the General tab selected displays information about the document type, size, and location. Click the Summary tab and fields display such as title, subject, author, company, category, keywords, and comments. Some fields may contain data and others may be blank. You can insert, edit, or delete text in the fields. With the Statistics tab selected, information displays such as the number of pages, paragraphs, lines, words, characters, and bytes. You can view the document without bringing it to the document screen by clicking the Contents tab. This displays a portion of the document in a viewing window. Click the Custom tab and the Properties dialog box displays as shown in Figure 5.10.

FIGURE 5.10 Properties Dialog Box with Custom Tab Selected

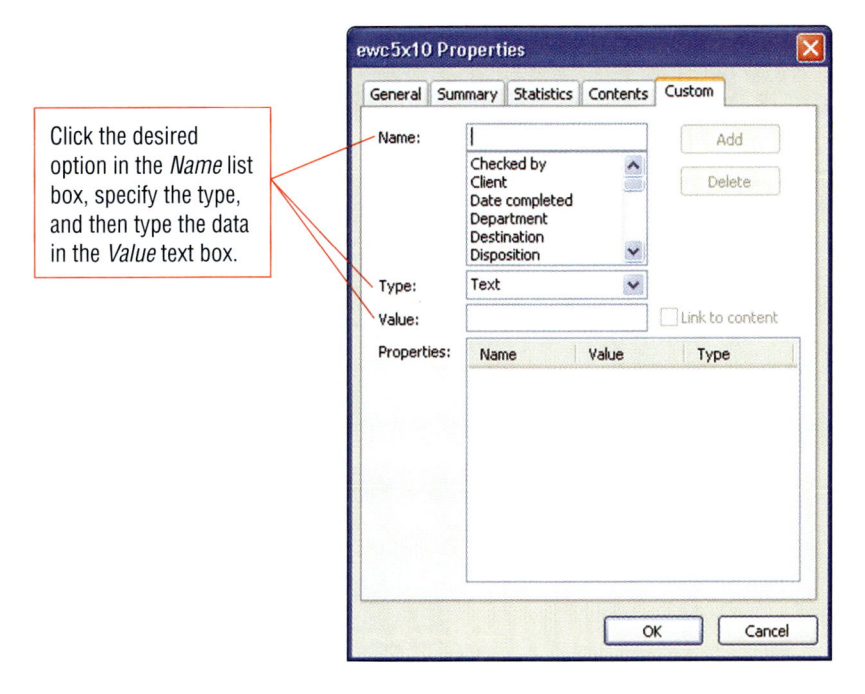

Click the desired option in the *Name* list box, specify the type, and then type the data in the *Value* text box.

Use the options at the Properties dialog box with the Custom tab selected to add custom properties to the document. For example, you can add a property that displays the date the document was completed, information on the department in which the document was created, and much more. The list box below the *Name* option box displays the predesigned properties provided by Word. You can choose a predesigned property or create your own.

To choose a predesigned property, select the desired property in the list box, specify what type of property it is (value, date, number, yes/no), and then type a value. For example, to specify the department in which the document was created, you would click *Department* in the list box, make sure the *Type* displays as *Text*, click in the *Value* text box, and then type the name of the department.

QUICK STEPS

Customize Documents Properties
1. Click File, Properties.
2. Click Custom tab.
3. Click desired property in *Name* list box.
4. Specify the type of property.
5. Type a value.
6. Click OK.

exercise 10   INSERTING AND CUSTOMIZING DOCUMENT PROPERTIES

1. Open **WordAnnualReport**.
2. Save the document with Save As and name it **ewc5x10**.
3. Click File and then click Properties.
4. At the ewc5x10 Properties dialog box, make sure the Summary tab is selected, and then type the following text in the specified text boxes:

   Subject = 2005 Annual Report
   Category = Annual Report
   Keywords = Research, Development, Manufacturing, Sales, Marketing
   Comments = This document contains the 2005 corporate information from the following departments: Research and Development, Manufacturing, and Sales and Marketing

5. Add custom information by completing the following steps:
   a. With the ewc5x10 Properties dialog box still open, click the Custom tab.
   b. Click *Checked by* in the *Name* list box.
   c. Make sure *Text* displays in the *Type* list box.
   d. Click in the *Value* text box and then type your first and last names.
   e. Click the Add button.
   f. Click *Date completed* in the *Name* list box.
   g. Click the down-pointing arrow at the right of the *Type* option box and then click *Date*.
   h. Click in the *Value* text box and then type today's date in figures (##/##/####).
   i. Click the Add button.
   j. Click *Status* in the *Name* list box. (You will need to scroll down the list to display this option.)
   k. Click the down-pointing arrow at the right of the *Type* option box and then click *Text*.
   l. Click in the *Value* text box and then type **First Draft**.
   m. Click the Add button.
   n. Click OK to close the ewc5x10 Properties dialog box.
6. Print the document properties by completing the following steps:
   a. Click File and then Print.
   b. At the Print dialog box, click the down-pointing arrow at the right side of the *Print what* option and then click *Document properties*.
   c. Click OK. (The printing of the document properties will include a variety of information about the document such as Filename, Directory, Last Saved On, Last Saved By, as well as summary information. However, the custom information you entered does not print.)
7. Save and then close **ewc5x10**.

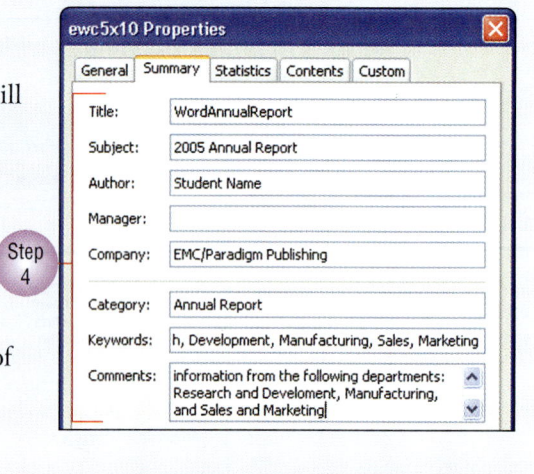

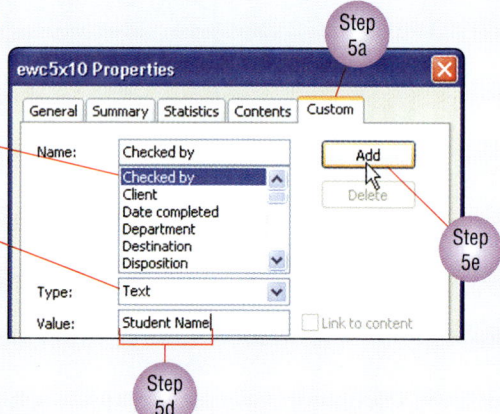

Changing the Default Font

QUICK STEPS

Change the Default Font
1. Click Format, Font.
2. Click the desired font, font style, and/or font size.
3. Click Default button.
4. Click Yes.

A Word document is based on the Normal template document. This template document contains default paragraph and font formatting. The default font for the Normal template document is generally 12-point Times New Roman. This default can be changed at the Font dialog box.

You can change the default font by displaying the Font dialog box, choosing the desired font, font style, and font size, and then clicking the Default button. At the message that displays asking if you want to change the default to the selected font and telling you that the change will affect all new documents based on the Normal template, click the Yes button. You can also change the default font by opening a document containing the desired font formatting and then selecting text formatted with the desired font. Display the Font dialog box, click the Default button, and then click Yes at the message.

Searching for Specific Documents

Use options at the Basic File Search task pane shown in Figure 5.11 to search for specific documents. To display this task pane, click File and then File Search. (If the Advanced File Search task pane displays, click the Basic File Search hyperlink located toward the bottom of the task pane.) In the *Search text* box, enter one or more words specific to the documents for which you are searching. The word or words can be contained in the document name, the text of the document, keywords assigned to the document, or in the document properties. After entering the search word or words, click the Go button (or press Enter) and documents matching the search criteria display in the Search Results task pane.

HINT
Consider installing the Fast search feature, which extracts information from files and organizes it in a way that makes the files quicker and easier to find.

FIGURE 5.11 Basic File Search Task Pane

Enter in this text box one or more words specific to the document and then click the Go button.

Specify the locations to search with the *Search in* option. Click the down-pointing arrow at the right side of the *Search in* option box. This displays a drop-down list containing folders and network places. Click the plus symbol preceding a folder name to expand the display to include any subfolders. Insert a check mark in the check box next to any folder you want searched. Click a check box once and a check mark is inserted in the box and only that folder is searched. Click a check box a second time to specify that you want the folder and all subfolders searched. When you click the check box a second time, the check box changes to a cascading check box (check boxes overlapping). Click a check box a third time and the folder is deselected but all subfolders remain selected. Click a check box a fourth time and all subfolders are deselected.

Specify the types of files to search with the *Results should be* option. Click the down-pointing arrow at the right side of the *Results should be* option box and then, at the drop-down list that displays, insert a check mark in the check boxes before the types of files you want searched. For example, if you want only Word files displayed, insert a check mark in the Word Files check box.

QUICK STEPS

Search for Specific Document
1. Click File, File Search.
2. Click in *Search text* box.
3. Type desired word or words.
4. Specify the locations to search.
5. Specify the types of files to search.
6. Click Go button.

WORD — Working with Shared Documents — E203

exercise 11

FINDING DOCUMENTS CONTAINING SPECIFIC TEXT

1. At a clear document screen, click File and then File Search. (If the Advanced File Search task pane displays, click the Basic File Search hyperlink located toward the bottom of the task pane.)
2. Search for all Word documents on your disk in drive A that contain the word *telecommunications* by completing the following steps:
    a. Click in the *Search text* box. (If text displays in the text box, select the text and then delete it.)
    b. Type **telecommunications** in the *Search text* box.
    c. Click the down-pointing arrow at the right side of the *Search in* option box.
    d. Click the plus symbol that precedes *My Computer*.
    e. Click in the *3½ Floppy (A:)* check box *twice* to insert a check mark (and to cascade the check box). (Make sure that it is the only check box containing a check mark.)
    f. Click in the task pane outside the *Search in* list box to remove the list.
    g. Click the down-pointing arrow at the right side of the *Results should be* option box.
    h. At the drop-down list, click in the *Word Files* check box to insert a check mark. (Make sure that it is the only check box containing a check mark.)
    i. Click in the task pane outside the *Results should be* list box to remove the list.
    j. Click the Go button. (In a few moments, the Search Results task pane will display with document names containing *telecommunications*.)
3. You decide to change the default font for all future documents and want to base the new font on an existing document about Terra Energy Corporation. Complete a search for the Terra Energy Corporation document and then use that document to change the default font by completing the following steps:
    a. Click the Modify button located toward the bottom of the Search Results task pane.
    b. Type **Terra Energy Corporation** in the *Search text* box.
    c. Leave the *Search in* option set at *3½ Floppy (A:)* and the *Results should be* option set at *Word Files*.
    d. Click the Go button.
    e. When the document displays in the Search Results task pane, double-click *WordDocument07* in the list box.
    f. Select a portion of text in the first paragraph. (Do not select the title or any headings. Select text that is not bold.)
    g. Click Format and then Font.

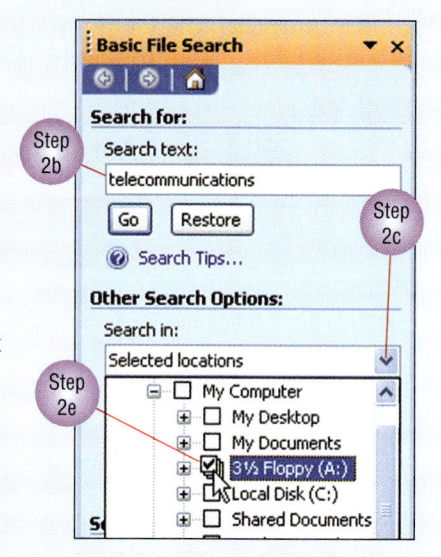

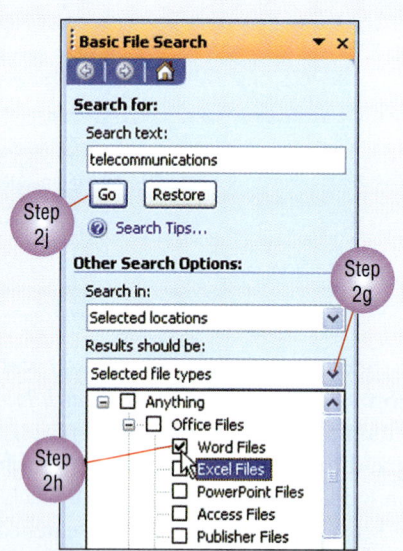

E204 Chapter Five

h. At the Font dialog box, click the Default button.
i. At the message asking if you want to change the default to the selected font and telling you that the change will affect all new document based on the Normal template, click the Yes button. (This closes the dialog box and returns you to the clear document screen, which now uses Bookman Old Style as the default font.)
4. Close **WordDocument07** without saving the changes.
5. Close the Search Results task pane.
6. Click the New Blank Document button on the Standard toolbar.
7. Type the text shown in Figure 5.12. (Make sure you set the appropriate tabs.)
8. Save the document and name it **ewc5x11**.
9. Print and then close **ewc5x11**.
10. Display a clear document screen and then return the default font for the Normal template back to Times New Roman by completing steps similar to those in Steps 3g through 3i.

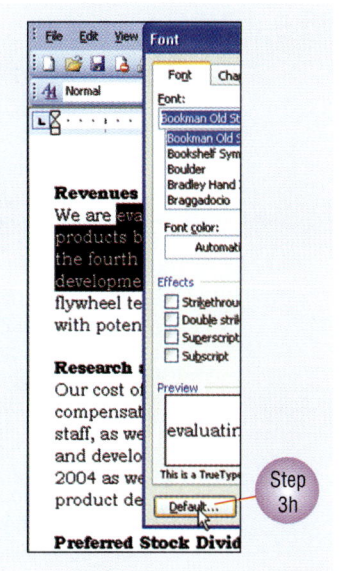

FIGURE 5.12 *Exercise 11*

TABLE OF CONTENTS

PART I

Business	4
Properties	11
Legal Proceedings	12
Security	15

PART II

Marketing	16
Financial Data	19
Analysis of Financial Condition	26
Financial Statements and Supplementary Data	30

Completing Advanced Searches

Click the Advanced File Search hyperlink located toward the bottom of the Basic File Search task pane and the Advanced File Search task pane displays as shown in Figure 5.13. Use options at this task pane to narrow your search.

FIGURE 5.13 Advanced File Search Task Pane

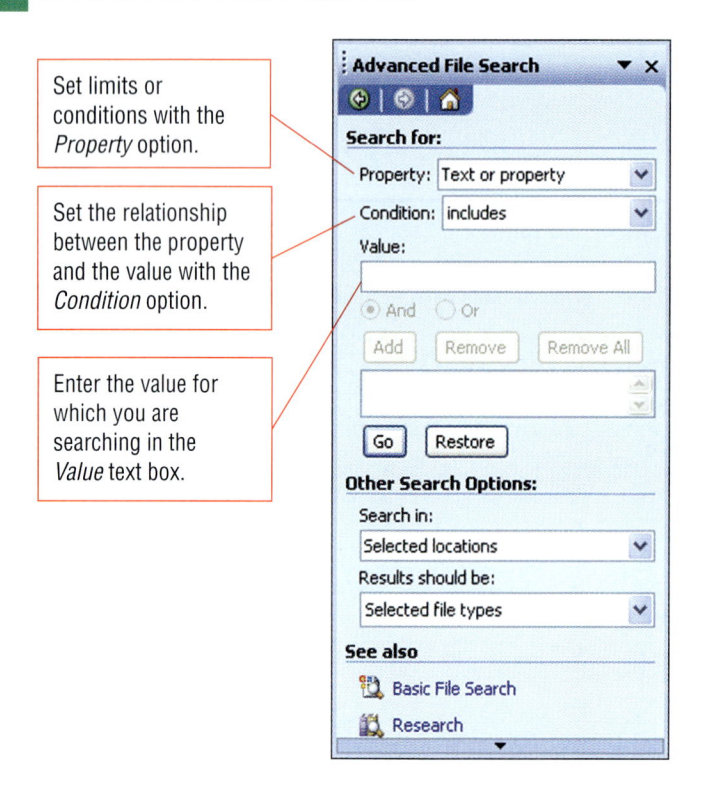

Set limits or conditions with the *Property* option.

Set the relationship between the property and the value with the *Condition* option.

Enter the value for which you are searching in the *Value* text box.

In the *Property* option box, select the property on which you want to set limits or conditions. For example, you can select the number of words, paragraphs, or pages as the property on which you are searching or specify the category, comments, or file size as the search property. Use the *Condition* option to set the relationship between the property and the value. For example, you can complete a search for documents containing a specific number of words. In the *Value* text box, enter the value for which you are searching. Click the Add button and the search criterion is added to the option box below the Add, Remove, and Remove All buttons. As an example of how to use these options, in Exercise 12 you will set the *Property* option to *Number of words*, the *Condition* option to *more than*, and type **600** in the *Value* text box. This narrows the search to files containing more than 600 words.

You can conduct an advanced search on more than one criterion. To do this, specify the desired property, condition, and value and then click the Add button. Specify the additional desired property, condition, and value. Click the Go button and then click the Add button. For example, in Exercise 12 you will search for all documents containing the words *desktop personal computer* and are greater than 500 words in length. After completing a search, click the Remove All button to remove the search criteria.

E206 Chapter Five WORD

exercise 12

COMPLETING ADVANCED SEARCHES FOR SPECIFIC DOCUMENTS

1. At a clear document screen, click File and then File Search.
2. Click the Advanced File Search hyperlink located toward the bottom of the Basic File Search task pane. (Skip this step if the Advanced File Search task pane is already displayed.) 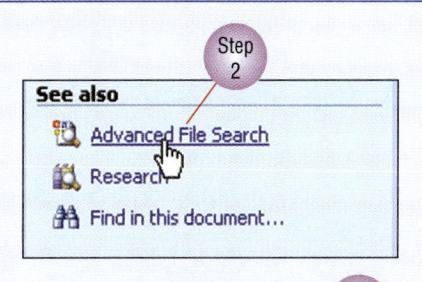
3. Search for all Word documents on your disk in drive A that contain more than 600 words by completing the following steps:
   a. Click the down-pointing arrow at the right side of the *Property* option box and then click *Number of words* at the drop-down list. 
   b. Click the down-pointing arrow at the right side of the *Condition* option box and then click *more than* in the drop-down list. 
   c. Click in the *Value* text box and then type **600**.
   d. Click the Add button. (This adds the search criterion to the option box below the Add button.)
   e. Make sure the *Search in* option is set at *3½ Floppy (A:)* and the *Results should be* option is set at *Word Files*.
   f. Click the Go button. 
4. Search for all documents on the disk in drive A containing more than 500 words and containing the words *desktop publishing* by completing the following steps:
   a. Click the Modify button located toward the bottom of the Search Results task pane.
   b. Click the Remove All button. (This removes all search criteria in the box below the Add button.)
   c. Click the down-pointing arrow at the right side of the *Property* option box and then click *Number of words* at the drop-down list.
   d. Click the down-pointing arrow at the right side of the *Condition* option box and then click *more than* in the drop-down list.
   e. Click in the *Value* text box and then type **500**.
   f. Click the Add button. (This adds the search criterion to the box below the Add button.)
   g. Click the down-pointing arrow at the right side of the *Property* option box and then click *Text or property* at the drop-down list.

WORD Working with Shared Documents E207

h. Click in the *Value* text box and then type **desktop publishing**.
i. Click the Add button. (This adds the search criterion to the box below the Add button.)
j. Leave the *Search in* option set at *3½ Floppy (A:)* and the *Results should be* option set at *Word Files*.
k. Click the Go button.
l. When the Search Results task pane displays (with *WordReport04* listed), click the Modify button.
m. At the Advanced File Search task pane, click the Remove All button to remove all search criteria.
n. Click the Basic File Search hyperlink that displays toward the bottom of the task pane.
5. Close the Basic File Search task pane.

Creating a Custom Dictionary

QUICK STEPS

Create Custom Dictionary
1. Click Tools, Options.
2. Click Spelling & Grammar tab.
3. Click Custom Dictionaries button.
4. Click New button.
5. Type name for dictionary.
6. Press Enter.

When completing a spelling check on a document, Word uses the CUSTOM.DIC custom dictionary by default. You can add or remove words from this default dictionary. In a multiple-user environment, you might also consider adding your own custom dictionary and then selecting that dictionary as the default. In this way, multiple users can create their own dictionary to use when spell checking a document.

To create a custom dictionary, click Tools and then Options. At the Options dialog box, click the Spelling & Grammar tab and then click the Custom Dictionaries button. This displays the Custom Dictionaries dialog box shown in Figure 5.14. To create a new dictionary, click the New button. At the Create Custom Dictionary dialog box, type a name for the dictionary in the *File name* text box and then press Enter. The new dictionary name will display in the *Dictionary list* box in the Custom Dictionaries dialog box. You can use more than one dictionary when spell checking a document. Insert a check mark in the check box next to any dictionary you want to use.

FIGURE 5.14 *Custom Dictionaries Dialog Box*

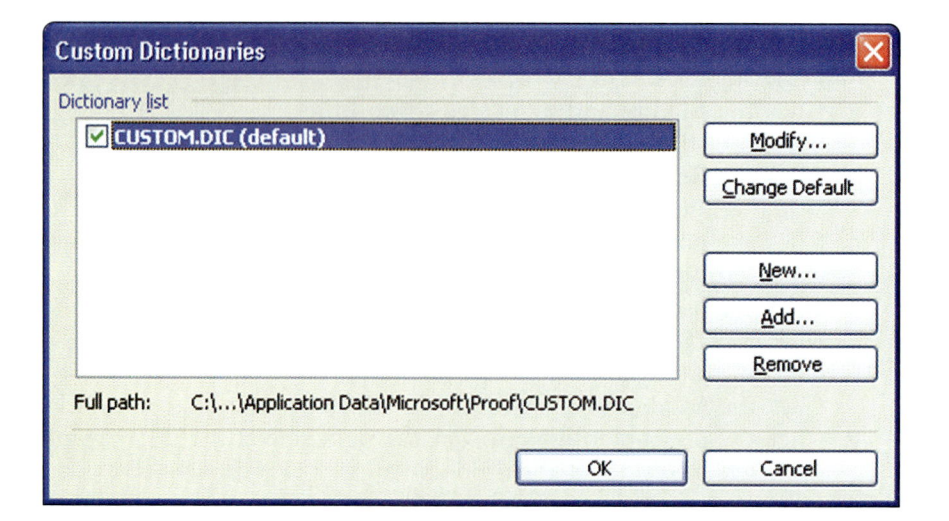

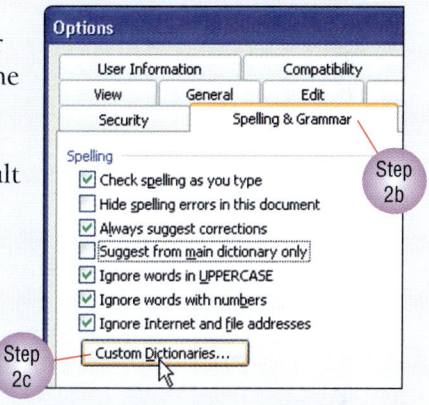

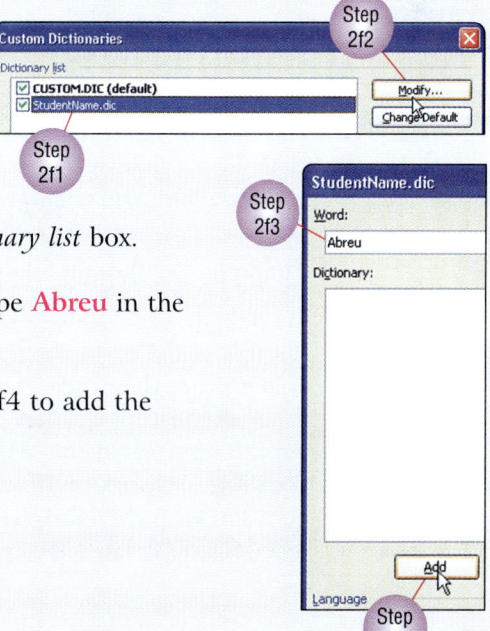

Changing the Default Dictionary

At the Custom Dictionaries dialog box, the default dictionary displays in the *Dictionaries list* box followed by *(default)*. You can change this default by clicking the desired dictionary name in the list box and then clicking the Change Default button.

Removing a Dictionary

Remove a custom dictionary with the Remove button at the Custom Dictionaries dialog box. To remove a dictionary, display the Custom Dictionaries dialog box, click the dictionary name in the *Dictionary list* box, and then click the Remove button. You are not prompted to confirm the removal so make sure you select the correct dictionary name before clicking the Remove button.

exercise 13
CREATING A CUSTOM DICTIONARY AND CHANGING THE DEFAULT DICTIONARY

1. Open **WordDocument08**, notice the wavy red lines indicating words not recognized by the spelling checker (words not in the custom dictionary), and then close the document.
2. At a clear document screen, create a custom dictionary, add words to the dictionary, and then change the default dictionary by completing the following steps:
    a. Click Tools and then Options.
    b. At the Options dialog box, click the Spelling & Grammar tab.
    c. Click the Custom Dictionaries button.
    d. At the Custom Dictionaries dialog box, click the New button.
    e. At the Create Custom Dictionary dialog box, type your first and last names (without a space between) in the *File name* text box, and then press Enter.
    f. At the Custom Dictionaries dialog box, add a word to your dictionary by completing the following steps:
        1) Click your dictionary name in the *Dictionary list* box.
        2) Click the Modify button.
        3) At your custom dictionary dialog box, type **Abreu** in the *Word* text box.
        4) Click the Add button.
    g. Complete steps similar to those in 2f3 and 2f4 to add the following words:
        Banco
        Itau
        Bradesco
        Unibanco
        Monteiro
        Lipschultz

h. When all the words have been added, click the OK button to close the dialog box.

i. At the Custom Dictionaries dialog box with your dictionary name selected in the *Dictionary list* box, click the Change Default button. (Notice that the word *(default)* displays after your custom dictionary.)

j. Click OK to close the Custom Dictionaries dialog box.

k. Click OK to close the Options dialog box.

3. Open **WordDocument08**.
4. Save the document with Save As and name it **ewc5x13**.
5. Click the Spelling and Grammar button on the Standard toolbar and then complete a spelling and grammar check of the document. (The spelling checker will not stop at the words you added to your custom dictionary.)
6. After completing the spelling and grammar check, save, print, and then close **ewc5x14**.
7. Change the default dictionary and then remove your custom dictionary by completing the following steps:
   a. At a clear document screen, click Tools and then Options.
   b. At the Options dialog box, make sure the Spelling & Grammar tab is selected, and then click the Custom Dictionaries button.
   c. At the Custom Dictionaries dialog box, click *CUSTOM.DIC* in the *Dictionary list* box.
   d. Click the Change Default button. (This changes the default back to the CUSTOM.DIC dictionary.)
   e. Click your dictionary name in the *Dictionary list* box.
   f. Click the Remove button. (If you receive the message that removing the custom dictionary could affect other dictionaries, click OK to continue.)
   g. Click OK to close the Custom Dictionaries dialog box.
   h. Click OK to close the Options dialog box.

QUICK STEPS

Change Default File Location for Workgroup Templates
1. Click Tools, Options.
2. Click File Locations tab.
3. Click *Workgroup templates*.
4. Click Modify button.
5. Navigate to desired location.
6. Double-click desired folder.
7. Click OK.
8. Click OK.

Creating a Template

A document that will be used in the future as a framework for other documents can be saved as a template. To save a document as a template, display the Save As dialog box, change the *Save as type* option to *Document Template*, type a name for the template, and then press Enter.

Changing the Default File Location for Workgroup Templates

By default a template is saved in the Templates folder and will display at the Templates dialog box with the General tab selected. You can save a template in a folder other than the default by specifying the folder. If you are working in a company setting with an intranet, consider saving templates that will be shared on the network in the Workgroup templates file location. You can specify the file location for Workgroup templates at the Options dialog box. Specify the file location with the *Workgroup templates* option at the Options dialog box with the File Locations tab selected as shown in Figure 5.15.

FIGURE

5.15 Options Dialog Box with File Locations Tab Selected

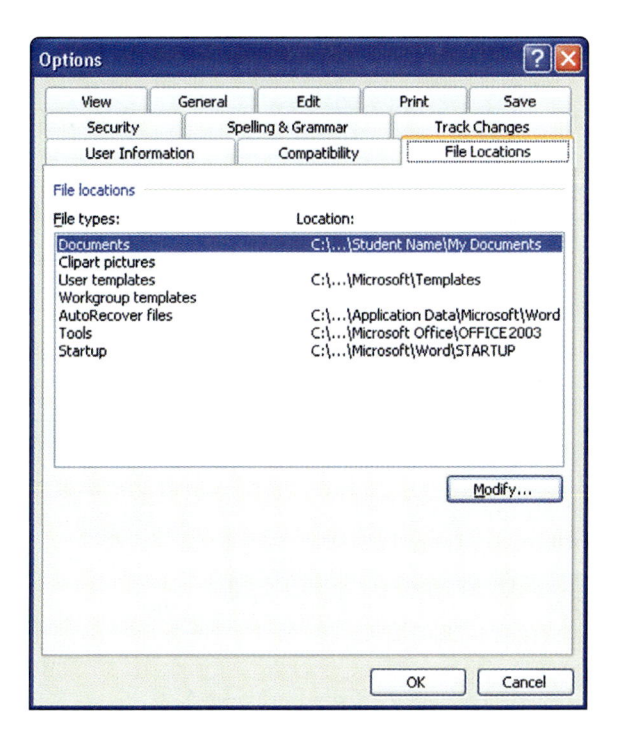

In Exercise 14 you will be change the location of Workgroup templates to a Templates folder you will create on your disk. In a company setting, the Workgroup templates location would probably be a folder on the network. Before completing Exercise 14, check with your instructor to determine if you can change file locations.

exercise 14 (OPTIONAL) CHANGING FILE LOCATION AND CREATING A TEMPLATE DOCUMENT

1. Create a Templates folder on your disk by completing the following steps:
   a. Display the Open dialog box.
   b. Make active the drive where your disk is located (do not make WordChapter05E the active folder).
   c. Click the Create New Folder button on the Open dialog box toolbar.
   d. At the New Folder dialog box, type **Templates** in the *Name* text box.
   e. Click OK or press Enter to close the dialog box.
   f. Click the Cancel button to close the Open dialog box.
2. At a clear document screen, specify the Templates folder on your disk as the location for Workgroup templates by completing the following steps:
   a. Make sure your disk (containing the Templates folder) is inserted in the appropriate drive.
   b. Click Tools and then Options.
   c. At the Options dialog box, click the File Locations tab.
   d. At the Options dialog box with the File Locations tab selected, make a note of the current location for Workgroup templates that displays in the *File types* list box (the

WORD
Working with Shared Documents E211

location may be blank). (You will be returning the location back to this default at the end of the exercise.)
   e. Click *Workgroup templates* in the *File types* list box.
   f. Click the Modify button.
   g. At the Modify Location dialog box, click the down-pointing arrow at the right side of the *Look in* option box and then click *3½ Floppy (A:)* (or the drive letter where your disk is located).
   h. Double-click the *Templates* folder.
   i. Click OK to close the Modify Location dialog box.
   j. Click OK to close the Options dialog box.
3. Open **WordLegal02**.
4. Save the document as a template named Summons in the Templates folder on your disk by completing the following steps:
   a. Click File and then Save As.
   b. At the Save As dialog box, click the down-pointing arrow at the right side of the *Save as type* option box, and then click *Document Template*. (This automatically changes the folder to the Microsoft Templates folder.)
   c. Change to the Templates folder on your disk by completing the following steps:
      1) Click the down-pointing arrow at the right side of the *Save in* option box.
      2) At the drop-down list that displays, click the drive where your disk is located.
      3) Double-click the *Templates* folder.
   d. Select the name in the *File name* text box and then type **Summons**.
   e. Press Enter or click the Save button.
5. Close the Summons template.
6. Open the Summons template by completing the following steps:
   a. Click File and then New.
   b. Click the On my computer hyperlink in the New Document task pane.
   c. At the Templates dialog box with the General tab selected, double-click the *Summons* icon.
7. With the Summons template document open, make the following find and replaces:
   a. Find *NAME1* and replace with *AMY GARCIA*.
   b. Find *NAME2* and replace with *NEIL CARLIN*.
   c. Fine *NUMBER* and replace with *C-98002*.
8. Save the document in the WordChapter05E folder on your disk and name it **ewc5x14**.
9. Print and then close **ewc5x14**.
10. Remove the Summons template from the Templates dialog box by completing the following steps:

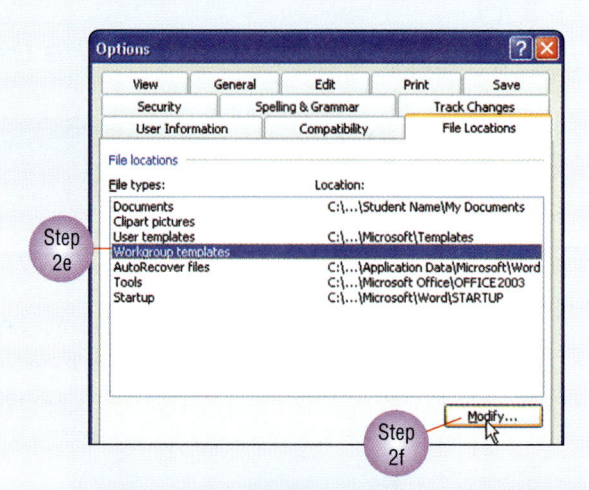

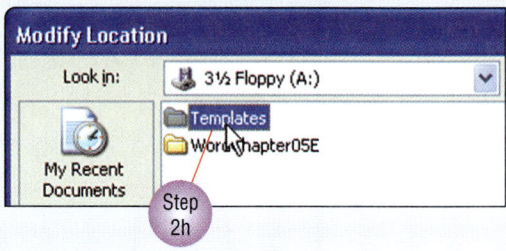

a. Click File and then New.
   b. Click the On my computer hyperlink in the New Document task pane.
   c. At the Templates dialog box with the General tab selected, right-click on the *Summons* icon.
   d. At the shortcut menu that displays, click the Delete option.
   e. At the Confirm File Delete message, click Yes.
   f. Click Cancel to close the New dialog box.
11. Return the Workgroup templates back to the default location by completing the following steps:
   a. At a document screen, click Tools and then Options.
   b. At the Options dialog box, click the File Locations tab.
   c. At the Options dialog box with the File Locations tab selected, click *Workgroup templates* in the *File types* list box.
   d. Click the Modify button.
   e. At the Modify Location dialog box, change to the default Workgroup templates folder. (If the default location was blank, select any text currently displayed in the *Folder name* text box and then press the Delete key.)
   f. Click OK to close the Modify Location dialog box.
   g. Click OK to close the Options dialog box.

CHAPTER summary

- Use the tracking feature when more than one person is reviewing a document and making editing changes. Turn on tracking by clicking the Track Changes button on the Reviewing toolbar.
- Control how editing markings display in a document with the Display for Review button on the Reviewing pane. Control the marking changes that Word displays in a document with options at the Show button drop-down menu.
- Change tracking default settings with options at the Track Changes dialog box. Display this dialog box by clicking the Show button on the Reviewing toolbar and then clicking Options.
- Use the versioning feature to save multiple versions of a document in the same document. Save a version of a document and delete a version of a document at the Versions in (Document Name) dialog box. An earlier version of a document can be opened and then viewed next to the current version.
- Restrict formatting and editing in a document as well as apply a password to a document with options at the Protect Document task pane. Display this task pane by clicking Tools and then Protect Document.
- Restrict formatting by specifying the styles that are allowed and not allowed in a document. Do this at the Formatting Restrictions dialog box. Display this dialog box by clicking the Settings hyperlink in the Protect Document task pane.
- To restrict editing in a document, click the *Allow only this type of editing in a document* option at the Protect Document task pane, click the down-pointing arrow at the right of the option box, and then click the desired option.

- When you choose certain options at the *Allow only this type of editing in a document* option box, the *Exceptions (optional)* option displays. Use this option to select specific parts of a document that you will allow certain users to edit.
- Enforce restrictions you specified by clicking the Yes, Start Enforcing Protection button in the Protect Document task pane, and then make desired changes at the Start Enforcing Protection dialog box.
- Add users to the *Editing restrictions* section of the task pane by clicking the More users hyperlink. At the Add Users dialog box, type the name (or e-mail address) for the individual you want added.
- Protect a document with a password using options at the Start Enforcing Protection dialog box or with options at the Options dialog box with the Security tab selected.
- Specify a document as read-only with options at the Options dialog box with the Security tab selected.
- Apply a digital signature (an encryption-based electronic stamp) to a document to vouch for the authenticity of the document. Obtain a digital signature from a commercial certification authority or create your own using the Selfcert.exe tool.
- Insert and customize document information with options at the Properties dialog box.
- The Normal template document contains default formatting including a default font. Change this default font by selecting the desired font at the Font dialog box and then clicking the Default button.
- Use options at the Basic File Search task pane to search for specific documents. Display this task pane by clicking File and then File Search.
- Use options at the Advanced File Search task pane to narrow the search for documents to specific criteria. Display this task pane by clicking the Advanced File Search hyperlink in the Basic File Search task pane.
- Word uses the CUSTOM.DIC custom dictionary when spell checking a document. Add your own custom dictionary at the Custom Dictionaries dialog box. Display this dialog box by clicking the Custom Dictionaries button at the Options dialog box with the Spelling & Grammar tab selected.
- Specify file locations with options at the Options dialog box with the File Locations tab selected.

FEATURES summary

FEATURE	BUTTON	MENU	KEYBOARD
Tracking		Tools, Track Changes	Ctrl + Shift + E
Track Changes dialog box		Show button on Reviewing toolbar, Options; or Tools, Options, Track Changes	
Versions in (Document name) dialog box		File, Versions	
Protect Document task pane		Tools, Protect Document	

Options dialog box	Tools, Options	
Font dialog box	Format, Font	Ctrl + D
Basic File Search task pane	File, File Search	
Properties dialog box	File, Properties	

CONCEPTS check

Completion: On a blank sheet of paper, indicate the correct term, command, or number for each description.

1. Change the default tracking colors with options at this dialog box.
2. Use this feature to save multiple versions of a document in the same document.
3. Display the Save Version dialog box by clicking this button at the Versions in (Document Name) dialog box.
4. Limit what formatting users can perform on text in a document with options in this section of the Protect Document task pane.
5. Use options in this section of the Protect Document task pane to limit the types of changes a user can make to a document.
6. Click this button in the Protect Document task pane to display the Start enforcing protection dialog box.
7. Protect a document with a password with options at the Options dialog box with this tab selected.
8. Include information about the document such as the name of the person checking the document, the department in which the document was created, and the status of the document with options at the Properties dialog box with this tab selected.
9. Click File and then this option to display the Basic File Search task pane.
10. Use options at this task pane to narrow a file search to specific properties, conditions, and/or values.
11. Display the Custom Dictionaries dialog box by clicking the Custom Dictionaries button at the Options dialog box with this tab selected.
12. Specify a location for Workgroup templates with options at this dialog box with the File Locations tab selected.

SKILLS check

Assessment 1

1. Open **WordDocument09**.
2. Save the document with Save As and name it **ewc5sc01**.
3. Change to the Print Layout view, turn on tracking, and then make the following changes:
   a. Insert the words *open-end* in the first sentence of the first paragraph between the number *12* and the word *mutual*.
   b. Insert the words *Long-Short* between *Global* and *Fund* in the first bulleted item in the *Global Funds* section.

c. Delete *World Fund*, which is the last bulleted item in the *Global Funds* section.
   d. Delete the last sentence in the document (the sentence that begins *These special considerations…*).
4. Display the Options dialog box with the User Information tab selected, change the name to *Mitchell Costas*, the initials to *MC*, and then close the dialog box.
5. With tracking on, make the following changes to the document:
   a. Apply 14-point Arial bold formatting to the title *INVESTMENT CHOICES*.
   b. Apply 12-point Arial bold formatting to the five headings: *Global Funds*, *Foreign Funds*, *Regional Funds*, *Emerging Market Funds*, and *Global Bond Funds*.
   c. Insert the word *Foreign* between the words *Smaller* and *Companies* that is located in the second bulleted item in the *Foreign Funds* section.
   d. Insert the words *and governments* between the words *companies* and *of* in the sentence below the heading *Global Bond Funds*.
   e. Delete the word *heightened* located in the third sentence in the last paragraph of the document.
6. Save and then print **ewc5sc01**.
7. Customize tracking options with the following specifications:
   a. Display the Track Changes dialog box.
   b. Change the *Formatting* option to *Underline* and the color to *Pink*.
   c. Change the *Use Balloons (Print and Web Layout)* option to *Only for comments/formatting*.
   d. Change the Paper orientation to *Force landscape*.
   e. Close the Track Changes dialog box.
8. Print **ewc5sc01**.
9. Do not display changes made by Mitchell Costas.
10. Print **ewc5sc01**.
11. Click the Display for Review button and then click *Final*.
12. Print **ewc5sc01**.
13. Make the following changes:
    a. Click th Display for Review button and then click *Final Showing Markup*.
    b. Display all reviewers.
    c. Accept all changes in the document.
    d. Change the User Information back to the information that displayed before you changed it.
    e. Display the Track Changes dialog box, return the tracking options back to the default, and then close the dialog box.
14. Save and then close **ewc5sc01**.

Assessment 2

1. Open **WordLegal02**.
2. Save the document with Save As and name it **ewc5sc02**.
3. Create a version of the original document by completing the following steps:
   a. Display the Versions in ewc5sc02 dialog box.
   b. Click the Save Now button to display the Save Version dialog box.
   c. At the Save Version dialog box, type **First draft of Summons** in the *Comments on version* text box.
   d. Click OK to close the dialog box.
4. Make the following editing changes to the document:
   a. Delete the words *a copy of which is* at the end of the first paragraph and replace them with *two copies of which are*.
   b. Insert the word *written* between the words *without* and *notice* located at the end of the first sentence in the second paragraph.

5. Create another version of the document with the comment *Second draft of Summons*.
6. Make the following editing changes to the document:
   a. Delete the sentence *A default judgment is one where the plaintiff, NAME1, is entitled to what plaintiff asks for because you have not responded.* that displays at the end of the second paragraph.
   b. Insert the words *null and* between the words *be* and *void* located at the end of the third paragraph.
7. Create another version of the document with the comment *Third draft of Summons*.
8. Open the First draft of Summons version of the document. ***(Hint: Be sure to do this at the Versions in ewc5sc02 dialog box.)***
9. After viewing the first draft version, save the version as a separate document named **SummonsFirstDraft**.
10. Close the **SummonsFirstDraft** document.
11. Maximize the **ewc5sc02** window.
12. Delete the second draft version of the document. ***(Hint: Be sure to do this at the Versions in ewc5sc02 dialog box.)***
13. Save and then close **ewc5sc02**.
14. Open **SummonsFirstDraft** and then compare the document with **ewc5sc02**. (Save the results in a new document.)
15. Save the new document and name it **ewc5sc02ComDoc**.
16. Print and then close **ewc5sc02ComDoc**.
17. Close **SummonsFirstDraft**.

Assessment 3

1. Open **WordReport04**.
2. Save the document with Save As and name it **ewc5sc03**.
3. Display the Protect Document task pane and then restrict formatting to the Heading 2 and Heading 3 styles.
4. Enforce the protection and include the password *computers*.
5. Save and then close **ewc5sc03**.
6. Open **ewc5sc03**.
7. If necessary, display the Protect Document task pane. ***(Hint: Click View and then Task Pane.)***
8. Click the Available styles hyperlink.
9. Apply the *Heading 2* style to the two titles: *COMPUTERS IN COMMUNICATIONS* and *COMPUTERS IN ENTERTAINMENT*.
10. Apply the *Heading 3* style to the five headings: *Telecommunications, Publishing, News Services, Television and Film,* and *Home Entertainment*.
11. Close the Protect Document task pane.
12. Save the document and then print only page 1.
13. Save and then close **ewc5sc03**.

Assessment 4

1. Open **WordDocument07**.
2. Save the document with Save As and name it **ewc5sc04**.
3. Display the Protect Document task pane, restrict editing to only comments, and then start enforcing the protection (do not include a password).
4. Save and then close **ewc5sc04**.
5. Open **ewc5sc04**.
6. Insert the following comment immediately after the period that ends the paragraph in the *Revenues* section: **Include the total amount of generated revenues.**

7. Insert the following comment immediately after the period that ends the paragraph in the *Research and Development* section: **Provide a more detailed explanation of how costs decreased.**
8. Print only the comments.
9. Save and then close **ewc5sc04**.

Assessment 5

1. Open **WordLegalBrief**.
2. Save the document with Save As and name it **ewc5sc05**.
3. Display the ewc5sc05 Properties dialog box.
4. Add the following text to the Properties dialog box with the Summary tab selected:

    Subject = **Larsen Brief**
    Category = **Legal Brief**
    Comments = **This legal brief was prepared by Amanda Meyers for petitioner, William G. Larsen, and submitted October 17, 2005.**

5. Add the following custom information to the Properties dialog box with the Custom tab selected:
    a. Click *Client* in the *Name* list box, leave the *Type* option box set at *Text*, enter *William G. Larsen* in the *Value* text box, and then click the Add button.
    b. Click *Disposition* in the *Name* list box, leave the *Type* option box set at *Text*, enter *Submitted October 17, 2005* in the *Value* text box, and then click the Add button.
6. Print only the document properties.
7. Save and then close **ewc5sc05**.

Assessment 6

1. At a clear document screen, create a custom dictionary named with the initials of your first and last names, and then add the following words to your dictionary:

    Avner
    Ronen
    Odigo
    Maskit
    Sella

2. Make your dictionary the default dictionary.
3. Open **WordDocument06**.
4. Save the document with Save As and name it **ewc5sc06**.
5. Click the Spelling and Grammar button on the Standard toolbar and then complete a spelling and grammar check of the document.
6. After completing the spelling and grammar check, save, print, and then close **ewc5sc06**.
7. Remove your custom dictionary from the Custom Dictionaries dialog box.

CHAPTER challenge

Case study

You work in the design department of a local research company. Since many of the employees are continually creating written reports, the need for a consistent cover page has emerged. Create an attractive template, using various fonts and font sizes, which can be used as a cover page. The cover page should include placeholders for the following: <title>, <subtitle>, prepared by <first and last name>, and <current date>. Insert a logo or an appropriate graphic. Protect the document and restrict the editing in appropriate areas of the document. Save the template as **Cover Page**.

HELP?

Much of the research done at this company is focused around specific objects. The employees writing the reports have asked for your help with inserting pictures taken with their digital cameras. Others would like to scan in existing pictures. Use the Help feature to learn how to insert pictures from a scanner or with a digital camera. Then appropriately insert either a scanned picture or a picture taken with a digital camera into the cover page created in the first part of the Chapter Challenge. Save the document as **Cover Page with Picture**.

INTEGRATED

The cover page completed in the first part of the Chapter Challenge is ready to be distributed and used by the employees; however, it needs approval. The individual who is to approve of this project is out of town for two weeks, but does have access to e-mail. Create an e-mail message with the cover page as an attachment and send it to her (your professor).

CHAPTER 6

SHARING DATA

PERFORMANCE OBJECTIVES

Upon successful completion of Chapter 6, you will be able to:
- Import data from an Excel worksheet into a chart
- Copy, link, and embed an Excel worksheet in a Word document
- Edit a linked worksheet and modify an embedded worksheet
- Link and edit objects in Word documents
- Create a form template and fill in a form document
- Print, edit, and customize a form
- Draw a table in a form template
- Create a master document and subdocuments
- Expand, collapse, open, close, rearrange, split, combine, remove, and rename subdocuments

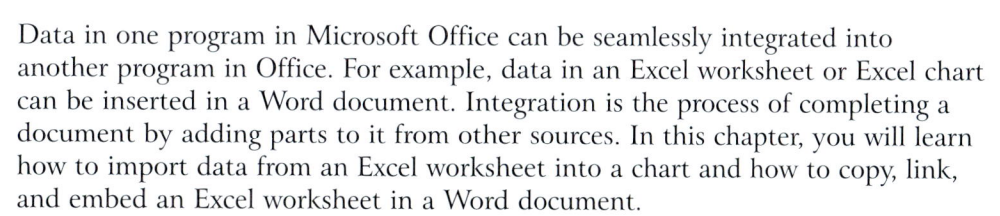

Data in one program in Microsoft Office can be seamlessly integrated into another program in Office. For example, data in an Excel worksheet or Excel chart can be inserted in a Word document. Integration is the process of completing a document by adding parts to it from other sources. In this chapter, you will learn how to import data from an Excel worksheet into a chart and how to copy, link, and embed an Excel worksheet in a Word document.

Many businesses use preprinted forms that are generally filled in by hand, with a typewriter, or using a computer. These forms require additional storage space and also cost the company money. With Word's form feature, you can create your own forms, eliminating the need for preprinted forms. In this chapter, you will learn how to create a template document for a form that includes text boxes, check boxes, and pull-down lists. You will learn how to save the form as a protected document and then open the form and type information in the fill-in boxes. You will create basic form documents in this chapter. For ideas on creating advanced forms, please refer to Word's Help.

For some documents such as a book or procedures manual, consider creating a master document. A master document contains a number of separate documents called subdocuments. In this chapter, you will learn how to create a master document using subdocuments.

Importing Data

The Microsoft Office suite contains a program named Excel, which is a complete spreadsheet program. While numbers can be calculated in a Word table, for extensive calculations, use Excel. In this section, you will import and modify data from Excel into a chart and import, modify, and create worksheets in a table.

If Excel is not available, you will still be able to complete many of the exercises in this section. Two Excel worksheets have already been created and are available in the WordChapter06E folder. To import and edit a worksheet, you will need access to Excel. Before completing exercises in this section, check with your instructor.

Import File

Importing Data into a Chart

Data in an Excel worksheet can be imported into a chart. To do this, you would complete these basic steps:

QUICK STEPS

Import Data into a Chart
1. Click Insert, Object.
2. Double-click *Microsoft Graph Chart* in *Object type* list box.
3. Click Import File button.
4. Double-click desired worksheet name.
5. Click OK at Import Data Options dialog box.

1. Click Insert and then Object.
2. At the Object dialog box with the Create New tab selected, double-click *Microsoft Graph Chart* in the *Object type* list box. (You will need to scroll down the list to display this program.)
3. With the default datasheet and chart displayed, click the Import File button on the Graph Standard toolbar.
4. At the Import File dialog box, double-click the desired worksheet name.
5. At the Import Data Options dialog box, shown in Figure 6.1, specify whether you want the entire worksheet or a specific range of cells, and then click OK.
6. Click in the document screen outside the chart and datasheet to return to the document and view the chart.

FIGURE 6.1 *Import Data Options Dialog Box*

Edit data in a chart created with Excel data in the normal manner. Open Graph by double-clicking the chart. Make the desired changes in the datasheet and then click outside the datasheet to close Graph.

exercise 1
IMPORTING AN EXCEL WORKSHEET INTO A CHART

1. Open and save an Excel worksheet. To begin, open Excel by clicking the Start button on the Taskbar, pointing to All Programs, pointing to Microsoft Office, and then clicking Microsoft Office Excel 2003. (These steps may vary.)
2. In Excel, click the Open button on the Standard toolbar.
3. At the Open dialog box, make sure the WordChapter06E folder on your disk is the active folder, and then double-click *ExcelWorksheet01*.
4. With **ExcelWorksheet01** open, click File and then Save As.
5. At the Save As dialog box, type Excelc6x01 and then press Enter.
6. Click File and then Close to close **Excelc6x01**.
7. Click File and then Exit to exit Excel.
8. In Word, import **Excelc6x01** into a chart by completing the following steps:
   a. At a clear document screen, click Insert and then Object.
   b. At the Object dialog box with the Create New tab selected, double-click *Microsoft Graph Chart* in the *Object type* list box. (You will need to scroll down the list to display this program.)
   c. With the default datasheet and chart displayed, click the Import File button on the Graph Standard toolbar.
   d. At the Import File dialog box, make sure the WordChapter06E folder on your disk is the active folder, and then double-click *Excelc6x01*.
   e. At the Import Data Options dialog box, make sure *Entire sheet* is selected in the *Import* section, and then click OK.
   f. Click in the document screen outside the chart and datasheet to return to the document and view the chart.
9. Save the document and name it **ewc6x01**.
10. Print **ewc6x01**.
11. With **ewc6x01** still open, revise data in the chart by completing the following steps:
    a. Double-click the chart.
    b. Click in the cell containing the number 795,460 and then type 590200.
    c. Click in the cell containing the number 890,425 and then type 603565.
    d. Click outside the datasheet to close Graph.
12. Save, print, and then close **ewc6x01**.

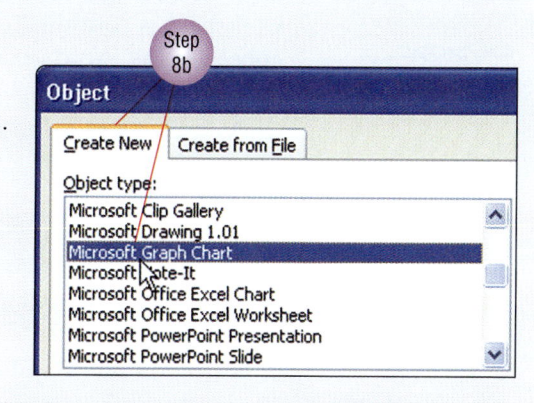

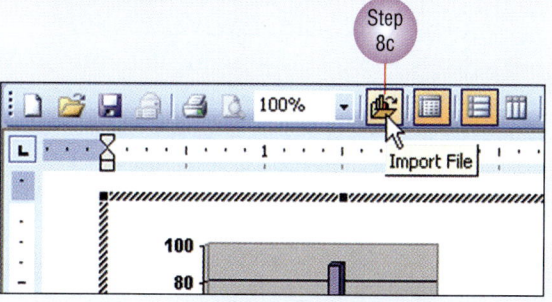

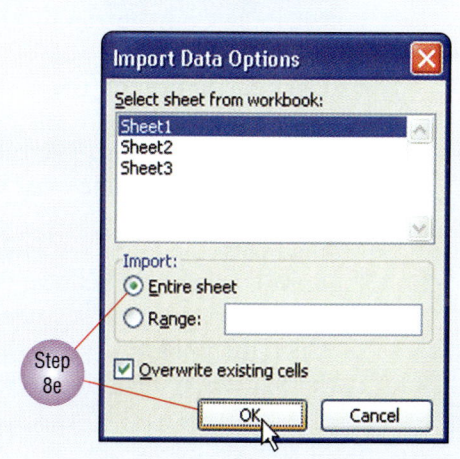

WORD Sharing Data E223

QUICK STEPS

Link Worksheet with Word Document
1. Open Excel and then open worksheet.
2. Select cells.
3. Click Copy button.
4. Open Word and then open document.
5. Click Edit, Paste Special.
6. Click *Microsoft Excel Worksheet Object.*
7. Click *Paste link.*
8. Click OK.

Importing a Worksheet into a Table

Several methods are available for importing a Microsoft Excel worksheet into a Word document. The methods include copying a worksheet in Excel and pasting it into a Word document, linking the worksheet to a Word document, or embedding the worksheet as an object. Consider the following when choosing a method:

- Copy an Excel worksheet into a Word document in situations where the worksheet will not need to be edited.
- Link an Excel worksheet with a Word document in situations where the worksheet is continually updated in Excel and you want the updates to appear in the Word document.
- Embed an Excel worksheet in a Word document in situations where the worksheet will be edited in the Word document.

HINT The main differences between linking and embedding a worksheet are where the data is stored and how it is updated after it is placed in the document.

exercise 2

COPYING AN EXCEL WORKSHEET INTO A WORD DOCUMENT

1. Make sure Word is open and a clear document screen displays.
2. Open Microsoft Excel.
3. Click the Open button on the Standard toolbar.
4. At the Open dialog box, make sure WordChapter06E is the active folder, and then double-click *ExcelWorksheet01*.
5. Copy the cells containing data into a Word document by completing the following steps:
   a. Select cells A1 through E5. (To do this, position the cell pointer [white plus symbol] in cell A1, hold down the left mouse button, drag down to cell E5, and then release the mouse button.)
   b. Click the Copy button on the Standard toolbar.
   c. Click the button on the Taskbar representing Word.
   d. At the clear document screen, click the Paste button.
6. Make the following changes to the document:
   a. Press Ctrl + Home to move the insertion point to the beginning of the document and then press the Enter key three times. (This inserts blank lines above the worksheet and moves the worksheet down the screen.)
   b. Press the Up Arrow key once.
   c. Click the Bold button on the Formatting toolbar and then type **2004 REGIONAL SALES**.
   d. If gray gridlines do not display in the table, click in any cell in the table, click Table, and then Show Gridlines.
7. Save the document with Save As and name it **ewc6x02**.

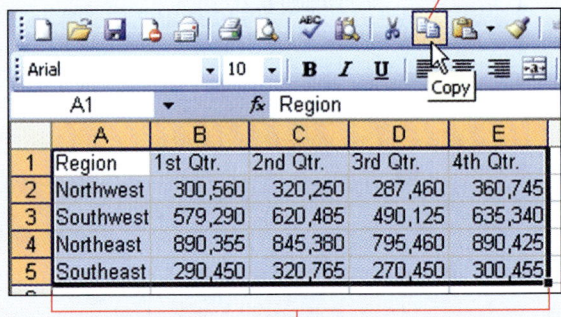

8. Print and then close **ewc6x02**. (The worksheet border gridlines will not print.)
9. Click the button on the Taskbar representing **ExcelWorksheet01**.
10. Close **ExcelWorksheet01** and then exit Excel.

exercise 3 — LINKING AN EXCEL WORKSHEET WITH A WORD DOCUMENT

1. In Word, open **WordMemo01**.
2. Save the memo document and name it **ewc6x03**.
3. Link an Excel worksheet with **ewc6x03** by completing the following steps:
    a. Open Excel.
    b. Click the Open button on the Standard toolbar.
    c. At the Open dialog box, make sure the WordChapter06E folder on your disk is the active folder, and then double-click *ExcelWorksheet02*.
    d. With **ExcelWorksheet02** open, click File and then Save As.
    e. At the Save As dialog box, type Excelc6x03 and then press Enter.
    f. Select cells A1 through D7. (To do this, position the mouse pointer in cell A1, hold down the left mouse button, drag down to cell D7, and then release the mouse button.)
    g. Click the Copy button on the Standard toolbar.
    h. Make Word the active program (click the button on the Taskbar representing the Word document **ewc6x03**).
    i. With **ewc6x03** open, position the insertion point between the first and second paragraphs of text in the body of the memo.
    j. Click Edit and then Paste Special.
    k. At the Paste Special dialog box, click *Microsoft Office Excel Worksheet Object* in the *As* list box.
    l. Click *Paste link*.
    m. Click OK to close the dialog box. (If you only see a border with no numbers inside, display the Options dialog box with the View tab selected and remove the check mark from the *Picture placeholders* check box, and then close the dialog box.)
4. Save, print, and then close **ewc6x03**. (The worksheet border lines will not print.)
5. Exit Word.
6. With Excel the active program, close **Excelc6x03**.
7. Exit Excel by clicking File and then Exit.

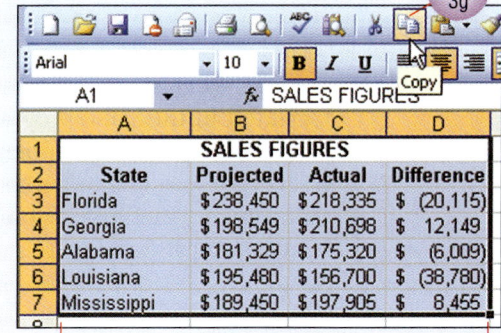

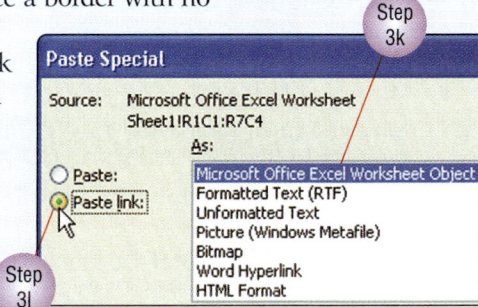

exercise 4 — EDITING A LINKED WORKSHEET

1. Open Excel.
2. Click the Open button on the Standard toolbar.
3. At the Open dialog box, make sure WordChapter06E on your disk is the active folder, and then double-click *Excelc6x03*.

4. Change some of the numbers in cells by completing the following steps:
   a. Position the mouse pointer (thick white plus sign) over the cell containing the number *$218,335* (cell C3) and then click the left mouse button.
   b. Type **230578** (over *$218,335*).
   c. Press the Enter key. (Notice that the number in cell D3 [the Difference column] automatically changed. This is because the cell contains a formula.)
   d. Change the number in cell B5 from *181,329* to *195,200*.
   e. Change the number in cell C7 from *197,905* to *188,370*. (Be sure to press the Enter key.)
5. Save the revised worksheet by clicking the Save button on the Standard toolbar.
6. Close **Excelc6x03** by clicking File and then Close.
7. Exit Excel by clicking File and then Exit.
8. Open Word and then open **ewc6x03**. If a message displays telling you that the document contains links and asking if you want to update the document, click the Yes button. (Notice how the numbers in the worksheet are updated to reflect the changes made to **Excelc6x03**.)
9. Save the document with Save As and name it **ewc6x04**.
10. Print and then close **ewc6x04**.

HINT
Linking can help minimize the size of a Word document.

Linking does not have to be between two different programs—documents created in the same program also can be linked. For example, you can create an object in a Word document and then link it with another Word document (or several Word documents). If a change is made to the object in the original document, the linked object in the other document (or documents) is automatically updated.

exercise 5

LINKING OBJECTS IN WORD DOCUMENTS

1. At a clear Word document screen, open **WordMemo02**.
2. Save the document and name it **ewc6LinkDoc01**.
3. Change to the Print Layout view and then change the Zoom to Whole Page.
4. With **ewc6LinkDoc01** still open, open **WordTable08**.
5. Save the document with Save As and name it **WordTableC06**.
6. Copy and link the table by completing the following steps:
   a. With **WordTableC06** the active document, select the table.
   b. Click the Copy button on the Standard toolbar.
   c. Click the button on the Taskbar representing **ewc6LinkDoc01**.
   d. With **ewc6LinkDoc01** the active document, click Edit and then Paste Special.
   e. At the Paste Special dialog box, click *Microsoft Word Document Object* in the *As* list box, and then click *Paste link*.

E226 Chapter Six

f. Click OK to close the dialog box.
7. Move the table by completing the following steps:
    a. Make sure the Drawing toolbar displays.
    b. Click the table once to select it (black sizing handles display around the table).
    c. Click the Draw button on the Drawing toolbar, point to Text Wrapping, and then click Top and Bottom. (This change the sizing handles to white circles.)
    d. Drag the table so it is positioned between the paragraph of text in the memo and the reference initials.
8. Change the Zoom back to 100%.
9. Save and then print **ewc6LinkDoc01**.
10. Change the name and title after TO: from *Kyle Kovach, Manager, Novelty Items* to *Regina Stewart, Manager, Catalog Services*.
11. Save the document with Save As and name it **ewc6LinkDoc02**.
12. Print and then close **ewc6LinkDoc02**.
13. Deselect the table, print, and then close **WordTableC06**.

exercise 6 — CHANGING DATA IN A LINKED OBJECT IN A WORD DOCUMENT

1. With Word the active program, open **WordTableC06**.
2. Change the following quantities in the On-Hand Qty. column:
    Change *450* to *365*
    Change *500* to *425*
    Change *230* to *170*
    Change *400* to *310*
    Change *140* to *106*
3. Change the following quantities in the Weekly Usage column:
    Change *85* to *67*
    Change *60* to *45*
    Change *34* to *20*
4. Save the edited document with the same name (**WordTableC06**).
5. Print and then close **WordTableC06**.
6. Open **ewc6LinkDoc01**. If a message displays telling you that the document contains links and asking if you want to update the document, click the Yes button.
7. Change the date from *March 8, 2005* to *March 15, 2005*.
8. Save, print, and then close **ewc6LinkDoc01**.
9. Open **ewc6LinkDoc02**. If a message displays telling you that the document contains links and asking if you want to update the document, click the Yes button.
10. Change the date from *March 8, 2005* to *March 15, 2005*.
11. Save, print, and then close **ewc6LinkDoc02**.

Embed an Excel worksheet in a Word document using the Insert Microsoft Excel Worksheet button located on the Standard toolbar. Click this button and a grid displays below the button. This grid is similar to the grid that displays when you click the Insert Table button. Select the desired number of rows and columns and then click the left mouse button. This opens the Microsoft Excel program

Insert Microsoft Excel Worksheet

and inserts the worksheet in the document. Figure 6.2 shows the embedded worksheet you will create in Exercise 7. The Excel toolbars and Formula bar are identified in the figure.

FIGURE 6.2 *Embedded Excel Worksheet*

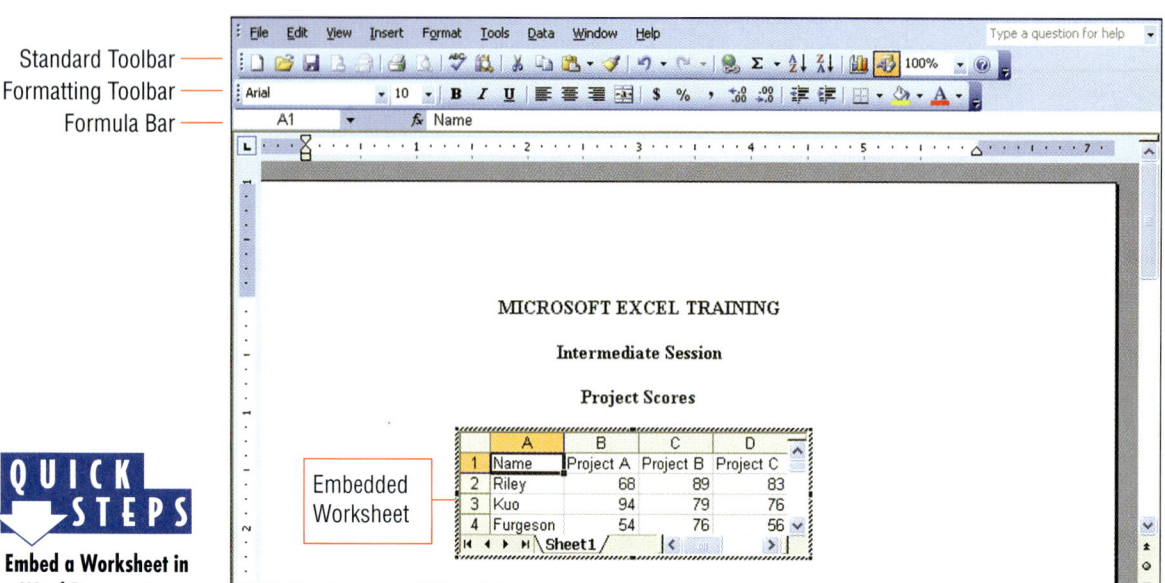

Embed a Worksheet in a Word Document
1. Click Insert Microsoft Excel Worksheet button.
2. Drag to create desired rows and columns.
3. Type text in cells.

When an Excel worksheet is inserted in a Word document using the Insert Microsoft Excel Worksheet button, Excel opens and all of the toolbars and Excel features are available for creating, modifying, or editing the worksheet. After creating or editing the worksheet, return to Word by clicking in the document screen, outside the worksheet.

exercise 7

EMBEDDING AN EXCEL WORKSHEET IN A WORD DOCUMENT

1. At a clear document screen, click the Center button on the Formatting toolbar, click the Bold button, and then type the three lines of text shown at the beginning of Figure 6.3.
2. With the insertion point positioned a triple space below the text (centered), create the text shown in the table in the figure as an Excel worksheet by completing the following steps:
    a. Click the Insert Microsoft Excel Worksheet button on the Standard toolbar.
    b. Drag down and to the right until four rows and four columns are selected on the grid. (The numbers below the grid display as *4 × 4 Spreadsheet*.)
    c. Click the left mouse button.

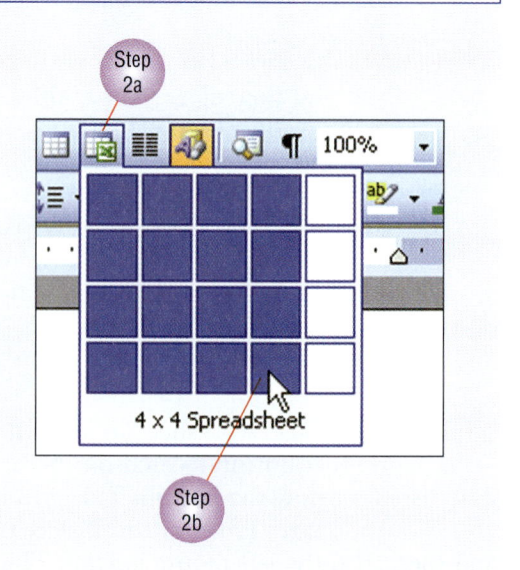

E228 Chapter Six

d. Type the text in the cells as shown in Figure 6.3. (Type the text in the cells in the same manner as you would in a table.)

e. When all of the text is entered in the worksheet, click in the document screen outside the worksheet.

3. Save the document and name it **ewc6x07**.
4. Print and then close **ewc6x07**.

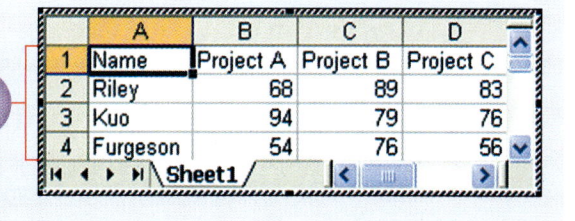

FIGURE 6.3 *Exercise 7*

MICROSOFT EXCEL TRAINING

Intermediate Session

Project Scores

Name	Project A	Project B	Project C
Riley	68	89	83
Kuo	94	79	76
Furgeson	54	76	56

One of the advantages to embedding an Excel worksheet in a Word document is the ability to modify the worksheet. To modify an embedded worksheet, open the Word document containing the worksheet, and then double-click the worksheet. This opens Microsoft Excel and provides all of the toolbars and editing features of Excel.

exercise 8 — MODIFYING AN EMBEDDED EXCEL WORKSHEET

1. Open **ewc6x07**.
2. Save the document with Save As and name it **ewc6x08**.
3. Add a column to the worksheet by completing the following steps:
   a. Double-click the worksheet. (This opens Microsoft Excel.)
   b. Increase the size of the worksheet so columns E and F display by completing the following steps:
      1) Position the mouse pointer on the small square black sizing handle that displays in the middle at the right side of the worksheet until the pointer turns into a double-headed arrow pointing left and right.
      2) Hold down the left mouse button, drag to the right so the right border jumps twice (approximately 2 inches), and then release the mouse button.

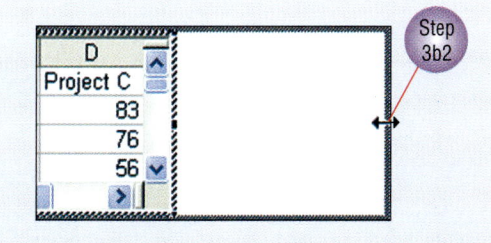

WORD Sharing Data E229

c. Click once in cell E1 and then type **Average**.
4. Insert a formula to calculate the average of the project scores by completing the following steps:
   a. Click once in cell E2.
   b. Click inside the white text box that displays immediately after an equals sign on the Formula bar. (The Formula bar displays above the Ruler.)
   c. Type **=AVERAGE(B2:D2)** and then press Enter.

   Step 4c

5. Copy the formula down to cells E3 and E4 by completing the following steps:
   a. Click once in cell E2 to make it active.
   b. Position the mouse pointer on the small black square that displays in the lower right corner of cell E2 until the pointer turns into a thin black cross. (The small black square is called the "fill handle.")
   c. With the mouse pointer displayed as a thin black cross, hold down the left mouse button, drag down to cell E4, and then release the mouse button.
6. Decrease the size of the worksheet so column F is no longer visible by completing the following steps:
   a. Position the mouse pointer on the small square black sizing handle that displays in the middle at the right side of the worksheet until the pointer turns into a double-headed arrow pointing left and right.
   b. Hold down the left mouse button, drag to the left so the right border jumps once, and then release the mouse button.

   Step 5c

7. Apply the following formatting to the cells:
   a. Select cells A1 through E1.
   b. Click the Bold button and then the Center button on the Formatting toolbar.
   c. Select cells B2 through E4.
   d. Click the Center button on the Formatting toolbar.
8. Click in the document screen outside the worksheet.
9. Save, print, and then close **ewc6x08**.

Copying an Object

Because of the integration of the programs in the Office suite, you can easily copy an object from one program and insert it in another program within the suite. For example, you can copy an Excel worksheet and paste it into a Word document as you did in Exercise 2 or you can copy a diagram from a PowerPoint presentation into a Word document as you will do in Exercise 9.

exercise 9

COPYING A DIAGRAM FROM POWERPOINT TO WORD

1. At a clear document screen, change the font to 18-point Arial bold, change the alignment to center, type the title shown in Figure 6.4 (*Local Area Network*), and then press the Enter key.
2. Open PowerPoint by clicking the Start button on the Taskbar, pointing to All Programs, pointing to Microsoft Office, and then clicking Microsoft Office PowerPoint 2003. (These steps may vary.)

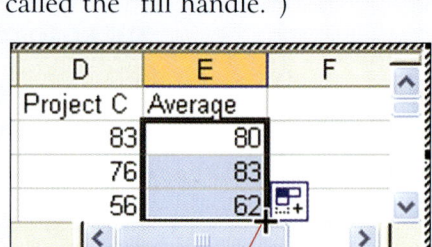

3. Open the file named **PPDiagram** that is located in the WordChapter06E folder.
4. With the presentation open (one slide), click near the diagram to select it (white circle sizing handles display around the diagram).
5. Click the Copy button on the Standard toolbar.
6. Click the button on the Taskbar representing Word.
7. Click the Paste button. (This inserts the diagram in the document.)
8. Change the Zoom to Whole Page.
9. Size and move the diagram so it is the size and position shown at the right.
10. With the diagram still selected (and the Diagram toolbar visible), click the AutoFormat button and then double-click *Primary Colors* at the Diagram Style Gallery dialog box.
11. Change the Zoom back to 100%.
12. Edit each circle so that the text displays more centered in the circle. To do this, click at the beginning of the word in the circle and then press the Enter key twice. (You will need to do this for each circle. Your diagram should appear similar to what you see in Figure 6.4.)
13. Save the document and name it **ewc6x09**.
14. Print and then close **ewc6x09**.
15. Click the button on the Taskbar representing PowerPoint, close the **PPDiagram** presentation, and then exit PowerPoint.

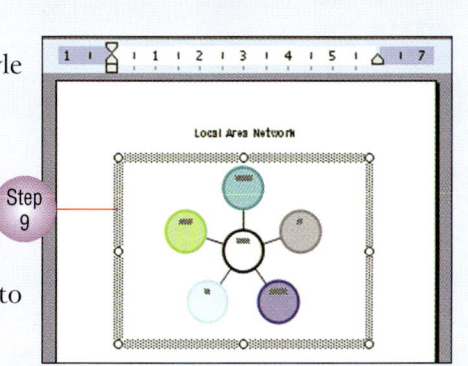

FIGURE 6.4 *Exercise 9*

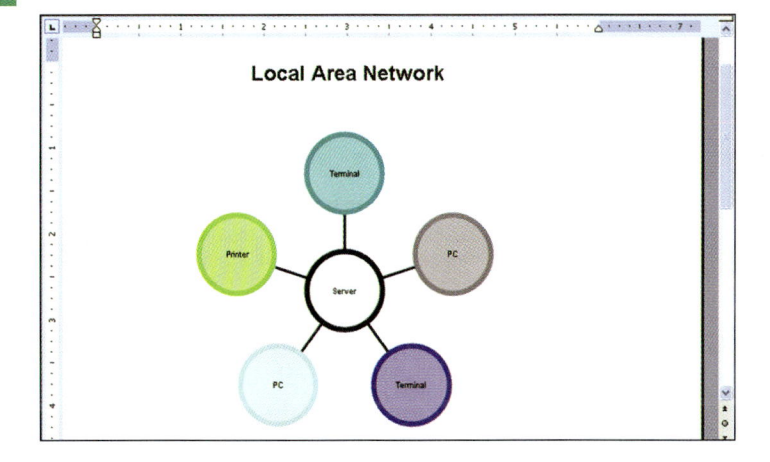

Creating a Form

In Word, a *form* is a protected document that includes fields where information is entered. A form document contains *form fields* that are locations in the document where one of three things is performed: text is entered, a check box is turned on or off, or information is selected from a drop-down list. Three basic steps are completed when creating a form:

HINT
Before creating a form, sketch a layout of the form.

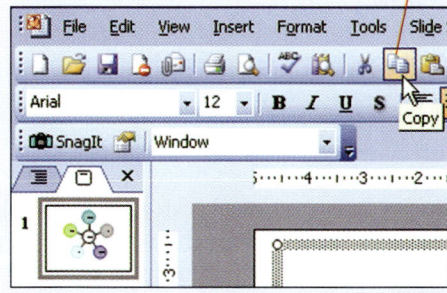

QUICK STEPS

Create a Form
1. Click File, New.
2. Click *On my computer* hyperlink.
3. Click *Template* in *Create New* section.
4. Click OK.
5. Click View, Toolbars, Forms.
6. Type text to create form and use buttons on Forms toolbar to insert text boxes, check boxes, and drop-down lists.
7. Save form template document.

HINT
Consider using an existing form as a guide for designing a new form.

1. Create a form document based on a template and build the structure of the form.
2. Insert form fields where information is to be entered at the keyboard.
3. Save the form as a protected document.

Creating the Form Template

A form is created as a template so that when someone fills in the form they are working on a copy of the form, not the original. The original is the template document that is saved as a protected document. In this way, a form can be used over and over again without changing the original form. When a form is created from the template form document that has been protected, information can be typed only in the fields designated when the form was created.

Figure 6.6 shows an example of a form document created with the form feature. (You will create this form in Exercise 10.) You can create forms that contain fields for text, such as the fields *Name:*, *Address:*, *Date of Birth:*, and so on, shown in Figure 6.6. Forms can also contain check boxes, such as the boxes after *Yes* and *No*, shown in Figure 6.6. Forms can also contain drop-down lists (not used in the form shown in Figure 6.6). You will learn about drop-down lists later in this chapter.

Word provides a Forms toolbar with buttons you can use to easily insert a text box, check box, or other form fields into a form template document. To display the Forms toolbar shown in Figure 6.5, position the arrow pointer on either the Standard or Formatting toolbar, click the *right* mouse button, and then click Forms at the drop-down menu. You can also display the Forms toolbar by clicking View, pointing to Toolbars, and then clicking Forms.

FIGURE 6.5 Forms Toolbar

Generally, a form is created based on the default template document (called the Normal template). The form is created and then saved as a protected template document. To learn how to create a form document, complete Exercise 10.

Changing File Locations

By default, Word saves template documents in a Templates subfolder within the Microsoft Office program. In this chapter, you will create form template documents and save them to this subfolder. In some situations, you may want to change the location of template documents. Do this at the Options dialog box with the File Locations tab selected. At the Options dialog box, click *User templates* in the *File types* list box, and then click the Modify button. At the Modify Location dialog box, specify the desired folder, and then click OK. Click OK to close the Options dialog box.

exercise 10 — CREATING A FORM DOCUMENT

1. Create the form shown in Figure 6.6 as a template document. To begin, click File and then New.
2. Click the <u>On my computer</u> hyperlink in the New Document task pane.
3. At the Templates dialog box with the General tab selected, make sure *Blank Document* is selected in the list box.
4. Click *Template* in the *Create New* section at the bottom right corner of the dialog box.
5. Click OK.
6. At the document screen, make sure the default font is 12-point Times New Roman. (If it is not, display the Font dialog box, change the size to 12, and then click the Default button. At the question asking if you want to change the default font, click Yes.)
7. Type the beginning portion of the form shown in Figure 6.6 up to the colon after *Name:*. After typing the colon, press the spacebar once, and then insert a form field where the name will be typed by completing the following steps:
    a. Turn on the display of the Forms toolbar by clicking View, pointing to Toolbars, and then clicking Forms.
    b. At the Forms toolbar shown in Figure 6.5, click the Text Form Field button. (The form field displays as a shaded area in the document screen.)
8. After inserting the form field, press the Enter key, and then create the remaining text and text form fields as shown in Figure 6.6. To create the check boxes after *Yes* and *No*, position the insertion point where you want the check box to display, and then click the Check Box Form Field button on the Forms toolbar.
9. After the form is completed, protect the document by clicking the Protect Form button on the Forms toolbar.
10. Turn off the display of the Forms toolbar by clicking the Close button located at the right side of the Forms toolbar Title bar.
11. Save the document and name it **XXXTemplateDocument**. (Use your initials in place of the *XXX*.)
12. Print **XXXTemplateDocument**. (The form field gray shading will not print.)
13. Close **XXXTemplateDocument**.

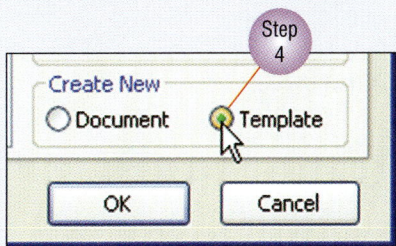

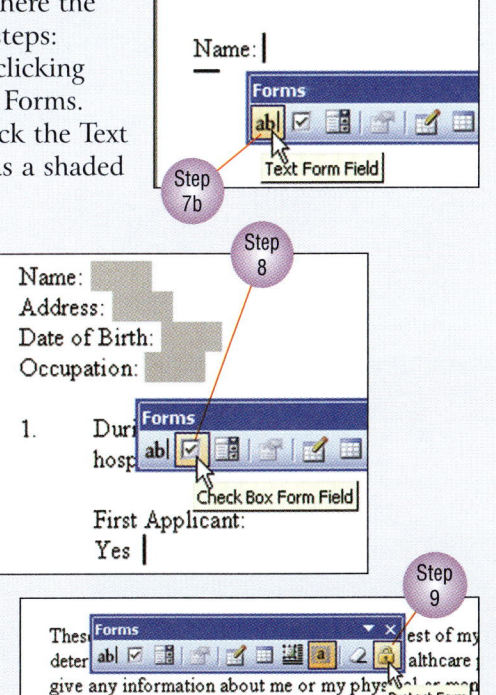

FIGURE 6.6 Exercise 10

LIFETIME ANNUITY INSURANCE APPLICATION

FIRST APPLICANT

Name:
Address:
Date of Birth:
Occupation:

SECOND APPLICANT

Name:
Address:
Date of Birth:
Occupation:

1. During the past 3 years, have you for any reason consulted a doctor or been hospitalized?

    First Applicant: Second Applicant:
    Yes ☐   No ☐   Yes ☐   No ☐

2. Have you ever been treated for or advised that you had any of the following: heart, lung, kidney, or liver disorder; high blood pressure; drug abuse, including alcohol; cancer or tumor; diabetes; or any disorder of your immune system?

    First Applicant: Second Applicant:
    Yes ☐   No ☐   Yes ☐   No ☐

These answers are true and complete to the best of my knowledge and belief. To determine my insurability, I authorize any healthcare provider or insurance company to give any information about me or my physical or mental health.

FIRST APPLICANT'S SIGNATURE   SECOND APPLICANT'S SIGNATURE

_____   _____

QUICK STEPS

Filling in a Form Template Document
1. Click File, New.
2. Click On my computer hyperlink.
3. Click *Document* in *Create New* section.
4. Double-click form template document.
5. Type text in first field.
6. Press Tab to move to next field.
7. Continue typing text and/or pressing Tab until form is completed.
8. Save form with a new name.

Filling in a Form Document

After a template form document is created, protected, and saved, the template can be used to create a personalized form document. When you open a form template document that has been protected, the insertion point is automatically inserted in the first form field. Type the information for the data field and then press the Tab key to move the insertion point to the next form field. You can move the insertion point to a preceding form field by pressing Shift + Tab. To fill in a check box form field, click in the check box, or move the insertion point to the check box and then press the spacebar. Complete the same steps to remove an *X* from a check box form field. As an example of how to fill in a form template, complete Exercise 11.

exercise 11

FILLING IN A TEMPLATE FORM DOCUMENT

1. Create a form with the **XXXTemplateDocument** form template. To begin, click File and then New.
2. Click the On my computer hyperlink in the New Document task pane.
3. At the Templates dialog box with the General tab selected, click *Document* in the *Create New* section of the dialog box.
4. Double-click the **XXXTemplateDocument** icon (where your initials display instead of the *XXX*).
5. Word displays the form document with the insertion point positioned in the first form field after *Name:*. Type the name **Dennis Utley** (as shown in Figure 6.7).
6. Press the Tab key to move to the next form field.
7. Fill in the remaining text and check box form fields as shown in Figure 6.7. Press the Tab key to move the insertion point to the next form field. Press Shift + Tab to move the insertion point to the preceding form field. (To insert the *X* in a check box, click in the check box, or move the insertion point to the check box, and then press the spacebar.)
8. When the form is completed, save the document in the WordChapter06E folder on your disk and name it **ewc6x11**.
9. Print and then close **ewc6x11**.

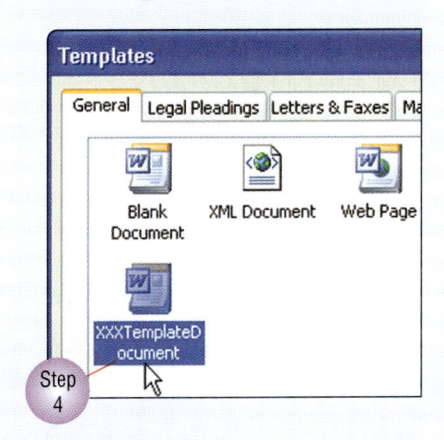

FIGURE 6.7 Exercise 11

LIFETIME ANNUITY INSURANCE APPLICATION

FIRST APPLICANT

Name: Dennis Utley
Address: 11315 Lomas Drive, Seattle, WA 98123
Date of Birth: 02/23/1959
Occupation: Accountant

SECOND APPLICANT

Name: Geneva Utley
Address: 11315 Lomas Drive, Seattle, WA 98123
Date of Birth: 09/04/1962
Occupation: Social Worker

1. During the past 3 years, have you for any reason consulted a doctor or been hospitalized?

   First Applicant: Second Applicant:
   Yes ☐   No ☒   Yes ☐   No ☒

2. Have you ever been treated for or advised that you had any of the following: heart, lung, kidney, or liver disorder; high blood pressure; drug abuse, including alcohol; cancer or tumor; diabetes; or any disorder of your immune system?

   First Applicant: Second Applicant:
   Yes ☐   No ☒   Yes ☐   No ☒

These answers are true and complete to the best of my knowledge and belief. To determine my insurability, I authorize any healthcare provider or insurance company to give any information about me or my physical or mental health.

FIRST APPLICANT'S SIGNATURE   SECOND APPLICANT'S SIGNATURE

_____   _____

Printing a Form

After the form fields in a form document have been filled in, the form can be printed in the normal manner. In some situations, you may want to print just the data (not the entire form) or print the form and not the fill-in data.

If you are using a preprinted form that is inserted in the printer, you will want to print just the data. Word will print the data in the same location on the page as it appears in the form document. To print just the data in a form, click Tools and then Options. At the Options dialog box, click the Print tab. At the Options dialog box with the Print tab selected, click *Print data only for forms* in the *Options for current document only* section (this inserts a check mark in the check box), and then click OK. Click the Print button on the Standard toolbar. After printing only the data, complete similar steps to remove the check mark from the *Print data only for forms* check box.

> **HINT**
> Form field shading does not print.

To print only the form without the data, you would click File and then New, and then click the On my computer hyperlink in the New Document task pane. At the Templates dialog box, select the desired template document in the list box, and then click OK. With the form document displayed in the document screen, click the Print button on the Standard toolbar, and then close the document.

exercise 12

PRINTING ONLY THE DATA IN A FORM DOCUMENT

1. Open **ewc6x11**.
2. Print only the data in the form fields by completing the following steps:
   a. Click Tools and then Options.
   b. At the Options dialog box, click the Print tab.
   c. At the Options dialog box with the Print tab selected, click *Print data only for forms* in the *Options for current document only* section. (This inserts a check mark in the check box.)
   d. Click OK.
   e. Click the Print button on the Standard toolbar.
3. After printing, remove the check mark from the *Print data only for forms* option by completing the following steps:
   a. Click Tools and then Options.
   b. At the Options dialog box with the Print tab selected, click *Print data only for forms* in the *Options for current document only* section. (This removes the check mark from the check box.)
   c. Click OK.
4. Close **ewc6x11** without saving the changes.

Editing a Form Template

When a form template is created and then protected, the text in the template cannot be changed. If you need to make changes to a form template, you must open the template document, unprotect the document, and then make the changes. After making the changes, protect the document again.

To unprotect a template document, click the Protect Form button on the Forms toolbar to deactivate it. You can also unprotect a document by clicking Tools and then Unprotect Document. Make any necessary changes to the document and then protect it again by clicking the Protect Form button on the Forms toolbar or by clicking Tools and then Protect Document.

> **HINT**
> To apply formatting to a form field, select the form field and then apply the desired formatting. Use Format Painter to apply the same formatting to other form fields.

Protect Form

Opening a Template Document

Word, by default, saves a template document in a Templates folder. The location of this folder will vary depending on your system configuration. In Exercise 13, you will click My Recent Documents in the My Places bar located at the left side of the dialog box. This displays the most recently opened documents in the Recent folder. If your template document does not display in the Recent folder, check with your instructor to determine the location of the Templates folder.

exercise 13

EDITING A TEMPLATE FORM

1. Add the text shown in Figure 6.8 to the **XXXTemplateDocument** form. To begin, click the Open button on the Standard toolbar.
2. At the Open dialog box, click My Recent Documents in the My Places bar (located at the left side of the dialog box).
3. With the Recent folder selected, click the down-pointing arrow to the right of the *Files of type* option box (located at the bottom left corner of the dialog box), and then click *All Files*.
4. Double-click **XXXTemplateDocument** in the list box (where *XXX* indicates your initials).
5. Display the Forms toolbar.
6. Unprotect the template document by clicking the Protect Form button on the Forms toolbar to deactivate it.
7. Add the paragraph and the check boxes shown in Figure 6.8 to the form.
8. Protect the document again by clicking the Protect Form button on the Forms toolbar.
9. Turn off the display of the Forms toolbar.
10. Save, print, and then close **XXXTemplateDocument**.

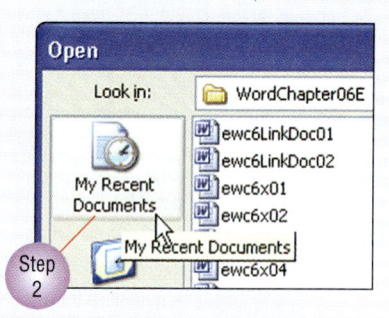

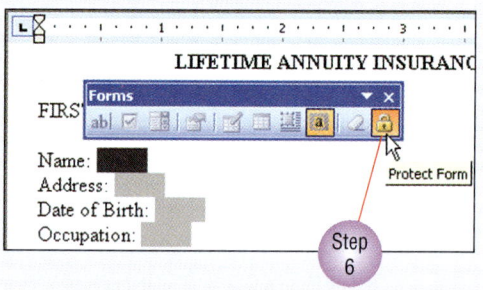

FIGURE 6.8 Exercise 13

3. During the past 3 years, have you for any reason been denied life insurance by any other insurance company?

   First Applicant: Second Applicant:
   Yes ☐   No ☐   Yes ☐   No ☐

E238 Chapter Six — WORD

Customizing Form Field Options

A drop-down list, text box, or check box form field is inserted in a document with default options. You can change these default options for each form field. Options at the Drop-Down Form Field Options dialog box can be used to create form fields with drop-down lists.

Drop-Down Form Field

Form Field Options

Creating Form Fields with Drop-Down Lists

When creating form fields for a form document, there may be some fields where you want the person entering the information to choose from specific options, rather than typing the data. To do this, create a form field with a drop-down list. Open the template document, unprotect the template document, type the field name, and then click the Drop-Down Form Field button on the Forms toolbar. After inserting the drop-down form field, click the Form Field Options button on the Forms toolbar. This displays the Drop-Down Form Field Options dialog box shown in Figure 6.9.

FIGURE 6.9 *Drop-Down Form Field Options Dialog Box*

Type the option you want to display in the drop-down list and then click the Add button.

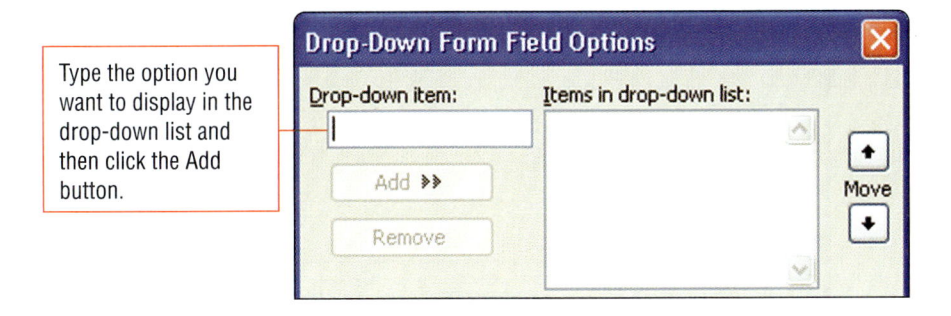

At the Drop-Down Form Field Options dialog box, type the first option you want to display in the drop-down list, and then click the Add button. Continue in this manner until all drop-down list items have been added and then click OK or press Enter to close the Drop-Down Form Field Options dialog box. Protect and then save the template document. A drop-down form field in a form document displays as a gray box with a down-pointing arrow at the right side of the box. You can remove drop-down items at the Drop-Down Form Field Options dialog box by selecting the item in the *Items in drop-down list* box and then clicking the Remove button.

HINT
Insert a drop-down list box to restrict choices to those in the list box.

When filling in a form field in a form template document that contains a drop-down list, position the insertion point in the drop-down form field, and then complete one of the following steps:

- Click the down-pointing arrow at the right side of the form field.
- Press F4.
- Press Alt + Down Arrow key.

HINT
To remove an item in the *Items in drop-down list* box, click the item and then click the Remove button.

Sharing Data   E239

When you choose one of the methods above, a drop-down list displays with the choices for the form field. Click the desired choice, or press the Up or Down Arrow key to select the desired choice, and then press the Enter key.

Changing Text Form Field Options

To change options for a text form field, position the insertion point on the text form field you want to change and then click the Form Field Options button on the Forms toolbar. This displays the Text Form Field Options dialog box shown in Figure 6.10.

FIGURE 6.10 *Text Form Field Options Dialog Box*

Change the type of text to be inserted in the form field with options from this text box.

Specify an exact measurement for a form field at this text box.

At the Text Form Field Options dialog box, you can change the type of text that is to be inserted in the form field. The default setting at the *Type* option box is *Regular text*. This can be changed to *Number, Date, Current date, Current time,* or *Calculation*.

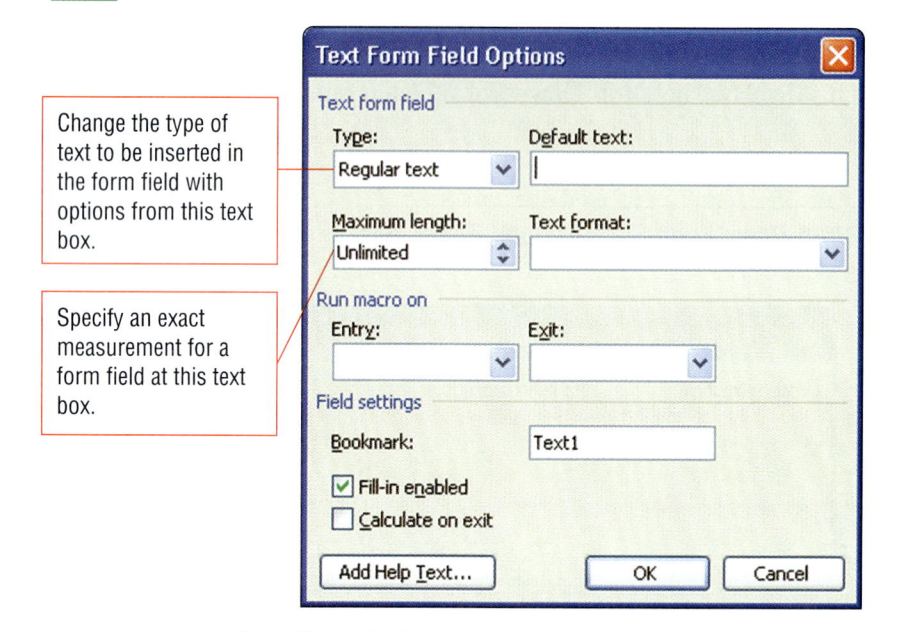

HINT *You can specify a default entry in a text form field.*

If you change the *Type* option, Word will display an error message if the correct type of information is not entered in the form field. For example, if you change the form field type to *Number* in the *Type* option box, only a number can be entered in the form field. If something other than a number is entered, Word displays an error message, the entry is selected, and the insertion point stays in the form field until a number is entered.

If a particular text form field will generally need the same information, type that information in the *Default text* box. This default text will display in the form field. If you want to leave the default text in the form document, just press the Tab key or the Enter key when filling in the form. If you want to change the default text, type the new text over the default text when filling in the form.

With the *Maximum length* option at the Text Form Field Options dialog box, you can specify an exact measurement for a form field. This option has a default setting of *Unlimited*.

E240 Chapter Six

Formatting options for text in a form field can be applied with options at the *Text format* option box. For example, if you want text to display in all uppercase letters, click the down-pointing arrow at the right side of the *Text format* option box, and then click *Uppercase* at the drop-down list. When you type text in the form field while filling in the form, the text is converted to uppercase letters as soon as you press the Tab key or Enter key. The *Text format* options will vary depending on what is selected in the *Type* option box.

Changing Check Box Form Field Options

Check Box form field options can be changed at the Check Box Form Field Options dialog box shown in Figure 6.11. To display this dialog box, position the insertion point on a check box form field and then click the Form Field Options button on the Forms toolbar.

FIGURE

6.11 *Check Box Form Field Options Dialog Box*

Change the size of a check box by choosing *Exactly* and then typing the desired point size.

By default, Word inserts a check box in a form template document in the same size as the adjacent text. This is because *Auto* is selected at the *Check box size* section of the Check Box Form Field Options dialog box. If you want to specify an exact size for the check box, click *Exactly*, and then type the desired point measurement in the *Exactly* text box.

A check box form field is empty by default. If you want the check box to be checked by default, click the *Checked* option in the *Default value* section of the dialog box.

exercise 14

CREATING A FORM WITH TEXT FIELDS, CHECK BOXES, AND DROP-DOWN LISTS

1. Create the form shown in Figure 6.12 as a template document. To begin, click File and then New.
2. Click the On my computer hyperlink in the New Document task pane.
3. At the Templates dialog box with the General tab selected, make sure *Blank Document* is selected in the list box.
4. Click *Template* in the *Create New* section at the bottom right corner of the dialog box and then click OK.

5. At the document screen, make sure the default font is 12-point Times New Roman.
6. Turn on the display of the Forms toolbar.
7. Type the title of the form, *APPLICATION FOR PREFERRED INSURANCE*, centered and bolded. Press the Enter key three times, turn off bold, and then return the paragraph alignment to left. Type **Date:**, press the spacebar once, and then insert a text form field that inserts the current date by completing the following steps:
   a. Click the Text Form Field button on the Forms toolbar.
   b. Click the Form Field Options button on the Forms toolbar.
   c. At the Text Form Field Options dialog box, click the down-pointing arrow at the right side of the *Type* option box, and then click *Current date* at the drop-down list. 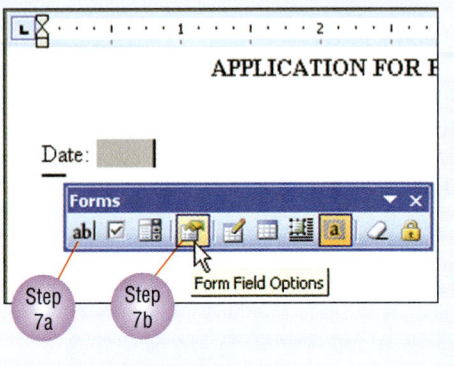 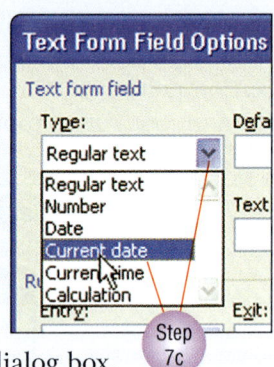
   d. Click OK or press Enter to close the Text Form Field Options dialog box.
   e. Press the Right Arrow key to deselect the field and move the insertion point to the right side of the field. (You can also position the mouse pointer immediately right of the field and then click the left mouse button.)
8. Press the Enter key twice, type **Name:**, press the spacebar once, and then create the text form field. Do the same for *Address:* and *Date of Birth:*.
9. Type **Social Security Number:** and then create a text form field that allows a maximum of 11 characters (the number required for the Social Security number including the hyphens) by completing the following steps:
   a. Press the spacebar once after typing *Social Security Number:*.
   b. Click the Text Form Field button on the Forms toolbar.
   c. Click the Form Field Options button on the Forms toolbar.
   d. At the Text Form Field Options dialog box, select *Unlimited* that displays in the *Maximum length* text box, and then type **11**.
   e. Click OK or press Enter to close the Text Form Field Options dialog box.
   f. Press the Right Arrow key to deselect the field and move the insertion point to the right side of the field. (You can also position the mouse pointer immediately right of the field and then click the left mouse button.) 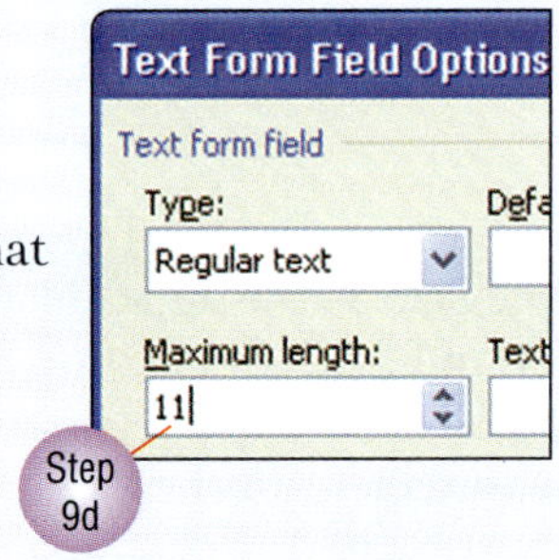
10. Press the Enter key twice, type **Gender:**, and then press the Tab key. Create the text and check boxes after *Gender:* as shown in Figure 6.12.
11. After creating the check box after *Male*, press the Enter key twice, type **Nonprofit Employer:**, press the spacebar once, and then create a drop-down form field with three choices by completing the following steps:
    a. Click the Drop-Down Form Field button on the Forms toolbar.
    b. Click the Form Field Options button on the Forms toolbar.

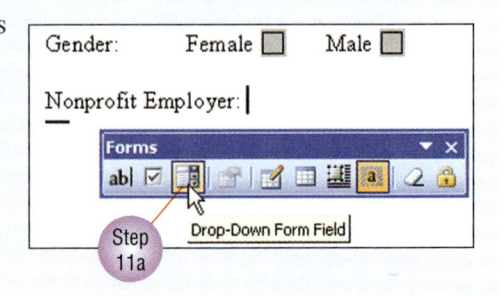

c. At the Drop-Down Form Field Options dialog box, type **College** in the *Drop-down item* text box.
  d. Click the Add button.
  e. Type **Public School** in the *Drop-down item* text box.
  f. Click the Add button.
  g. Type **Private School** in the *Drop-down item* text box.
  h. Click the Add button.
  i. Click OK or press Enter to close the Drop-Down Form Field Options dialog box.
  j. Press the Right Arrow key to deselect the field and move the insertion point to the right side of the field. (You can also position the mouse pointer immediately right of the field and then click the left mouse button.)
12. Press the Enter key twice, type **How are premiums to be paid?**, press the spacebar once, and then create a drop-down form field with the choices *Annually*, *Semiannually*, and *Quarterly* by completing steps similar to those in Step 11.
13. Continue creating the remainder of the form as shown in Figure 6.12.
14. After the form is completed, protect the document by clicking the Protect Form button on the Forms toolbar.
15. Close the Forms toolbar.
16. Save the document and name it **XXXewc6x14**. (Use your initials in place of the *XXX*.)
17. Print and then close **XXXewc6x14**.

TABLE 6.12 Exercise 14

APPLICATION FOR PREFERRED INSURANCE

Date:

Name:

Address:

Date of Birth:

Social Security Number:

Gender: Female ☐   Male ☐

Nonprofit Employer:

How are premiums to be paid?

1. Will this insurance replace any existing insurance or annuity?
   Yes ☐   No ☐

2. Within the past 3 years has your driver's license been suspended or revoked, or have you been convicted for driving under the influence of alcohol or drugs?
   Yes ☐   No ☐

3. Do you have any intention of traveling or residing outside the United States or Canada within the next 12 months?
   Yes ☐   No ☐

Signature of proposed insured:

_____   Date _____

exercise 15

FILLING IN A TEMPLATE FORM DOCUMENT

1. Create a form with the **XXXewc6x14** form template. To begin, click File and then New.
2. Click the On my computer hyperlink in the New Document task pane.
3. At the Templates dialog box with the General tab selected, click *Document* in the *Create New* section.
4. Double-click **XXXewc6x14** (where your initials display instead of the *XXX*).
5. Word displays the form document with the insertion point positioned in the *Name:* form field. Fill in the text and check boxes as shown in Figure 6.13. (Press the Tab key to move the insertion point to the next form field. Press Shift + Tab to move the insertion point to the preceding form field.) To fill in the form fields with drop-down lists, complete the following steps:
   a. With the insertion point in the drop-down list form field, click the down-pointing arrow at the right side of the option box.
   b. Click the desired option at the drop-down list.
6. When the form is completed, save the document in the WordChapter06E folder on your disk and name it **ewc6x15**.
7. Print and then close **ewc6x15**.

FIGURE 6.13 *Exercise 15*

APPLICATION FOR PREFERRED INSURANCE

Date: (current date)

Name: Jennifer Reynolds

Address: 2309 North Cascade, Renton, WA 98051

Date of Birth: 12/18/1963

Social Security Number: 411-23-6800

Gender: Female ☒   Male ☐

Nonprofit Employer: Public School

How are premiums to be paid? Quarterly

1. Will this insurance replace any existing insurance or annuity?
   Yes ☐   No ☒

2. Within the past 3 years has your driver's license been suspended or revoked, or have you been convicted for driving under the influence of alcohol or drugs?
   Yes ☐   No ☒

3. Do you have any intention of traveling or residing outside the United States or Canada within the next 12 months?
   Yes ☐   No ☒

Signature of proposed insured:

_____   Date _____

Creating Tables in a Form Template

A table can be very useful when creating a form with form fields. A table can be customized to create a business form such as an invoice or a purchase order. Figure 6.14 shows an example of a form you will create in Exercise 16 using the table feature.

exercise 16 — CREATING A FORM USING THE TABLE FEATURE

1. Create the form shown in Figure 6.14 as a template document and name it **XXXewc6x16** (where *XXX* are your initials). To begin, click File and then New.
2. Click the On my computer hyperlink in the New Document task pane.
3. At the Templates dialog box with the General tab selected, make sure *Blank Document* is selected in the list box.
4. Click *Template* in the *Create New* section at the bottom right corner of the dialog box.
5. Click OK.
6. At the document screen, make sure the default font is 12-point Times New Roman.
7. Display the Forms toolbar.

8. Click the Draw Table button on the Forms toolbar.
9. Use the buttons on the Tables and Borders toolbar to draw the table lines as shown in Figure 6.14.
10. Change the text alignment to Align Center for specific cells by completing the following steps:
    a. Select the cells that will contain the text *Date, Description, Amount,* and *Ref #*.
    b. Click the down-pointing arrow at the right side of the Align Top Left button on the Tables and Borders toolbar.
    c. At the drop-down palette of choices, click Align Center (second option from the left in the second row).
11. Turn off the display of the Tables and Borders toolbar.
12. Type the text in the cells as shown in Figure 6.14. Insert text form fields as shown in the figure. (To insert the three text form fields in the Date column, insert the first text form field and then press the Enter key. This moves the insertion point down to the next line within the cell. Continue in this manner until all three text form fields are inserted. Complete similar steps for the three text form fields in the *Description, Amount,* and *Ref #* columns.)
13. After the table is completed, protect the document by clicking the Protect Form button on the Forms toolbar.
14. Close the Forms toolbar.
15. Save the document and name it **XXXewc6x16**. (Use your initials in place of the *XXX*.)
16. Print and then close **XXXewc6x16**.

FIGURE 6.14 *Exercise 16*

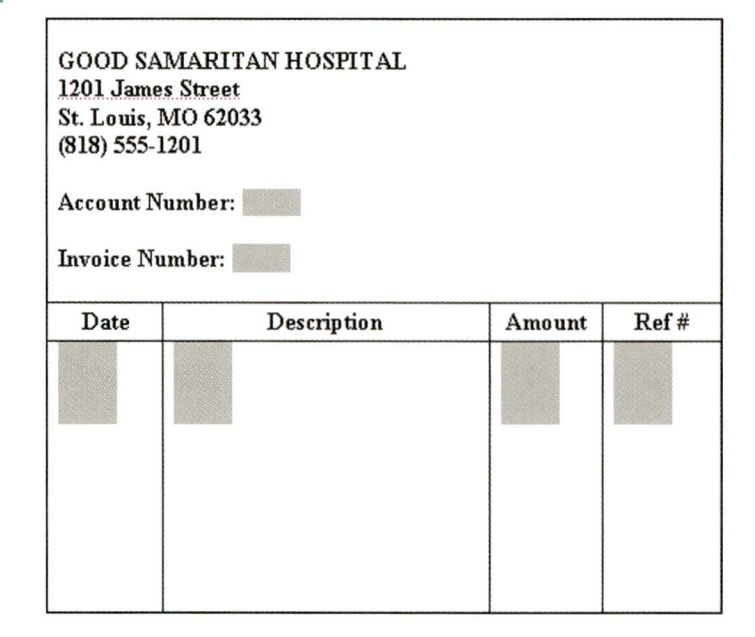

exercise 17

FILLING IN A TEMPLATE TABLE FORM

1. Create a form with the **XXXewc6x16** form template. To begin, click File and then New.
2. Click the <u>On my computer</u> hyperlink in the New Document task pane.
3. At the Templates dialog box with the General tab selected, click *Document* in the *Create New* section.
4. Double-click **XXXewc6x16** (where your initials are displayed instead of the *XXX*).
5. Word displays the form document with the insertion point positioned in the first form field. Fill in the text as shown in Figure 6.15. (Press the Tab key to move the insertion point to the next form field. Press Shift + Tab to move the insertion point to the preceding form field.)
6. When the form is completed, save the document and name it **ewc6x17**.
7. Print and then close **ewc6x17**.

FIGURE

6.15 *Exercise 17*

GOOD SAMARITAN HOSPITAL
1201 James Street
St. Louis, MO 62033
(818) 555-1201

Account Number: 3423-001

Invoice Number: 342

Date	Description	Amount	Ref #
04/11/2005	Bed linens	$984.50	5403
04/19/2005	Hospital slippers	$204.00	9422
04/23/2005	Hospital gowns	$750.25	6645

Creating a Master Document and Subdocuments

For projects containing a variety of parts or sections such as a reference guide or book, consider using a ***master document***. A master document contains a number of separate documents referred to as ***subdocuments***. A master document might be useful in a situation where several people are working on one project. Each person prepares a document for his or her part of the project and then the documents are included in a master document. A master document allows for easier editing of subdocuments. Rather than opening a large document for editing, you can open a subdocument, make changes, and those changes are reflected in the master document.

Create a new master document or format an existing document as a master document at the Outline view and the Master Document view. When you change to the Outline view, the Outlining toolbar displays with buttons for working with master documents and subdocuments. These buttons are shown in Figure 6.16.

HINT
By setting up a master document and saving it to a network, several people can work simultaneously on subdocuments within the master document.

QUICK STEPS

Create a Master Document
1. Change to the Outline view.
2. Apply heading-level styles to headings.
3. Select heading and text.
4. Click Create Subdocument button.

The names and functions of some of the Outlining toolbar buttons for working with master documents and subdocuments may vary depending on what is selected in the document. Some buttons may display activated and other deactivated. An activated button displays on the toolbar with a blue border.

FIGURE

6.16 *Outlining Toolbar Master Document Buttons*

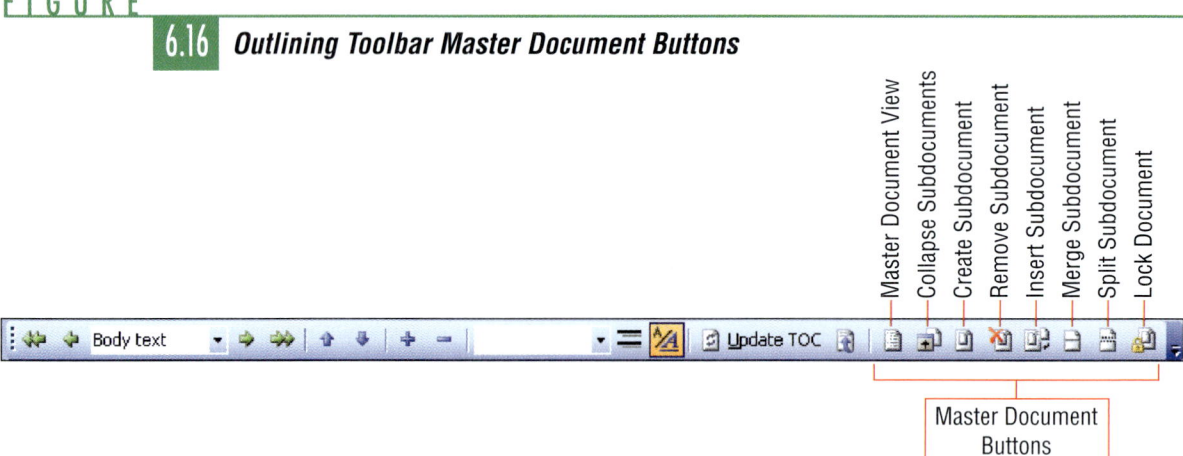

When Outline view is selected, the Master Document View button on the Outlining toolbar is automatically activated. With this button activated, collapsed subdocuments display surrounded by a light gray border line, and subdocument icons display.

Master Document View

Creating a Master Document

To create a master document, start at a clear document screen and then type the text for the document; or, open an existing document. Identify the subdocuments by completing the following steps:

1. Change to the Outline view.
2. Make sure the Master Document View button is activated.
3. Make sure heading-level styles are applied to headings in the document.
4. Select the heading and text to be divided into a subdocument.
5. Click the Create Subdocument button on the Outlining toolbar. (Text specified as a subdocument displays surrounded by a thin gray line border and a subdocument icon displays in the upper left corner of the border.)

Create Subdocument

HINT Word assigns names to each subdocument based on the text used in the outline headings.

Word creates a subdocument for each heading at the top level within the selected text. For example, if selected text begins with Heading 1 text, Word creates a new subdocument at each Heading 1 in the selected text. Save the master document in the same manner as a normal document. Word automatically assigns a document name to each subdocument using the first characters in the subdocument heading.

Opening and Closing a Master Document and Subdocument

Open a master document at the Open dialog box in the same manner as a normal document. Subdocuments in a master document display collapsed in the master document as shown in Figure 6.17. This figure displays the master document named MasterDocc6x18 you will create in Exercise 18. Notice that Word automatically converts subdocument names into hyperlinks. To open a subdocument, hold down the Ctrl key and then click the subdocument hyperlink. This displays the subdocument and also displays the Web toolbar.

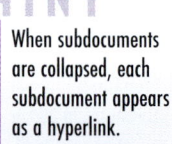

HINT When subdocuments are collapsed, each subdocument appears as a hyperlink.

FIGURE

6.17 MasterDocc6x18

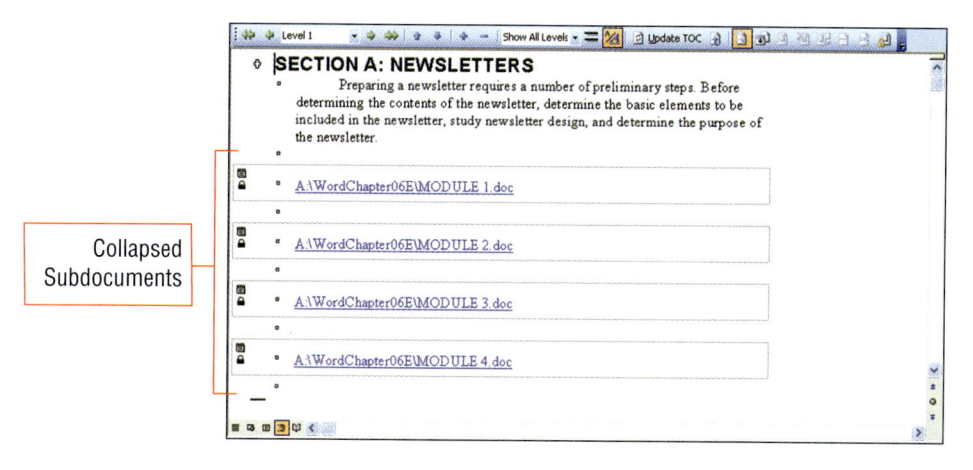

Collapsed Subdocuments

SECTION A: NEWSLETTERS
Preparing a newsletter requires a number of preliminary steps. Before determining the contents of the newsletter, determine the basic elements to be included in the newsletter, study newsletter design, and determine the purpose of the newsletter.

A:\WordChapter06E\MODULE 1.doc
A:\WordChapter06E\MODULE 2.doc
A:\WordChapter06E\MODULE 3.doc
A:\WordChapter06E\MODULE 4.doc

To close a subdocument, click File and then Close or click the Close button that displays at the right side of the Menu bar. If you made any changes to the document, you will be asked if you want to save the changes. Closing a subdocument redisplays the master document and the subdocument hyperlink displays in a different color (identifying that the hyperlink has been used). Close a master document in the normal manner. You may also want to turn off the display of the Web toolbar.

Expanding/Collapsing Subdocuments

Open a master document and subdocuments are automatically collapsed. To expand subdocuments, click the Expand Subdocuments button on the Outlining toolbar. To collapse expanded subdocuments, click the Collapse Subdocuments button on the Outlining toolbar.

Expand Subdocuments

Locking/Unlocking a Subdocument

By default, a subdocument is unlocked so that the subdocument can be viewed or edited. If you want a subdocument available for viewing but not editing, lock the subdocument by clicking the Lock Document button on the Outlining toolbar. Word will automatically lock a subdocument if the subdocument name is set as a read-only document or if another user is currently working on the subdocument.

Collapse Subdocuments

When subdocuments are collapsed, all subdocuments appear to be locked. A lock icon displays below the subdocument icon at the left side of the subdocument name. A document is locked only if the lock icon displays below the subdocument icon when subdocuments are expanded.

Lock Document

exercise 18

CREATING A MASTER DOCUMENT AND EXPANDING/COLLAPSING SUBDOCUMENTS

1. At a clear document screen, change the line spacing to double, and then type the text shown in Figure 6.18. (Press the Enter key after typing the text.)
2. With the insertion positioned at the end of the document, insert the document named **WordReport05**. (To do this, click Insert and then File. At the Insert File dialog box, make sure the WordChapter06E folder is active, and then double-click **WordReport05**.)

3. With the insertion point positioned at the end of the document, insert the document named **WordReport06**. (Click Insert and then File.)
4. Move the insertion point to the beginning of the document.
5. Change to Outline view.
6. Make sure the Master Document View button on the Outlining toolbar is active (displays with an orange background). If it is not active, click the Master Document View button.
7. Format the title with a style by completing the following steps:
    a. Position the insertion point on any character in the title *SECTION A: NEWSLETTERS*.
    b. Click the down-pointing arrow at the right side of the Style button (located toward the left side of the Formatting toolbar).
    c. At the drop-down list that displays, click *Heading 1*.
8. Complete steps similar to those in Step 7 to apply the specified styles to the following headings:

MODULE 1: DEFINING NEWSLETTER ELEMENTS	=	Heading 2
Designing a Newsletter	=	Heading 3
Defining Basic Newsletter Elements	=	Heading 3
MODULE 2: PLANNING A NEWSLETTER	=	Heading 2
Defining the Purpose of a Newsletter	=	Heading 3
MODULE 3: DESIGNING A NEWSLETTER	=	Heading 2
Applying Desktop Publishing Guidelines	=	Heading 3
MODULE 4: CREATING NEWSLETTER LAYOUT	=	Heading 2
Choosing Paper Size and Type	=	Heading 3
Choosing Paper Weight	=	Heading 3
Creating Margins for Newsletters	=	Heading 3

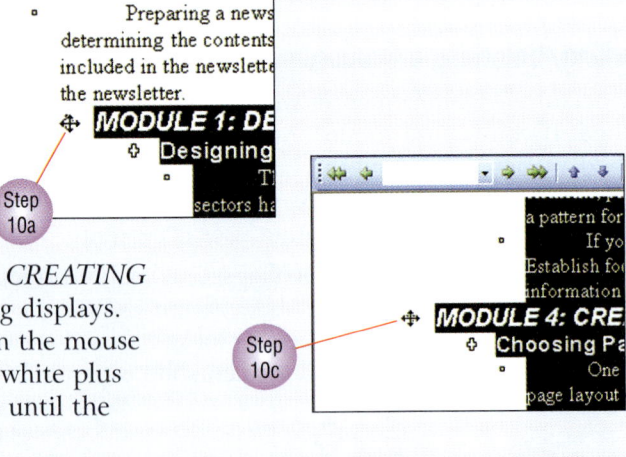

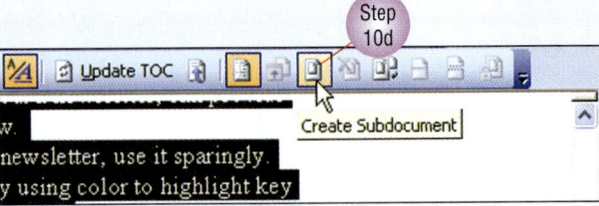

9. Save the document and name it **MasterDocc6x18**.
10. Create subdocuments with the module text by completing the following steps:
    a. Position the mouse pointer on the selection symbol (white plus sign) that displays immediately left of the heading *MODULE 1: DEFINING NEWSLETTER ELEMENTS* until the pointer turns into a four-headed arrow, and then click the left mouse button.
    b. Scroll through the document until the *MODULE 4: CREATING NEWSLETTER LAYOUT* heading displays.
    c. Hold down the Shift key, position the mouse pointer on the selection symbol (white plus sign) immediately left of the title until the pointer turns into a four-headed arrow, and then click the left mouse button. (This selects all of the text in modules 1, 2, 3, and 4.)
    d. With the text selected, click the Create Subdocument button on the Outlining toolbar.

11. Save and then close **MasterDocc6x18**.
12. Open **MasterDocc6x18**.
13. Print **MasterDocc6x18** by completing the following steps:
    a. Click the Print button on the Standard toolbar.
    b. At the question asking if you want to open the subdocuments, click No. (The document will print collapsed as shown in the document screen.)
14. Edit the MODULE 1 subdocument by completing the following steps:
    a. Hold down the Ctrl key and then click the *A:\WordChapter06E\MODULE 1.doc* hyperlink.
    b. With the **MODULE 1.doc** document displayed, edit the title so it reads MODULE 1: DEFINING ELEMENTS.
    c. Change the heading *Designing a Newsletter* so it displays as *Designing*.
    d. Change the heading *Defining Basic Newsletter Elements* so it displays as *Defining Basic Elements*.
15. Save the subdocument by clicking the Save button on the Standard toolbar.
16. Close the subdocument.
17. Expand the subdocuments by clicking the Expand Subdocuments button on the Outlining toolbar.
18. Print page 1 of the master document.
19. Collapse the subdocuments by clicking the Collapse Subdocuments button on the Outlining toolbar.
20. Save and then close **MasterDocc6x18**.

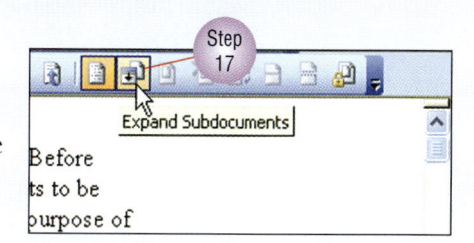

FIGURE

6.18 *Exercise 18*

SECTION A: NEWSLETTERS

Preparing a newsletter requires a number of preliminary steps. Before determining the contents of the newsletter, determine the basic elements to be included in the newsletter, study newsletter design, and determine the purpose of the newsletter.

Rearranging Subdocuments

Many of the features of a master document are similar to an outline. For example, expanding and collapsing an outline is very similar to expanding and collapsing subdocuments. Also, like headings in an outline, subdocuments in a master document can be moved or rearranged.

To rearrange the order of subdocuments, collapse the subdocuments. Position the mouse pointer on a subdocument icon, hold down the left mouse button (mouse pointer turns into a four-headed arrow), drag to the location where you want the subdocument moved, and then release the mouse button. As you drag with the mouse, a dark gray horizontal line displays identifying where the subdocument will be inserted. Use this dark gray line to insert the subdocument in the desired location.

When moving a collapsed subdocument, the dark gray horizontal line must be positioned above the white square that displays above a subdocument. If you position the dark gray horizontal line between the white square and the top border of a collapsed subdocument, Word will display a message telling you that you cannot change a locked subdocument or master document. With the dark gray horizontal line positioned immediately above the subdocument border, Word assumes you want to insert the selected subdocument into the subdocument. This cannot be done because subdocuments are locked.

Removing a Subdocument

Remove a subdocument from a master document by clicking the subdocument icon and then pressing the Delete key. This removes the subdocument from the master document but not from the original location. For example, in Exercise 19, you will remove the MODULE 3 subdocument from the MasterDocc6x18 master document, but the document named MODULE 3 still remains on your disk.

Splitting/Combining Subdocuments

A subdocument can be split into smaller subdocuments or subdocuments can be combined into one. To split a subdocument, expand subdocuments, select the specific text within the subdocument, and then click the Split Subdocument button on the Outlining toolbar. Word assigns a document name based on the first characters in the subdocument heading.

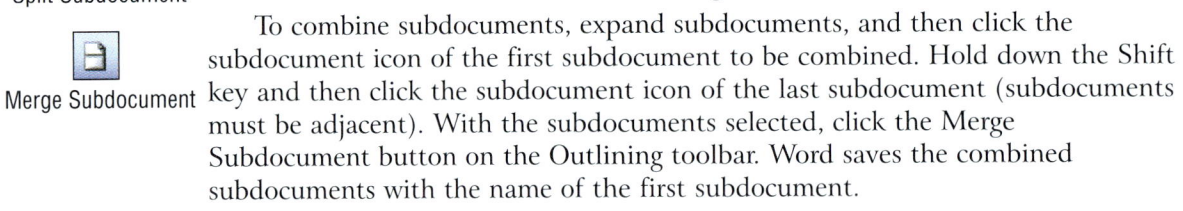

Split Subdocument

To combine subdocuments, expand subdocuments, and then click the subdocument icon of the first subdocument to be combined. Hold down the Shift key and then click the subdocument icon of the last subdocument (subdocuments must be adjacent). With the subdocuments selected, click the Merge Subdocument button on the Outlining toolbar. Word saves the combined subdocuments with the name of the first subdocument.

Merge Subdocument

Renaming a Subdocument

If you need to rename a subdocument, do it through the master document. To rename a subdocument, display the master document containing the subdocument, and then click the subdocument hyperlink. With the subdocument displayed, click File and then Save As. At the Save As dialog box, type a new name for the subdocument, and then press Enter or click the Save button. This renames the document in its original location as well as within the master document.

exercise 19 — REARRANGING, SPLITTING, REMOVING, AND RENAMING SUBDOCUMENTS

1. Open **MasterDocc6x18**.
2. Save the document with Save As and name it **MasterDocc6x19**.
3. Move the Module 4 subdocument above the Module 3 subdocument by completing the following steps:
    a. Position the arrow pointer on the subdocument icon that displays to the left of the **A:\WordChapter06E\MODULE 4.doc** subdocument. (The pointer turns into an arrow pointing up and to the right.)

b. Hold down the left mouse button, drag up so the dark gray horizontal line displays between the MODULE 2 and MODULE 3 subdocuments (above the white square between the modules), and then release the mouse button.

4. Print **MasterDocc6x19**. (At the prompt asking if you want to open the subdocuments, click No.)

5. Remove the **A:\WordChapter06E\MODULE 3.doc** subdocument by completing the following steps:
   a. Click the subdocument icon that displays to the left of the **A:\WordChapter06E\MODULE 3.doc** subdocument.
   b. Press the Delete key.

6. Split the MODULE 1 subdocument by completing the following steps:
   a. Click the Expand Subdocuments button on the Outlining toolbar.
   b. Move the insertion point to the MODULE 1 subdocument.
   c. In the MODULE 1 subdocument, edit the heading *Defining Basic Elements* so it displays as *MODULE 2: DEFINING BASIC ELEMENTS*. (You may need to scroll down the document to display this heading.)
   d. Change the heading style of the heading *MODULE 2: DEFINING BASIC ELEMENTS* from Heading 3 to Heading 2. *(Hint: Use the Style button on the Formatting toolbar.)*
   e. Position the mouse pointer on the selection symbol (white plus sign) that displays immediately left of the heading *MODULE 2: DEFINING BASIC ELEMENTS* until the pointer turns into a four-headed arrow, and then click the left mouse button.
   f. With the text selected, click the Split Subdocument button on the Outlining toolbar.
   g. Click the Collapse Subdocuments button on the Outlining toolbar. At the question asking if you want to save the changes to the master document, click OK.

7. Rename the MODULE 1 subdocument by completing the following steps:
   a. Hold down the Ctrl key and then click the A:\WordChapter06E\MODULE 1.doc hyperlink.
   b. With the subdocument open, click File and then Save As.
   c. At the Save As dialog box, type **NewMod1** and then press Enter.
   d. Close the subdocument.

8. Rename the MODULE 5 subdocument by completing the following steps:
   a. Hold down the Ctrl key and then click the A:\WordChapter06E\MODULE 5.doc hyperlink.
   b. With the subdocument open, click File and then Save As.

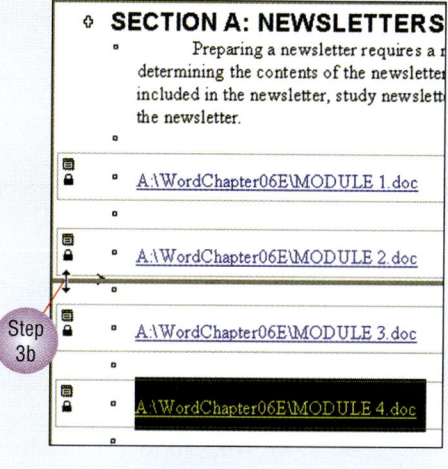

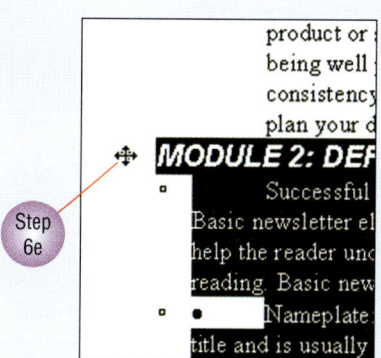

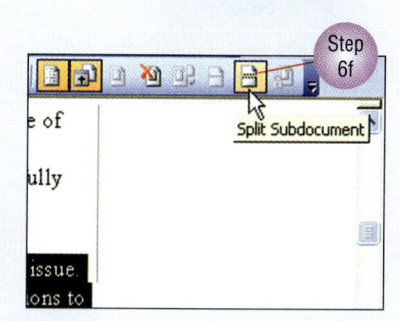

c. At the Save As dialog box, type **NewMod2** and then press Enter.
d. Close the subdocument.
9. Rename and edit the MODULE 2 subdocument by completing the following steps:
   a. Hold down the Ctrl key and then click the A:\WordChapter06E\MODULE 2.doc hyperlink.
   b. With the subdocument open, edit the *MODULE 2: PLANNING A NEWSLETTER* heading so it reads *MODULE 3: PLANNING A NEWSLETTER*.
   c. Click File and then Save As.
   d. At the Save As dialog box, type **NewMod3** and then press Enter.
   e. Close the subdocument.
10. Rename the MODULE 4 subdocument by completing the following steps:
    a. Hold down the Ctrl key and then click the A:\WordChapter06E\MODULE 4.doc hyperlink.
    b. With the subdocument open, click File and then Save As.
    c. At the Save As dialog box, type **NewMod4** and then press Enter.
    d. Close the subdocument.
11. Save and then print **MasterDocc6x19**. (The master document will print with the subdocuments collapsed.)
12. Close **MasterDocc6x19**.

CHAPTER summary

➤ You can import data from an Excel worksheet into a chart in a Word document with Microsoft Graph Chart. This feature is available at the Object dialog box with the Create New tab selected.

➤ Several methods are available for importing a Microsoft Excel worksheet into a Word document such as copying a worksheet into a Word document, linking the worksheet to a Word document, or embedding the worksheet as an object.

➤ Copy an Excel worksheet into a Word document in situations where the worksheet will not need to be edited. Link an Excel worksheet with a Word document in situations where the worksheet is continually updated. Embed an Excel worksheet in a Word document in situations where the worksheet will be edited in the Word document.

➤ You can copy an object from one program in the Office suite into another program.

➤ You can create your own forms with Word's form feature, thus eliminating the need for preprinted forms. A form is created as a template document that contains Fill-in fields. Information based on the form template is typed in the fields when a document is opened.

➤ A form document contains form fields where one of three actions is performed: text is entered, a check box is turned on or off, or information is selected from a drop-down list.

➤ Three basic steps are involved in creating a form: 1) create a form document based on a template and build the structure of the form; 2) insert form fields where information is to be entered at the keyboard; and 3) save the form as a protected document.

➤ Create a template document by clicking Template at the Templates dialog box.

➤ Word provides a Forms toolbar with buttons you can use to easily insert a text box, check box, or other form field into a form template document.

➤ After a template form document is created, protected, and saved, the template can be used to create a personalized form document.

- After the form fields have been filled in, the form can be printed in the normal manner, or you can print just the data from the Options dialog box with the Print tab selected.
- When a form template is created and then protected, the text in the template cannot be changed. To edit a template document, you must open the document, unprotect it, make the necessary changes, and then protect the document again.
- Use options at the Drop-Down Form Field Options dialog box to create form fields with drop-down lists. Change options for a text form field at the Text Form Field Options dialog box. Change check box form field options at the Check Box Form Field Options dialog box.
- Click the Draw Table button on the Forms toolbar and then draw table lines to create a form.
- A master document contains a number of separate documents called subdocuments. Create a master document or format an existing document as a master document at the Outline view and the Master Document view.
- The Outlining toolbar contains buttons for working with master documents and subdocuments. Clicking the Create Subdocument button on the Outlining toolbar causes Word to create a subdocument for each heading at the top level within the selected text.
- Save a master document in the normal manner. Word automatically assigns a document name to each subdocument using the first characters in the subdocument heading.
- Using buttons on the Outlining toolbar, you can expand and collapse subdocuments, lock/unlock subdocuments, and rearrange, remove, split, combine, and rename subdocuments.

FEATURES summary

FEATURE	BUTTON	MENU	KEYBOARD
Object dialog box		Insert, Object	
Paste Special dialog box		Edit, Paste Special	
Forms toolbar		View, Toolbars, Forms	
Options dialog box		Tools, Options	
Templates dialog box		File, New, On my computer hyperlink	
Drop-Down Form Field Options dialog box			
Text Form Field Options dialog box	ab|		
Check Box Form Field Options dialog box			
Outline view		View, Outline	Alt + Ctrl + O
Master Document view			

CONCEPTS check

Completion: On a blank sheet of paper, indicate the correct term, command, or symbol for each description.

1. The Microsoft Graph Chart feature is available at the Object dialog box with this tab selected.
2. Do this to an Excel worksheet you want inserted in a Word document when the worksheet will be continually updated.
3. Do this to an Excel worksheet you want inserted in a Word document when the worksheet will be edited in Word.
4. Generally, a form is created based on this default template document.
5. A fill-in form can include text boxes, check boxes, and/or these.
6. To display the Text Form Field Options dialog box, position the insertion point on a text form field, and then click this button on the Forms toolbar.
7. To protect a form, click this button on the Forms toolbar.
8. If you want the user to fill in a form by choosing from specific options, create this type of form field.
9. To fill in a check box form field, move the insertion point to the check box, and then press this key on the keyboard.
10. This is the default setting for the *Maximum length* option at the Text Form Field Options dialog box.
11. When filling in a form template document, press this key to move the insertion point to the next form field.
12. In Outline view and this view, collapsed subdocuments display surrounded by a light gray border line and subdocument icons display.
13. This toolbar contains buttons for working with master documents and subdocuments.
14. Expand subdocuments with the Expand Subdocuments button on this toolbar.

SKILLS check

Assessment 1

1. In Word, import **ExcelWorksheet04** into a chart using Microsoft Graph Chart.
2. Save the document with Save As and name it **ewc6sc01**.
3. Print and then close **ewc6sc01**.

Assessment 2

1. Open **WordMemo03**.
2. Save the document and name it **ewc6sc02**.
3. Open Excel and then open **ExcelWorksheet03**.
4. Save the worksheet with Save As and name it **Excelc6sc02**.

5. Select cells A1 through C5, copy the cells, and then link the cells so the worksheet displays in **ewc6sc05** between the first and second paragraphs. (Make sure you use the Paste Special dialog box [and select the *Paste link* option in the dialog box].)
6. Save, print, and then close **ewc6sc02**.
7. Make Excel the active program, close **Excelc6sc02**, and then exit Excel.

Assessment 3

1. Open the Microsoft Excel program.
2. Open **Excelc6sc02** and then make the following changes:
   a. Change the percentage in cell B3 from *8.3* to *8.4*.
   b. Change the percentage in cell C3 from *7.4* to *8.1*.
   c. Change the percentage in cell B5 from *17.4* to *17.3*.
   d. Change the percentage in cell C5 from *17.6* to *17.0*.
   e. Save the revised worksheet by clicking the Save button on the Excel Standard toolbar.
3. Close **Excelc6sc02**.
4. Exit Microsoft Excel.
5. Open Word and then open **ewc6sc02**. (Notice how the numbers in the worksheet are updated to reflect the changes made to **Excelc6sc02**.)
6. Save the document with Save As and name it **ewc6sc03**.
7. Print and then close **ewc6sc03**.

Assessment 4

1. Create the form shown in Figure 6.19 (next page) as a template document named **XXXc6sc04**. Insert text form fields and check box form fields in the document as shown in the figure.
2. Print and then close **XXXc6sc04**.

FIGURE 6.19 Assessment 4

GOOD SAMARITAN HOSPITAL

APPLICATION FOR FUNDING

Project Title: ▭

Department Applying: ▭

Facility: SFH ☐   LC ☐   SCC ☐

Contact Person(s): ▭

Check the statement(s) that best describe(s) how this proposal will meet the eligibility criteria:

☐ Improved patient care outcomes

☐ Cost reduction

☐ Improved customer satisfaction

☐ Reduced outcome variation

☐ Compliance with quality standards

_____   _____
Signature   Date

_____   _____
Department   Extension

Assessment 5

1. Create a form with the **XXXc6sc04** form template. Insert the following information in the form:
    Project Title: **Quality Improvement Project**
    Department Applying: **Pediatrics**
    Facility: (check *SFH*)
    Contact Person(s): **Alyce Arevalo**
    Check all the statements describing the proposal except *Cost reduction*.
2. When the form is completed, save the document in the WordChapter06E folder on your disk and name it **ewc6sc05**.
3. Print and then close **ewc6sc05**.

Assessment 6

1. Create the form shown in Figure 6.20 as a template document named **XXXc6sc06**. Customize the table as shown in Figure 6.20. Insert text form fields and check box form fields in the table as shown in the figure.
2. Print and then close **XXXc6sc06**.

FIGURE 6.20 Assessment 6

LIFETIME ANNUITY

PROFESSIONAL LIABILITY INSURANCE APPLICATION

Name:

Address:

| **County:** | **SSN:** | **DOB:** |

Type of Deduction:
- ☐ Flat
- ☐ Participating

Deduction Amount:
- ☐ None   ☐ $2,500
- ☐ $1,000   ☐ $5,000

Check if this insurance is to be part of a program.
- ☐ AANA   ☐ AAOMS   ☐ APTA-PPS   ☐ None

Check your specific professional occupation.

- ☐ Chiropractor
- ☐ Dental Anesthesia
- ☐ Dental Hygienist
- ☐ Dietitian/Nutritionist
- ☐ Laboratory Director
- ☐ Medical Office Assistant

- ☐ Medical Technician
- ☐ Nurse
- ☐ Nurse Practitioner
- ☐ Occupational Therapist
- ☐ Optometrist
- ☐ Paramedic/EMT

Signature: **Date:**

Assessment 7

1. Create a form with the **XXXc6sc06** form template. Insert the following information in the form:

   Name: Steven Katori
   Address: 11502 South 32nd Street, Bellevue, WA 98049
   County: King
   SSN: 230-52-9812
   DOB: 11/20/1960

   Type of Deduction: (check *Flat*)
   Deduction Amount: (check *$1,000*)
   Part of insurance program? (check *None*)
   Occupation: (check *Nurse Practitioner*)

2. When the form is completed, save the document in the WordChapter06E folder on your disk and name it **ewc6sc07**.
3. Print and then close **ewc6sc07**.

Assessment 8

1. Delete the **XXXTemplateDocument** form document created in Exercise 10 by completing the following steps:
   a. Click File and then New.
   b. Click the On my computer hyperlink in the New Document task pane.
   c. At the Templates dialog box, position the arrow pointer on the **XXXTemplateDocument** template form, and then click the *right* mouse button.
   d. From the pop-up menu that displays, click Delete.
   e. At the question asking if you want to delete the document, click Yes.
2. Complete similar steps to delete the other template documents containing your initials created in this chapter.

Assessment 9

1. Open **WordReport01**.
2. Save the document with Save As and name it **MasterDocc6sc09**.
3. Make the following changes to the document:
   a. Delete the title *DESKTOP PUBLISHING* and the blank line below the title.
   b. Change to the Outline view.
   c. Apply the Heading 1 style to the following headings:
      Defining Desktop Publishing
      Initiating the Desktop Publishing Process
      Planning the Publication
      Creating the Content
   d. Make sure the Master Document View button on the Outlining toolbar is activated.
   e. Create subdocuments by selecting the entire document and then clicking the Create Subdocument button on the Outlining toolbar.
4. Save and then close **MasterDocc6sc09**.
5. Open **MasterDocc6sc09** and then print the document. (Subdocuments will be collapsed.)
6. Close **MasterDocc6sc09**.

Assessment 10

1. Open **MasterDocc6sc09**.
2. Save the document with Save As and name it **MasterDocc6sc10**.
3. Make the following changes to the document:
   a. Remove the *Defining Desktop Publishing* subdocument.
   b. Move the *Planning the Publication* subdocument above the *Initiating the Desktop Publishing Process* subdocument. (Make sure the dark gray horizontal line is positioned above the white square immediately above the *Initiating the Desktop Publishing Process* subdocument before you release the mouse button.)
4. Save, print, and then close **MasterDocc6sc10**.

CHAPTER challenge

Case study

You have been hired as the payroll clerk for Reilly's Retail Store. The current printed time sheets are ready to be updated. Create a template document for a form that can be used as a monthly time sheet. Include the following fields: first name, last name, address, city, state, ZIP, and total wage. Add five more fields of your choice. The fields should be formatted as text boxes, check boxes, or pull-down lists. (Include at least one of each.) Use field options for each of the fields to ensure accuracy and help reduce the amount of potential errors. Protect, save (as **Monthly Time Sheet**), and print the form with your own data.

Help

Being able to quickly access other documents and Web pages while in Word can easily be accomplished through the use of a hyperlink. Use the Help feature to learn about hyperlinks. Create an Excel worksheet that includes at least three employees' names, their hours worked, overtime (if applicable), wage earned per hour, and total wages (use a formula to calculate). Save the workbook as **Daily Log**. Strategically insert a hyperlink in the **Monthly Time Sheet** form created in the first part of the Chapter Challenge to open the Excel worksheet. Save the time sheet again.

Integrated

Using the workbook created in the second part of the Chapter Challenge, link the cell containing the total wage for one employee to the total wage field in the **Monthly Time Sheet** form.

CHAPTER 7

CREATING SPECIALIZED TABLES AND INDEXES

PERFORMANCE OBJECTIVES

Upon successful completion of Chapter 7, you will be able to:
➤ Create, compile, and update a table of contents
➤ Create, compile, and update an index
➤ Create, compile, and update a table of figures
➤ Create, compile, and update a table of authorities

HINT
You can use a table of contents to quickly navigate in a document and to get an overview of the topics covered in the document.

A book, textbook, report, or manuscript often includes sections such as a table of contents, index, and table of figures in the document. Creating these sections can be tedious when done manually. With Word, these functions can be automated to create the sections quickly and easily. In this chapter, you will learn the steps to mark text for a table of contents, index, table of figures, and table of authorities, and then compile the table or list.

Creating a Table of Contents

A table of contents appears at the beginning of a book, manuscript, or report and contains headings and subheadings with page numbers. Figure 7.1 shows an example of a table of contents. Text to be included in a table of contents can be identified by applying a heading style, assigning an outline level, or text can be marked as a field entry.

QUICK STEPS

Create a Table of Contents
1. Apply heading styles.
2. Click Insert, Reference, Index and Tables.
3. Click Table of Contents tab.
4. Select the desired format.
5. Click OK.

TABLE

7.1 Table of Contents

TABLE OF CONTENTS

Chapter 1: Trends in Telecommunications..2
Telecommunications at Work...2
Evolution in Telecommunications..4
Chapter Summary...8
Terminology Review..9
Check Your Understanding..10

> **HINT**
> Apply heading styles to text in a document and you can quickly create a table of contents.

Marking Table of Contents Entries as Styles

A table of contents can be created by applying heading styles to text to be included in the table of contents. When creating a table of contents, two steps are involved in creating the table of contents. The first step is to apply the appropriate styles to the text that will be included in the table of contents and the second step is to compile the table of contents.

Word automatically includes text that is formatted with a heading style in a table of contents. In Chapter 4, you learned that Word contains heading styles you can apply to text. If you have already applied styles to headings in a document, the same headings are included in the table of contents. If the styles have not previously been applied, you can apply them with the Style button on the Formatting toolbar, or with buttons on the Outlining toolbar in the Outline view. To apply styles for a table of contents, position the insertion point on any character in the text you want included in the table of contents, click the down-pointing arrow to the right of the Style button on the Formatting toolbar, and then click the desired style. Continue in this manner until all styles have been applied to titles, headings, and subheadings in the document.

Compiling a Table of Contents

After the necessary heading styles have been applied to text that you want included in the table of contents, the next step is to compile the table of contents. To do this, position the insertion point where you want the table to appear, click Insert, point to Reference, and then click Index and Tables. At the Index and Tables dialog box, click the Table of Contents tab. This displays the Index and Tables dialog box as shown in Figure 7.2. At this dialog box, make any desired changes, and then click OK.

FIGURE 7.2 *Index and Tables Dialog Box with Table of Contents Tab Selected*

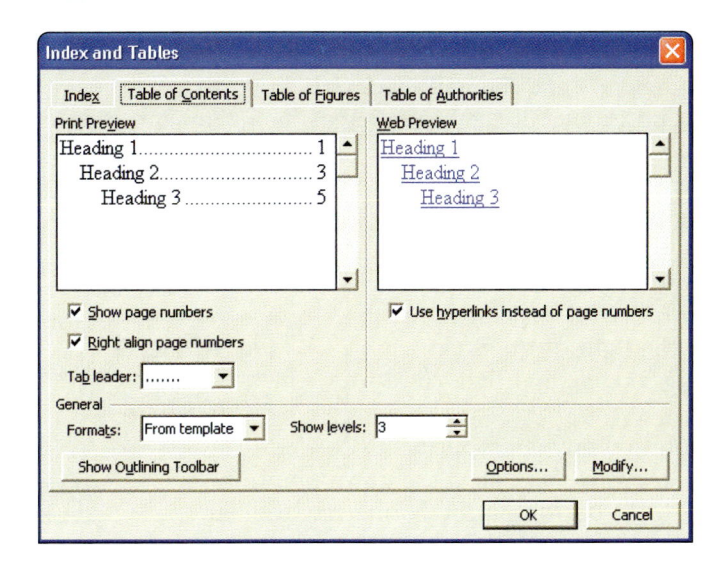

At the Index and Tables dialog box with the Table of Contents tab selected, a sample table of contents displays in the *Print Preview* section. You can change the table of contents format by clicking the down-pointing arrow at the right side of the *Formats* option box (located in the *General* section). At the drop-down list that displays, click the desired format. When a different format is selected, that format displays in the *Print Preview* section. Page numbers in a table of contents will display after the text or aligned at the right margin depending on what options are selected. The number of levels displayed depends on the number of heading levels specified in the document.

Tab leaders help guide the reader's eyes from the table of contents heading to the page number. The default tab leader is a period. To choose a different leader, click the down-pointing arrow at the right side of the *Tab leader* option box, and then click the desired leader character from the drop-down list.

If you want the table of contents to print on a page separate from the document text, insert a section break that begins a new page between the table of contents and the title of the document. If the beginning of the text in the document, rather than the table of contents, should be numbered as page 1, change the starting page number for the section. A table of contents is generally numbered with lowercase Roman numerals.

Word automatically identifies headings in a table of contents as hyperlinks. You can use these hyperlinks to move the insertion point to a specific location in the document. To move the insertion point, position the mouse pointer on the desired heading in a table of contents, hold down the Ctrl key (the mouse pointer turns into a hand), and then click the left mouse button.

exercise 1
APPLYING STYLES AND COMPILING A TABLE OF CONTENTS

1. Open **WordReport01**.
2. Save the document with Save As and name it **ewc7x01**.
3. With the insertion point positioned at the beginning of the document, press the Enter key once. (This adds room for the table of contents you will be inserting later.)
4. Select the entire document and then change the line spacing to single.
5. Position the insertion point on any character in the title *DESKTOP PUBLISHING*, click the down-pointing arrow to the right of the Style button on the Formatting toolbar, and then click *Heading 1*.
6. Position the insertion point on any character in the heading *Defining Desktop Publishing*, click the down-pointing arrow to the right of the Style button on the Formatting toolbar, and then click *Heading 2*.
7. Apply the Heading 2 style to the following headings:
    Initiating the Desktop Publishing Process
    Planning the Publication
    Creating the Content
8. Position the insertion point immediately left of the *D* in *DESKTOP PUBLISHING* and then insert a section break by completing the following steps:
    a. Click Insert and then Break.
    b. At the Break dialog box, click *Next page*.
    c. Click OK or press Enter.
9. With the insertion point positioned below the section break, insert page numbering and change the beginning number to 1 by completing the following steps:
    a. Click Insert and then Page Numbers.
    b. At the Page Numbers dialog box, click the down-pointing arrow at the right side of the *Alignment* option, and then click *Center* at the drop-down list.
    c. Click the Format button (in the dialog box, not on the Menu bar).
    d. At the Page Number Format dialog box, click *Start at*. (This inserts *1* in the *Start at* text box.)
    e. Click OK or press Enter to close the Page Number Format dialog box.
    f. At the Page Numbers dialog box, click OK or press Enter. (The view automatically changes to Print Layout.)
10. Compile and insert a table of contents at the beginning of the document by completing the following steps:
    a. Press Ctrl + Home to move the insertion point to the beginning of the document (on the new page).
    b. Turn on bold, type **TABLE OF CONTENTS** centered, and then turn off bold.

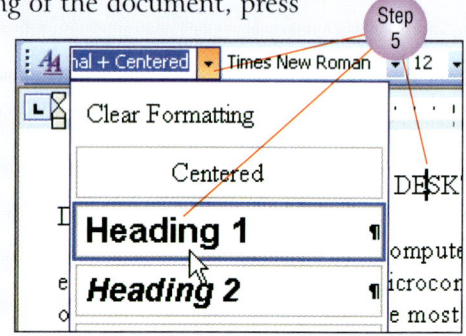

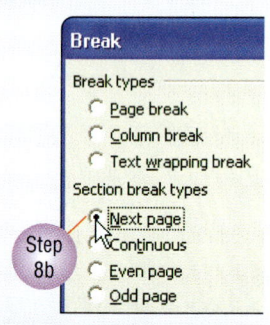

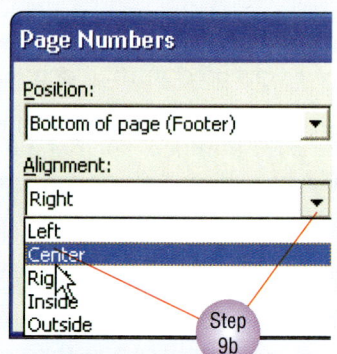

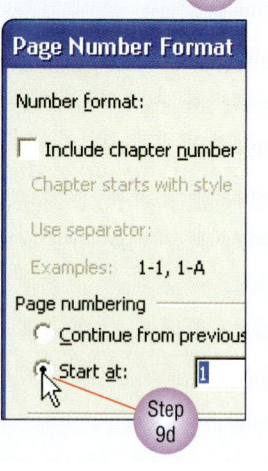

c. Press the Enter key once and then change the paragraph alignment back to left.
d. Click Insert, point to Reference, and then click Index and Tables.
e. At the Index and Tables dialog box, click the Table of Contents tab.
f. At the Index and Tables dialog box with the Table of Contents tab selected, click the down-pointing arrow at the right side of the *Formats* option box, and then click *Formal* at the drop-down list.
g. Click OK or press Enter.
11. Position the insertion point on any character in the title, *TABLE OF CONTENTS*, and then apply the Heading 1 style. (This will change the font to 16-point Arial bold and also change the alignment to left.)
12. Insert page numbering in the Table of Contents page by completing the following steps:
a. Click Insert and then Page Numbers.
b. At the Page Numbers dialog box, click the Format button.
c. At the Page Number Format dialog box, click the down-pointing arrow at the right side of the *Number format* text box, and then click *i, ii, iii, ...* at the drop-down list.
d. Click *Start at*. (This inserts *i* in the *Start at* text box.)
e. Click OK or press Enter to close the Page Number Format dialog box.
f. At the Page Numbers dialog box, click OK or press Enter.
13. Save the document again and then print the table of contents page. (Check with your instructor to see if you should print the other pages of the document.)
14. Close **ewc7x01**. (If a message displays asking if you want to save the changes to the document, click Yes.)

Assigning Levels to Table of Contents Entries

Applying styles to text applies specific formatting. If you want to identify titles and/or headings for a table of contents but you do not want heading style formatting applied, assign an outline level. To do this, open the document in Normal or Print Layout view, and then display the Outlining toolbar. Move the insertion point to a title or heading you want included in the table of contents. Click the down-pointing arrow at the right side of the Outline Level button on the Outlining toolbar and then click the desired level at the drop-down list. After assigning levels to titles and/or headings, compile the table of contents.

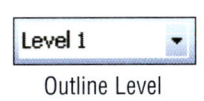

Outline Level

exercise 2

ASSIGNING LEVELS AND COMPILING A TABLE OF CONTENTS

1. Open **WordReport05**.
2. Save the document with Save As and name it **ewc7x02**.
3. Make sure the Normal view is selected.
4. With the insertion point positioned at the beginning of the document, press the Enter key once. (This adds room for the table of contents you will insert later.)
5. Click View, Toolbars, and then Outlining to turn on the display of the Outlining toolbar.

6. Assign levels to titles and headings by completing the following steps:
   a. Position the insertion point on any character in the title *MODULE 1: DEFINING NEWSLETTER ELEMENTS*, click the down-pointing arrow to the right of the Outline Level button on the Outlining toolbar, and then click *Level 1* at the drop-down list.
   b. Assign level 1 to the title *MODULE 2: PLANNING A NEWSLETTER*. (This title is located approximately on the third page.)
   c. Position the insertion point on any character in the heading *Designing a Newsletter* (located toward the beginning of the document), click the down-pointing arrow to the right of the Outline Level button on the Outlining toolbar, and then click *Level 2*.
   d. Assign level 2 to the headings *Defining Basic Newsletter Elements* and *Defining the Purpose of a Newsletter*.
7. Position the insertion point immediately left of the *M* in *MODULE 1: DEFINING NEWSLETTER ELEMENTS* and then insert a section break that begins a new page. *(Hint: Refer to Exercise 1, Step 8.)*
8. With the insertion point positioned below the section break, insert page numbering at the bottom center of each page of the section and change the starting number to 1. *(Hint: Refer to Exercise 1, Step 9.)*
9. Compile and insert a table of contents at the beginning of the document by completing the following steps:
   a. Press Ctrl + Home to move the insertion point to the beginning of the document (on the new page).
   b. Turn on bold, type **TABLE OF CONTENTS** centered, and then turn off bold.
   c. Press the Enter key once and then change the paragraph alignment back to left.
   d. Click Insert, point to Reference, and then click Index and Tables.
   e. At the Index and Tables dialog box, click the Table of Contents tab.
   f. At the Index and Tables dialog box with the Table of Contents tab selected, click the down-pointing arrow at the right side of the *Formats* option box, and then click *Distinctive* at the drop-down list.
   g. Click OK or press Enter.
10. Insert page numbering on the Table of Contents page at the bottom center. *(Hint: Refer to Exercise 1, Step 12.)*
11. Save the document again and then print the table of contents page. (Check with your instructor to see if you should print the other pages of the document.)
12. Close **ewc7x02**. (If a message displays asking if you want to save the changes to the document, click Yes.)

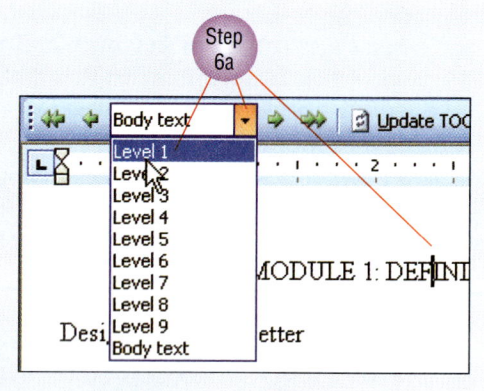

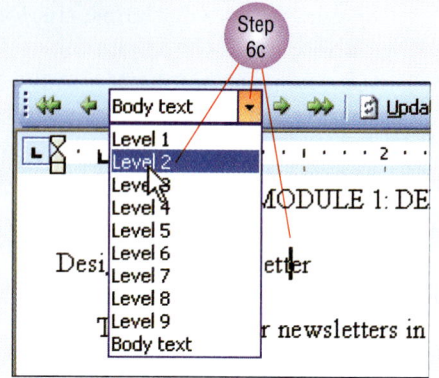

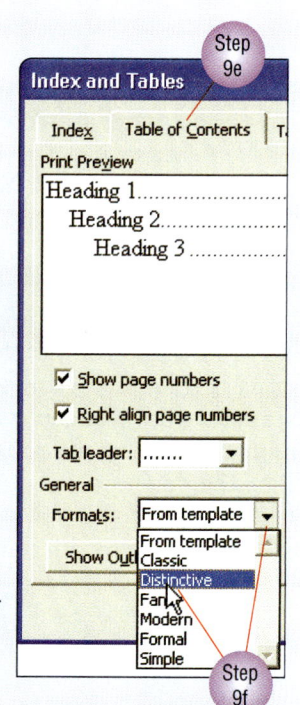

Marking Table of Contents Entries as Fields

Another method for marking text for a table of contents is to mark the text as a field entry. To do this, select the text you want included in the table of contents and then press Alt + Shift + O. This displays the Mark Table of Contents Entry dialog box shown in Figure 7.3. The text you selected in the document displays in the *Entry* text box. At this dialog box, specify the text level using the *Level* option, and then click the Mark button. This turns on the display of nonprinting symbols in the document and also inserts a field code immediately after the selected text. For example, when you select the first title in Exercise 3, the following code is inserted immediately after the title: { TC "MODULE 3: DESIGNING A NEWSLETTER" \f C \l " 1 " }. The Mark Table of Contents Entry dialog box also remains open. To mark the next entry for the table of contents, select the text, and then click the title bar of the Mark Table of Contents Entry dialog box. Specify the level and then click the Mark button. Continue in this manner until all table of contents entries have been marked.

HINT Switch to Web Layout view and the table of contents headings display as hyperlinks. Click a hyperlink to jump to that heading in the document.

FIGURE 7.3 Mark Table of Contents Entry Dialog Box

Click the Mark button to identify the text in the *Entry* text box as a table of contents field.

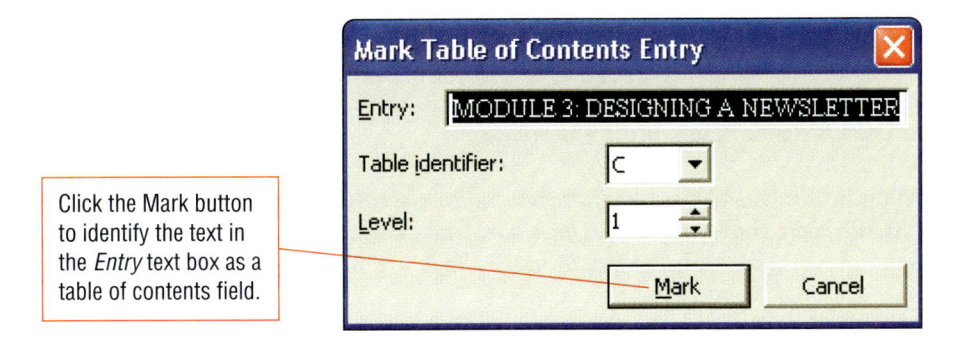

If you mark table of contents entries as fields, you will need to activate the *Table entry fields* option when compiling the table of contents. To do this, display the Index and Tables dialog box with the Table of Contents tab selected, and then click the Options button. At the Table of Contents Options dialog box, click in the *Table entry fields* text box to insert a check mark, and then click OK.

exercise 3

MARKING HEADINGS AS FIELDS AND THEN COMPILING A TABLE OF CONTENTS

1. Open **WordReport06**.
2. Save the document with Save As and name it **ewc7x03**.
3. Mark the titles and headings as fields for a table of contents by completing the following steps:
    a. With the insertion point positioned at the beginning of the document, press the Enter key once. (This adds room for the table of contents you will be inserting later.)
    b. Select the title MODULE 3: DESIGNING A NEWSLETTER.
    c. Press Alt + Shift + O.

d. At the Mark Table of Contents Entry dialog box, make sure the *Level* is set at *1*, and then click the Mark button. (This turns on the display of nonprinting symbols.)
   e. Click in the document and then select the heading *Applying Desktop Publishing Guidelines*.
   f. Click the up-pointing arrow at the right side of the *Level* text box in the Mark Table of Contents Entry dialog box until *2* displays.
   g. Click the Mark button.
   h. Click in the document and then scroll down the document until the Module 4 title displays.
   i. Select the title MODULE 4: CREATING NEWSLETTER LAYOUT.
   j. Click the down-pointing arrow at the right side of the *Level* text box in the Mark Table of Contents Entry dialog box until *1* displays.
   k. Click the Mark button.
   l. Mark the following headings as level 2 **(Hint: You must select the heading, click the up-pointing arrow at the right side of the Level *text box*, and then click the down-pointing arrow at the right side of the Level *text box to make the Mark button active.*)**:
      Choosing Paper Size and Type
      Choosing Paper Weight
      Creating Margins for Newsletters
   m. Click the Close button to close the Mark Table of Contents Entry dialog box.
4. Position the insertion point immediately left of the *M* in the title *MODULE 3: DESIGNING A NEWSLETTER* and then insert a section break that begins a new page. **(Hint: Refer to Exercise 1, Step 8.)**
5. With the insertion point positioned below the section break, insert page numbering at the bottom center of each page of the section and change the starting number to 1. **(Hint: Refer to exercise 1, Step 9.)**
6. Compile and insert a table of contents at the beginning of the document by completing the following steps:
   a. Press Ctrl + Home to position the insertion point at the beginning of the document (on the new page).
   b. Type **TABLE OF CONTENTS** centered and bolded.
   c. Press the Enter key once, turn off bold, and then change the paragraph alignment back to left.
   d. Click Insert, point to Reference, and then click Index and Tables.
   e. At the Index and Tables dialog box, click the Table of Contents tab.
   f. At the Index and Tables dialog box with the Table of Contents tab selected, click the down-pointing arrow at the right side of the *Formats* option box, and then click *Fancy* at the drop-down list.

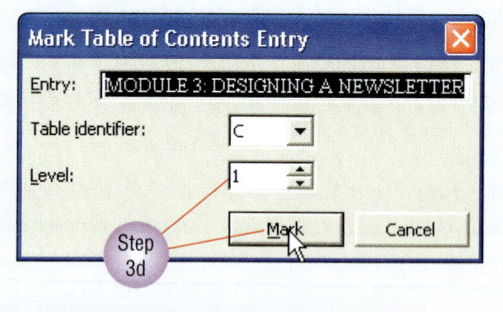

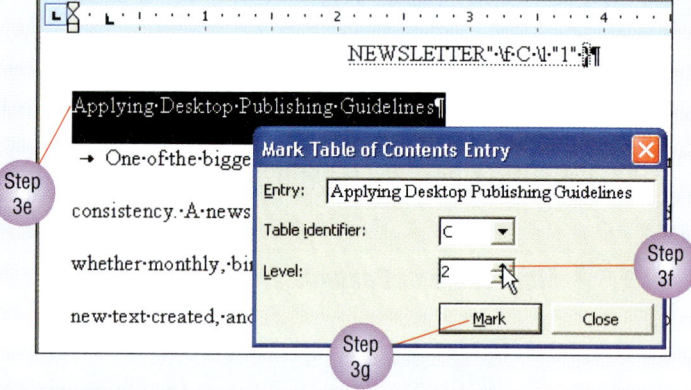

g. Click the Options button.
h. At the Table of Contents Options dialog box, click *Table entry fields* to insert a check mark in the check box. (This option is located in the bottom left corner of the dialog box.)
i. Click OK or press Enter to close the Table of Contents Options dialog box.
j. Click OK or press Enter to close the Index and Tables dialog box.

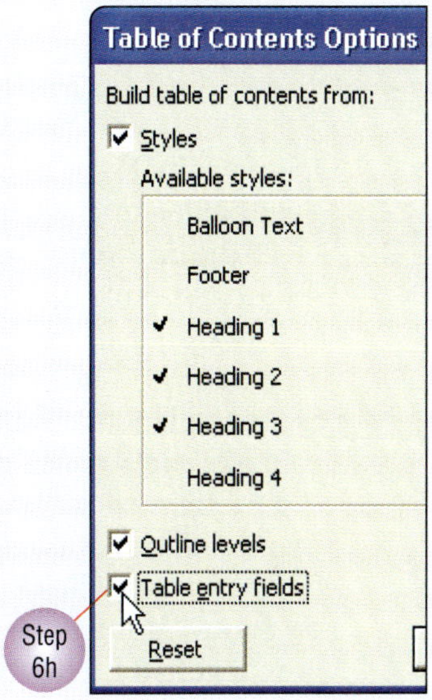

7. Insert page numbering on the Table of Contents page at the bottom center. *(Hint: Refer to Exercise 1, Step 12.)*
8. Turn off the display of nonprinting symbols.
9. Check the page breaks in the document and, if necessary, adjust the page breaks.
10. Save the document again and then print the table of contents page. (Before printing, make sure that hidden text will not print. To do this, click the Options button at the Print dialog box. At the Print dialog box with the Print tab selected, make sure *Hidden text* option does not contain a check mark.) (Check with your instructor to see if you should print the entire document.)
11. Close **ewc7x03**. (If a message displays asking if you want to save the changes to the document, click Yes.)

Updating a Table of Contents

If you make changes to a document after compiling a table of contents, update the table of contents. To do this, click anywhere within the current table of contents and then press F9 (the Update Field key) or click the Update TOC button on the Outlining toolbar. At the Update Table of Contents dialog box shown in Figure 7.4, click *Update page numbers only* if changes occur only to the page numbers, or click *Update entire table* if changes were made to headings or subheadings within the table. Click OK or press Enter to close the dialog box.

HINT
If you add, delete, move, or edit headings or other text in a document, update the table of contents.

FIGURE 7.4 Update Table of Contents Dialog Box

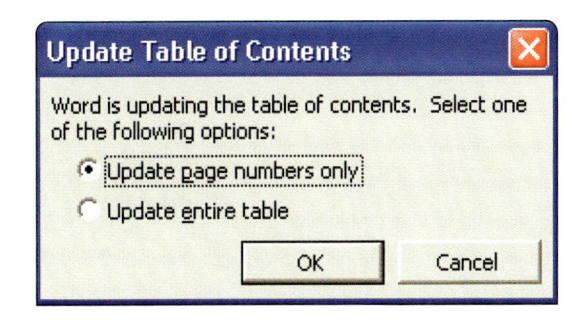

QUICK STEPS

Update a Table of Contents
1. Click in table of contents.
2. Press F9.
3. Click OK at Update Table of Contents dialog box.

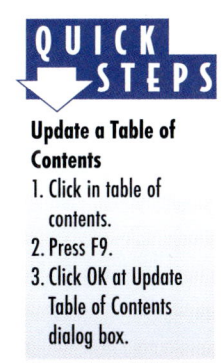

exercise 4

UPDATING A TABLE OF CONTENTS

1. Open **ewc7x01**.
2. Save the document with Save As and name it **ewc7x04**.
3. Select the entire document and then change the line spacing to double.
4. Update the table of contents by completing the following steps:
    a. Click once in the table of contents.
    b. Press F9. (This is the Update Field key.)
    c. At the Update Table of Contents dialog box, make sure *Update page numbers only* is selected, and then click OK or press Enter.
5. Save the document again and then print the table of contents page. (Check with your instructor to see if you should print the entire document.)
6. Close **ewc7x04**. (If a message displays asking if you want to save the changes to the document, click Yes.)

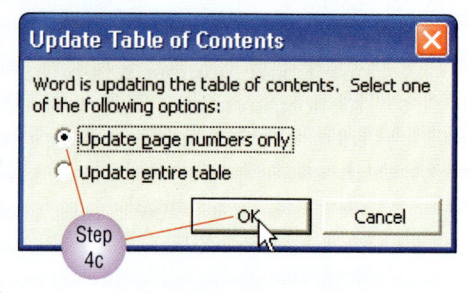

Deleting a Table of Contents

A table of contents that has been compiled in a document can be deleted. To do this, select the entire table of contents in the normal manner, and then press the Delete key. You can also select the table of contents by clicking the Go to TOC button on the Outlining toolbar.

Creating an Index

An index is a list of topics contained in a publication and the pages where those topics are discussed. Word lets you automate the process of creating an index in a manner similar to that used for creating a table of contents. When creating an index, you mark a word or words that you want included in the index. Creating an index takes some thought and consideration. The author of the book, manuscript, or report must determine the main entries desired and what subentries will be listed under main entries. An index may include such items as the main idea of a document, the main subject of a chapter or section, variations of a heading or subheading, and abbreviations. Figure 7.5 shows an example of an index.

FIGURE 7.5 Index

INDEX

A
Alignment, 12, 16
ASCII, 22, 24, 35
    data processing, 41
    word processing, 39

B
Backmatter, 120
    page numbering, 123
Balance, 67-69
Banners, 145

C
Callouts, 78
Captions, 156
Color, 192-195
    ink for offset printing, 193
    process color, 195

D
Databases, 124-129
    fields, 124
    records, 124
Directional flow, 70-71

Marking Text for an Index

A selected word or words can be marked for inclusion in an index. Before marking words for an index, determine what main entries and subentries are to be included in the index. Selected text is marked as an index entry at the Mark Index Entry text box.

To mark text for an index, select the word or words, and then press Alt + Shift + X. At the Mark Index Entry dialog box, shown in Figure 7.6, the selected word(s) appears in the *Main entry* text box. Make any necessary changes to the dialog box, and then click the Mark button. (When you click the Mark button, Word automatically turns on the display of nonprinting symbols and displays the index field code.) Click the Close button to close the Mark Index Entry dialog box.

> **QUICK STEPS**
>
> **Mark Text for an Index**
> 1. Select text.
> 2. Press Alt + Shift + X.
> 3. Click Mark button.

FIGURE 7.6 Mark Index Entry Dialog Box

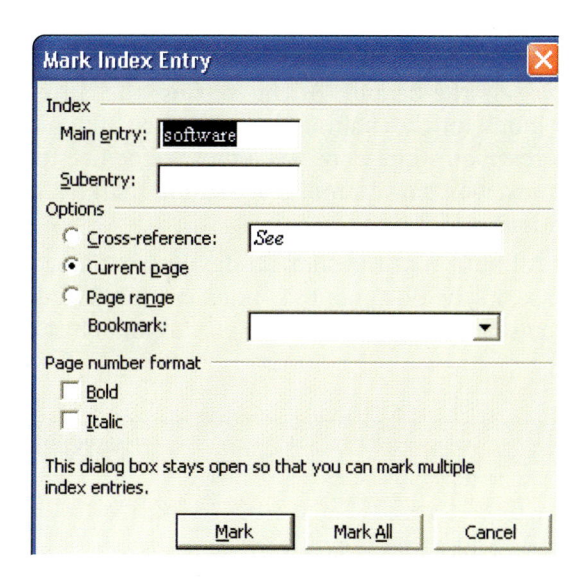

At the Mark Index Entry dialog box, the selected word or words displays in the *Main entry* text box. If the text is a main entry, leave it as displayed. If, however, the selected text is a subentry, type the main entry in the *Main entry* text box, click in the *Subentry* text box, and then type the selected text. For example, suppose a publication includes the terms *Page layout* and *Portrait*. The words *Page layout* are to be marked as a main entry for the index and *Portrait* is to be marked as a subentry below *Page layout*. To mark these words for an index, you would complete the following steps:

1. Select *Page layout*.
2. Press Alt + Shift + X.
3. At the Mark Index Entry dialog box, click the Mark button. (This turns on the display of nonprinting symbols.)
4. With the Mark Index Entry dialog box still displayed on the screen, click in the document to make the document active, and then select *Portrait*.
5. Click the Mark Index Entry dialog box Title bar to make it active.
6. Select *Portrait* in the *Main entry* text box and then type **Page layout**.
7. Click in the *Subentry* text box and then type **Portrait**.
8. Click the Mark button.
9. Click the Close button.

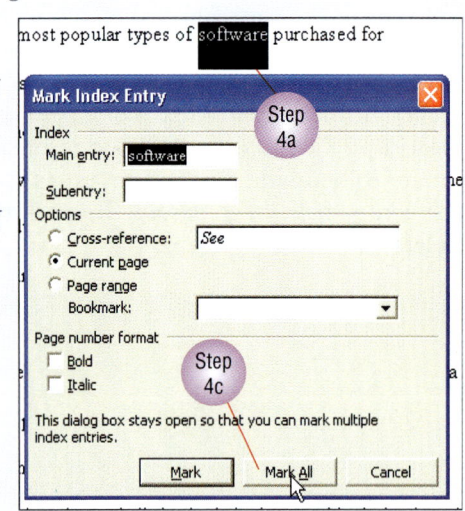

The main entry and subentry do not have to be the same as the selected text. You can select text for an index, type the text you want to display in the *Main entry* or *Subentry* text box, and then click Mark. At the Mark Index Entry dialog box, you can apply bold and/or italic formatting to the page numbers that will appear in the index. To apply formatting, click *Bold* and/or *Italic* to insert a check mark in the check box.

The *Options* section of the Mark Index Entry dialog box contains several options, with *Current page* the default. At this setting, the current page number will be listed in the index for the main and/or subentry. If you click *Cross-reference*, you would type the text you want to use as a cross-reference for the index entry in the *Cross-reference* text box. For example, you could mark the word *Serif* and cross reference it to *Typefaces*.

Click the Mark All button at the Mark Index Entry dialog box to mark all occurrences of the text in the document as index entries. Word marks only those entries whose uppercase and lowercase letters exactly match the index entry.

exercise 5 — MARKING WORDS FOR AN INDEX

1. Open **WordReport01**.
2. Save the document with Save As and name it **ewc7x05**.
3. Make the following changes to the document:
   a. Number pages at the bottom center of each page.
   b. Set the title DESKTOP PUBLISHING and the headings *Defining Desktop Publishing*, *Initiating the Desktop Publishing Process*, *Planning the Publication*, and *Creating the Content* in 14-point Times New Roman bold.
4. Mark the word *software* in the first paragraph for the index as a main entry and mark *word processing* in the first paragraph as a subentry below *software* by completing the following steps:
   a. Select *software* (located in the last sentence of the first paragraph).
   b. Press Alt + Shift + X.
   c. At the Mark Index Entry dialog box, click the Mark All button. (This turns on the display of nonprinting symbols.)

E274 Chapter Seven

d. With the Mark Index Entry dialog box still displayed, click in the document to make the document active, and then select *word processing* (located in the last sentence of the first paragraph). (You may want to drag the dialog box down the screen so more of the document text is visible.)
e. Click the Mark Index Entry dialog box Title bar to make it active.
f. Select *word processing* in the *Main entry* text box and then type **software**.
g. Click in the *Subentry* text box and then type **word processing**.
h. Click the Mark All button.
i. With the Mark Index Entry dialog box still displayed, complete steps similar to those in Steps 4d through 4h to mark the *first* occurrence of the following words as main entries or subentries for the index:

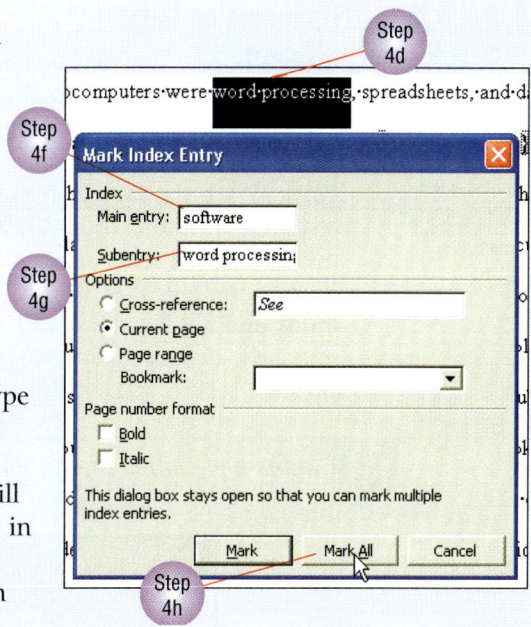

In the first paragraph in the *Defining Desktop Publishing* section:
spreadsheets = subentry (main entry = *software*)
database = subentry (main entry = *software*)

In the second paragraph in the *Defining Desktop Publishing* section:
publishing = main entry
desktop = subentry (main entry = *publishing*)
printer = main entry
laser = subentry (main entry = *printer*)

In the third paragraph in the *Defining Desktop Publishing* section:
design = main entry

In the fourth paragraph in the *Defining Desktop Publishing* section:
traditional = subentry (main entry = *publishing*)

In the first paragraph in the *Initiating the Desktop Publishing Process* section:
publication = main entry
planning = subentry (main entry = *publication*)
creating = subentry (main entry = *publication*)
intended audience = subentry (main entry = *publication*)
content = subentry (main entry = *publication*)

In the third paragraph in the *Planning the Publication* section:
message = main entry

j. Click Close to close the Mark Index Entry dialog box.
k. Click the Show/Hide ¶ button on the Standard toolbar to turn off the display of nonprinting symbols.
5. Save and then close **ewc7x05**.

QUICK STEPS

Compile an Index
1. Click Insert, Reference, Index and Tables.
2. Click Index tab.
3. Select the desired format.
4. Click OK.

Compiling an Index

After all necessary text has been marked as a main entry or subentry for the index, the next step is to compile the index. An index should appear at the end of a document, generally beginning on a separate page. To compile the index, position the insertion point at the end of the document, and then insert a page break. With the insertion point positioned below the page break, type **INDEX** centered and bolded, and then press the Enter key. With the insertion point positioned at the left margin, click Insert, point to Reference, and then click Index and Tables. At the Index and Tables dialog box, click the Index tab. At the Index and Tables dialog box with the Index tab selected, as shown in Figure 7.7, select the desired formatting, and then click OK or press Enter.

FIGURE 7.7 *Index and Tables Dialog Box with Index Tab Selected*

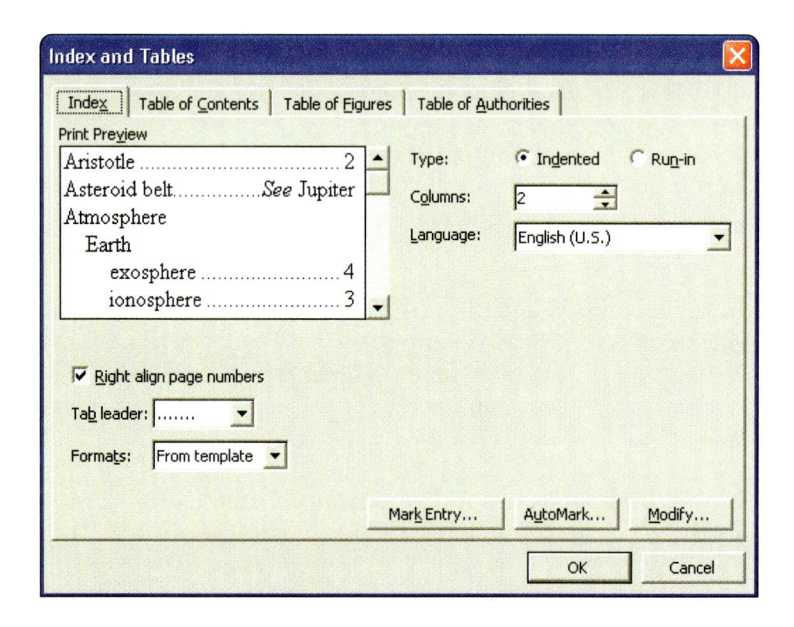

Word compiles the index and then inserts it at the location of the insertion point with the formatting selected at the Index and Tables dialog box. Word also inserts a section break above and below the index text.

At the Index and Tables dialog box with the Index tab selected, you can specify how the index entries will appear. The *Print Preview* section shows how the index will display in the document. The *Columns* option has a default setting of *2*. At this setting, the index will display in two newspaper columns. This number can be increased or decreased.

By default, numbers are right-aligned in the index. If you do not want numbers right-aligned, click the *Right align page numbers* check box to remove the check mark. The *Tab leader* option is dimmed for all formats except *Formal*. If you click *Formal* in the *Formats* option box, the *Tab leader* option displays in black. The default tab leader character is a period. To change to a different character, click the down-pointing arrow at the right of the text box, and then click the desired character.

In the *Type* section, the *Indented* option is selected by default. At this setting, subentries will appear indented below main entries. If you click *Run-in*, subentries will display on the same line as main entries.

Click the down-pointing arrow at the right side of the *Formats* option box and a list of formatting choices displays. At this list, click the desired formatting and the *Print Preview* box will display how the index will appear in the document.

exercise 6

COMPILING AN INDEX

1. Open **ewc7x05**.
2. Save the document with Save As and name it **ewc7x06**.
3. Compile the index and insert it in the document by completing the following steps:
    a. Position the insertion point at the end of the document.
    b. Insert a page break.
    c. With the insertion point positioned below the page break, type **INDEX** centered and bolded.
    d. Press the Enter key twice, turn off bold, and then change the paragraph alignment back to left.
    e. Click Insert, point to Reference, and then click Index and Tables.
    f. At the Index and Tables dialog box, click the Index tab.
    g. At the Index and Tables dialog box with the Index tab selected, click the down-pointing arrow at the right side of the *Formats* option box, and then click *Modern* at the drop-down list.
    h. Click OK to close the dialog box.
    i. Select the title *INDEX* and then set it in 14-point Times New Roman bold.
4. Save the document again and then print the index (last page). (Check with your instructor to see if you should print the entire document.)
5. Close **ewc7x06**.

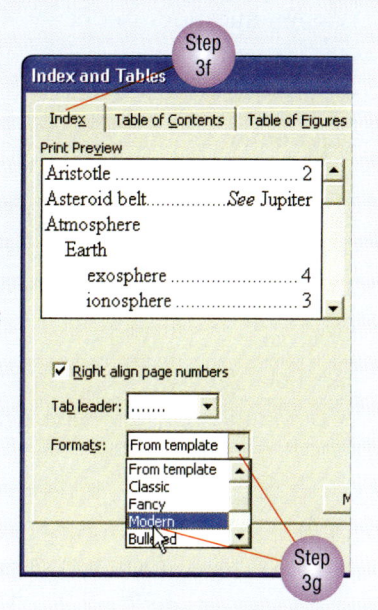

Creating a Concordance File

Words that appear frequently in a document can be saved as a concordance file. This saves you from having to mark each reference in a document. A concordance file is a regular Word document containing a single, two-column table with no text outside the table. In the first column of the table, you enter words you want to index. In the second column, you enter the main entry and subentry that should appear in the index. To create a subentry, separate each main entry from a subentry by a colon. Figure 7.8 shows an example of a completed concordance file.

QUICK STEPS

Create a Concordance File
1. Click Insert Table button.
2. Drag to create a 1 × 2 table.
3. In first column, type words you want to index.
4. In second column, type the main entry and subentry.
5. Save document.

WORD
Creating Specialized Tables and Indexes E277

FIGURE 7.8 Concordance File

World War I	World War I
Technology	Technology
technology	Technology
Teletypewriters	Technology: teletypewriters
motion pictures	Technology: motion pictures
Television	Technology: television
Radio Corporation of America	Radio Corporation of America
coaxial cable	Coaxial cable
Telephone	Technology: telephone
Communications Act of 1934	Communications Act of 1934
World War II	World War II
radar system	Technology: radar system
Computer	Computer
Atanasoff Berry Computer	Computer: Atanasoff Berry Computer
Korean War	Korean War
Columbia Broadcasting System	Columbia Broadcasting System
Cold War	Cold War
Vietnam	Vietnam
artificial satellite	Technology: artificial satellite
Communications Satellite Act of 1962	Communications Satellite Act of 1962

In the concordance file shown in Figure 7.8, the text as it appears in the document is inserted in the first column (such as *World War I*, *Technology*, and *technology*). The second column contains the text as it should appear in the index specifying whether it is a main entry or subentry. For example, the text *motion pictures* in the concordance file will appear in the index as a subentry under the main entry *Technology*.

After a concordance file has been created, it can be used to quickly mark text for an index in a document. To do this, open the document containing text you want marked for the index, display the Index and Tables dialog box with the Index tab selected, and then click the AutoMark button. At the Open Index AutoMark File dialog box, double-click the concordance file name in the list box. Word turns on the display of nonprinting symbols, searches through the document for text that matches the text in the concordance file, and then marks it accordingly. After marking text for the index, insert the index in the document as described earlier.

When creating the concordance file in Exercise 7, Word's AutoCorrect feature will automatically capitalize the first letter of the first word entered in each cell. In Figure 7.9, you can see that several of the first words in the first column do not begin with a capital letter. Before completing the exercise, consider turning off this AutoCorrect capitalization feature. To do this, click Tools and then AutoCorrect Options. At the AutoCorrect dialog box click the *Capitalize first letter of table cells* check box to remove the check mark. Click OK to close the dialog box.

exercise 7
CREATING A CONCORDANCE FILE

1. At a clear document screen, create the text shown in Figure 7.9 as a concordance file by completing the following steps:
   a. Click the Insert Table button on the Standard toolbar.
   b. Drag down and to the right until *1 × 2 Table* displays at the bottom of the grid and then click the left mouse button.
   c. Type the text in the cells as shown in Figure 7.9. Press the Tab key to move to the next cell. (If you did not remove the check mark before the *Capitalize first letter of table cells* option at the AutoCorrect dialog box, the *n* in the first word in the first cell, *newsletters*, is automatically capitalized. Delete the capital *N*, type an **n**, press the Down Arrow key [this will capitalize it again], and then click the Undo button. You will need to repeat this for each cell entry in the first column that should begin with a lowercase letter.)
2. Save the document and name it **ewc7ConcordFile**.
3. Print and then close **ewc7ConcordFile**.

FIGURE 7.9 Exercise 7

newsletters	Newsletters
Newsletters	Newsletters
Software	Software
Desktop publishing	Software: desktop publishing
word processing	Software: word processing
Printers	Printers
Laser	Printers: laser
Design	Design
Communication	Communication
Consistency	Design: consistency
Elements	Elements
Nameplate	Elements: nameplate
Logo	Elements: logo
Subtitle	Elements: subtitle
Folio	Elements: folio
Headlines	Elements: headlines
Subheads	Elements: subheads
Byline	Elements: byline
Body Copy	Elements: body copy
Graphics Images	Elements: graphics images
Audience	Newsletters: audience
Purpose	Newsletters: purpose
focal point	Newsletters: focal point

WORD Creating Specialized Tables and Indexes

If you removed the check mark before the *Capitalize first letter of table cells* option at the AutoCorrect dialog box, you may need to turn this feature back on. To do this, click Tools and then AutoCorrect Options. At the AutoCorrect dialog box, click the *Capitalize first letter of table cells* check box to insert the check mark, and then click OK to close the dialog box.

exercise 8 — COMPILING AN INDEX USING A CONCORDANCE FILE

1. Open **WordReport05**.
2. Save the document with Save As and name it **ewc7x08**.
3. Make the following changes to the document:
    a. Select the entire document and then change the font to 12-point Bookman Old Style (or a similar serif typeface).
    b. Set the titles and headings in the document in 14-point Bookman Old Style bold.
4. Mark text for the index using the concordance file by completing the following steps:
    a. Click Insert, point to Reference, and then click Index and Tables.
    b. At the Index and Tables dialog box with the Index tab selected, click the AutoMark button.
    c. At the Open Index AutoMark File dialog box, double-click ***ewc7ConcordFile*** in the list box. (This turns on the display of the nonprinting symbols.)
5. Compile and insert the index in the document by completing the following steps:
    a. Position the insertion point at the end of the document.
    b. Insert a page break.
    c. Type **INDEX** bolded and centered.
    d. Press the Enter key twice, turn off bold, and then return the paragraph alignment to left.
    e. Click Insert, point to Reference, and then click Index and Tables.
    f. At the Index and Tables dialog box, click the Index tab.
    g. At the Index and Tables dialog box with the Index tab selected, click the down-pointing arrow at the right side of the *Formats* option box, and then click *Formal* at the drop-down list.
    h. Click OK to close the dialog box.
    i. Click the Show/Hide ¶ button on the Standard toolbar to turn off the display of nonprinting symbols.
    j. Set the title *INDEX* in 14-point Bookman Old Style bold.
6. Save the document again and then print the index (last page). (Check with your instructor to see if you should print the entire document.)
7. Close **ewc7x08**.

HINT
If you edit an index entry and move it to a different page, update the index.

Updating or Deleting an Index

If you make changes to a document after inserting an index, update the index. To do this, click anywhere within the index and then press F9. To delete an index, select the entire index using either the mouse or the keyboard, and then press the Delete key.

QUICK STEPS
Update Index
1. Click in index.
2. Press F9.

exercise 9

UPDATING AN INDEX

1. Open **ewc7x08**.
2. Save the document with Save As and name it **ewc7x09**.
3. Insert a page break at the beginning of the title *MODULE 2: PLANNING A NEWSLETTER*.
4. Update the index by clicking anywhere in the index and then pressing F9.
5. Save the document again and then print only the index. (Check with your instructor to see if you should print the entire document.)
6. Close **ewc7x09**.

Creating a Table of Figures

A document that contains figures should include a list (table) of figures so the reader can quickly locate a specific figure. Figure 7.10 shows an example of a table of figures. A table of figures can be created using a variety of methods. The easiest method is to mark figure names as captions and then use the caption names to create the table of figures.

FIGURE 7.10 *Table of Figures*

```
                    TABLE OF FIGURES

    FIGURE 1 SCANNED LINE ART .................................................... 3
    FIGURE 2 DIGITAL HALFTONE MATRIX .................................... 8
    FIGURE 3 BAR CHARTS ........................................................... 12
    FIGURE 4 LINE CHARTS .......................................................... 15
    FIGURE 5 DETAIL VS. WEIGHT ................................................ 18
```

Creating Captions

A variety of methods are available for creating a caption for text. One method is to select the text, click Insert, point to Reference, and then click Caption. At the Caption dialog box shown in Figure 7.11, make sure *Figure 1* displays in the *Caption* text box and the insertion point is positioned after *Figure 1*. Type the name for the caption, and then click OK or press Enter. Word inserts *Figure 1 (caption name)* below the selected text.

QUICK STEPS

Create a Caption
1. Select text.
2. Click Insert, Reference, Caption.
3. Type caption name.
4. Click OK.

WORD — Creating Specialized Tables and Indexes — **E281**

FIGURE 7.11 Caption Dialog Box

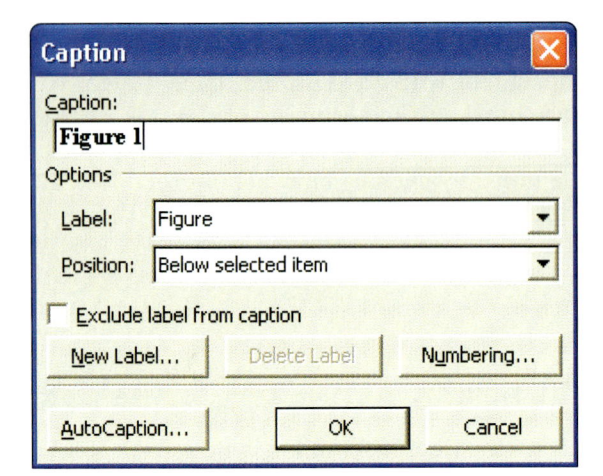

QUICK STEPS

Compile a Table of Figures
1. Click Insert, Reference, Index and Tables.
2. Click Table of Figures tab.
3. Select the desired format.
4. Click OK.

Compiling a Table of Figures

Once figures have been marked as captions in a document, compile the table of figures. A table of figures generally displays at the beginning of the document, after the table of contents. To compile the table of figures, display the Index and Tables dialog box with the Table of Figures tab selected as shown in Figure 7.12, make any necessary changes, and then click OK to close the dialog box.

FIGURE 7.12 Index and Tables Dialog Box with the Table of Figures Tab Selected

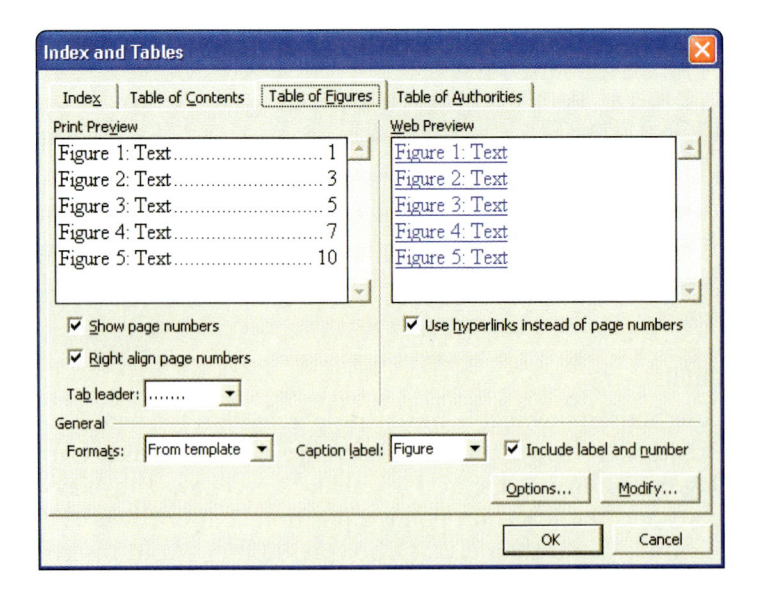

The options at the Index and Tables dialog box with the Table of Figures tab selected are similar to those options available at the dialog box with the Table of Contents tab selected. For example, you can choose a format for the table of figures from the *Formats* option box, change the alignment of the page number, or add leaders before page numbers.

exercise 10

CREATING A LIST OF FIGURES

1. Open **WordReport03**.
2. Save the document with Save As and name it **ewc7x10**.
3. Add the caption *Figure 1 Basic Hardware* to the bulleted text, and the lines above and below the bulleted text, that displays in the middle of page 2 by completing the following steps:
   a. Move the insertion point to the middle of page 2 and then select from just below the top horizontal line to just above the bottom horizontal line (see the figure at the right).
   b. Click Insert, point to Reference, and then click Caption.
   c. At the Caption dialog box, press the spacebar once, and then type **Basic Hardware**. (The insertion point is automatically positioned in the *Caption* text box, immediately after *Figure 1*.)
   d. Click OK or press Enter.
4. Complete steps similar to those in Step 3 to create the caption *Figure 2 Input Devices* for the bulleted text toward the bottom of the second page. (Be sure to include the lines above and below the bulleted text.)
5. Complete steps similar to those in Step 3 to create the caption *Figure 3 Output Devices* for the bulleted text that displays at the bottom of the second page and the top of the third page (the location may vary slightly). (Be sure to include the lines above and below the bulleted text.)
6. Compile and insert a table of figures at the beginning of the document by completing the following steps:
   a. Position the insertion point at the beginning of the document, press the Enter key, and then insert a page break.
   b. Move the insertion point above the page break and then type **TABLE OF FIGURES** bolded and centered.
   c. Press the Enter key, turn off bold, and then change the paragraph alignment back to left.
   d. Click Insert, point to Reference, and then click Index and Tables.
   e. At the Index and Tables dialog box, click the Table of Figures tab.
   f. At the Index and Tables dialog box with the Table of Figures tab selected, click the down-pointing arrow at the right side of the *Formats* option box, and then click *Formal* at the drop-down list.
   g. Click OK or press Enter.
7. Check the page breaks in the document and, if necessary, adjust the page breaks.
8. Save the document again and then print the Table of Figures page. (Check with your instructor to see if you should print the entire document.)
9. Close **ewc7x10**.

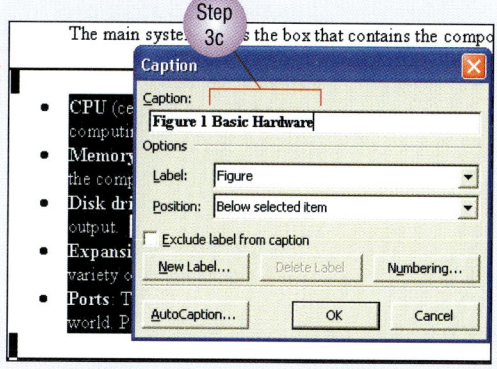

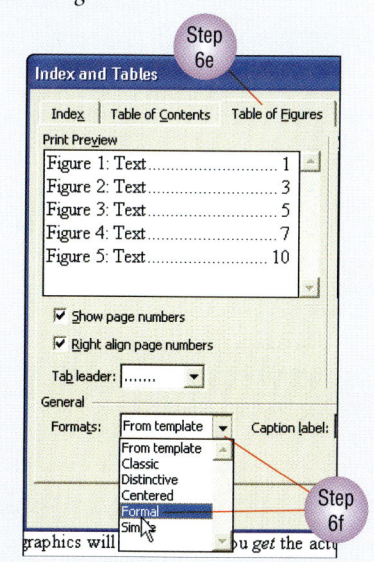

WORD Creating Specialized Tables and Indexes E283

QUICK STEPS

Update Table of Figures
1. Click in table of figures.
2. Press F9.
3. Click OK at the Update Table of Figures dialog box.

Updating or Deleting a Table of Figures

If you make changes to a document after inserting a table of figures, update the table. To do this, click anywhere within the table of figures, and then press F9. At the Update Table of Figures dialog box, click *Update page numbers only* if the changes occur only to the page numbers, or click *Update entire table* if changes were made to headings or subheadings within the table. Click OK or press Enter to close the dialog box. To delete a table of figures, select the entire table using either the mouse or the keyboard, and then press the Delete key.

Creating a Table of Authorities

A table of authorities is a list of citations identifying the pages where the citations appear in a legal brief or other legal document. Word provides many common categories under which citations can be organized. Word includes Cases, Statutes, Other Authorities, Rules, Treatises, Regulations, and Constitutional Provisions. Within each category, Word alphabetizes the citations. Figure 7.13 shows an example of a table of authorities.

FIGURE 7.13 *Table of Authorities*

```
                    TABLE OF AUTHORITIES

                            CASES

Mansfield v. Rydell, 72 Wn.2d 200, 433 P.2d 723 (1983)...............3
State v. Fletcher, 73 Wn.2d 332, 124 P.2d 503 (1981).................5
Yang v. Buchwald, 21 Wn.2d 385, 233 P.2d 609 (1991)..................7

                          STATUTES

RCW 8.12.230(2)......................................................4
RCW 6.23.590........................................................7
RCW 5.23.103(3)....................................................10
```

Some thought goes into planning a table of authorities. Before marking any text in a legal document, you need to determine what section headings you want and what should be contained in the sections. When marking text for a table of authorities, you need to find the first occurrence of the citation, mark it as a full citation with the complete name, and then specify a short citation. To mark a citation for a table of authorities, you would complete the following steps:

1. Select the first occurrence of the citation.
2. Press Alt + Shift + I.
3. At the Mark Citation dialog box shown in Figure 7.14, edit and format the text in the *Selected text* box as you want it to appear in the table of authorities. Edit and format the text in the *Short citation* text box so it matches the short citation you want Word to search for in the document.
4. Click the down-pointing arrow at the right of the *Category* text box and then click the category from the drop-down list that applies to the citation.
5. Click the Mark button to mark the selected citation or click the Mark All button if you want Word to mark all long and short citations in the document that match those displayed in the Mark Citation dialog box.
6. The Mark Citation dialog box remains on the document screen so you can mark other citations. To find the next citation in a document, click the Next Citation button. (This causes Word to search through the document for the next occurrence of text commonly found in a citation such as *in re* or *v.*)
7. Select the text for the next citation and then complete Steps 3 through 5.
8. After marking all citations, click the Close button to close the Mark Citations dialog box.

QUICK STEPS

Mark Citation for a Table of Authorities
1. Select first occurrence of citation.
2. Press Alt + Shift + I.
3. At Mark Citation dialog box, edit and format text.
4. Specify the category.
5. Click the Mark button.

FIGURE 7.14 *Mark Citation Dialog Box*

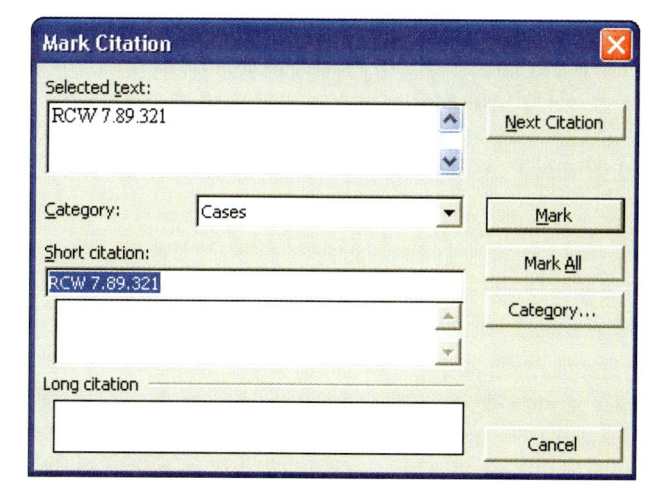

Compiling a Table of Authorities

Once citations have been marked in a document, the table of authorities can be compiled and inserted in the document. A table of authorities is compiled in a document in a manner similar to a table of contents or figures. A table of authorities generally displays at the beginning of the document. To compile a table of authorities in a document containing text marked as citations, display the Index and Tables dialog box with the Table of Authorities tab selected, as shown in Figure 7.15, make any necessary changes, and then click OK to close the dialog box.

QUICK STEPS

Compile a Table of Authorities
1. Click Insert, Reference, Index and Tables.
2. Click the Table of Authorities tab.
3. Select the desired format.
4. Click OK.

WORD — Creating Specialized Tables and Indexes — E285

FIGURE 7.15 Index and Tables Dialog Box with the Table of Authorities Tab Selected

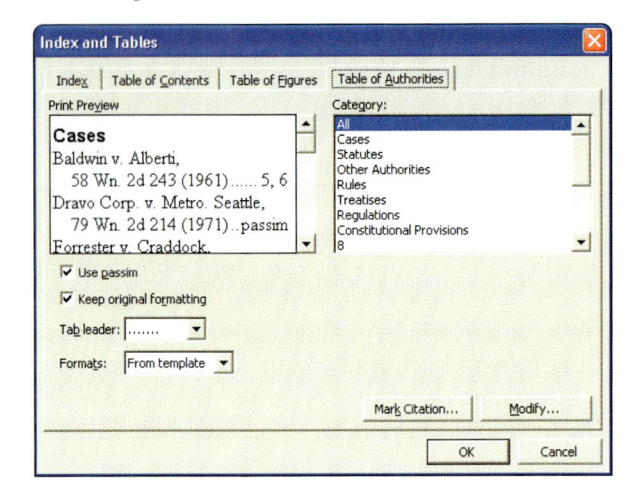

If you want the table of authorities to print on a page separate from the document text, insert a section break that begins a new page between the table of authorities and the title of the document. If the beginning of the text in the document, rather than the table of authorities, should be numbered as page 1, change the starting page number for the section.

The Index and Tables dialog box with the Table of Authorities tab selected contains options for formatting a table of authorities. The *Use passim* option is active by default (the check box contains a check mark). When it is active, Word replaces five or more page references to the same authority with *passim*. With the *Keep original formatting* check box active, Word will retain the formatting of the citation as it appears in the document. Click the *Tab leader* option if you want to change the leader character. By default, Word compiles all categories for the table of authorities. If you want to compile citations for a specific category, select that category from the *Category* list box.

exercise 11

COMPILING A TABLE OF AUTHORITIES

1. Open **WordLegalBrief**.
2. Save the document with Save As and name it **ewc7x11**.
3. Mark *RCW 7.89.321* as a statute citation by completing the following steps:
   a. Select *RCW 7.89.321*. (This citation is located toward the middle of the second page. **Hint: Use the Find feature to help you locate this citation**.)
   b. Press Alt + Shift + I.
   c. At the Mark Citation dialog box, click the down-pointing arrow at the right side of the *Category* option box, and then click *Statutes* at the drop-down list.
   d. Click the Mark All button. (This turns on the display of nonprinting symbols.)

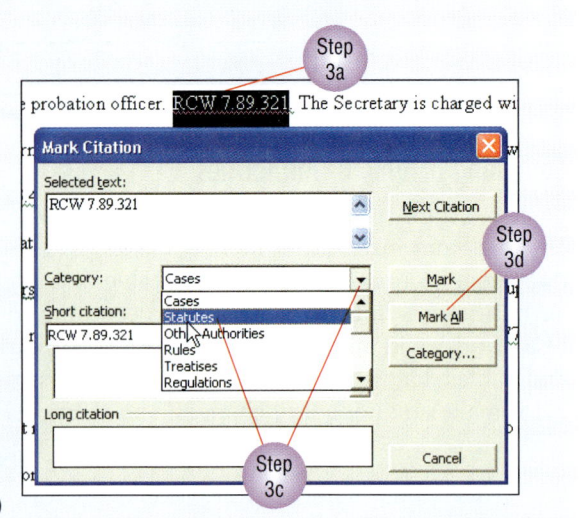

e. Click the Close button to close the Mark Citation dialog box.
4. Complete steps similar to those in Step 3 to mark *RCW 7.53.443* as a statute citation. (This citation is located toward the middle of the second page.)
5. Complete steps similar to those in Step 3 to mark *RCW 7.72A.432(2)* as a statute citation. (This citation is located toward the top of the third page.)
6. Complete steps similar to those in Step 3 to mark *RCW 7.42A.429(1)* as a statute citation. (This citation is located toward the top of the third page.)
7. Mark *State v. Connors, 73 W.2d 743, 430 P.2d 199 (1974)* as a case citation by completing the following steps:
    a. Select *State v. Connors, 73 W.2d 743, 430 P.2d 199 (1974)*. (This citation is located toward the bottom of the second page. **Hint: Use the Find feature to help you locate this citation**.)
    b. Press Alt + Shift + I.
    c. At the Mark Citation dialog box, type **State v. Connors** in the *Short citation* text box.
    d. Click the down-pointing arrow at the right side of the *Category* option box, and then click *Cases* at the drop-down list.
    e. Click the Mark All button.

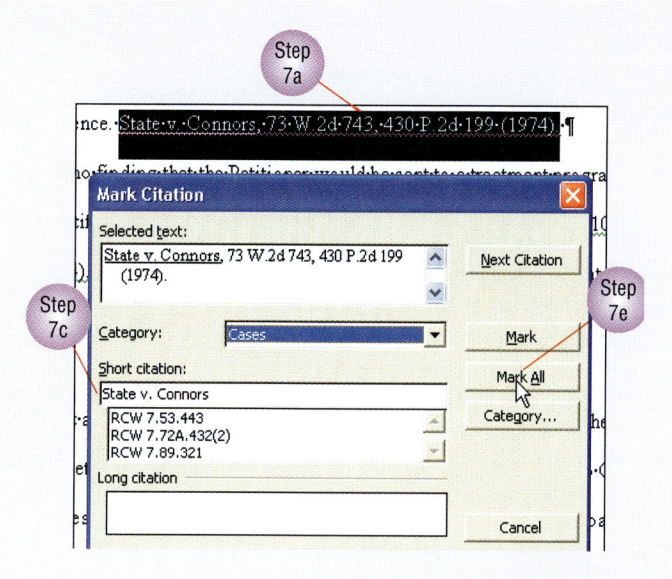

    f. Click the Close button to close the Mark Citation dialog box.
8. Complete steps similar to those in Step 7 to mark *State v. Bertelli, 63 W.2d 77, 542 P.2d 751 (1971)*. Enter **State v. Bertelli** as the short citation. (This citation is located toward the bottom of the second page.)
9. Complete steps similar to those in Step 7 to mark *State v. Landers, 103 W.2d 432, 893 P.2d 2 (1984)*. Enter **State v. Landers** as the short citation. (This citation is located toward the top of the third page.)

10. Turn on page numbering and compile the table of authorities by completing the following steps:
    a. Position the insertion point at the beginning of the document and then press the Enter key once.
    b. Position the insertion point immediately left of the *S* in STATEMENT OF CASE and then insert a section break that begins a new page.
    c. With the insertion point positioned below the section break, turn on page numbering at the bottom center of each page and change the starting number to 1.
    d. Position the insertion point above the section break and then type **TABLE OF AUTHORITIES** centered and bolded.
    e. Press the Enter key, turn off bold, and then change the paragraph alignment back to left.
    f. Click Insert, point to Reference, and then click Index and Tables.
    g. At the Index and Tables dialog box, click the Table of Authorities tab.
    h. At the Index and Tables dialog box with the Table of Authorities tab selected, click the down-pointing arrow at the right side of the *Formats* option box, and then click *Formal* at the drop-down list.
    i. Click OK or press Enter.
11. With the insertion point positioned anywhere in the table of authorities, turn on page numbering at the bottom center of each page and change the numbering format to lowercase Roman numerals.
12. Turn off the display of nonprinting symbols.
13. Save the document again and then print the table of authorities. (Check with your instructor to see if you should print the entire document.)
14. Close **ewc7x11**.

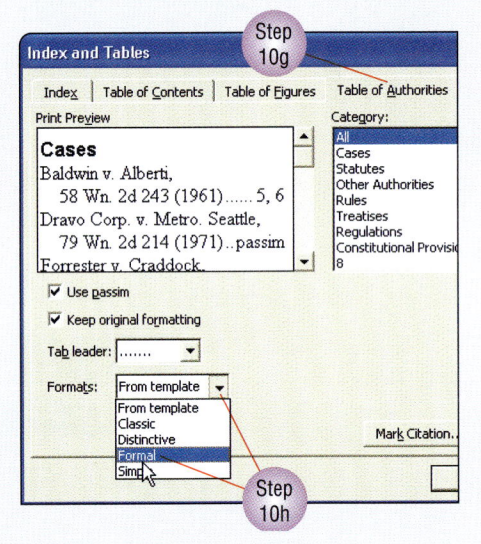

HINT

If you need to make changes to a citation in a document containing a table of authorities, modify the citation in the body of the document and not the citation in the table of authorities; otherwise, the next time you update the table, your change will be lost.

Updating or Deleting a Table of Authorities

If you make changes to a document after inserting a table of authorities, update the table. To do this, click anywhere within the table of authorities, and then press F9. To delete a table of authorities, select the entire table of authorities using either the mouse or the keyboard, and then press the Delete key.

CHAPTER summary

- Word contains options for automating the creation of a table of contents, index, list, or table of authorities.
- Text to be included in a table of contents can be identified by applying a heading style, assigning an outline level, or text can be marked as a field entry.
- One method for marking text for a table of contents is to mark the text as a field entry at the Mark Table of Contents dialog box. Display this dialog box by pressing Alt + Shift + O.
- Two steps are involved in creating a table of contents: apply the appropriate styles to the text that will be included, and compile the table of contents in the document.
- To compile the table of contents, position the insertion point where you want the table of contents to appear, display the Index and Tables dialog box with the Table of Contents tab selected, make any desired changes, and then click OK.
- If you want the table of contents to print on a page separate from the document text, insert a section break that begins a new page between the table of contents and the title of the document. You may need to adjust the page numbering also.
- If you make changes to a document after compiling a table of contents, update the table of contents by clicking anywhere in the table and then pressing F9. Update an index, table of figures, or table of authorities in a similar manner.
- To delete a table of contents, select the entire table of contents, and then press the Delete key. Delete an index, a table of figures, or a table of authorities in the same manner.
- An index is a list of topics contained in a publication and the pages where those topics are discussed. Word lets you automate the process of creating an index in a manner similar to that for creating a table of contents.
- Mark text for an index at the Mark Index Entry dialog box. Display this dialog box by pressing Alt + Shift + X.
- After all necessary text has been marked as a main entry or subentry for the index, the next step is to compile the index so that it appears at the end of the document beginning on a separate page.
- Word provides seven formatting choices for an index at the *Formats* option box at the Index and Tables dialog box.
- Words that appear frequently in a document can be saved as a concordance file so that you need not mark each reference in a document. A concordance file is a regular document containing a single, two-column table created at the Insert Table dialog box.
- Create a table of figures by marking specific text as captions and then using the caption names to create the table of figures. Mark captions at the Caption dialog box. Display this dialog box by clicking Insert, pointing to Reference, and then clicking Caption.
- A table of figures is compiled in a document in a manner similar to a table of contents and generally displays at the beginning of the document, after the table of contents.
- A table of authorities is a list of citations identifying the pages where the citations appear in a legal brief or other legal document.

➤ When marking text for a table of authorities, find the first occurrence of the citation, mark it as a full citation with the complete name, and then specify a short citation at the Mark Citation dialog box. Display this dialog box by pressing Alt + Shift + I.

➤ A table of authorities is compiled in a document in a manner similar to a table of contents or figures. A table of authorities generally displays at the beginning of the document.

FEATURES summary

FEATURE	BUTTON	MENU	KEYBOARD
Index and Tables dialog box		Insert, Reference, Index and Tables	
Mark Table of Contents Entry dialog box			Alt + Shift + O
Display Mark Index Entry dialog box			Alt + Shift + X
Update index, table of figures, or table of authorities	Update TOC		F9
Captions dialog box		Insert, Reference, Caption	
Mark Citation dialog box			Alt + Shift + I

CONCEPTS check

Matching: On a blank sheet of paper, indicate the letter of the term that matches each description. (Terms may be used more than once.)

- Ⓐ Alt + Shift + A
- Ⓑ Alt + Shift + I
- Ⓒ Alt + Shift + O
- Ⓓ Alt + Shift + X
- Ⓔ Alt + Shift + T
- Ⓕ Captions
- Ⓖ Compiling
- Ⓗ Concordance
- Ⓘ F9
- Ⓙ F10
- Ⓚ Index
- Ⓛ Index and Tables dialog box
- Ⓜ Subentries
- Ⓝ Table of authorities
- Ⓞ Table of contents
- Ⓟ Table of figures

1. File that helps save time when marking text for an index.
2. Identifies citations in a legal brief.
3. Generally placed at the end of a document.
4. Generally placed at the beginning of a document.
5. This is a list of topics contained in a publication.
6. Pressing these keys displays the Mark Table of Contents Entry dialog box.
7. If included in a document, it usually follows the Table of Contents.
8. Pressing these keys displays the Mark Index Entry dialog box.
9. The easiest way to create a table of figures is to use these.
10. Choose a preformatted table of contents at this dialog box.
11. Pressing this key updates a table of authorities.

SKILLS check

Assessment 1

1. At a clear document screen, create the text shown in Figure 7.16 as a concordance file.
2. Save the document and name it **ewc7scCFile**.
3. Print and then close **ewc7scCFile**.
4. Open **WordReport06**.
5. Save the document with Save As and name it **ewc7sc01**.
6. Make the following changes to the document:
    a. Mark text for an index using the concordance file **ewc7scCFile**.
    b. Compile the index at the end of the document.
7. Save the document again and then print the index. (Check with your instructor to see if you should print the entire document.)
8. Close **ewc7sc01**.

FIGURE 7.16 Assessment 1

NEWSLETTER	Newsletter
Newsletter	Newsletter
Consistency	Newsletter: consistency
Element	Elements
Margins	Elements: margins
column layout	Elements: column layout
Nameplate	Elements: nameplate
Location	Elements: location
Logos	Elements: logo
Color	Elements: color
ruled lines	Elements: ruled lines
Focus	Elements: focus

Balance	Elements: balance
graphics images	Graphics images
Photos	Photos
Headlines	Newsletter: headlines
Subheads	Newsletter: subheads
White space	White space
directional flow	Newsletter: directional flow
Paper	Paper
Size	Paper: size
Type	Paper: type
Weight	Paper: weight
Stock	Paper: stock
margin size	Newsletter: margin size

Assessment 2

1. Open **ewc7sc01**.
2. Save the document with Save As and name it **ewc7sc02**.
3. Apply the following styles:
   MODULE 3: DESIGNING A NEWSLETTER = Heading 1
   Applying Desktop Publishing Guidelines = Heading 2
   MODULE 4: CREATING NEWSLETTER LAYOUT = Heading 1
   Choosing Paper Size and Type = Heading 2
   Choosing Paper Weight = Heading 2
   Creating Margins for Newsletters = Heading 2
   INDEX = Heading 1
4. Number the pages at the bottom center of each page.
5. Compile the table of contents. (Include a title for the table of contents.)
6. Number the table of contents page at the bottom center of the page. (Change the number to a lowercase Roman numeral.)
7. Save the document again and then print the table of contents page. (Check with your instructor to see if you should print the entire document.)
8. Close **ewc7sc02**.

Assessment 3

1. Open **ewc7sc02**.
2. Save the document with Save As and name it **ewc7sc03**.
3. Insert a page break at the beginning of the title *MODULE 4: CREATING NEWSLETTER LAYOUT*.
4. Update the table of contents and the index.
5. Save the document again, print the table of contents, and then print the index. (Check with your instructor to see if you should print the entire document.)
6. Close **ewc7sc03**.

CHAPTER challenge

Case study

Using the content from Chapter 7, create a document that includes the side headings and subheadings for the first 20 pages. Position the headings and subheadings in the document in the approximate locations as you see them in the book, leaving space where the paragraphs and exercises appear. Prepare to compile a table of contents by applying appropriate styles to the headings. When you are finished, save the document as **Chapter 7 with Table of Contents**. At the top of the document, insert a new page and key the title **Table of Contents**. Then generate a table of contents, using formatting of your choice. Save the document again.

HELP?

Word inserts the TOC (Table of Contents) field when the Index and Tables command from the Reference submenu on the Insert menu is used. If the Table of Contents is not being used or is consuming too much space in the document, it is possible to temporarily remove the Table of Contents by turning on the Table of Contents field code. Use the Help feature to learn about switching from results to field codes. Then switch the Table of Contents to a field code. Save the document as **Hidden Table of Contents**.

INTEGRATED

In an e-mail, send the table of contents (not the entire document) created in the first part of the Chapter Challenge as an attachment to your professor. In the e-mail, explain how you were able to send the table of contents without sending the entire document.

CHAPTER 8

USING XML IN WORD 2003

PERFORMANCE OBJECTIVES

Upon successful completion of Chapter 8, you will be able to:
- Attach an XML schema to a Word document
- Load XML data into an Excel worksheet
- Use a schema as a template
- Validate a schema
- Display XML options
- Enhance a schema
- Transform XML
- Open a file in Internet Explorer
- Add a solution
- Delete schemas and solutions

Microsoft Office 2003 offers the XML feature, which allows you to identify specific data in files and then extract that data for use in other applications. If you determine that you want to extract data from a Word 2003 document for use in other applications, you can attach a schema to the document and then map specific data within the document to specific data definitions within the schema. In this chapter, you will learn how to attach a schema to a Word document, save XML data from a document, modify schemas, create fill-in forms using XML documents, and transform XML data using XML style sheets.

Introducing XML

Since the early days of computing, one of the most persistent problems has been the exchange of data between different computer applications. Word processors, spreadsheets, databases, and e-mail applications, just to name a few, all use different file structures to store information. Even among applications of a similar type, such as word processing, each manufacturer will store documents in its own unique file format. The explosive growth of the global Internet has significantly increased the number of users who want to exchange all types of information with other users who often use different applications or different operating systems. One reason often cited for the rapid growth of the World Wide Web is that, despite the dizzying variety of information on the Web, it uses a common method of text formatting called *Hypertext Markup Language (HTML)*. HTML is a pure text format designed to make text information easy to read. Using HTML, documents of all types, from graduate theses to advertising publications, can be made accessible to a wide range of computer users.

Many Internet pioneers wondered if, by using HTML as a model, a better method for exchanging complex sets of data could be developed. The result of their efforts is *Extensible Markup Language (XML)*. Computer languages, unlike human languages, typically have been created with a fixed vocabulary of keywords, which are the only instructions that can be used in coding that language. An extensible language is one that allows for the invention of new terms. In an extensible computer language, terms are restricted only by a set of rules, that is, a grammar, that defines how new terms can be added to code written in that language.

While HTML and XML have many similar attributes, the way in which they are intended to be used is different. A document using HTML is meant to be a complete, finished document ready for display. XML typically is used as one part of a more complicated application. In Word 2003, XML files are used along with other Word features to create documents and exchange data.

An important characteristic of XML is that it is *self-documenting*. While XML documents contain data, they also contain information about what those data items represent and how they relate to each other.

Providing Structure with XML Schemas

A Word document allows you a great degree of freedom about how you organize your text. If you create a letter or a resume, you are free to decide where in the document you prefer to place any item of information. However, XML documents require a high degree of structure so that data items destined for exchange with other users are organized clearly and consistently.

The designers of XML anticipated this problem and devised a special type of XML document called a *schema*, which enables non-XML applications, like Word, to properly structure an XML data document. Schema files are roughly the XML equivalent of Word templates. Like templates, schema files can be attached to a Word document. Once a schema file is attached to a Word document, Word uses the structure described in the schema to guide you through various operations that relate text in your Word document to the structure of an XML file.

Working with XML Schemas in Word 2003

The average Word user is not expected to have the technical knowledge to handle the complex task of creating XML schema files. This is typically done by programmers or database designers who know the type of application that will use the XML information you create in Word. On the other hand, once a schema is created it can be distributed among many users so they can use the schema to facilitate the sharing of data in new and useful ways. No matter how different the documents may look, if they are organized using the same XML schema, XML applications will be able to utilize the information. As an example, look at the letter shown in

Figure 8.1. The letter is part of an internship program in which interns are required to submit personal and contact information in a Word document that is sent to the company as an e-mail attachment.

FIGURE 8.1 *Letter Containing Data*

> Thank you for the opportunity to intern in the Human Resources Department at Grayson Investments. I am excited about the opportunity to work for such a highly respected investment company. As you requested in our telephone conversation, my contact information includes:
>
> Susan Little
> 4812 Southport Avenue
> Long Beach, CA 94011
> (212) 555-3402
> slittle@emcp.net
>
> My internship will be monitored by the business administration advisor as well as the coordinator of the internship program. The telephone numbers for these two individuals are:
>
> Jeremy Carter, (412) 555-3499
> Sylvia Mansfield, (412) 555-7885
>
> Thank you again for the opportunity to work for Grayson Investments. I look forward to seeing you June 20.

The letter in Figure 8.1 appears to be just text. But if you think about the purpose of the letter, you will see that it is actually a mix of two very different types of information. Some standard text displays, such as *Thank you for the opportunity...*, while other portions of specific data are found throughout the letter. Figure 8.2 identifies the significant information contained in the letter.

FIGURE 8.2 **Highlighted Letter Data**

> Thank you for the opportunity to intern in the Human Resources Department at Grayson Investments. I am excited about the opportunity to work for such a highly respected investment company. As you requested in our telephone conversation, my contact information includes:
>
> ==Susan Little==
> ==4812 Southport Avenue==
> ==Long Beach, CA 94011==
> ==(212) 555-3402==
> ==slittle@emcp.net==
>
> My internship will be monitored by the business administration advisor as well as the coordinator of the internship program. The telephone numbers for these two individuals are:
>
> ==Jeremy Carter, (412) 555-3499==
> ==Sylvia Mansfield, (412) 555-7885==
>
> Thank you again for the opportunity to work for Grayson Investments. I look forward to seeing you June 20.

Suppose that your job is to receive letters (as Word documents) similar to the one shown in Figure 8.1 and then convert the information contained in the letter to a format that could be loaded into a database file, which would maintain records for all of the interns. In most cases, that would require you to retype the information into another format or application.

Word 2003 and XML schemas provide a new solution. The key is to have the database developer create an XML schema that defines the information that needs to be extracted from each of the incoming letters. In Word 2003, you can add an XML schema to the Schema library and then attach the schema to a document allowing you to map specific items within the document to specific data definitions within the XML schema. You can then have Word extract the data from the document and convert it to an XML document. All of this can be accomplished without having to retype any data. Also, the original document is retained as an XML-enhanced Word document, which combines the best of both types of format.

Although Word 2003 does not have any special features that help you create XML schema files, Excel 2003 and Access 2003 do have features that will automatically generate XML schemas based on data stored in worksheets or tables.

Attaching an XML Schema

After the XML schema is created, you can attach the schema to a document. Attaching a schema generally involves two steps—adding the schema to the Schema library and attaching the schema to the document. If you attach a schema to a document, Word automatically adds the schema to the Schema library. Once the schema is attached to a document, elements in the schema are used to tag data in the Word document.

To attach an XML schema to a document, begin by displaying the XML Structure task pane shown in Figure 8.3. To do this, click File and then New. At the New Document task pane, click the XML document hyperlink. Or, click the Other Task Panes button on any currently displayed task pane, and then click *XML Structure*.

FIGURE

8.3 *XML Structure Task Pane*

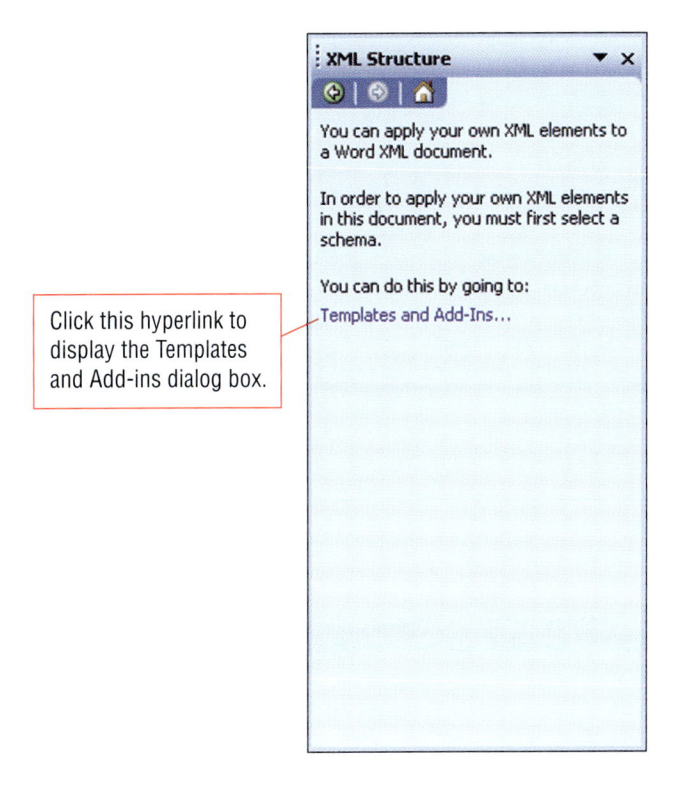

Click this hyperlink to display the Templates and Add-ins dialog box.

At the XML Structure task pane, click the Templates and Add-Ins hyperlink. This displays the Templates and Add-ins dialog box with the XML Schema tab selected as shown in Figure 8.4. At this dialog box, click the Add Schema button to display the Add Schema dialog box. At the Add Schema dialog box, navigate to the folder containing the desired file and then double-click the file name. Word displays the Schema Settings dialog box shown in Figure 8.5. At this dialog box, the *URI* (Universal Resource Identifier) text box is filled in with the URI contained in the schema file. The *Location* text box is also filled with the actual file location of the schema file. The *Alias* text box allows you to enter a descriptive name of your own choosing that will identity the schema in Word. The alias name you assign appears in the list of schemas currently added to the Word Schema library.

FIGURE 8.4 Templates and Add-Ins Dialog Box with XML Schema Tab Selected

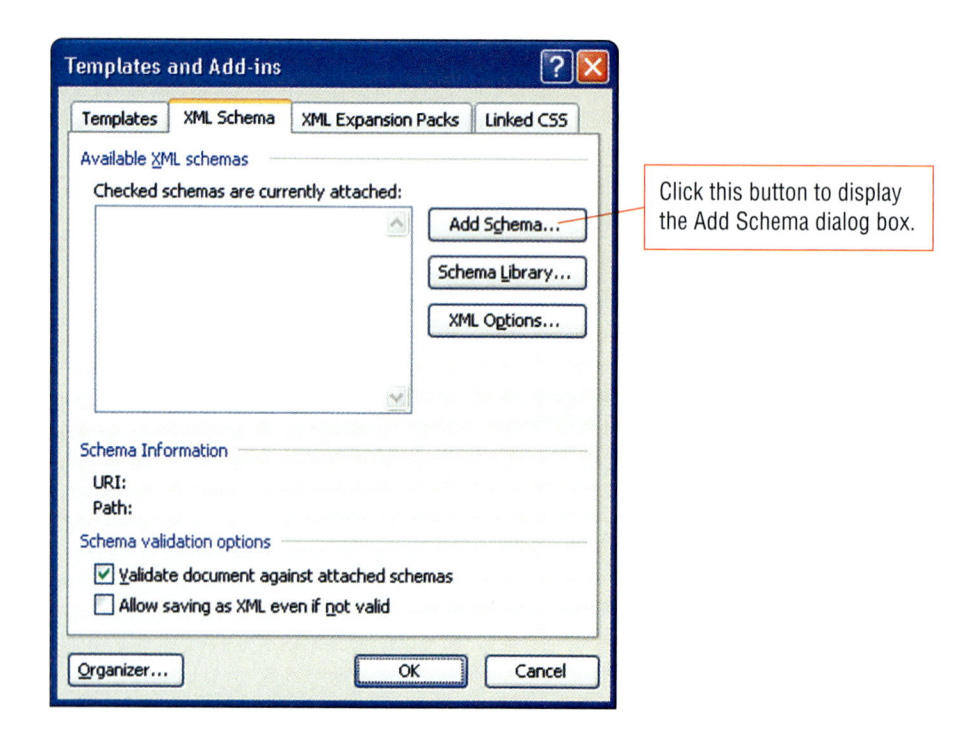

Click this button to display the Add Schema dialog box.

FIGURE 8.5 Schema Settings Dialog Box

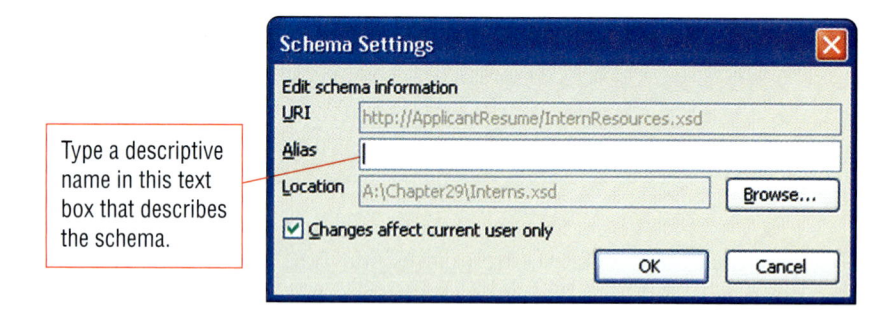

Type a descriptive name in this text box that describes the schema.

When an XML schema is attached to a document, the XML Structure task pane displays information that reflects the elements defined in the schema. Figure 8.6 displays information about the InternResources.xsd schema you will attach to a document in Exercise 1.

FIGURE

8.6 *XML Structure Task Pane with Schema Attached*

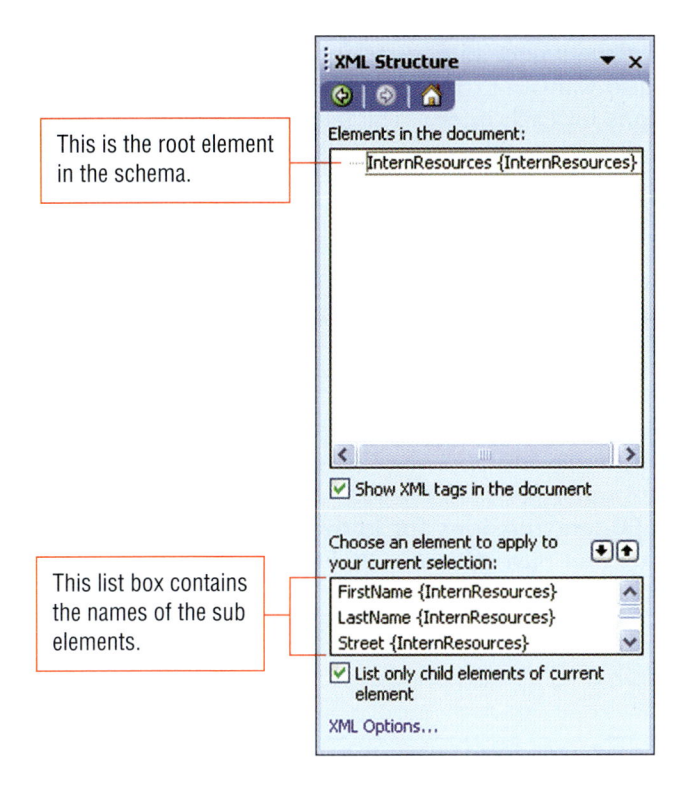

- This is the root element in the schema. → InternResources {InternResources}
- This list box contains the names of the sub elements. → FirstName {InternResources}, LastName {InternResources}, Street {InternResources}

The elements in the XML schema must be mapped to the corresponding data items in the Word document. Once the schema is mapped to the text, you can use Word to produce an XML file that can be used in other applications (such as Excel 2003 and Access 2003) to load and manipulate the information contained in the Word document.

When applying XML elements to the document, you need to apply the root element of the schema to the entire document. Once the root is applied, the elements below the root become available for mapping to specific blocks of text. ***Mapping*** refers to the process in which data in a document is linked to elements in an XML schema. When data is mapped to an XML schema, Word knows which parts of the document are XML items and which parts of the document are Word data.

Extracting Data as XML

Once you have added XML to a Word document, you have two options for saving the document. If you save it as an XML document most of your normal Word structure and formatting is discarded and all the information is organized as XML. An alternative is to save the document as a WordML document. The WordML document retains all of the normal Word formatting as well as the XML information. If you want to use the document again in Word, save it as a WordML document. When you want to convert the data to non-Word XML use the XML document file type.

In Exercise 1, you will assume you are working as an intern coordinator for a company. You have asked all the interns to prepare a letter in Word that includes their personal information as well as their contacts' information. You have asked them to send that letter to you as an e-mail or an attachment to an e-mail. You will use the information for preparing future documents, spreadsheets, and database tables. However, since each letter may arrange the information differently, you ask the database designer in your company to create an XML schema you can use to extract the name, address, telephone number, and e-mail address of each intern. You also want to extract the names and telephone numbers of the contact persons for each intern. The database designer has created a schema named Interns.xsd that you will use in Exercise 1 to add to the Schema library, attach to the Word document sent by the intern, and then map data in the Word document by linking specific text to elements in the XML schema.

Note: To complete exercises in this chapter, you will need to turn on the display of file extensions. If file extensions display, skip to Exercise 1. If not, complete the following steps to display file extensions:

1. *Display the Control Panel.*
2. *Double-click the* Folder Options *icon.*
3. *At the Folder Options dialog box, click the View tab.*
4. *At the Folder Options dialog box with the View tab selected, remove the check mark from the* Hide extensions for known file types *option.*
5. *Click the Apply button and then click the OK button.*
6. *Close the Control Panel.*

exercise 1

ATTACHING AN XML SCHEMA TO A WORD DOCUMENT

1. Open the document named **Resources.doc**.
2. Display the XML Structure task pane by completing the following steps:
   a. Click View and then Task Pane.
   b. At the task pane, click the Other Task Panes button and then click *XML Structure* at the drop-down list.
3. Attach a schema to the document by completing the following steps:
   a. Click the Templates and Add-Ins hyperlink in the XML Structure task pane.
   b. At the Templates and Add-ins dialog box, make sure the XML Schema tab is selected and then click the Add Schema button.
   c. At the Add Schema dialog box, navigate to the WordChapter08E folder on your disk and then double-click the **Interns.xsd** file name.

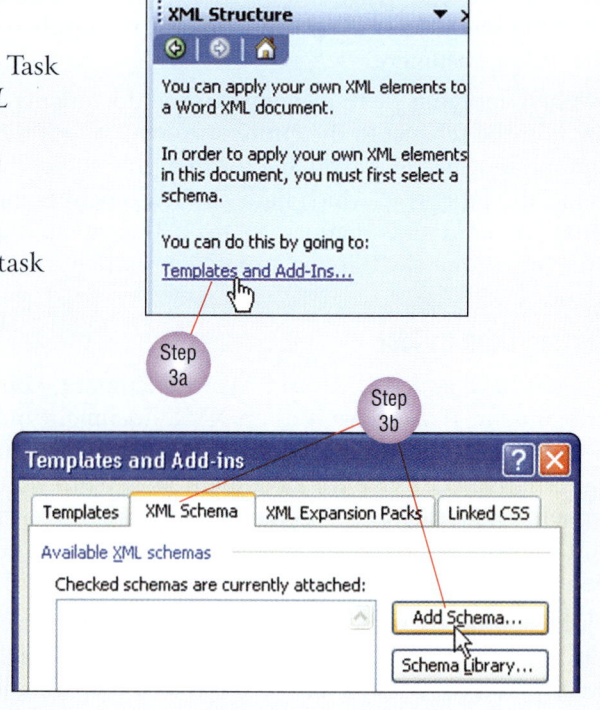

E302 Chapter Eight

d. At the Schema Settings dialog box, type **InternResources** in the *Alias* text box and then click OK. (This displays the Templates and Add-ins dialog box with the *InternResources* schema listed in the *Checked schemas are currently attached* list box.)
e. Click OK to close the Templates and Add-ins dialog box.

4. The schema is now attached to the document (and it was also automatically added to the Schema library so it will be available for future use). The next step is to apply the root element of the schema to the entire document. To do this, complete the following steps:
   a. Select the entire document by clicking Edit and then Select All.
   b. In the XML Structure task pane, click *InternResources* in the *Choose an element to apply to your current selection* list box.
   c. At the message asking whether your want to apply the XML element to the entire document or the current selection, click the Apply to Entire Document button.

5. Map elements in the schema to specific text in the letter by completing the following steps:
   a. Map the FirstName element to the intern's first name by double-clicking *Susan* in the letter and then clicking *FirstName* in the *Choose an element to apply to your current selection* list box in the XML Structure task pane.

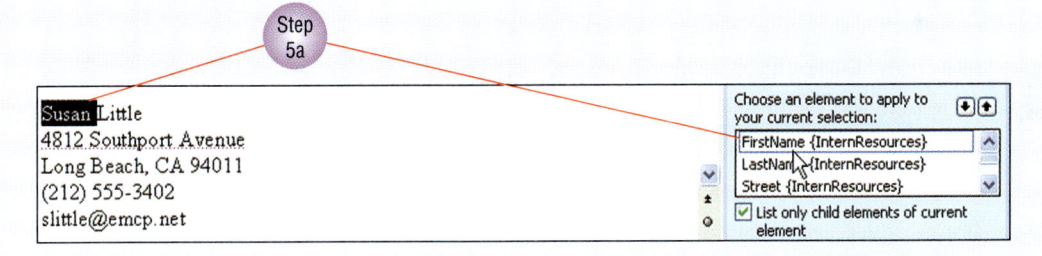

   b. Map the last name by double-clicking *Little* and then clicking the *LastName* element in the *Choose an element to apply to your current selection* list box.
   c. Select the text *4812 Southport Avenue* and then click the *Street* element.
   d. Select *Long Beach* in the letter and then click the *City* element.
   e. Double-click *CA* in the letter and then click the *State* element.
   f. Double-click *94011* in the letter and then click the *Zip* element.
   g. Select *(212) 555-3402* and then click the *Phone* element.
   h. Select *slittle@emcp.net* and then click the *Email* element.

6. Map the sub elements in the schema to specific text in the letter by completing the following steps:
   a. Select the text *Jeremy Carter, (412) 555-3499* and then click the *Reference* element in the task pane.
   b. Select the text *Sylvia Mansfield, (412) 555-7885* and then click the *Reference* element in the task pane.

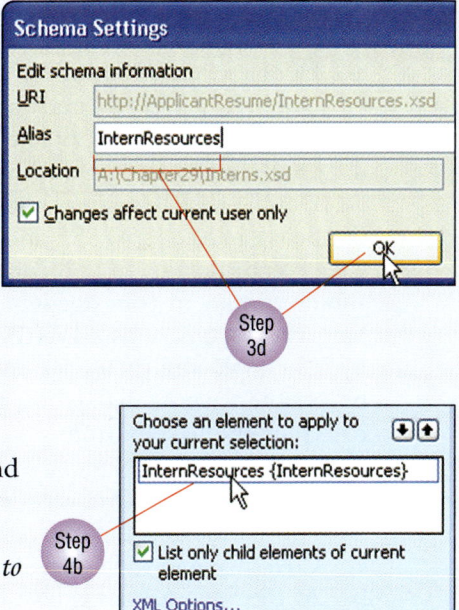

7. Map the items in each reference to the detailed reference elements in the schema by completing the following steps:
   a. Double-click *Jeremy,* and then click the *ReferenceFirst* element.
   b. Double-click *Carter,* and then click the *ReferenceLast* element.
   c. Select *(412) 555-3499* and then click the *ReferencePhone* element.
   d. Double-click *Sylvia,* and then click the *ReferenceFirst* element.
   e. Double-click *Mansfield,* and then click the *ReferenceLast* element.
   f. Select *(412) 555-7885* and then click the *ReferencePhone* element.
8. Check your document and compare it with the document in Figure 8.7. XML tags should display in your document as shown in the figure.
9. Save the document as a WordML document by completing the following steps:
   a. Click File and then Save As.
   b. At the Save As dialog box, type **ResourcesWithXML**.
   c. Click the Save button.
10. Close the document.
11. Open *ResourcesWithXML.doc.* (The XML icons appear along with the text.)
12. Save only the XML data by completing the following steps:
    a. Click File and then Save As.
    b. At the Save As dialog box, click the down-pointing arrow at the right of the *Save as type* list box, and then click *XML Document (*.xml)* at the drop-down list.
    c. Click the *Save data only* check box to insert a check mark.
    d. Select the name that currently displays in the *File name* text box and then type **slittle**.
    e. Click the Save button.

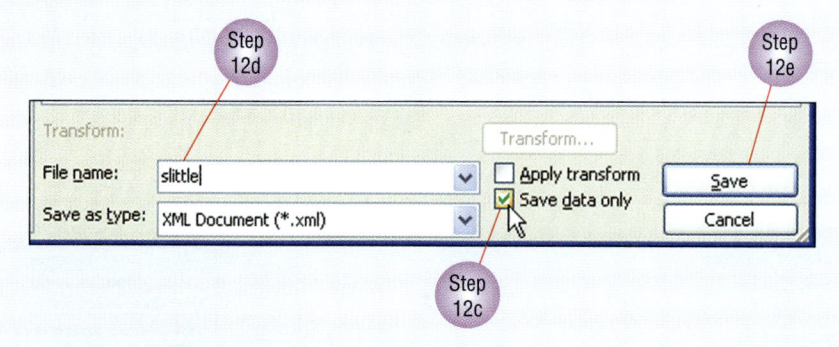

    f. At the message asking if you to confirm that you wish to save the contents of the document as XML, click the Continue button.
13. Close the XML Structure task pane and then close the document.

FIGURE 8.7 Exercise 1

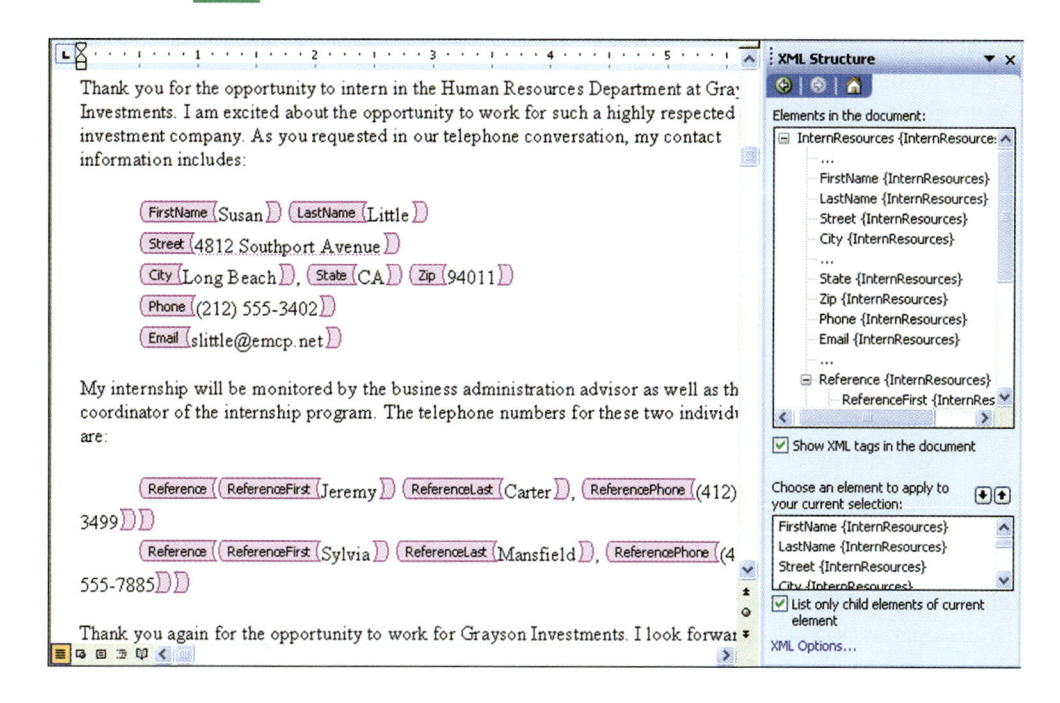

[Screenshot of a Word 2003 document showing an XML-tagged internship letter with the XML Structure task pane open on the right. The letter begins "Thank you for the opportunity to intern in the Human Resources Department at Grayson Investments..." with tagged elements including FirstName (Susan), LastName (Little), Street (4812 Southport Avenue), City (Long Beach), State (CA), Zip (94011), Phone ((212) 555-3402), Email (slittle@emcp.net), and Reference entries for Jeremy Carter and Sylvia Mansfield.]

Using the XML Data in a Different Application

The purpose of creating an XML document is to place information in a format that can be accessed by different applications including non-Windows applications. Excel 2003, like Word 2003, is capable of using XML files and understanding their structure. Because XML is self-documenting, when Excel loads an XML file prepared in Word it loads not only the data but the structure. Because Excel understands the structure of the XML document, it will automatically generate its own way of displaying and organizing the data.

exercise 2 — LOADING XML DATA INTO AN EXCEL WORKSHEET

(Note: Before completing this exercise, check with your instructor to determine if Excel 2003 is available and the steps to open Excel.)

1. Open Excel 2003.
2. Open the **slittle.xml** file you created in Exercise 1 into the blank worksheet by completing the following steps:
   a. Click the Open button on the Standard toolbar.
   b. At the Open dialog box, navigate to the WordChapter08E folder on your disk.
   c. Change the *Files of type* option to *All Files (*.*)*.
   d. Double-click **slittle.xml** in the list box.

WORD — Using XML in Word 2003 **E305**

3. At the Open XML dialog box, make sure the *As an XML list* option is selected and then click OK. (The *As an XML list* option loads both the XML data and the XML structure.)
4. Excel displays the message *The specified XML source does not refer to a schema. Excel will create a schema based on the XML source data*. At this message, click OK. (This message indicates that Excel will use the self-documenting information in the XML file to create a schema automatically. Your document should appear as shown in Figure 8.8.)
5. Display the XML Source Task pane by completing the following steps:
   a. Click View and then Task Pane.
   b. At the task pane, click the Other Task Panes button and then click *XML Source* at the drop-down list. (The XML Source task pane shows the XML schema generated by Excel from the information included in the XML document. This schema is identical in structure to the one used in Word to create the **slittle.xml** document.)
6. Scroll the worksheet to the right until you can view columns I through K. Note that because Excel is organized in rows and columns it interpreted the XML document as containing two rows, one for each reference. In order for each row to be complete, Excel duplicated the applicant's information on each row.
7. Each column heading has a down-pointing arrow that opens a drop-down list. You can use the options at the drop-down list to sort or select items. Click the down-pointing arrow at the right of the *ReferencePhone* column heading and then click *Sort Descending*. (The rows are now sorted in descending order by telephone number.)

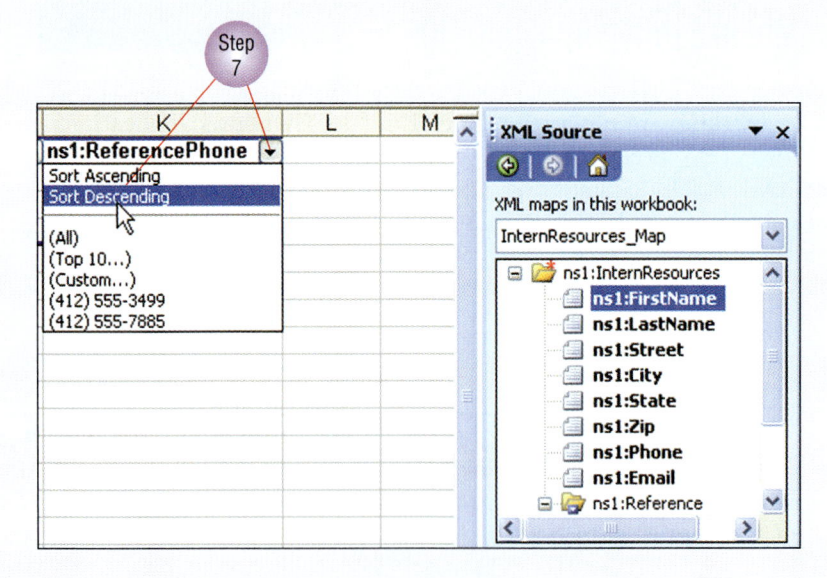

8. Print the worksheet in landscape orientation by completing the following steps:
   a. Click File and then Page Setup.
   b. At the Page Setup dialog box make sure the Page tab is selected.
   c. Click the *Landscape* option.
   d. Click the Print button.
   e. At the Print dialog box, click OK.
9. Save the worksheet by completing the following steps:
   a. Click the Save button on the Standard toolbar.

b. At the Save As dialog box, navigate to the WordChapter08E folder on your disk.
c. Click in the *File name* text box and then type **Excelewc8x02**.
d. Press Enter.
10. Click File and then Close to close the worksheet.
11. Click File and then Exit to exit Excel.

FIGURE 8.8 Exercise 2

	A	B	C	D	E	F	G	H
1	ns1:FirstName	ns1:LastName	ns1:Street	ns1:City	ns1:State	ns1:Zip	ns1:Phone	ns1:Email
2	Susan	Little	4812 Southport Avenue	Long Beach	CA	94011	(212) 555-3402	slittle@emc
3	Susan	Little	4812 Southport Avenue	Long Beach	CA	94011	(212) 555-3402	slittle@emc
4	*							
5								
6								

Using Schemas as Templates

In Exercise 1, you used an XML schema to convert an already existing document into an XML document in order to facilitate loading the data from the letter into other applications. Another way to take advantage of the WordML feature is to create a fill-in document based on an XML schema and use this document to create XML files. For example, suppose that you are responsible for creating XML files that will be loaded into a class scheduling application. You start with an XML schema that defines the data elements you need to enter into the XML registration file and then build a Word fill-in template to actually enter the data, which is in turn saved into a standard XML format.

Validating a Schema

In Exercise 3, you will create a fill-in form in Word and map items in the form to elements in the ClassRegistration.xsd schema. After adding the schema to the Schema library and then attaching it to your document, you will apply the ClassReg root element to the document. When you first apply the root element, the XML Structure task pane will display as shown in Figure 8.9. The icon containing a question mark on a yellow background that displays in the *Elements in the document* list box is part of the schema validation capability of Word 2003. XML allows schemas to specify requirements and restrictions for XML documents constructed with that schema. The ClassRegistration.xsd schema requires that the document contains each of the five sub elements listed in the *Choose an element to apply to your current selection* list box.

Requiring an XML document to conform to the restrictions and requirements specified in an XML schema is referred to as ***validation***. Validation compares the structure of the document to the structure of a schema. By default, Word will only save XML documents that are validated by the schema to which the document is attached. When you apply the sub elements to the document in Exercise 3, the icons containing a question mark will disappear from the task pane.

FIGURE

8.9 XML Structure Task Pane with Icon Displayed for Validation

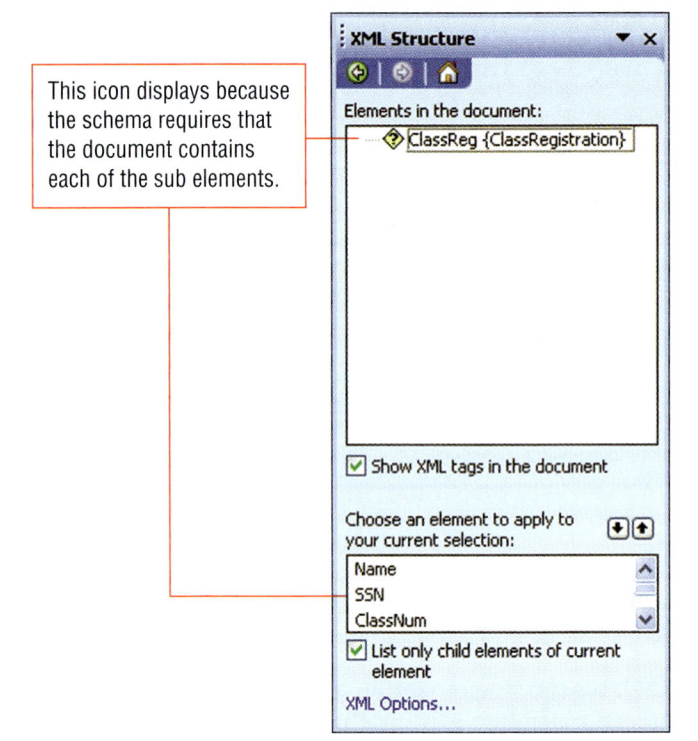

This icon displays because the schema requires that the document contains each of the sub elements.

exercise 3

ATTACHING AND VALIDATING A SCHEMA

1. At a blank Word screen, click File and then New.
2. At the New Document task pane, click the <u>XML document</u> hyperlink.
3. At the clear document screen with the XML Structure task pane displayed, attach an XML template to the blank document by completing the following steps:
   a. Click the <u>Templates and Add-Ins</u> hyperlink located in the XML Structure task pane.
   b. At the Templates and Add-ins dialog box, click the Schema Library button.
   c. At the Schema Library dialog box, click the Add Schema button.
   d. At the Add Schema dialog box, navigate to the WordChapter08E folder on your disk and then double-click *ClassRegistration.xsd*.
   e. At the Schema Settings dialog box, type **ClassReg** in the *URI* text box.
   f. Press the Tab key to move the insertion point to the *Alias* text box, type **ClassRegistration**, and then click OK.

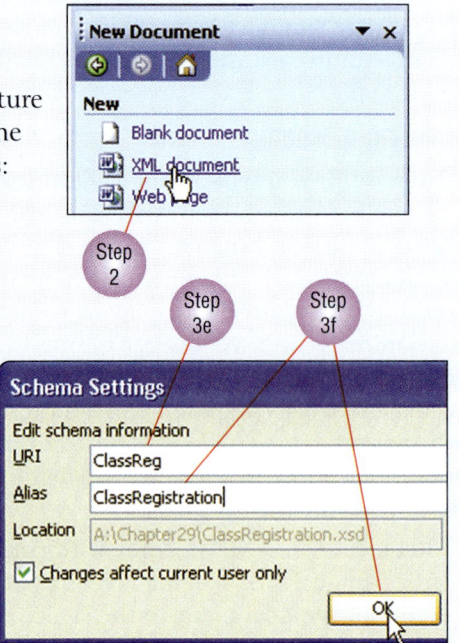

g. Click OK to close the Schema Library dialog box.
h. At the Templates and Add-ins dialog box, click the check box immediately left of *ClassRegistration* in the list box to insert a check mark.
i. Make sure a check mark appears in the *Validate document against attached schemas* option.
j. Click OK.
4. At the document window, press Ctrl + Alt + 1 to set the paragraph style to Heading 1.
5. Type **Class Registration Form** and then press the Enter key.
6. Apply the root element schema using a shortcut menu by completing the following steps:
    a. Right-click in the document window, point to Apply XML Element, and then click ClassReg.
    b. At the message asking how the element should be applied, click the Apply to Entire Document button. (This message displays because ClassReg is the root element.)
7. Notice the icon containing a question mark that appears in the *Elements in the document* list box in the XML Structure task pane. This icon displays because the five sub elements have not been applied to the document. Apply these sub elements by completing the following steps:
    a. Press the Right Arrow key on the keyboard to move the insertion point so that it is positioned immediately left of the end ClassReg tab.
    b. Click *Name* in the *Choose an element to apply to your current selection*.
    c. Press the Right Arrow key (to move the insertion to the right of the *Name* tag), and then press the Enter key.
    d. Click *SSN* in the list box, press the Right Arrow key, and then press the Enter key.
    e. Click *ClassNum* in the list box, press the Right Arrow key, and then press the Enter key.
    f. Click *Semester* in the list box, press the Right Arrow key, and then press the Enter key.
    g. Click *Phone* in the list box, press the Right Arrow key, and then press the Enter key. (Your document should now appear as shown in Figure 8.10.)
8. Save the document by completing the following steps:
    a. Click the Save button on the Standard toolbar.
    b. At the Save As dialog box, type **ClassForm** in the *File name* text box.
    c. Make sure the *Save as type* option is set at *XML Document (*.xml)* and then click the Save button.
9. Close **ClassForm.xml**.

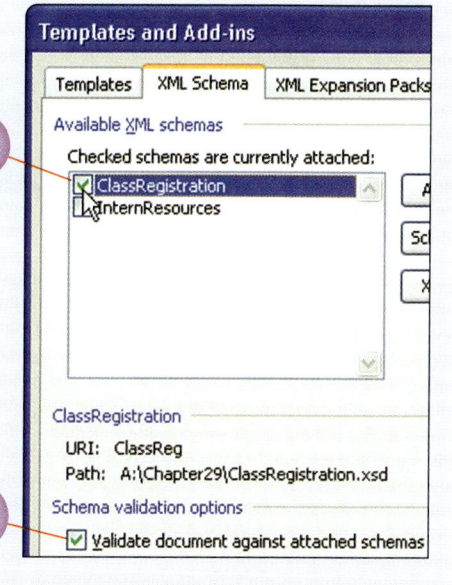

FIGURE 8.10 Exercise 3

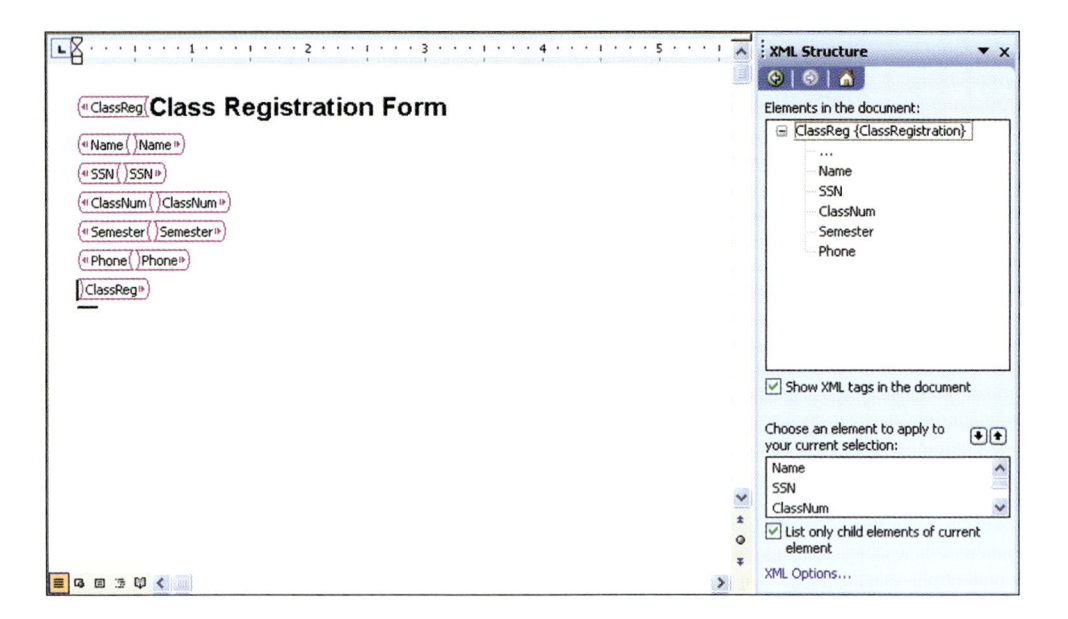

[Screenshot of Class Registration Form in Word with XML Structure task pane showing ClassReg {ClassRegistration} with child elements Name, SSN, ClassNum, Semester, Phone]

Enforcing Validation Rules

XML schema files define the elements that are included within an XML data file. The schema serves as a guide or a template for organizing information into a specific XML document format. In addition to simply listing the possible elements that an XML data file may contain, the schema can actually enforce rules that define more specifically what type of information you should enter into a given XML element. XML supports three general types of data validation.

- **Required Elements:** Schema files can require that some or all of the elements in the schema be included in any data file created with that schema. For example, an XML data entry about a book might require the name of the author and publisher in addition to the title.

- **Define Entry:** You can specify that the data entered into a given element be a whole number, a decimal number, a date, or an Internet URL.

- **Restrict Values:** Schema files can specify in detail the sort of data that is valid for an element. For example, you could restrict the entry to a decimal number between 1 and 25. You can even limit the entry of text to a list of specific phrases such as *Textbook, Reference,* or *Fiction*. If you enter anything other than those items, the element is not valid according to the schema.

Displaying XML Options

If a validation error occurs in a document, a question mark icon displays immediately left of the XML element in the XML Structure task pane. Position the mouse pointer on the question mark icon, and a message displays providing information about the validation error. You can provide more information about the error by selecting an option at the XML Options dialog box shown in Figure 8.11. Display this dialog box by clicking the XML Options hyperlink located toward the bottom of the XML Structure task pane.

To display more information about the validation error, insert a check mark in the *Show advanced XML error messages* check box at the XML Options dialog box. With this option active, a more detailed validation error message will display when you position the mouse pointer on a question mark icon.

FIGURE 8.11 XML Options Dialog Box

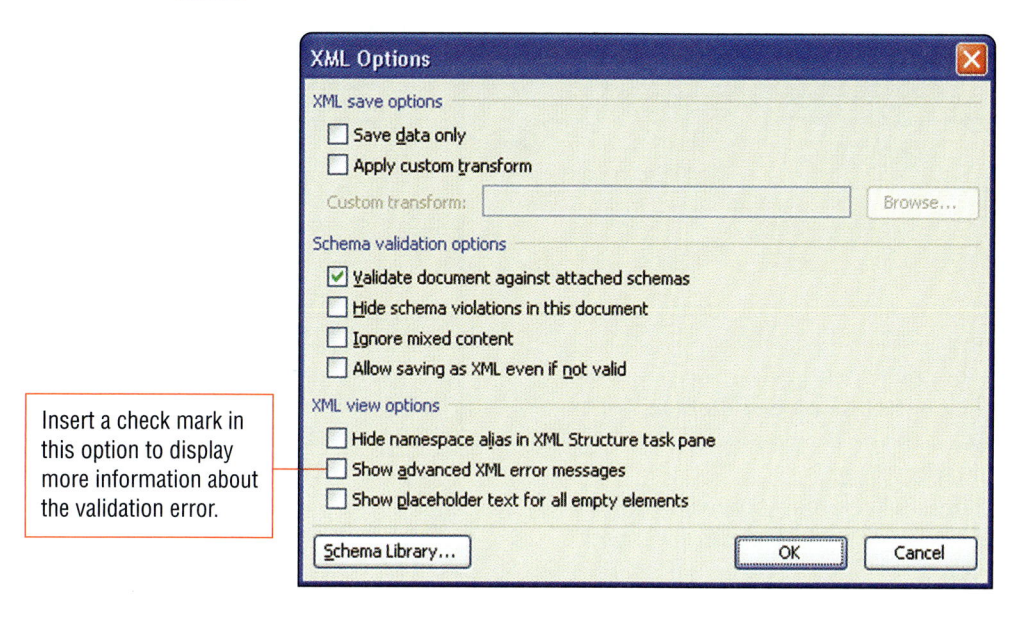

Insert a check mark in this option to display more information about the validation error.

In the following exercise you will attach a schema to validate a simple XML document you are creating that is designed to be a Reading List for a college course. The schema file you will apply to the document will enforce various rules about the content of the XML elements and the document as a whole.

exercise 4 — ENFORCING VALIDATION RULES

1. At a blank document window, click File and then New.
2. Click the XML document hyperlink in the *New* section of the New Document task pane.
3. At the clear document screen with the XML Structure task pane displayed, attach an XML template to the blank document by completing the following steps:
   a. Click the Templates and Add-Ins hyperlink in the XML Structure task pane.
   b. At the Templates and Add-ins dialog box, click the Schema Library button.
   c. At the Schema Library dialog box, click the Add Schema button.
   d. At the Add Schema dialog box, navigate to the WordChapter08E folder on your disk and then double-click ***Books.xsd***.

e. At the Schema Settings dialog box, type **ReadList** in the *URI* text box.
f. Press the Tab key, type **ReadingList** in the *Alias* text box, and then click OK.

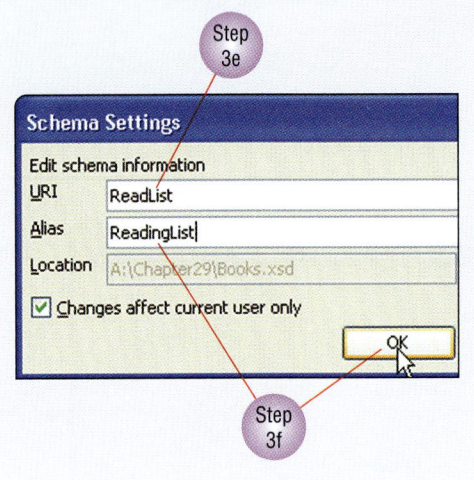

g. Click OK to close the Schema Library dialog box.
h. At the Templates and Add-ins dialog box, click the check box immediately left of *ReadingList* in the list box to insert a check mark.
i. Make sure a check mark appears in the *Validate document against attached schemas* check box.
j. Click OK.

4. At the document window, begin to enter the XML elements and read about validation errors by completing the following steps:
   a. Right-click in the document window, point to Apply XML Element, and then click Booklist.
   b. Press Enter to start a new line between the tags.
   c. Click *Book* in the *Choose an element to apply to your current selection* section of the XML Structure task pane. (Notice the icon containing a question mark on a yellow background that displays immediately left of *Book* in the *Elements in the document* section of the XML Structure task pane.)
   d. Position the mouse pointer on the question mark icon and Word displays the message *This must contain other elements*. Word displays this message because the schema requires that elements within Book are to be included in a valid document.
   e. Show more detail about the schema error message by clicking the XML Options hyperlink located towards the bottom of the task pane.
   f. At the XML Options dialog box, click the *Show advanced XML error messages* check box to insert a check mark and then click OK.
   g. Position the mouse pointer on the question mark icon and the message now displays as *Element 'Book' cannot be empty according to the DTD/Schema*. (This is a more detailed explanation of the validation error.)

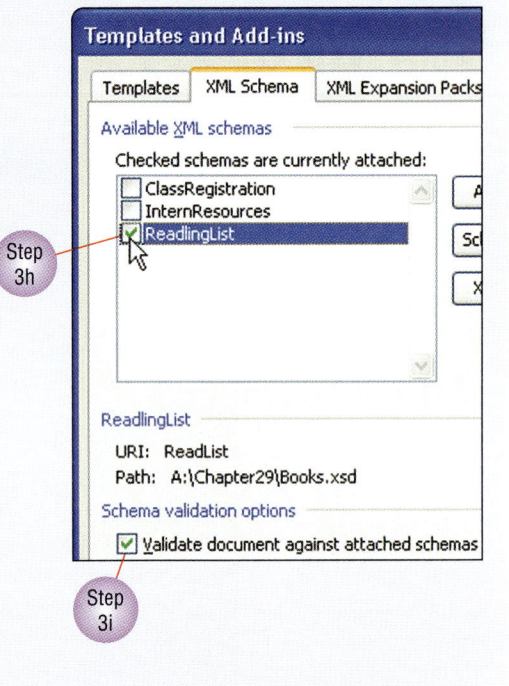

E312 Chapter Eight

h. Press the Enter key twice and then press the Up Arrow key to position the insertion point on a blank line between the Book tags. This element requires all sub elements to be included in the document. When you have inserted all sub elements in the document, the icon will disappear.)

5. Insert the Title sub element by completing the following steps:
   a. Click *Title* in the *Choose an element to apply to your current selection* section of the XML Structure task pane.
   b. Type **Understanding and Using XML**.
   c. Press the End key, and then press the Enter key.

6. Insert the Author sub element by completing the following steps:
   a. Click *Author* in the *Choose an element to apply to your current selection* section of the task pane.
   b. Type **Arnold Driver**.
   c. Press the End key, and then press the Enter key.

7. Insert the Publisher sub element by completing the following steps:
   a. Click *Publisher* in the *Choose an element to apply to your current selection* section of the task pane.
   b. Type **Advanced Technology Publishing**.
   c. Press the End key, and then the Enter key.

8. Insert the Year sub element by completing the following steps:
   a. Click *Year* in the *Choose an element to apply to your current selection* section of the task pane. (An icon appears next to *Year*.)
   b. Type **99**. The icon remains because the data type must be a valid four-digit number. Position the mouse pointer on the icon and the validation error message displays.
   c. Delete *99* and then type **1999**.
   d. Press the End key and then press the Enter key. (The icon disappears because the restriction has been satisfied.)

9. Insert the Current Price sub element by completing the following steps:
   a. Click *CurrentPrice* in the *Choose an element to apply to your current selection* section of the task pane. (An icon appears next to *CurrentPrice*.)
   b. Type **29.95**. The icon remains because the element requires a restriction that the value must be less than 25. Position the mouse pointer on the icon preceding *CurrentPrice* and read the validation error message.
   c. Delete *29.95,* and then type **24.95**. (Notice that the icon disappears.)
   d. Press the End key, and then press the Enter key.

10. Insert the Category sub element by completing the following steps:
    a. Click *Category* in the *Choose an element to apply to your current selection* section of the task pane.
    b. Position the mouse pointer on the icon left of *Category* and a message displays indicating that an enumeration violation occurred. (The element contains an enumeration restriction limiting an entry to *Textbook*, *Reference*, or *Fiction*.)
    c. Type **textbook**. (The icon is not removed because the enumeration is case sensitive.)
    d. Change *textbook* to *Textbook*. (Notice that the icon disappears. Your document should look like the document shown in Figure 8.12.)

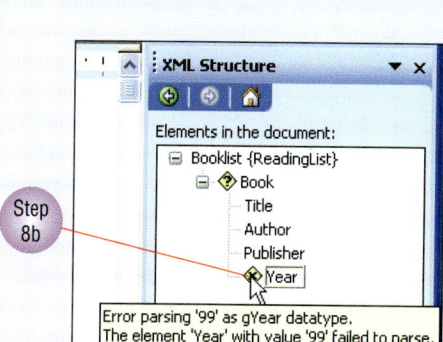

11. The document no longer contains any validation icons. This means that the document you created has been validated by the attached schema. Save the document by completing the following steps:
    a. Click the Save button on the Standard toolbar.
    b. At the Save As dialog box, type **BookInfo** in the *File name* text box.
    c. Insert a check mark in the *Save data only* check box.
    d. Click the Save button.
    e. At the message asking you to confirm that you wish to save the contents of the document as XML, click the Continue button.
12. Print the document. (Only the data prints since you saved only the data in the document.)
13. Close the XML Structure task pane, and then close the document.

FIGURE 8.12 Exercise 4

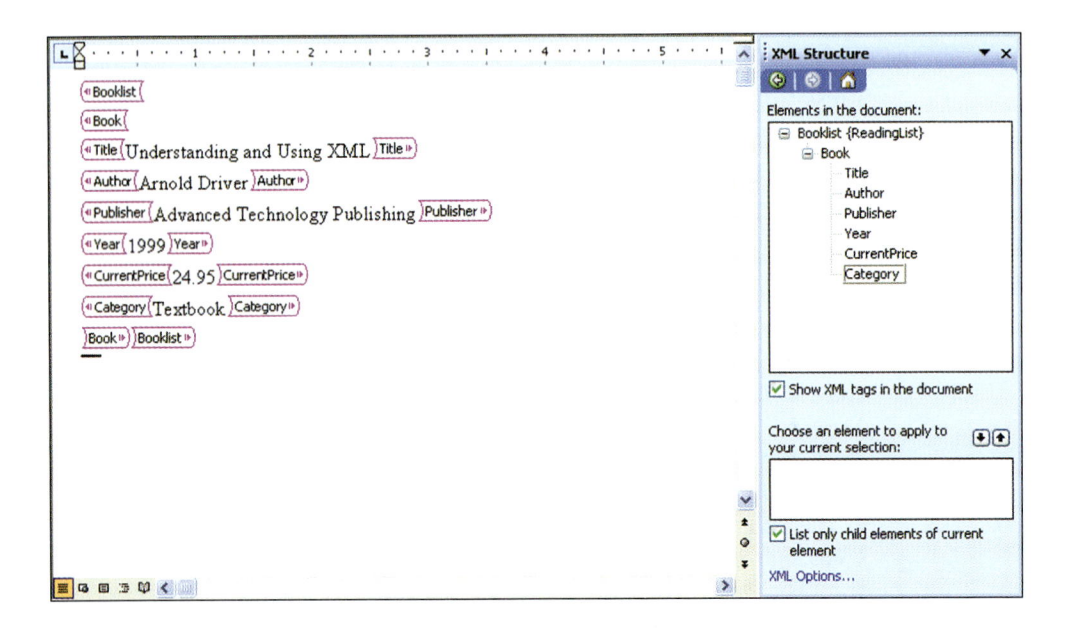

By default Word will not allow you to save an invalid XML document. In some situations, you may want to save an XML document that contains schema violations. To do this, click the XML Options hyperlink located toward the bottom of the XML Structure task pane. At the XML Options dialog box, insert a check mark in the *Allow saving as XML even if not valid* check box, and then click OK.

Enhancing the Schema

Figure 8.10 shows the XML document you created in Exercise 3 with the standard XML tag names, as specified by the schema. These tags indicate the location in the document where data entry should be made. Word 2003 allows you to replace this raw XML display with one that looks more like a typical Word fill-in document while still maintaining the ability to save the data as XML. This is accomplished by adding placeholder text to the elements.

To enhance the display of tags, right-click a tag, and then click Attributes at the shortcut menu. At the Attributes dialog box shown, click in the *Placeholder text* box, type the desired text, and then click OK. The text that you type in the *Placeholder text* box is inserted between the start and ending tags.

exercise 5
ENHANCING A SCHEMA

1. Open **ClassForm.xml**. (You created this file in Exercise 3.)
2. Display the XML Structure task pane.
3. Enhance the schema so the document appears as shown in Figure 8.13 by completing the following steps:
    a. Right-click *Name* in the *Elements in the document* list box in the XML Structure task pane, and then click Attributes at the shortcut menu. 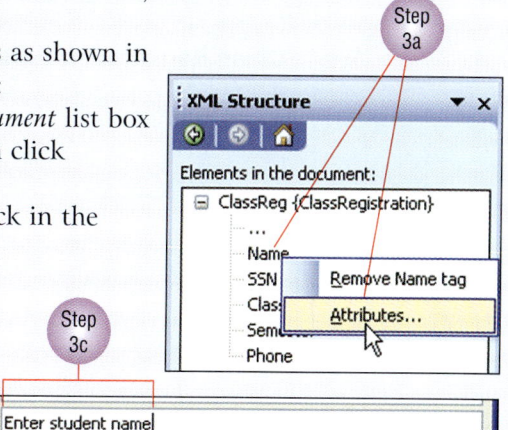
    b. At the Attributes for Name dialog box, click in the *Placeholder text* box.
    c. Type **Enter student name** and then press Enter. 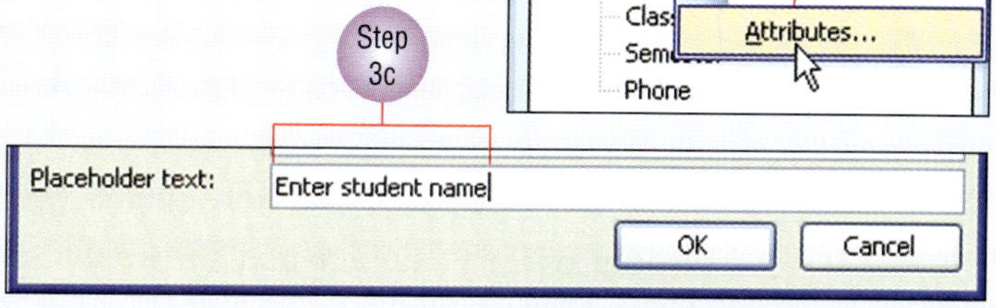
    d. Toggle off the display of the XML icons and display the text you typed in the Attributes for Name dialog box by removing the check mark from the *Show XML tags in the document* check box. To do this, click the check box, in the XML Structure task pane. 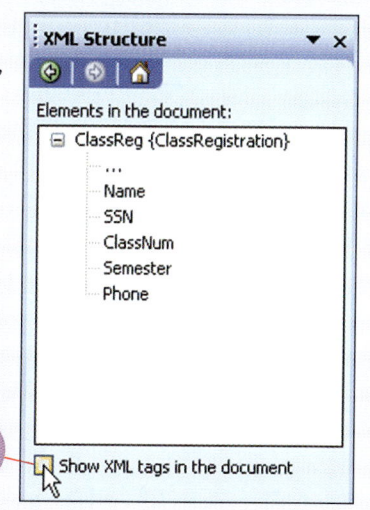
    e. Right-click *SSN* in the *Elements in the document* list box and then click Attributes.
    f. At the Attributes for SSN dialog box, click in the *Placeholder text* box type **Enter student Social Security Number**, and then press Enter.
    g. Right-click *ClassNum* in the *Elements in the document* list box, and then click Attributes.
    h. At the Attributes for ClassNum dialog box, click in the *Placeholder text* box, type **Enter class number**, and then press Enter.
    i. Right-click *Semester* in the *Elements in the document* list box, and then click Attributes.
    j. At the Attributes for Semester dialog box, click in the *Placeholder text* box, type **Enter semester**, and then press Enter.
    k. Right-click *Phone* in the *Elements in the document* list box, and then click Attributes.
    l. At the Attributes for Phone dialog box, click in the *Placeholder text* box, type **Enter student telephone number**, and then press Enter. (Your document should look like the document in Figure 8.13.)
4. Turn off the display of the XML Structure task pane.
5. Save the document by completing the following steps:
    a. Click File and then Save As.

b. At the Save As dialog box, type **ewc8x05** in the *File name* text box.
   c. Make sure the *Save as type* option is set at *XML Document (*.xml)* and then click the Save button.
6. Print and then close **ewc8x05.xml**.

FIGURE 8.13 Exercise 5

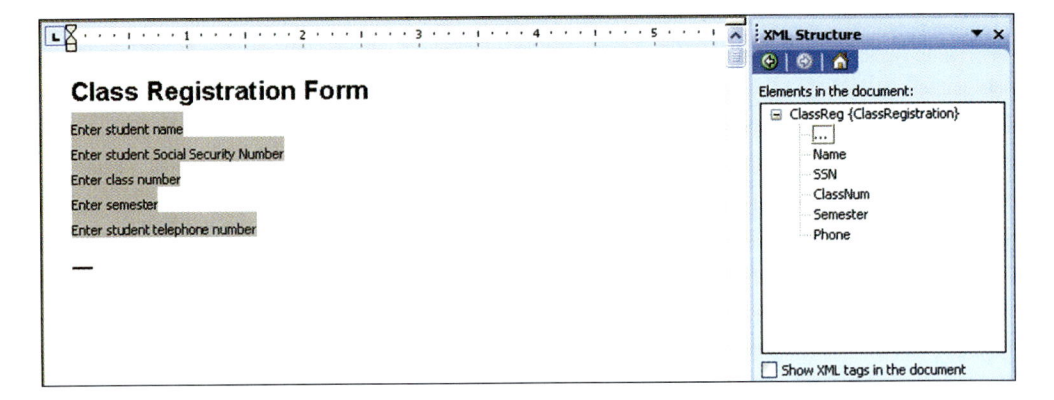

Using XML to Create Fill-In Documents

Adding the placeholder text to the document schema allows you to hide the actual XML elements while still showing where in the document you need to enter text in order to fill in the XML document with data. You can use the Document Protect feature in Word 2003 to allow the XML document to function like a Word fill-in document with data fields. Document Protection used in conjunction with placeholder text eliminates the possibility of accidentally making typing mistakes that would damage the XML elements in the document. Once the Document Protection is turned on, the only editing you can do is to replace the placeholder text with data that you want to save in the XML format. All of the XML elements in the document are hidden and protected from editing.

By creating an XML fill-in document, you are able to take advantage of XML without having to deal directly with the complexities of XML. This means that once created, a user with no knowledge of XML can use it to create XML files quickly and accurately.

exercise 6 — PROTECTING AN XML DOCUMENT

1. Open **ewc8x05.xml**.
2. Protect the document by completing the following steps:
   a. Display the Protect Document task pane by clicking Tools and then Protect Document.
   b. Click *Enter student name* in the document. (This changes the highlight to a darker gray.)

c. In the Protect Document task pane, click the *Allow only this type of editing in the document* check box in the *Editing restrictions* section. (This inserts a check mark in the check box.)
d. Click the *Everyone* check box in the *Exceptions (optional)* section.
e. In the document, click *Enter student Social Security Number,* and then click the *Everyone* check box in the *Exceptions (optional)* section of the task pane.
f. In the document, click *Enter class number,* and then click the *Everyone* check box in the task pane.
g. In the document, click *Enter semester,* and then click the *Everyone* check box in the task pane.
h. In the document, click *Enter student telephone number,* and then click the *Everyone* check box in the task pane.
i. Click the Yes, Start Enforcing Protection button located toward the bottom of the task pane. (You may need to scroll down the task pane to display this button.)
j. At the Start Enforcing Protection dialog box, click OK. (You are not adding a password to the document.)
3. Turn off the display of the task pane.
4. Save the fill-in document as a WordML document by completing the following steps:
    a. Click File and then Save As.
    b. At the Save As dialog box, type **ClassRegForm** in the *File name* text box.
    c. Change the *Save as type* option to *Word Document (*.doc)*.
    d. Click the Save button.
5. Close **ClassRegForm.doc**.

Generating XML Data with a Form

The ClassRegForm.doc document you created can be used as a template. However, unlike ordinary Word templates, which produce a Word document when they are filled in, ClassRegForm.doc can be used to produce an XML file.

exercise 7

GENERATING XML DATA WITH A FORM

1. Open **ClassRegForm.doc**.
2. Display the Protect Document task pane by completing the following steps:
    a. Click View and then Task Pane.
    b. Click the Other Task Panes button in the upper-right corner of the task pane, and then click *Protect Document* at the drop-down list.

3. Enter data in the document by completing the following steps:
   a. Click *Enter student name,* and then type **Louis Richards**.
   b. In the Protect Document task pane, click the Find Next Region I Can Edit button. (This highlights *Enter student Social Security Number* in the document.)

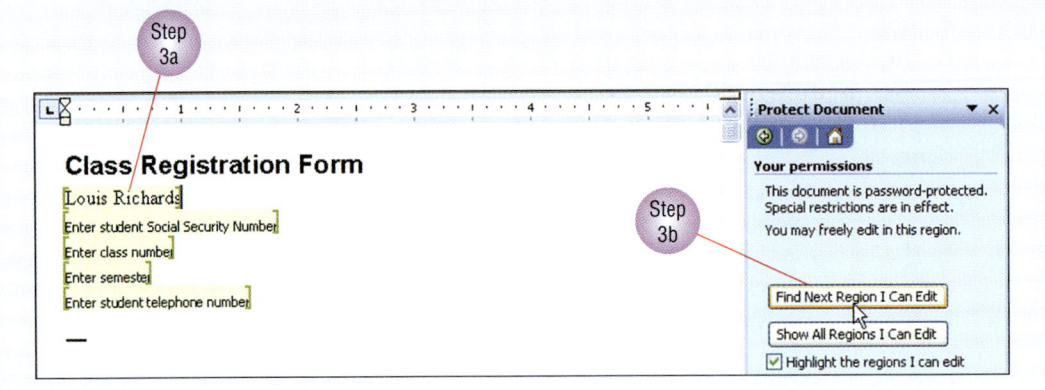

   c. Type **203-99-0000**.
   d. Click the Find Next Region I Can Edit button, and then type **6701B**.
   e. Click the Find Next Region I Can Edit button, and then type **Fall 2005**.
   f. Click the Find Next Region I Can Edit button, and then type **(010) 555-3455**.
4. Save the entries as an XML file by completing the following steps:
   a. Click File and then Save As.
   b. Type **Richards** in the *File name* text box.
   c. Change the *Save as type* option to *XML Document (*.xml)*.
   d. Click the *Save data only* check box to insert a check mark.
   e. Click the Save button.

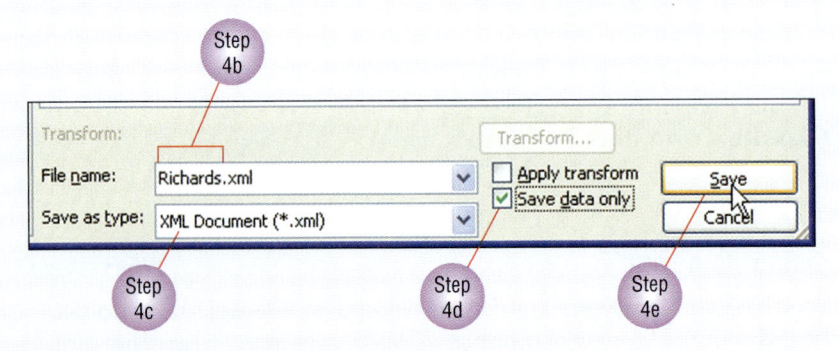

   f. At the message that displays, click the Continue button.
5. Close the **Richards.xml** file.
6. Open the **Richards.xml** file by completing the following steps:
   a. Click the Open button on the Standard toolbar.
   b. At the Open dialog box, change the *Files of type* option to *All Files (*.*)*.
   c. Navigate to the WordChapter08E folder on your disk and then double-click **Richards.xml** in the Open dialog box list box. (Notice the data that is inserted between the XML codes.)
7. Print the **Richards.xml** file. (Only the data prints.)
8. Close the task pane and then close the file.

Transforming XML with Style Sheets

An XML document consists of two basic elements—XML element tags and data inserted into those tags. Unlike Word, XML documents do not include information about how the information should be displayed and formatted. Instead XML uses XML style sheet files (.xsl extensions) to provide a method of using HTML formatting with XML data.

Word 2003 allows you to use style sheets in several different ways to automatically transform the data in an XML document into an HTML style Web page. Some of the methods include:

- **Browse with Style:** After you open an XML document, you can use the XML Document task pane to select an XML style sheet (XSL document) to alter the way the XML data appears in the document window.
- **Save as HTML:** When saving an XML document, you can select a style sheet. The resulting file is a fully-rendered HTML version, which combines the styles with the XML data.
- **Associate Style Sheets with Schemas:** In the schema library you can define a solution. A solution associates one or more style sheets with a schema file. When you load a document that uses a schema file it automatically formats its display.

All of these operations assume that one or more properly prepared XML style sheets exists for the XML document with which you are working. Creation of XML style sheets is a subject that goes beyond the scope of this chapter. In order to see how these features work, you will use two style sheets prepared in advance to work with the ClassRegistration.xsd schema.

exercise 8

DISPLAYING XML WITH A STYLESHEET

1. Open **Richards.xml**.
2. Apply the **SimpleRegForm.xsl** style sheet to the document by completing the following steps:
   a. In the XML Document task pane, click the *Browse* option in the list box.
   b. Navigate to the WordChapter08E folder on your disk and then double-click **SimpleRegForm.xsl**. (After applying the style sheet, your document should appear as shown in Figure 8.14.)
3. Click the Print button to print the document with the **SimpleRegForm.xsl** style sheet applied.
4. Apply the **FancyRegForm.xsl** style sheet by completing the following steps:
   a. Click the Browse option in the XML Document task pane.
   b. Navigate to the WordChapter08E folder on your disk and then double-click **FancyRegForm.xsl**. (After applying the style sheet, your document should appear as shown in Figure 8.15.)

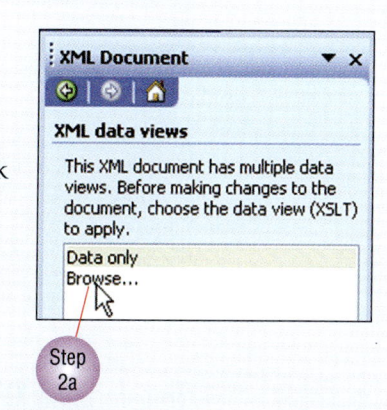

5. Click the Print button to print the document with the **FancyRegForm.xsl** style sheet applied.
6. Click **SimpleRegForm.xsl** in the XML Document task pane list box. (You can easily switch between style sheets by clicking the desired file name in the XML Document task pane.)
7. Close the task pane and then close **Richards.xml**.

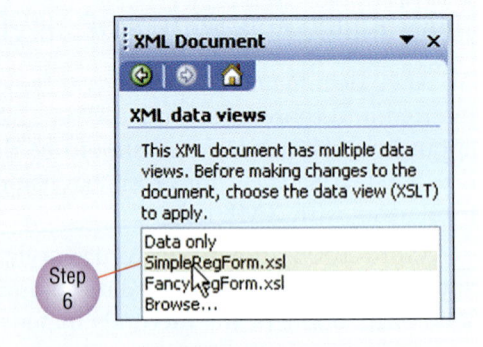

F I G U R E

8.14 *Exercise 8: Richards.xml File with SimpleRegForm.xsl Style Sheet Applied*

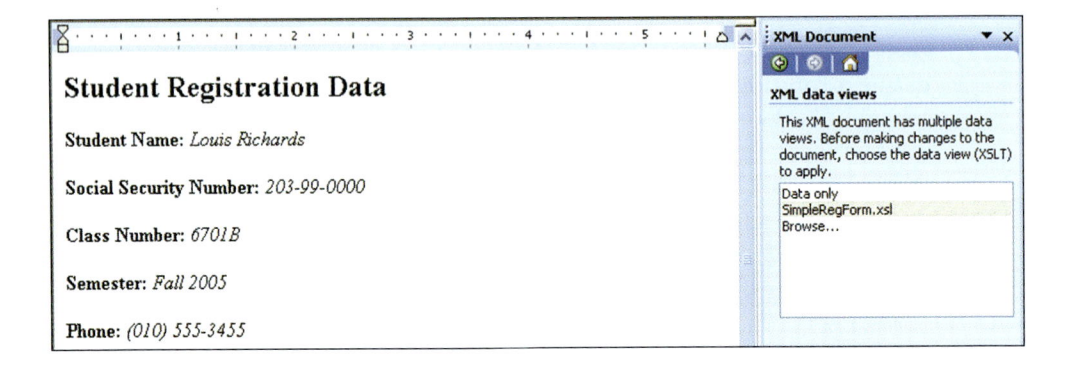

F I G U R E

8.15 *Exercise 8: Richards.xml File with FancyRegForm.xsl Style Sheet Applied*

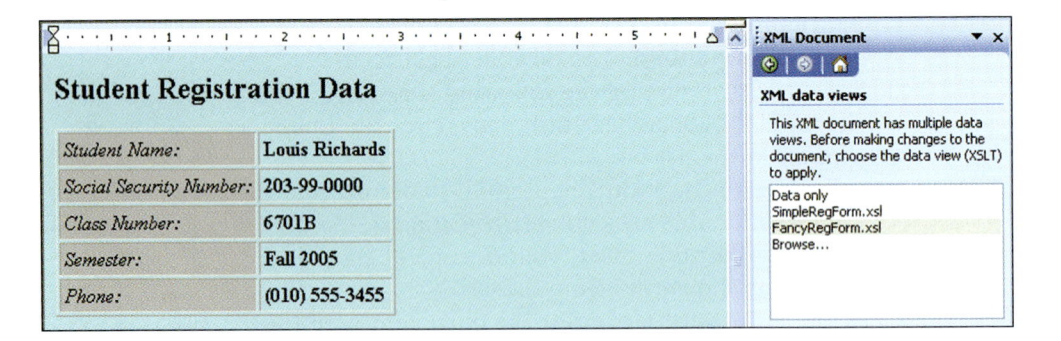

Transforming XML

Because XML and HTML are closely related, XML supports a process called **transformation**. Transformation is a process in which an XML document is converted to a standard Web HTML document using the XML style sheet as a formatting guide. Word has a similar feature that allows you to convert a Word document into an HTML file. The difference in this case is that the formatting information does not come from Word but from the XML style sheet.

In some cases, using an HTML representation of a document rather than the original XML file is simpler because the HTML file is a single file while XML often requires several related files, such as documents, schemas, and style sheets. For example, if you wanted to post an application on an internal company Web site you could convert it to HTML and add the HTML file to the Web site.

exercise 9 — TRANSFORMING XML BY SAVING WITH A STYLE SHEET

1. Open the **Miller.xml** document.
2. Save the document as an XML document by completing the following steps:
   a. Click File and then Save As.
   b. At the Save As dialog box, click the *Apply transform* check box to insert a check mark.
   c. Click the Transform button.
   d. At the Choose an XML Transformation dialog box, navigate to the WordChapter08E folder on your disk and then double-click *FancyRegForm.xsl*.
   e. At the Save As dialog box the name of the style sheet displays to the right of the *Transform* option. Select the current text in the *File name* text box and then type **MillerRegForm**.
   f. Click the Save button.
   g. At the message that displays, click the Continue button.
3. Close **MillerRegForm.xml**.

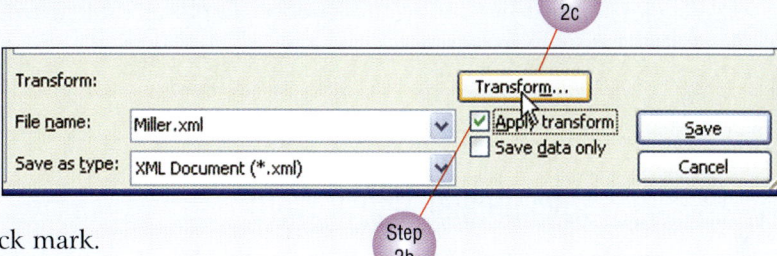

The file you saved in Exercise 9 is actually an HTML file, which can be displayed in any HTML-enabled application such as Internet Explorer. In Exercise 10, you will open the file you saved in Exercise 9 in Internet Explorer. Before opening the file in Internet Explorer, you will need to change the file extension from .xml to .htm. This is because Internet Explorer determines its display mode based on the extension of the file you are opening.

exercise 10 — OPENING A FILE IN INTERNET EXPLORER

(Note: Before completing this exercise, check with your instructor to determine if Internet Explorer is available for you to use.)

1. Open Internet Explorer by displaying the Windows desktop and then double-clicking the Internet Explorer icon. (These steps may vary.)
2. With Internet Explorer open, rename the **MillerRegForm.xml** file and then open the file by completing the following steps:

a. Click File and then Open.
  b. Click the Browse button in the Open dialog box.
  c. At the Microsoft Internet Explorer dialog box, navigate to the WordChapter08E folder on your disk.
  d. Change the *Files of type* option to *All Files*.
  e. Right-click **MillerRegForm.xml** in the dialog box list box, and then click Rename at the shortcut menu.
  f. Delete the .xml extension in the file name type **.htm**, and then press Enter.
  g. At the message telling you that changing a file name extension may make the file unusable and asking if you are sure you want to change it, click the Yes button.
  h. Double-click **MillerRegForm.htm** in the list box.
  i. At the Open dialog box, click OK.
3. Click the Print button on the Internet Explorer toolbar to print the file.
4. Close Internet Explorer.

Streamlining XML in Word

Microsoft Office applications like Word and Excel can store data, formatting, and other information in a single document or spreadsheet file. On the other hand, XML often requires the use of multiple files (documents, schemas, and style sheets) to get the desired result. In order to help streamline the process of relating documents, schemas, and style sheets, the Schema library contains a feature called a ***solution***, which allows you to associate one or more style sheets with a given schema. You can also designate one of the style sheets as the default style for that schema. A solution simplifies some XML operations because Word can then automatically apply the default style sheet to the XML document when the schema is selected.

exercise 11

ASSOCIATING STYLE SHEETS WITH SCHEMA

1. At a blank Word screen, click File and then New.
2. Click the XML document hyperlink in the New Document task pane.
3. Click the Templates and Add-Ins hyperlink in the XML Structure task pane.
4. At the Templates and Add-ins dialog box, click the Schema Library button.
5. At the Schema Library dialog box, click *ClassRegistration* in the *Select a schema* list box.

6. Click the Add Solution button.
7. At the Add Solution dialog box, navigate to the WordChapter08E folder on your disk and then double-click *SimpleRegForm.xsl*.
8. At the Solution Settings dialog box, type **SimpleForm** in the *Alias* text box, and then click OK. (The **SimpleRegForm.xsl** style sheet is now associated with the ClassRegistration.xsd schema.)
9. Associate another schema with a style sheet completing the following steps:
   a. Click the Add Solution button.
   b. At the Add Solution dialog box, navigate to the WordChapter08E folder on your disk and then double-click *FancyRegForm.xsl*.
   c. At the Solution Settings dialog box, type **FancyForm** in the *Alias* text box, and then click OK.
10. Click the down-pointing arrow at the right of the *Default solution* option box, and then click *SimpleForm* at the drop-down list. (This sets the default style sheet when more than one style sheet is associated with a schema.)
11. Click OK to close the Schema Library dialog box.
12. Click OK to close the Templates and Add-ins dialog box.
13. Open the **Richards.xml** file (located in the WordChapter08E folder on your disk). (Word automatically applies the Simple Form style sheet to the document because the document was created with the ClassRegistration.xsd schema. The ClassRegistration.xsd schema is associated with the SimpleForm style sheet in the schema library. Notice that the FancyForm style sheet is also listed as one of the available transformations. You can have as many different style sheets as you need associated with a given schema.)
14. Click the *FancyForm* option in the *XML data views* list box in the XML Document task pane.
15. Close the task pane and then close **Richards.xml**.

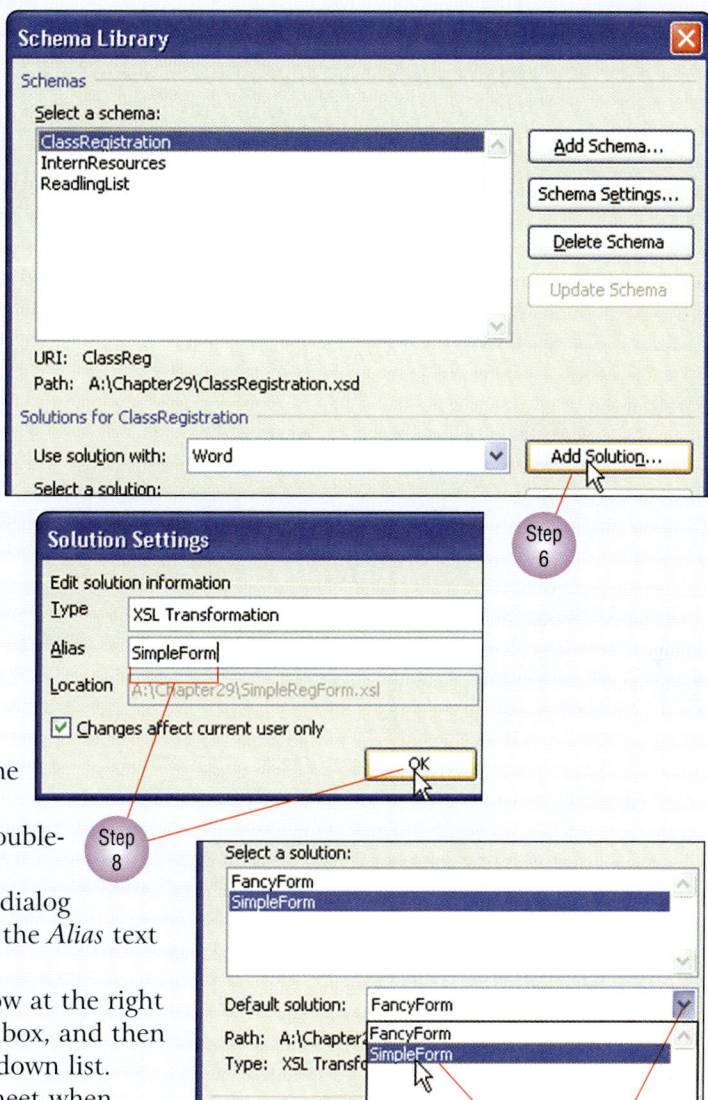

WORD

Using XML in Word 2003   E323

Deleting Schemas and Solutions

Manage schemas and solutions with options at the Schema Library dialog box shown in Figure 8.16. In previous exercises, you clicked the Add Schema button to add a schema to the Schema Library and attach the schema to a document, and you clicked the Add Solution button to associate a style sheet with a specific schema. Delete schemas and solutions at the Schema Library dialog box. To delete a schema, click the desired schema in the *Select a schema* list box, and then click the Delete Schema button. To delete a solution, click the specific schema in the *Select a schema* list box, click the specific solution in the *Select a solution* list box, and then click the Delete Solution button.

FIGURE

8.16 **Schema Library Dialog Box**

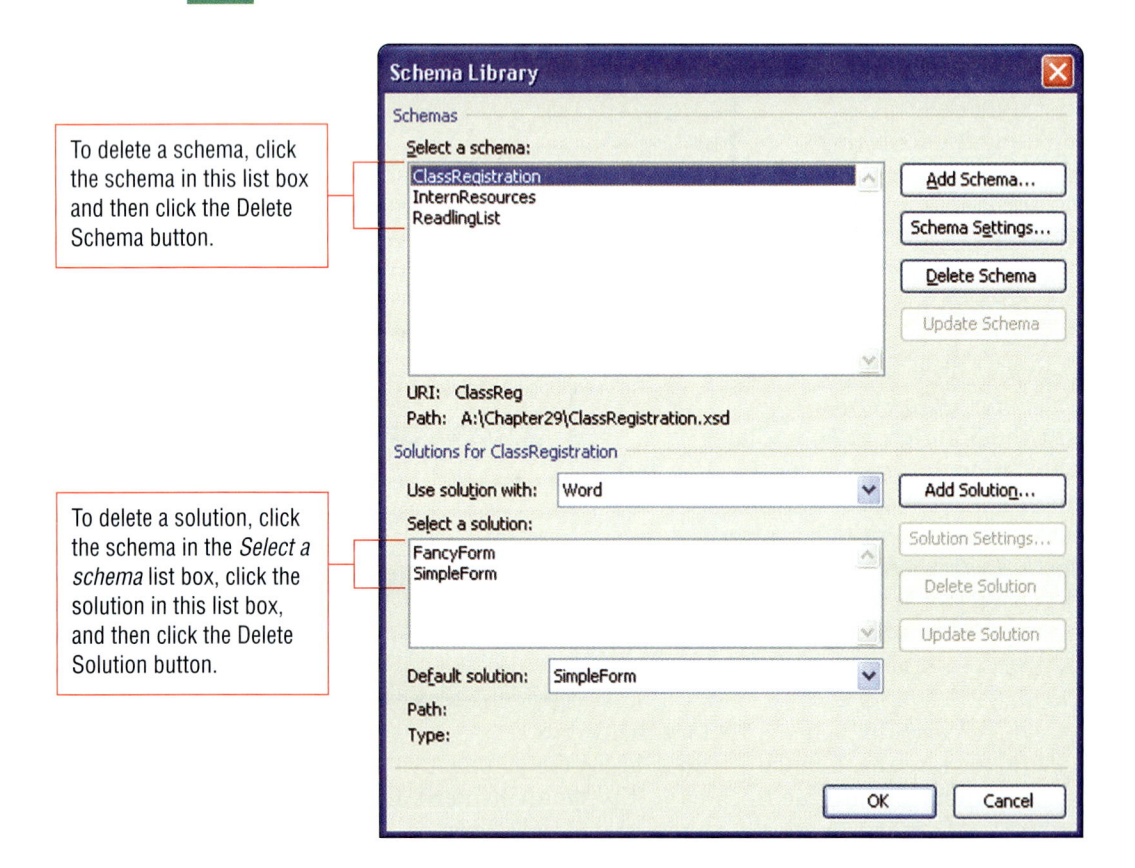

To delete a schema, click the schema in this list box and then click the Delete Schema button.

To delete a solution, click the schema in the *Select a schema* list box, click the solution in this list box, and then click the Delete Solution button.

exercise 12

DELETING A SCHEMA AND A SOLUTION

1. At a clear document screen click Tools and then Templates and Add-ins.
2. At the Templates and Add-ins dialog box, make sure the XML Schema tab is selected and then click the Schema Library button.
3. At the Schema Library dialog box, delete the InternResources.xsd schema by completing the following steps:

a. Click *InternResources* in the *Select a schema* list box.
b. Click the Delete Schema button.
c. At the message that displays, click the Yes button.
4. Delete a solution by completing the following steps:
   a. Click *ClassRegistration* in the *Select a schema* list box.
   b. Click *SimpleForm* in the *Select a solution* list box.
   c. Click the Delete Solution button.
   d. At the message that displays, click the Yes button.
5. Click OK to close the Schema Library dialog box.
6. Click OK to close the Templates and Add-ins dialog box.

CHAPTER summary

- Use the XML feature to identify specific data in files and then extract that data for use in other applications.
- To extract data from a document, attach a schema to the document and then map specific data within the document to specific data definitions in the schema.
- A schema enables non-XML applications to properly structure an XML data document and is usually designed by a programmer or database designer.
- Once a schema is designed, it can be attached to a document with options at the Schema Library dialog box.
- When an XML schema is attached to a document, the XML Structure task pane displays information that reflects the elements in the schema. Map these elements to data in the document. Mapping refers to the process in which data in the document is linked to items in the XML schema.
- The purpose of creating an XML document is to place information in a format that can be accessed by different applications.
- XML allows schemas to specify requirements and restrictions. Requiring an XML document to conform to the restrictions and requirements specified in the schema is referred to as validation.
- XML supports three general types of data validation—required elements, define entry, and restrict values.
- If a validation error occurs in a document, an icon displays immediately left of the XML element in the XML Structure task pane. Position the mouse pointer on the icon to display an error message.

- Enhance a schema with options at the Attributes dialog box. Display this dialog box by right-clicking an XML tag, and then clicking Attributes.
- An XML document consists of two basic elements—XML element tags and data inserted into those tags. XML uses XML style sheet files to provide a method of using HTML formatting with XML data.
- XML supports a process called transformation, which is a process in which an XML document is converted to a standard Web HTML document using an XML style sheet as a formatting guide.
- XML generally requires multiple files to get desired results. To streamline the process of relating documents, use a solution to associate one or more style sheets with a given schema.
- Add and delete schemas and solutions with options at the Schema Library dialog box.

COMMANDS review

Feature	Mouse/Keyboard
Display XML Structure task pane	Click File, New, XML document hyperlink or click Other Task Panes button, *XML Structure*
Display Templates and Add-ins dialog box	Click Templates and Add-Ins hyperlink at XML Structure task pane or click Tools, Templates and Add-Ins
Display XML Options dialog box	Click XML Options hyperlink at XML Structure task pane
Display Schema Library dialog box	Click Schema Library button at Templates and Add-ins dialog box

CONCEPTS check

Completion: On a blank sheet of paper, indicate the correct term, command, or symbol for each description.

1. The letters XML are an abbreviation for this.
2. Attaching a schema generally involves two steps—adding the schema to this and then attaching the schema to the document.
3. Display the XML Structure task pane by clicking this hyperlink at the New Document task pane.
4. Requiring an XML document to conform to restrictions and requirements specified in an XML schema is referred to as this.
5. XML supports three general types of data validation—required elements, define entry, and this.
6. This term refers to the process in which an XML document is converted to a standard Web HTML document using an XML style sheet as a formatting guide.
7. To streamline the process of relating documents, use this to associate one or more style sheets with a given schema.
8. Add and delete schemas and solutions with options at this dialog box.

SKILLS check

Assessment 1

1. Open the document named **Characters.doc** located in the WordChapter08E folder on your disk.
2. Attach the schema **FilmCharacters.xsd** to the document by completing the following steps:
    a. Display the XML Structure task pane. (*Hint: To do this, click View and then Task Pane. Click the Other Task Panes button, and then click XML Structure.*)
    b. Click the Templates and Add-Ins hyperlink in the XML Structure task pane.
    c. At the Templates and Add-ins dialog box, click the Add Schema button.
    d. At the Add Schema dialog box, navigate to the WordChapter08E folder on your disk and then double-click the **FilmCharacters.xsd** file name.
    e. At the Schema Settings dialog box, type **Roles** in the *URI* text box, type **Heroes and Villains** in the *Alias* text box, and then click OK.
    f. Click OK to close the Templates and Add-ins dialog box.
3. Map the following elements in the schema to specific date in the document:
    a. Apply the root element *FilmCharacters* to the entire document. (*Hint: Select the document and then click* **FilmCharacters** *in the* **Choose an element to apply to your current selection** *section of the XML Structure task pane.*)
    b. Select all of the information for the film character *Norman Bates* (from *Character: Norman Bates* through *Hair: Florence Bush*) and then apply the *Performance* element to the selected text.
    c. Select all of the information for the film character *Jack Torrance* and then apply the *Performance* element.
    d. Map each of the sub elements (*Character, Film, Year, Actor, Director,* and *Producer*) within the *Performance* element to the specific data in the document that relates to the sub element (e.g., select *Norman Bates* and then apply the *Character* element). Make sure you map all of the sub elements for both characters.
4. Save only the XML data by completing the following steps:
    a. Click File and then Save As.
    b. At the Save As dialog box, click the down-pointing arrow at the right of the *Save as type* list box and then click *XML Document (*.xml)* at the drop-down list.
    c. Click the *Save data only* check box to insert a check mark.
    d. Select the name that currently displays in the *File name* text box and then type **Roles**.
    e. Click the Save button.
    f. At the message asking if you to confirm that you wish to save the contents of the document as XML, click the Continue button.
5. Close the XML Structure task pane and then close the file.

Assessment 2

1. Open Excel 2003.
2. Open the **Roles.xml** file you created in Assessment 1 by completing these steps:
   a. Click the Open button on the Standard toolbar.
   b. At the open dialog box, navigate to the WordChapter08E folder on your disk.
   c. Change the *Files of type* option to *All Files (*.*)*.
   d. Double-click **Roles.xml**.
   e. At the Open XML dialog box, click OK.
   f. At the second message that displays, click OK.
3. Save the Excel worksheet and name it **ewc8sc02**.
4. Print the worksheet.
5. Close the worksheet and then exit Excel.

Assessment 3

1. Create a Word fill-in form based on the **NominationForm.xml** document. To begin, open **NominationForm.xml**.
2. Display the XML Structure task pane.
3. Enhance the schema by completing the following basic steps:
   a. Right-click *Character* in the *Elements in the document* list box in the XML Structure task pane and then click Attributes at the shortcut menu.
   b. At the Attributes for Character dialog box, click in the *Placeholder text* box, type **Name of character**, and then press Enter.
   c. Toggle off the display of the XML icons and display the text you typed in the Attributes for Name dialog box by removing the check mark from the *Show XML tags in the document* option.
   d. Complete steps similar to those in Steps 3a and 3b to add placeholder text for the remaining elements as shown below:

Film:	**Name of film**
Actor:	**Actor portraying character**
Director:	**Name of director**
HeroOrVillain:	**Type of character**

4. Display the Protect Document task pane.
5. Click the *Allow only this type of editing in the document* option to insert a check mark.
6. Click the placeholder for each XML element, and then click *Everyone* in the *Exceptions (optional)* list box.
7. Click the Yes, Start Enforcing Protection button (located toward the bottom of the Protect Document task pane). (Do not enter a password.)
8. Save the fill-in form as a WordML document by completing the following steps:
   a. Click File and then Save As.
   b. At the Save As dialog box, type **NominateForm** in the *File name* text box.
   c. Change the *Save as type* option to *Word Document (*.doc)*.
   d. Click the Save button.
9. Close **NominateForm.doc**.

Assessment 4

1. Open **NominateForm.doc**.
2. Display the Protect Document task pane.
3. Enter data in the document by completing the following steps:
   a. Click *Name of character* and then type **Rhett Butler**.
   b. In the Protect Document task pane, click the Find Next Region I Can Edit button. (This highlights *Name of film* in the document.)
   c. Type **Gone with the Wind**.
   d. Click the Find Next Region I Can Edit button and then type **Clark Gable**.
   e. Click the Find Next Region I Can Edit button and then type **Victor Fleming**.
   f. Click the Find Next Region I Can Edit button and then type **Hero**.
4. Save the entries as an XML file named **RhettButler.xml**. (Make sure you change the *Save as type* option to *XML Document (*.xml)* and that a check mark displays in the *Save data only* checkbox. At the message that displays when saving the document, click the Continue button.)
5. Close the **RhettButler.xml** file.
6. Open and then print the **RhettButler.xml** file. (Only the data prints.)
7. Close the task pane and then close the file.

Assessment 5

1. Display the New Document task pane and then click the XML document hyperlink.
2. Click the Templates and Add-Ins hyperlink.
3. At the Templates and Add-ins dialog box, click the Schema Library button.
4. At the Schema Library dialog box, click the Add Schema button.
5. Navigate to the WordChapter08E folder on your disk and then double-click **Heroes.xsd**.
6. At the Schema Settings dialog box, click OK. (Do not enter any text in the *Alias* text box.)
7. Associate a style sheet with the schema by completing the following steps:
   a. Make sure *Heroes* is selected in the *Select a schema* list box.
   b. Click the Add Solution button.
   c. At the Add Solution dialog box, navigate to the WordChapter08E folder on your disk and then double-click **HeroesSimple.xsl**.
   d. At the Solution Settings dialog box, type **SimpleForm** in the *Alias* text box, and then click OK.
   e. Click the Add Solution button.
   f. Navigate to the WordChapter08E folder on your disk and then double-click **HeroesFancy.xsl**.
   g. At the Solution Settings dialog box, type **FancyForm** in the *Alias* text box, and then click OK.
8. Click OK to close the Schema Library dialog box.
9. Click OK to close the Templates and Add-ins dialog box.
10. Open the **Heroes.xml** file (located in the WordChapter08E folder on your disk).
11. Click the *FancyForm* option in the *XML data views* list box in the XML Document task pane.
12. Close the task pane and then close **Heroes.xml**.

CHAPTER challenge

Case study

You are the secretary for the local chapter of Phi Theta Kappa, the international honor society for two-year colleges. The local organization is planning an alumni dinner. You have been asked to create a fill-in form that will be sent to all alumni requesting their presence at the dinner. The form will be based on the schema template named **PTK_Alumni.xsd** and will include all of the fields from that schema. Organize the form so that it is easy to understand and is visually appealing. Protect and save the form as a Word file named **Alumni Dinner**.

HELP?

Now that the form has been created, it will be sent out to the alumni via e-mail. You would like to include an e-mail signature with your e-mail. Use the Help feature to learn about creating e-mail signatures. Then create an e-mail signature for yourself. Using the form created in the first part of the Chapter Challenge, send an e-mail message to the alumni (at least five students in your class) and attach the form as a Word document. Ask them to complete the form, save it as **Alumni Dinner – (their first name and last name)** and return it to you within a couple of days (prior to the professor's due date for this assignment).

INTEGRATED

Once the forms have been completed and returned, you decide that the information could be better managed if Microsoft Access were used. Prepare the returned forms from the second part of the Chapter Challenge to be imported into Access by saving each of them as an XML file. Then create a database in Access named **Phi Theta Kappa** and import data from each of the files into one table.

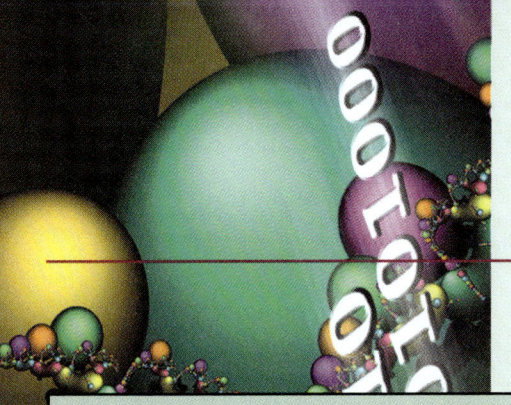

Workplace Ready

Sharing Information

ASSESSING proficiencies

In this unit, you learned about features for sharing documents within a workgroup and sharing data between programs and how to prepare specialized documents such as fill-in forms and documents with specialized tables such as tables of contents, indexes, figures, and tables of authorities. You also learned how to apply XML schemas to a document.

Assessment 1

1. Open **WordDocument10**.
2. Save the document with Save As and name it **ewu2pa01**.
3. Change to the Print Layout view, turn on tracking, and then make the following changes:
    a. Insert the word *highly* in the first sentence of the first paragraph between the words *a* and *diversified*.
    b. Delete the word *sectors* and the comma before *sectors* located in the second sentence of the first paragraph.
    c. Delete the second bulleted item in the *Fund Highlights* section.
    d. Move the insertion point to the end of the first paragraph in the *Fund Offerings* section and then type the following sentence: **Past performance does not guarantee future results.**
4. Display the Options dialog box with the User Information tab selected, change the name to *Lillian Reynolds*, the initials to *LR*, and then close the dialog box.
5. With tracking on, make the following changes to the document:
    a. Apply 14-point Arial bold formatting to the title *GRAYSON INVESTMENTS*.
    b. Apply 12-point Arial bold formatting to the headings *Fund Highlights* and *Fund Offerings*.
    c. Change *$7.5* in the second paragraph in the document to *$8.1*.
    d. Change *9.7%* in the first paragraph below the *Fund Offerings* heading to *10%*.
6. Save and then print **ewu2pa01**.
7. Customize tracking options with the following specifications:
    a. Display the Track Changes dialog box.
    b. Change the *Insertions* option to *Double underline*.
    c. Change the *Formatting* option to *Italic*.
    d. Change the *Paper orientation* to *Force Landscape*.

  e. Close the Track Changes dialog box.
8. Print **ewu2pa01**.
9. Click the Display for Review button, and then click *Final*.
10. Print **ewu2pa01**.
11. Click the Display for Review button, and then click *Final Showing Markup*.
12. Accept all changes in the document.
13. Display the Options dialog box with the User Information tab selected, change information back to the default, and then close the dialog box.
14. Display the Track Changes dialog box, and then return the settings that were in effect before you made the changes in Step 7.
15. Save and then close **ewu2pa01**.

Assessment 2

1. Open **WordLegal03**.
2. Save the document with Save As and name it **ewu2pa02**.
3. Create a version of the original document by completing the following steps:
  a. Display the Versions in ewu2pa02 dialog box.
  b. Click the Save Now button to display the Save Version dialog box.
  c. At the Save Version dialog box, type **First draft of Notice** in the *Comments on version* text box.
  d. Click OK to close the dialog box.
4. Make the following editing changes to the document:
  a. Insert **, attorneys at law,** after *Garcetti & Donovan* in the paragraph that begins *YOU AND EACH OF YOU*.
  b. Insert the word *waive* before the words *the Sixty-Day Rule* in the paragraph that begins *YOU AND EACH OF YOU*.
  c. Delete the word *heretofore* in paragraph 4.
5. Create another version of the document with the comment *Second draft of Notice*.
6. Make the following editing changes to the document:
  a. Insert **in this Summons** at the end of the sentence in paragraph 4 (between *requested* and the period).
  b. Delete paragraph 3.
  c. Renumber paragraph 4 to paragraph 3.
7. Create another version of the document with the comment *Third draft of Notice*.
8. Open the *First draft of Notice* version of the document.
9. After viewing the first draft version, save the version as a separate document named **NoticeFirstDraft**.
10. Close the **NoticeFirstDraft** document.
11. Maximize the **ewu2pa02** window.
12. Delete the second draft version of the document.
13. Save the document again with the same name (**ewu2pa02**).
14. Compare the **NoticeFirstDraft** document with the latest version into a new document.
15. Save the document with Save As and name it **ewu2ComDoc**.
16. Print and then close **ewu2ComDoc**.
17. Close **ewu2pa02**.

Assessment 3

1. Open **WordReport01**.
2. Save the document with Save As and name it **ewu2pa03**.
3. Change the line spacing to single for the entire document.
4. Display the Protect Document task pane and then restrict formatting the Heading 2 and Heading 3 styles.
5. Enforce the protection and include the password *report*.
6. Save and then close **ewu2pa03**.
7. Open **ewu2pa03**.
8. Display the Protect Document task pane. (***Hint: Click View and then Task Pane.***)
9. Click the Available styles hyperlink.
10. Apply the Heading 2 style to the title *DESKTOP PUBLISHING*.
11. Apply the Heading 3 style to the four headings *Defining Desktop Publishing*, *Initiating the Desktop Publishing Process*, *Planning the Publication*, and *Creating the Content*.
12. Close the Protect Document task pane.
13. Save the document and then print only page 1.
14. Save and then close **ewu2pa03**.

Assessment 4

1. Open **WordDocument11**.
2. Save the document with Save As and name it **ewu2pa04**.
3. Open Excel and then open **ExcelWorksheet05**.
4. Save the worksheet with Save As and name it **Excelu2pa04**.
5. Select cells A1 through D9, copy the cells, and then link the cells so the worksheet displays in **ewu2pa04** between the paragraph of text in the document and the name *Michael Kingston*. (Make sure you use the Paste Special dialog box [and select the *Paste link* option in the dialog box].)
6. Save, print, and then close **ewu2pa04**.
7. Make Excel the active program, close **Excelu2pa04**, and then exit Excel.

Assessment 5

1. Open the Microsoft Excel program.
2. Open **Excelu2pa04** and then make the following changes:
   a. Change the number in cell D3 from *98,244* to *80,932*.
   b. Change the number in cell D5 from *34,264* to *28,096*.
   c. Change the number in cell D7 from *45,209* to *37,650*.
   d. Save the revised worksheet by clicking the Save button on the Excel Standard toolbar.
3. Close **Excelu2pa04** and then exit Excel.
4. Make sure Word is open and then open **ewu2pa04**. (Notice how the numbers in the worksheet are updated to reflect the changes made to **Excelu2pa04**.)
5. Save the document with Save As and name it **ewu2pa05**.
6. Print and then close **ewu2pa05**.

Assessment 6

1. Create the table form shown in Figure U2.1 as a template document named **XXXu2pa06** (where your initials are inserted in place of the *XXX*). Customize the table as shown in Figure U2.1. Insert text form fields in the table as shown in the figure.
2. Print and then close **XXXu2pa06**.

REDWOOD COMMUNITY COLLEGE
312 South 122nd Street
Mendocino, CA 94220
(707) 555-7880

Name: ▢   Date: ▢

Department: ▢

Description	Qty.	Cost
▢	▢	▢

FIGURE U2.1 • Assessment 6

Assessment 7

1. Create a form with the **XXXu2pa06** form template. Insert the following information in the form:

    Name: **Ronald Jarvis**
    Date: (type the current date)
    Department: **Public Relations**

    Description: **Transfer Brochure**
    Qty.: **400**
    Cost: **$225.00**

Description: **Technology Degree Brochure**
Qty.: **250**
Cost: **$179.50**

Description: **College Newsletter**
Qty.: **2,000**
Cost: **$150.50**

2. When the form is completed, save the document and name it **ewu2pa07**.
3. Print and then close **ewu2pa07**.

Assessment 8

1. Open **WordReport07**.
2. Save the document with Save As and name it **MasterDocu2**.
3. Change to the Outline view.
4. Apply the following heading styles to the specified headings:

SECTION 1: COMPUTERS IN COMMUNICATIONS	=	Heading 1
Telecommunications	=	Heading 2
Publishing	=	Heading 2
News Services	=	Heading 2
SECTION 2: COMPUTERS IN ENTERTAINMENT	=	Heading 1
Television and Film	=	Heading 2
Home Entertainment	=	Heading 2
SECTION 3: COMPUTERS IN PUBLIC LIFE	=	Heading 1
Government	=	Heading 2
Law	=	Heading 2
Education	=	Heading 2

5. Make sure the Master Document View button on the Outlining toolbar is active.
6. Create subdocuments by selecting the entire document and then clicking the Create Subdocument button on the Outlining toolbar.
7. Save and then close **MasterDocu2**.
8. Open **MasterDocu2** and then print the document. (At the prompt asking if you want to open the subdocuments, click No.)
9. Make the following changes to the document:
   a. Delete the Section 2 subdocument.
   b. Move the Section 3 subdocument above the Section 1 subdocument. (Make sure the dark gray horizontal line displays above the white square above the Section 1 subdocument before releasing the mouse button.)
10. Save and then print **MasterDocu2**. (At the prompt asking if you want to open the subdocuments, click No.)
11. Close **MasterDocu2**.

Assessment 9

1. At a clear document screen, create the text shown in Figure U2.2 as a concordance file.
2. Save the document and name it **ewu2CF**.
3. Print and then close **ewu2CF**.

4. Open **WordReport02**.
5. Save the document with Save As and name it **ewu2pa09**.
6. Make the following changes to the document:
   a. Mark text for an index using the concordance file, **ewu2CF**.
   b. Compile the index at the end of the document.
   c. Mark the title and headings for a table of contents.
   d. Compile the table of contents at the beginning of the document.
7. Save the document and then print the table of contents and the index. (Check with your instructor to see if you should print the entire document.)
8. Close **ewu2pa09**.

Message	Message
Publication	Publication
Design	Design
Flyer	Flyer
Letterhead	Letterhead
Newsletter	Newsletter
Intent	Design: intent
Audience	Design: audience
Layout	Design: layout
Thumbnail	Thumbnail
Principles	Design: principles
Focus	Design: focus
Balance	Design: balance
Proportion	Design: proportion
Contrast	Design: contrast
directional flow	Design: directional flow
Consistency	Design: consistency
Color	Design: color
White space	White space
white space	White space
Legibility	Legibility
Headline	Headline
Subheads	Subheads

FIGURE U2.2 • Assessment 9

WRITING activities

The following writing activities give you the opportunity to practice your writing skills along with demonstrating an understanding of some of the important Word features you have mastered in this unit.

Activity 1

Situation: You manage a small business research company and are interested in learning more about how businesses use overnight or express shipping. Create a fill-in form template containing the information shown in Figure U2.3 that you plan to mail to selected small businesses. You determine the layout of the form and the types of form fields needed.

SHIPPING INFORMATION

1. What is the title of the person at your company who is most responsible for selecting small-package carriers?
   President/Owner
   Chief Financial Officer
   Controller
   Purchasing Manager
   Other

2. Does the person indicated above have access to a personal computer for use in shipping?
   Yes   No

3. How do you currently ship overnight letters or packages?
   Ground
   Domestic air express
   Neither

4. Do you receive a discount rate for domestic air express shipping?   Yes   No

5. Does your company ship or receive international express letters or packages?   Yes   No

6. If you currently do not ship or receive internationally, do you plan to do so within:
   Next month
   Next 6 months
   Next year
   Not likely

FIGURE U2.3 • Activity 1

After creating the form template, save the template document as **XXXu2act01**. Use the **XXXu2act01** form template to create a fill-in form. You make up information to fill in the form fields. After the form is filled in, save it and name it **ewu2act01**. Print and then close **ewu2act01**.

Activity 2

1. Display the Templates dialog box.
2. Delete the following template form documents:

    XXXu2pa06 (where your initials display rather than *XXX*)
    XXXu2act01 (where your initials display rather than *XXX*)

3. Close the Templates dialog box.

Activity 3

In this unit, you learned about copying, linking, and embedding objects in a document. Read the situations below and then write a report on which of the following procedures you would choose for the described situation:

- Copy and paste
- Copy and link
- Copy and embed

Situation 1: Each week you prepare a memo in Word to your supervisor that includes an Excel worksheet. The memo includes information about the number of products sold by your division, the current number of products on hand, and the number of products on order. This memo (with the worksheet) is updated each week. Which of the three procedures would you use for including the worksheet in the memo? Why?

Situation 2: Each year, you prepare an annual report for your company in Word that includes several Excel worksheets. This report and the worksheets are very different from year to year. Which of the three procedures would you use for including the worksheets in the report? Why?

Situation 3: You travel to various companies showing a PowerPoint presentation to prospective customers. The presentation includes several charts showing information such as quarterly sales figures, production figures, and projected sales. These charts are updated quarterly. Which of the three procedures would you use for including the charts in the presentation? Why?

Save the report document containing your responses to the three situations and name the document **ewu2act03**. Print and then close **ewu2act03**.

INTERNET project

Researching on the Internet

Make sure you are connected to the Internet and then use a search engine (you choose the search engine) to search for companies offering employment opportunities. Search for companies offering jobs in a field in which you are interested in working. Find at least three Web sites that interest you and then create a report in Word about the sites that includes the following:

- Site name, address, and URL
- A brief description of the site
- Employment opportunities

Create hyperlinks from your report to each of the three sites and include any other additional information pertinent to the sites. Apply formatting to enhance the document. When the document is completed, save it and name it **ewu2IntProject**. Print and then close **ewu2IntProject**.

JOB study

Developing Staff Guidelines for Reading Technical Manuals

As a staff member of a computer e-tailer, you are required to maintain cutting-edge technology skills, including being well versed in the use of new software programs such as Office 2003. Recently, you were asked to develop and distribute a set of strategies for reading technical and computer manuals that the staff will use as they learn new programs. In addition, you are to create a form to survey your staff regarding the publication and its contents. The project is co-sponsored by EMCParadigm Publishing, which will provide additional information at its Web site.

Use the concepts and techniques you learned in this unit to edit the guidelines report and create a survey form as follows:

1. Open **WordGuidelines** (located in the WordUnit02E folder) and then save the document with Save As and name it **u2Strategies**.
2. Edit the document using Word's track changes feature to highlight all changes in the document as you edit:
   a. Change all occurrences of *computer manuals* to *technical and computer manuals*.
   b. Format the document with appropriate heading and list styles.
   c. Insert at least two comments regarding the content and/or format of the document.
   d. Print the document with the tracked changes and the comments.
   e. Accept all of the tracked changes and then save the document again.
   f. Insert the EMCP logo attractively into the document. (Connect to your ISP and go to www.emcp.com. Download the EMCP logo located in the upper right-hand corner of the Web page.)
   g. Include page numbers, a hyperlink to www.emcp.com, and your name attractively formatted in a footer.
   h. Generate a table of contents.
3. Save and then close **u2Strategies**.
4. Create a survey form. Use Word's form feature to create a survey form document based on a template. Each member of your staff who received a copy of the guidelines will complete the form. The goal of the form is to help you determine whether or not the guidelines were helpful to your staff and whether or not they would like to see similar publications in the future. Add additional questions as you think appropriate. Be creative. Include text boxes, check boxes, and pull-down lists. Save the form as a protected document and print one copy.

INDEX

A

Add Users dialog box, 192, 214
Advanced button, 119
Advanced File Search task pane, 205, 206, 214
Advanced forms, 221
Advanced Layout dialog box, 90, 119
 formatting images at, 92-93
 with Picture Position tab selected, 91
 with Text Wrapping tab selected, 91
Advanced layout options, 90
Advanced searches: completing, 205-208
Alignment: of numbers in indexes, 276
Alphabetical sorts, 42
 by first and last name, 29
 for paragraphs, 28
 of text in tables, 34
Alphanumeric sorts, 26
Arabic numbers: footnotes numbered with, 77
Asterisk (*): for multiplication formulas, 65, 77
Attaching XML schema to, 298–300, 302–304
AutoCorrect: and concordance file creation, 278
AutoFormat dialog box, 141
AutoFormat feature, 140, 141-142, 161, 191
AutoMark button, 278
Autoshapes
 certificates created with aligned autoshapes, 96-97
 inserting, 119
 inserting and aligning, 95
AutoSummarize dialog box, 61, 62
AutoSummarize feature, 61, 62-63, 77
AVERAGE function, 65
Average sales: recalculating, 69

B

Background colors: applying, 120
Background formatting: applying, 114-116
Backgrounds
 applying to documents, 112
 for Web pages, 109
Background side menu, 113
Balloons
 page borders with, 85
 track changes options and, 183
Basic File Search task pane, 203, 214
Bookmark dialog box, 158, 159, 162
Bookmarks, 156, 169
 creating, 162
 deleting, 162
 inserting, 159, 162
 using, 158-159
Borders, 169
Borders and Shading dialog box, 119
 with Page Border tab selected, 83, 84, 85
Brackets ([ ]): around selected text for bookmarks, 159
Browsing: in XML documents, 319-320
Bullets and Numbering dialog box, 151

C

Calculations: on data in tables, 64-66
Capitalization: in concordance files, 278
Caption dialog box, 282, 289
Captions
 creating, 281
 marking, 289
Cells
 averaging numbers in, 65
 data direction changed in, 67
 rotating text in, 77
Certificates: creating with aligned autoshapes, 96-97
Certification authority: digital signatures obtained from, 198, 214
Changes: tracking in shared documents, 181-182
Change Text Direction button, 77
 on Tables and Borders toolbar, 67
Charts
 data imported into, 222
 data imported from Microsoft Excel worksheets into, 254
 Microsoft Excel worksheets imported into, 223
Check boxes, 221
 in Formatting Restrictions dialog box, 191
 forms created with, 231, 241-244
 inserting in forms, 239
 for record selection, 39
Check box form field options: changing, 241
Check Box Form Field Options dialog box, 241, 255

Check marks
  in Formatting Restrictions dialog box, 191
  removing from records, 38
Citations: in legal documents, 284, 290
Cities
  records containing, 40-41
  records selected for, 38
Clear All button, 38, 40
Clear Formatting style, 153
Clip art, 87
  editing components of, 94, 119
  inserting, 119
Clip Art task pane, 87, 95, 119
Collapse Subdocuments button, 249
Collapsing subdocuments, 249-251, 255
Color
  background, 112, 120
  border, 83
  images, 90
  tracking changes to document, 182
  watermark, 100
  WordArt text, 102, 108-109
Columns, 31
  sorted, 32
  sorting text in, 30-31, 42
Concordance files, 289
  creating, 277-280
  sample, 278
Contacts lists: as data sources, 19
Copying
  Excel worksheet into Word document, 224-225
  footnotes or endnotes, 60
  objects, 230-231
Copyright laws, 116

Create Subdocument button, 248, 255
Cross-Reference dialog box, 160
Cross-references, 156, 169
  creating, 160, 162
  inserting in documents, 160-161
Custom Dictionaries button, 214
Custom Dictionaries dialog box, 208, 209
Custom dictionaries: creating, 208-210
CUSTOM.DIC custom dictionary, 208, 214
Customize Address List dialog box, 41
Customize dialog box, 72, 77
  with Commands tab selected, 133, 134
Customize Keyboard dialog box, 146
Customizing
  document properties, 200-202
  form field options, 239-247
  images, 87-95
  menus, 74-76, 77
  toolbars, 72-74, 77
  track changes options, 183
  WordArt, 105-109, 119
Cut button, 60

D

Data
  calculations on in tables, 64-66
  changing in linked objects in Word documents, 227
  extracting, as XML, 301
  importing into charts, 222

  sorting in data source, 36-37
  sorting in specific field in ascending order, 42
  validating, using XML schemas, 310–314
Data direction: changing in cells, 67
Data sharing, 221-261
  features summary, 255
Data source
  data sorted in, 36-37
  merges completed with Outlook information as, 19
  records sorted in, 35
Data source fields: information for, 12
Data source files, 7, 8, 23, 41
  editing, 20-21
  and record selection, 38
Date sorts, 26
Default button, 202
Default dictionary: changing, 209
Default file locations: changing for workgroup templates, 210-213
Default fonts: changing, 202
Delete button, 161
Delete Frame button, 114
Delete key, 272, 280, 288, 289
Deleting
  footnotes or endnotes, 60, 77
  indexes, 280
  list of figures, 284
  macros, 131, 161
  styles, 153-154, 155
  table of authorities, 288
  table of contents, 272, 289
  versions of documents, 188
  XML schemas and solutions, 324–325

Diagrams: copying from PowerPoint to Word, 230-231
Dictionaries
  custom, 208-210
  removing, 209
Digital signatures, 189
  applying, 214
  creating and applying, 198-199
Directories
  customized, 7
  preparing with Mail Merge Wizard, 17
Directory list: preparing using Mail Merge Wizard, 17-19
Display for Review button, 182, 213
Document analysis: with readability statistics, 63-64
Document Map, 156
Document Map button, 157
Document Map pane, 162
  navigating with, 157
Document properties
  customizing, 200-202
  inserting and customizing, 201-202
Documents. *See also* Shared documents
  advanced searches for specific documents, 207-208
  automatically summarizing, 61-63
  customized, 7
  displaying Thumbnails and Document Map panes in, 157-158
  formatting and enhancing, 169-178
  read-only, 189, 197-198, 214
  saving as templates, 210
  searching for specific documents, 203-208
  with Thumbnails Pane displayed, 156
  XML, 301
Draw button, 95, 98
Drawing button, 87
Drawing toolbar, 95, 119
  customizing WordArt with buttons on, 107
  Draw button on, 95, 98
  Insert Clip Art button on, 87
Draw Table button, 255
Drop-Down Form Field button, 239
Drop-Down Form Field Options dialog box, 239, 255
Drop-down lists
  form fields created with, 239-240
  in forms, 231, 232, 241-244

E

Edit button, 161
Editing
  clip art images, 119
  data in charts, 222
  footnotes and endnotes, 59-60
  form templates, 237-238
  images, 94-95
  linked worksheets, 225-226
  macros, 138-140
  main documents, 42
  merge documents, 20-25
  restricting, 191-192, 195, 213
  saved Web pages, 117-118
  template documents, 255
Editing markings: controlling display of, 182, 213
Edit WordArt Text dialog box, 102
Electronic stamp, 198
E-mail communications: preparing guidelines for, 178
e-mail messages
  creation of merged with Outlook contact list, 19
  customized, 7
Embedded Microsoft Excel worksheets, 228
  modifying, 229-230
Em dash: searching for, 51
Encryption, 198
En dash: searching for, 51
Endnotes, 169
  creating, 55, 58-59
  deleting, 77
  moving, copying, and deleting, 60
  printing, 58, 77
  viewing and editing, 59-60
Enforcing Protection button, 192
Entries: in indexes, 273, 274
Envelopes
  customized, 7
  preparing with Mail Merge Wizard, 13-15
Exceptions: allowing, 192
Expanding subdocuments, 249-251, 255
Expand Subdocuments button, 249
Extensible Markup Language. *See* XML

F

Faxes: customized, 7
Field dialog box, 69, 70, 77, 136

Field entries: for table of contents, 263
Fields
  customized, 41
  form, 231
  inserting and modifying, 69-72
  inserting in tables, 77
  and Merge feature, 23
  predesigned, 8
  in records, 8, 41
  sorting on more than one, 31-32
  sorting on two, 32
  table of contents entries marked as, 269
File locations
  changing, 232-233
  specifying, 214
Fill effects: for Web page documents, 112
Fill Effects dialog box, 112, 120
Fill-in boxes, 221
Fill-in fields, 23, 42, 161
  adding to documents, 24-25
  recording macros with, 136-137
  running macros with, 138
Fill patterns: with WordArt, 102
Filter and Sort dialog box, 35, 40
  with Filter Records tab selected, 39
  with Sort Records tab selected, 36
Find and Replace dialog box: with Replace tab selected, 51
Find and replace feature, 51, 77
Flesch-Kincaid grade level, 63, 64

Flesch reading ease, 63, 64
Flipping objects, 98-99
Font dialog box, 202, 214
Fonts
  watermark, 100
  WordArt, 102
Footnote and Endnote dialog box, 55, 56, 58
Footnote pane, 56
Footnotes, 169
  creating, 55, 57
  deleting, 77
  editing and deleting, 60-61
  moving, copying, and deleting, 60-61
  printing, 58, 77
  viewing and editing, 59-60
Format Picture button, 90, 119
Format Picture dialog box, 119
  Advanced button on, 119
  formatting image at, 90-93
Formatting
  with AutoFormat, 141-142
  background, 114-116
  documents, 169-178
  form field text, 241
  images, 88-89, 119
  indexes, 289
  paragraph, 52
  restricting, 190-191, 193-194, 213
  special, 51
  styles, 161
  table of contents, 265
  text with styles, 140-142
  theme, 110
  Web pages, 109-116, 120
Formatting instructions and style modifications, 148
  within styles, 161
Formatting Restrictions dialog box, 191, 213

Formatting toolbar: Style button on, 140, 142, 162
Form documents
  creating, 233
  filling in, 235
  personalized, 254
  printing only data in, 237
Form feature, 221, 254
Form field options: customizing, 239-247
Form Field Options button, 239, 240
Form fields, 231, 236, 239-240, 254
Form letters: preparing using Mail Merge Wizard, 8-12
Forms, 231
  advanced, 221
  creating, 231-232, 254
  creating using Table feature, 245-246
  preprinted, 221, 237
  printing, 236-237, 255
  with text fields, check boxes, and drop-down lists, 241-244
Forms toolbar, 254
  buttons on, 232
  Draw Table button on, 255
  Protect Form button on, 237
Form templates
  creating, 232
  editing, 237-238
  tables created in, 245
Formula dialog box, 65, 77
Formulas
  example, 65-66
  operators for writing of, 65, 77
  recalculating, 69, 77
Forward slash (/): for division formulas, 65, 77

Frames
  inserting in document, 113-116, 120
  for Web pages, 109
Frames toolbar, 113, 120
  Delete Frame button on, 114
Functions, 65

G

Go to TOC button, 272
Graph Standard toolbar: Import File button on, 222

H

Header rows, 33, 42
Heading 1 style, 153
Headings
  creating with WordArt, 103-104
  marking as fields, 269-271
Heading styles: in table of contents, 263, 264
Horizontal layout options, 90
Horizontal Line dialog box, 85, 86, 119
Horizontal lines: inserting, 85-86, 119
HTML files: Web pages saved as, 116, 117
Hyperlinks: table of contents headings as, 265
Hypertext Markup Language, 296

I

Images, 169
  displaying in editable format, 94
  downloading and saving, 116-117
  formatting, 119
  formatting at Picture dialog box, 90-93
  formatting with buttons on Picture toolbar, 87
  inserting and aligning, 95
  inserting and customizing, 87-95
  inserting and formatting, 88-89
  moving, 119
  saving as separate files, 120
  sizing and moving, 88-89
Import Data Options dialog box, 222
Import File button, 222
Index and Tables dialog box, 264, 278
  with Index tab selected, 276
  with Table of Authorities tab selected, 285, 286
  with Table of Contents tab selected, 265, 269, 289
  with Table of Figures tab selected, 282
Indexes, 263, 289
  compiling, 276-277
  compiling using concordance file, 280
  creating, 272
  features summary, 290
  formatting, 289
  text marked for, 273-275
  updating or deleting, 280-281
Insert Clip Art button, 87
Insert Merge Field dialog box, 22
Insert Merge Fields button, 22
Insert Microsoft Excel Worksheet button, 227, 228
Insert Picture dialog box, 95, 118
Insert Word Field: Fill-in dialog box, 24
Insert Word Field button, 23
Integration, 230
Interactive Web pages, 110
Internet Explorer, 116
Internet project: Web site search, 177
Intranets, 210
Invoices, 245

J

Job study: preparing guidelines for e-mail communications, 178

K

Keyboard commands: assigning to macros, 131-133, 161

L

Labels
  customized, 7
  preparing with Mail Merge Wizard, 15-17
Layout: watermark, 100
Legal documents: table of authorities in, 284
Letterhead: creating and rotating an arrow, 98-99
Letters: customized, 7
Levels: assigning to table of contents entries, 267-268
Line breaks: manual, 52-53
Linked objects: changing data in, in Word document, 227
Linking
  Microsoft Excel worksheets with Word documents, 225, 254

objects in Word documents, 226-227
List of figures
  creating, 283
  updating or deleting, 284
List style: creating and modifying, 151-152
Lock Document button, 249
Locking/unlocking: subdocuments, 249
Logos: with WordArt, 102

M

Macro feature, 161
Macro recorder, 128
Macro Record toolbar, 128, 129
  Pause Recording button on, 131
Macros, 169
  adding/assigning to toolbars, 133-135, 161
  creating, 127, 161
  deleting, 131, 161
  digital signatures applied to, 198
  editing, 138-140
  features summary, 162
  keyboard commands assigned to, 131-133, 161
  pausing and then resuming, 131
  recording, 127, 128-129, 161
  recording, running, and editing, 139-140
  recording and assigning keyboard command to, 132-133
  recording with fill-in fields, 136-137
  running, 130-131, 161
  running with fill-in fields, 138

Macros dialog box, 129, 131, 138
Mail merge, 169
Mail Merge Recipients button, 22, 35
Mail Merge Recipients dialog box, 20, 35, 38, 42
Mail Merge toolbar, 35, 42, 69
  buttons on, 22
  editing merge documents with, 21-23
  Insert Word Field button on, 23
Mail Merge Wizard, 7, 41
  directory list prepared with, 17-19
  directory prepared with, 17
  editing merge documents with, 20
  envelopes prepared with, 13-15
  form letters prepared with, 8-12
  labels prepared with, 15-17
  merges completed with, 7-8
  task panes with, 8, 41
Main documents, 7, 8, 41
  editing, 20-21
  example, 13
  and record selection, 38
Main entries: in indexes, 273, 274
Manual line breaks: inserting, 52-53
Mark button, 269
Mark Citation dialog box, 285, 290
Mark Index Entry dialog box, 273, 274, 289
Mark Table of contents Entry dialog box, 269

Master documents, 221
  creating, 247-248, 255
  opening/closing, 248
  saving, 255
Master Document view, 247
Master Document View button, 248
Media images, 87
Menus: customizing, 74-76, 77
Merge documents
  editing, 20-25, 21
  editing using buttons on Mail Merge toolbar, 22-23
Merge feature, 23
Merges
  completing using Outlook information as data source, 19
  completing with Mail Merge Wizard, 7-8
  features summary, 43
  text input during, 23-24
Merge Subdocument button, 252
Merge to New Document button, 22
Merge to Printer button, 22
Microsoft Access files, 8
Microsoft Authenticode technology, 198
Microsoft Excel, 222
Microsoft Excel: loading XML data into, 305–307
Microsoft Excel worksheets
  calculations with, 64
  copying into Word document, 254
  data from inserted in Word document, 221
  embedded, 228-229, 254
  importing into charts, 223, 254
  importing into tables, 224

linking with Word
documents, 225
modifying embedded,
229-230
Microsoft Exchange Server
security features, 198
Microsoft Office: Microsoft
Authenticode technology
with, 198
Microsoft Outlook: contact
lists
in, 19
Microsoft Word
fields, 23
Web pages opened in, 117
Microsoft Word Picture
graphic editor, 94
Minus sign (-): for
subtraction formulas,
65, 77
Modify Style dialog box,
148, 149, 153, 162
Movie images, 87, 119
Multiple versions of
document: creating, 186
My Data Sources folder, 8

N

Names
bookmark, 158
reviewers, 182
styles, 142
Navigating in document
with bookmarks, 158-159
with cross-references,
160-161
with Document Map
pane, 157
with Thumbnails
pane, 156
New Document task
pane, 237
New Style dialog box,
142, 151

creating styles with,
143-144
Nonbreaking spaces
inserting, 49-50, 77
searching for, 51
Nonprinting elements:
finding and replacing,
51-52
Nonprinting symbols, 269
Normal style, 140, 161
Normal template:
copying/deleting style
to/from, 155-156
Normal template document,
140, 161, 202, 214
Numbering format:
specifying, 65
Numbers: sorting in table in
descending order, 34-35
Numeric sorts, 26, 42

O

Objects
copying, 230-231
copying from one program
to another, 254
flipping and rotating,
98-99
inserting, 119
inserting and aligning, 95
linking in Word
documents, 226-227
Open dialog box, 248
Open Index AutoMark File
dialog box, 278
Operators: for writing
formulas, 65, 77
Options dialog box, 158,
208, 214, 232, 237
with File Locations tab
selected, 211
Organizer, 154, 162
Organizer button, 154
Organizer dialog box,
154, 155

Outline Level button, 267
Outline levels
assigning to table of
contents entries, 267
in table of contents, 263
Outline view, 247
Outlining toolbar, 247, 267
Collapse Subdocuments
button on, 249
Create Subdocuments
button on, 255
Expand Subdocuments
button on, 249
Go to TOC button on, 272
Master Document buttons
on, 247, 248
Master Document View
button on, 248
Merge Subdocument
button on, 252
Split Subdocument button
on, 252
Update TOC button
on, 271

P

Page borders
balloons within, 85
inserting, 83-85, 119
Pagination: controlling,
53-55
Paragraph dialog box: with
Line and Page Breaks tab
selected, 53, 54, 77
Paragraph marks
paragraph formatting
stored in, 52
searching for, 51
Paragraphs
alphabetic sorts for, 28
keeping together, 54
sorting text in, 27, 42
styles applied to, 162
Passwords, 189, 197

Paste function option: at Formula dialog box, 65
Pattern: applying to WordArt text, 108-109
Pause Recording button, 131, 161
Periods: tab leaders as, 265
Photographs, 87, 119
Picture toolbar, 119
   buttons on, 88
   Format Picture button on, 90
   formatting images with buttons on, 87
   Text Wrapping button on, 88
Picture watermarks: creating, 100, 101
Plus sign (+): for addition formulas, 65, 77
PowerPoint: diagrams copied from to Word, 230-231
Predesigned fields, 8
Predesigned properties: choosing, 201
Predesigned styles, 140, 149
Preprinted forms, 221, 237
Print button, 237
Printed Watermark dialog box, 100
Printing
   footnotes and endnotes, 58, 77
   forms, 236-237, 255
Print Layout view: viewing footnotes and endnotes in, 59
Properties dialog box, 214
   with Custom tab selected, 201
   with General tab selected, 200
Protect Document task pane, 189, 190, 213, 214, 316–317

Protect Form button, 237
Protecting documents, 189-199, 316–317
Pull-down lists, 221
Purchase orders, 245

R

Readability statistics
   displaying, 64, 77
   document analysis with, 63-64
Read-only documents, 189, 214
   identifying, 197-198
Reanaming: subdocuments, 255
Recalculating: formulas, 69, 77
Recommended Minimum button, 191
Recording: macros, 127, 128-130, 139-140, 161
Record Macro dialog box, 128, 131, 161
Records, 8, 41
   features summary, 43
   selecting, 38-41
   selecting for merging with main document, 42
   selecting for specific city, 38, 40-41
   sorting, 42
   sorting in data source, 35
   with specific ZIP Codes, 39-40
Renaming
   styles, 153
   subdocuments, 252, 253-254
Reset Toolbar dialog box, 73
Restricting editing, 191-192, 195, 213
Restricting formatting, 190-191, 193-194, 213

Restrictions
   allowing exceptions to, 192
   enforcing, 192-193, 214
Reviewer markings: controlling display of, 182
Reviewing pane: Display for Review button on, 213
Reviewing toolbar
   Show button on, 183
   Track Changes button on, 213
Roman numerals
   endnotes numbered with, 58, 77
   table of contents numbered with, 265
Rotating: objects, 98-99
Run button, 130
Running macros, 130-131, 139-140, 161

S

Sales
   averaging, 68-69
   modifying table and calculating, 67-68
Save As dialog box, 210
Saved Web images: inserting, 118
Saved Web pages: opening and editing, 117-118
Save Now button, 186
Save Picture dialog box, 116
Save Version dialog box, 187
Save Web Page dialog box, 116
Saving
   master documents, 255
   versions of documents, 186-188
Schema Settings dialog box, 300–301

Searching
  advanced, 205-208
  for specific documents, 203-208
Section breaks: in table of contents, 265
Selecting, 169
Select Objects button, 95, 119
Selfcert.exe tool, 198, 199, 214
Shading: applying to WordArt text, 108-109
Shapes: inserting and aligning, 95
Shared documents
  creating multiple versions of, 186
  deleting versions of, 188
  features summary, 214-215
  opening, saving, deleting, and comparing versions of, 188-189
  opening earlier versions of, 188
  protecting, 189-199
  saving versions as separate documents, 188
  tracking and controlling changes in, 183-816
  tracking changes to, 181-182
Sharing data, 221-261
Shortcut key combinations
  assigning to style, 146
  removing, 147-148
  styles applied in documents with, 147
Show button, 182, 183, 213
Show Button drop-down menu, 182

Show/Hide button: nonprinting characters display and, 50
Sizing
  images, 88-89
  watermarks, 100
  WordArt, 104-105
Sizing handles: around WordArt text, 104, 119
Slant: of WordArt text, 104
Solutions: creating, in a schema library, 322–323
Solutions: deleting, 324–325
Sorted columns, 32
Sorting text, 26-37, 169
  on more than one field, 31-32
  on two fields, 32
Sort options: changing, 28-29
Sort Options dialog box, 28, 29, 30, 42
Sorts: types of, 26
Sort Text dialog box, 27, 29, 30, 33, 42
Sound clips, 87, 119
Source citations: from Internet, 116
Spaces: nonbreaking, 51
Special button, 51
Special button drop-down menu, 51
Special characters: finding and replacing, 51
Special features:
summary, 78
Split Subdocument button, 252
Standard toolbar
  adding/removing buttons from, 73-74

buttons drop-down list, 72
Cut button on, 60
Drawing button on, 87
Insert Microsoft Excel Worksheet button on, 227, 228
macros assigned to, 134-135
Print button on, 237
Tables and Borders button on, 67
Start Enforcing Protection button, 214
Start Enforcing Protection dialog box, 192, 193, 197
Style button, 140, 142, 145, 162
Style dialog box, 142
Style Gallery dialog box, 140
Styles, 169
  applying, 145
  applying in table of contents, 266-267
  applying to paragraphs, 162
  associating XML style sheets with schemas, 322–323
  changing/applying to text, 161
  copying to a template, 154
  creating, 142-144
  creating by example, 142-143
  creating by modifying existing style, 149
  deleting, 153-154
  displaying XML documents with, 319–320
  features summary, 162
  formatting, 161
  modifying, 148-156

new, 161
predesigned, 140, 149
removing from text, 153
renaming, 153
shortcut key combinations assigned to, 146
table of contents entries marked as, 264
text formatted with, 140-142
Styles and Formatting button, 142, 143
Styles and Formatting task pane, 145, 149, 151, 162
Subdocuments, 221
   creating, 247-248, 255
   expanding/collapsing, 249-251, 255
   locking/unlocking, 249, 255
   opening/closing, 248-249
   reanaming, 255
   rearranging, 251-252, 255
   rearranging, splitting, removing, and renaming, 252-254
   removing, 252
   renaming, 252, 253-254
   splitting/combining, 252, 255
Subentries: in indexes, 273, 274
SUM part of formula, 65
Symbols: manual line break, 52

T

Tab characters: searching for, 51
Tab leaders: in table of contents, 265

Table feature: form creation with, 245-246
Table formats and properties: modifying, 66-69
Table Grid style, 149-151
Table of authorities, 263, 289
   compiling, 285-287, 290
   creating, 284
   updating or deleting, 288
Table of contents
   compiling, 264-267, 289
   creating, 263, 289
   deleting, 272, 289
   entries marked as styles in, 264
   levels assigned to entries in, 267-268
   marking headings as fields and compiling, 269-271
   updating, 271, 272
Table of figures, 263
   compiling, 282, 290
   creating, 281, 289
Table Properties dialog box: with Table tab selected, 66
Tables
   calculating numbers in, 77
   creating in form templates, 245
   Excel worksheets imported into, 224
   features summary, 290
   fields inserted/modified in, 70-72, 77
   modifying and calculating sales, 67-68
   performing calculations on data in, 64-66

sorting numbers in descending order in, 34-35
sorting text in, 33-35
Tables and Borders button, 67
Tables and Borders toolbar: Change Text Direction button on, 67
Table styles: creating and modifying, 150
Template documents
   creating, 254
   editing, 255
   opening, 238
   unprotecting, 237
Template form document: filling in, 244
Templates
   creating, 210-213
   deleting style from, 155
   form, 232
   styles copied to, 154, 162
   using XML schemas as, 307–318
Templates dialog box, 237, 254, 300
   with General tab selected, 210
Templates folder, 210, 238
Templates subfolder, 232
Template table forms: filling in, 246-247
Text. *See also* WordArt
   bookmarks for selected text, 159
   finding documents containing specific text, 204-205
   formatting with styles, 140-142

inputting during merge, 23-24
keeping together, 54-55
in legal documents, 284
marking for indexes, 273-275
marking for Table of Authorities, 290
marking for Table of Contents, 289
removing a style from, 153
rotating in cells, 77
sorting, 26-37
sorting alphabetically in table, 34
sorting in columns, 30-31, 42
sorting in paragraphs, 27, 42
sorting in tables, 33-35
sorting on more than one field, 42
sorting with header row, 33
special, 51
Text boxes, 221
inserted in forms, 239
inserting, 119
inserting and aligning, 95
Text fields: forms created with, 241-244
Text form field options: changing, 240-241
Text Form Field Options dialog box, 240, 255
Text watermarks: creating, 100, 102
Text Wrapping button, 88
Theme dialog box, 110, 119
Themes
applying, 119
for Web pages, 109, 110

Three-dimensional effects: with WordArt, 102
Thumbnails, 156
Thumbnails pane, 162
navigating with, 156
Times New Roman: as default font, 202
Toolbar Options button, 72
Toolbars
customizing, 72-74, 77
macros added to, 161
Track Changes button, 182, 213
Track Changes dialog box, 183, 213
Track changes options: customizing, 183
Tracking changes to document, 181-182
Tracking default settings: changing, 213
Tracking feature, 181, 213
Transformation: of XML documents to HTML documents, 320–322

U

Undo button, 153
Universal Resource Identifier, 299
Update Table of Contents dialog box, 271
Update Table of Figures dialog box, 284
Update TOC button, 271
Users: adding, 196, 214

V

Variable information: in documents, 23
Versioning feature, 186, 213

Versions in (Document Name) dialog box, 186, 213
Vertical layout options, 90
Viewing
digital signatures, 199
footnotes and endnotes, 59
Visual appeal, 83, 169
Visual Basic Editor, 138, 139, 161
Visual elements
adding, 83-126
features summary, 120

W

Watermarks, 169
creating, 100-102, 119
Web images: inserting saved, 118
Web Layout view, 109
Web Layout View button, 109
Web pages
creating and formatting, 109-116
downloading and saving, 116-117
formatting, 120
frames inserted in, 113-116
interactive, 110
saving as separate files, 116, 117, 120
XML documents saved as, 320–322
Web Tools toolbar
buttons on, 111
formatting Web pages with buttons on, 110
Widow/orphan control: turning on/off, 54

Widows/orphans: controlling display of, 77
WordArt, 169
   creating, moving, and sizing text in, 105
   customizing, 105-109, 119
   headings created with, 103-104
   sizing and moving, 104-105
   using, 102-109
WordArt Gallery, 102, 103
WordArt text
   creating, 119
   creating and applying pattern, color, and shading to, 108-109
   creating and then customizing, 106-107
WordArt toolbar, 105
   buttons on, 106
WordChapter06E folder, 222
Word documents: saving as Web pages, 109
Words: marking for index, 274-275

WordML documents, 301
Word wrap, 49
Workgroups, 181
   protecting documents in, 189-199
Workgroup templates: changing default file location for, 210-213
Work in progress: formatting and enhancing documents, 169-178

X

XML (Extensible Markup Language), 295–296
XML documents
   creating HTML documents from, 320–322
   creating protected fill-in documents, 316–317
   loading into Microsoft Excel, 305–307
   saving Word documents as, 301
XML Document task pane, 319–320

XML files: generating, with forms, 317–318
XML Options dialog box, 310–311
XML schemas
   adding placeholder text to elements, 314–316
   attaching to a Word document, 298–300, 302–304
   generating, 298
   as templates, 307–318
   validating, 307–314
   working with, 296–298
XML Structure task pane, 299
XML style sheets, 319–322

Z

ZIP Codes: and record selection, 38, 39-40